China's Economic Revolution

In memory of Liu Ta-chung:
Pioneer in Chinese Economic Studies

CHINA'S ECONOMIC REVOLUTION

ALEXANDER ECKSTEIN

Formerly Professor of Economics and
Director of the Chinese Economic Studies Program
The University of Michigan

CAMBRIDGE UNIVERSITY PRESS

Cambridge

London New York Melbourne

Published by the Syndics of the Cambridge University Press
The Pitt Building, Trumpington Street, Cambridge, CB2 1RP
Bentley House, 200 Euston Road, London NW1 2DB
32 East 57th Street, New York, NY 10022, USA
296 Beaconsfield Parade, Middle Park, Melbourne 3206, Australia

First published 1977
Reprinted 1977

Printed in the United States of America
by Vail-Ballou Press, Inc., Binghamton, N.Y.

Library of Congress Cataloging in Publication Data

Eckstein, Alexander, 1915–1976

China's economic revolution.

Includes bibliographical references and index.

1. China – Economic policy. 2. China – Economic conditions – 1949-
I. Title.
HC427.9.E28 330.9'51'05 76–9176
ISBN 0 521 21283 9 hard covers
ISBN 0 521 29189 5 paperback

Publisher's note: Professor Alexander Eckstein died during the production of this book. He had completed the review of galley proofs at the time of his death.

Contents

Tables

Preface

The Communist leadership that came to power in 1949 has launched China on the path of modern economic growth within a socialist framework. Seen from the vantage point of 1975, the objectives postulated by the new leadership were not confined to rapid industrialization and economic growth. Rather, economic growth was combined with a commitment to improve income distribution, assure full employment free of inflation, and promote development with honor through a policy of self-reliance, that is, by minimizing or obviating China's dependence on foreign countries.

The pursuit of these objectives posed a number of dilemmas, both as to ends and means. Some of the objectives may be competitive rather than complementary at particular points in time. Decisions thus had to be made on which goals are more important and which less important, and trade-offs had to be defined. Different leaders and groups in Chinese society and polity attached differing weights and priorities to particular goals, and this then became a source of policy tensions within the top ranks of the Chinese Communist leadership. Similar differences arose as to the methods by which these goals should be pursued, particularly as to how much reliance should be placed on material rewards and incentives as compared to normative and psychic appeals. These issues are explored in some detail in Chapter 2.

The extent to which these objectives were actually attained in the past twenty or twenty-five years is assessed in the last four chapters of this book. The performance of the Chinese economy is appraised in terms of its quest for stability, the pursuit of economic growth, the degree of self-reliance attained, the improvements in income distribution and the way in which all of these form what one might term a Chinese development model. These outcomes were, in turn, made possible by the application of certain resource and institutional inputs.

The initial resources at the disposal of the new regime were necessarily those inherited from the past. They required a potent ideology – potent in the sense that it would be capable of providing a strong faith and motivational force for the broad masses of the population – to mobilize these resources. It also required organization provided through a set of new institutions to carry out, control, and shape this mobilization process. Therefore, the key inputs in China's development process since 1949 were (1) the resources and constraints – the assets and liabilities – inherited from the past, (2) an ideology that defined the broad objectives and supplied the motivational force but was also in part conditioned by the past, (3) a major institutional transformation in property relations and the whole system of economic organization to assure the new regime of far-reaching control over the resource-allocation process, and (4) a set of specific planning instruments designed to achieve the desired outputs with the foregoing inputs. The character of these inputs is explored and analyzed in the first four chapters of this book.

The basic approach of this book and the analytical framework on which it is based were formulated in the course on China's economic development that I have taught on and off for about ten years at the University of Michigan. These years have brought some marked changes in the Chinese economy, which have necessarily shaped and modified my understanding and views of the development process in the People's Republic. Moreover, information that had virtually dried up in the 1960s began to trickle out once more in the 1970s, although in a more fragmented and esoteric form than was the case in the 1950s. This too has contributed to a shift in perspective concerning rates and patterns of economic growth in China.

A book such as this owes a great deal to the contributions of a number of students of the Chinese economy. Among these, one of the seminal and pioneering contributions was that of Liu Ta-chung, to whom this book is dedicated. Professor Liu, whose tragic and premature death took from us an outstanding economist, started systematic, quantitatively oriented, high-quality work on the Chinese economy long before such studies were fashionable in the United States. He was the first to compile a set of national accounts for China (*China's National Income, 1931–36: An Exploratory Study*, published in 1946). This was followed some years later with a comprehensive and thoroughly researched study of the country's *National Income and Economic Development*, 1933–59 (Princeton, N.J., 1965) written in collaboration with K. C. Yeh. The latter represented a decisive advance in our understanding of China's economic structure and its transformation between the 1930s and the 1950s.

In writing this book I was fortunate in being able to draw not only on earlier studies of the Chinese economy but also on the comments and criticisms of several friends and colleagues. An earlier draft was read in full by A. Doak

Barnett, Kang Chao, David Denny, Robert Dernberger, Nicholas Lardy, Thomas Rawski, and an anonymous reader; Albert Feuerwerker and Michel Oksenberg read the first and last chapters. The detailed comments received from all these colleagues enabled me to greatly improve the quality of the manuscript. I am deeply indebted to them for this help. Needless to say, they do not bear any responsibility for the errors of fact or interpretation that may still remain in this book. It should be added that in some of the quotations in this book, I have added italics for emphasis.

This book and the additional research on which it is based could not have been completed without the invaluable support of the National Science and Andrew W. Mellon foundations, for which I wish to express my warmest appreciation. I was also assisted by an old and dear friend, Mrs. May Wittner, whose editorial talents significantly contributed to the readability of this work. Possibly my greatest obligation is to Janet Cady, my bright, patient, wonderful assistant, who was invaluable in ushering this manuscript through the various stages of production. Last but not least, I want to acknowledge the continuing and unstinting help of Ruth Eckstein, my wife, who was an ever-ready, penetrating, and most benevolent critic of both substance and style.

A. E.

September 1976

1

The economic heritage

The relevance of the past

The economic policy and performance of the People's Republic has been shaped by certain characteristics growing out of China's long history, the country's stage of development, and the 1949 revolution. In a fundamental sense China's economic development since 1949 is the product of both continuity and change. As revolutionary as the changes have been in the past twenty-five years, the actual course of development can be much better understood against the background of China's heritage.

One of the most crucial questions is what elements of the Chinese experience inherited from the past may have fostered or hampered China's economic development. Clearly there are no simple answers to this question. Moreover, the answers given would depend on whether one were exploring the problem in prospect – that is, before rapid and sustained development was started – or after it was fully and visibly underway for a certain period of time. Thus the assessment of the role of China's heritage in the country's economic development would almost certainly be quite different and much more pessimistic seen from the perspective of the 1930s as compared to that of the 1970s.

Similarly, an informed observer appraising the prospects for economic development and modernization in Asia from the vantage point of 1840 might have picked China – rather than Japan – as the most likely candidate. China was a vast empire more populous than Japan, much better endowed with mineral resources and large internal markets. Even in terms of social and political institutions, China might have appeared to be in the better position. Yet it was Japan that within approximately a hundred years (1870 to 1970) climbed close to the top of the world income scale, leaving China far behind.

What this suggests is that a study of conditions fostering or retarding economic development poses a highly elusive problem. Why did the industrial revolution come first to England in the late eighteenth century rather than to

Germany or Russia? Why did Japan embark on economic modernization a century later? Why was Japan the only country in Asia to start on the path to modern economic growth in the nineteenth century rather than in the middle of the twentieth? Moreover, to what extent is economic development due to certain economic, social, cultural, and political traits and institutions of the society we are studying and to what extent to certain patterns of interaction between different national economies and societies?

Conditions conducive to development in the eighteenth century may not at all be the same as those required in the twentieth century with its entirely different international environment and much more advanced stock of technology. As Alexander Gerschenkron has suggested, a crucial variable in the development process is the timing of the industrial revolution in a country, that is, whether a particular economy is a precursor or a follower, an early industrializer or a latecomer. He also emphasizes that it is doubtful that one can specify a unique and fixed bundle of characteristics that may be expected to yield rapid economic growth. Conditions are substitutable, and what may work under one set of circumstances may not work at a different time in a different place.[1]

Given the elusive nature of this problem, one of the few ways we can approach it is to compare the economic, social, and political conditions in countries that have broken through the development barrier at a particular time with those that have not. Therefore to illuminate the Chinese case we have to cast at least a brief glance at certain key countries or regions from around 1800 to 1850, but do so from the vantage point of the 1970s.

By that time England and parts of continental Europe were well on the way to industrialization. China, Japan, and India encompassed old civilizations, highly organized and complex societies subject to considerable population pressure on their arable land and hard pressed by European expansionism and colonialism. Parts of Southeast Asia, on the other hand, were much less densely populated, less highly organized, and had methods of farm production that even by pre-modern standards were less advanced than those of China or Japan. These characteristics of "backwardness" were even more pronounced in the Middle East and the parts of Africa that were quite sparsely populated. They relied to a considerable extent on much simpler and tribal forms of organization not based on permanent agricultural settlement, and employed a much more primitive technology.

It therefore seems that China, India, and Japan shared certain characteristics with pre-industrial Europe, since all these can be considered old and rich civilizations with highly complex societies. Yet Europe forged ahead in the early nineteenth century, Japan in the late nineteenth, while India's and China's development was postponed until the middle of the twentieth. Some of the elements contributing to this apparent paradox can perhaps be better understood through a somewhat more detailed comparison of conditions in pre-industrial Europe and China.[2]

Pre-industrial Europe and China

In both societies a primarily agrarian economy supported a small superstructure. In many ways this was a "natural economy," with a relatively low degree of commercialization and a limited use of money. The monetary system was inefficient. There were extensive barriers to trade in the form of tolls, dues, and taxes on the movement of goods. Roads and communication were poor, except for water transport. Capital was scarce, as illustrated by high and usurious rates of interest. All these factors placed severe constraints on internal trade.

As a result, these were in many ways what Eli Heckscher has called "storage economies," in which consumption depended largely upon accumulated stocks.[3] Such inventories of grain and other foodstuffs were needed not only to meet inter-harvest requirements, but also to serve as a protection against both natural and man-made disasters. Other similarities between pre-industrial Europe and China include the low status of the merchant and moneylender and the extensive use of guild organizations to protect and control merchant activities.

But perhaps even more notable are the dis-similarities between China and pre-industrial Europe. Possibly the most important factors contributing to the process of economic change in pre-industrial Europe were the scientific revolution and the cumulative character of scientific progress, the growth of foreign trade, and the growth of autonomous cities. Europe's development and expansion overseas after the voyages of discovery in the fifteenth century were marked by a widening in the extent of the market and the commercialization of the economy together with extensive capital accumulation, all facilitated by foreign trade. These developments also depended upon the growth of urban centers, with their legal status as chartered cities or city-states and the special privileges extended to the burghers.

None of these developments had a counterpart in China. As Joseph Needham has demonstrated, the Chinese were highly inventive people who made large numbers of discoveries in anticipation of the Europeans.[4] However, scientific development in China was handicapped by the absence of cumulative, mathematically based, abstract theory. Moreover, few of China's inventions were applied or translated into an ongoing stream of technological progress. The essence of traditional China's technological dilemma is perhaps best captured by R. H. Tawney's penetrating observation that China's peasants "ploughed with iron when Europe used wood, and continued to plough with it when Europe used steel."[5]

Foreign trade in proportion to the total economy, even during the Sung period, never reached the degree of importance that it had in Europe. The reasons for this smaller role of foreign trade in China are many and varied. First, the Chinese geographical configuration placed its centers of ancient population on the broad irrigated plains of the Wei and Yellow rivers. Only later, after China's social institutions had been well established, did dense populations accumulate in delta regions like those of Canton and Shanghai. When seaports eventually developed, their growth was handicapped by China's comparative isolation from other major states. Korea remained an appendage, accessible by land as well as sea. Japan and Annam were comparatively small and peripheral. Chinese expansion was chiefly absorbed in the sub-continent that constitutes modern China – for example, into the Southwest or Central Asia. With half a dozen provinces, each larger than any accessible foreign state, China's trade remained oriented toward the domestic market and was not based upon seafaring. This preponderantly inward orientation has characterized China's economy up to the present day, as will be shown in Chapter 7.

At the same time, the Chinese city was under the domination of officials rather than of merchants. The tradition of government monopoly or regulation of all forms of large-scale association and economic activity kept commercial growth subordinate to the political, administrative, and military interests of the non-commercial ruling strata.

Lying behind the contrast between China and Western Europe were the differing institutional frameworks and cultural values within which their economies developed. The West, except in Egypt, had little counterpart to the irrigated rice economy that had such far-reaching influence on Chinese life. The Mediterranean Basin facilitated the growth of city-states and sea trade, and Western European geography with its radiating peninsulas later fostered the development of nation-states and overseas explorations. These same factors promoted the introduction and diffusion of new technologies and ideas. In contrast, from the beginning the Chinese empire was turned in upon itself by the Central Asian landmass and the expanse of the Pacific Ocean. It early developed a bureaucratic empire in which the legal system remained a tool of the official class.

Feudalism in China was wiped out at the time of the Ch'in unification. From the Han period on, the bureaucratic network and the ideal of imperial unity militated against the rise of detached and particularistic political-economic areas. In spite of the barbarian inroads after the Han dynasties, the geographical environment and cultural and institutional inheritance of the Chinese people were so strong that they led to a revival of unified empire. This meant that the pluralistic and multi-focal institutional structure of Western Europe, with its struggles and rivalries among the crown, nobles, lesser gentry, cities, and burghers; between church and state; and between nation and nation within Christendom, had no counterpart in Chinese experience. While European development out of the chaos of feudalism stimulated dynamic and individualistic innovation and adventure, the Chinese empire remained a bureaucratic colossus bestriding all social life. This was reflected in the legal system, which did not protect the individual within the family nor the individual property holder nor, least of all, the merchant; and also in the Confucian ethic, which did not give the individual the same incentive as the Protestant ethic.

It is not surprising therefore that under the impact of all these developments, the "initial conditions" for industrialization and modern economic growth were more favorable in late eighteenth- or early nineteenth-century Europe than in early twentieth-century China. This is illustrated by the fact that average per capita product in pre-industrial England is estimated as possibly a fourfold multiple of that prevailing in China in the 1930s.[6] Demographic conditions were also more favorable in Europe, with lower birth rates and much less acute population pressure on arable land resources.

A *comparative view of China and Japan*

While there were marked differences – economic, political, social, cultural, and institutional – between pre-industrial England and China this was much less true for pre-industrial Japan and China. In both China and Japan irrigated rice cultures played a major role, small units of cultivation characterized modes of agricultural production, and the density of population on cultivated land was high.

Similarly, as of 1850 or 1870, the average product or income per capita in China and Japan was probably at more or less the same level. Both countries were virtually cut off from the outside world for two centuries or more between 1600 and 1800 or 1850. In the Japanese case this came about through the "closing of the country" (*sakoku*) by the Shogun, with just one port – Nagasaki – open to foreign trade. In China, the vast territorial expanse and geographic configuration of the country in and of itself dictated a preponderantly inward orientation; this was reinforced by prohibiting foreigners to reside in the country, except in Canton. Last but not least, the cultural distance between China and Japan was much shorter than between China and pre-industrial Europe. After all, the Japanese borrowed their writing, architectural styles, forms of clothing, and art from T'ang dynasty (618–907) China.

Yet following the Meiji restoration (1868), Japan embarked on rapid modernization and industrialization while China was left behind.[7] While the reasons for this are quite complex and far from fully understood, one can point to certain significant differences between the two economies that must have played a major role in accounting for the markedly different courses of development in the two countries.

Perhaps the most crucial differences are geographic configuration and governmental structure. China is a vast sub-continent that mainly relies on inland and overland transport. Therefore, communication lanes are long and pre-modern modes of transport are high-cost. In contrast, Japan is an island country, long and narrow. It is easily accessible through coastal and inter-port transport, which is much cheaper, with only relatively short overland hauls from any point. This factor alone tends to facilitate greater inter-regional specialization and trade in pre-modern Japan as compared to China.

Geographic configuration and lower-cost transport greatly facilitated all forms of communication. Once an innovation was brought to Japan at one point of entry, it could be much more easily diffused throughout the country than in the vast continental expanse of China.

Governmental structure reinforced geographic configuration in fostering greater commercialization in Japan as compared to China in the eighteenth or nineteenth century. Tokugawa government can be described as centralized feudalism, while China was ruled by a centralized bureaucratic empire. This meant that although the Tokugawa Shogun controlled both the largest fiefdom and the central government, the country itself was divided into 200 "baronies," each headed by a lord exercising authority within his fief and enjoying a certain and at times even a considerable degree of local autonomy.[8]

The seats of these local fiefdoms (known as *han*) were in castle towns. The seat of the Tokugawa *shogunate* was in Edo (present-day Tokyo). Kyoto was the imperial capital and Osaka the commercial capital. By 1730, Edo had a population of more than half a million and was perhaps the world's largest city. Osaka and Kyoto had populations of 400,000 or more by 1800 and, with two neighboring cities, comprised an urban center of nearly a million people.

It is estimated that by the middle of the eighteenth century about 22 percent of the people lived in cities.[9] Moreover, although the urban population was heavily concentrated in these three large cities, castle towns were so widely scattered that there were few villages more than twenty miles from a fair-sized town.

Commercialization was also fostered by another feature of government administration, the so-called *sankin kotai* (alternate residence) system. According to Tokugawa regulations, the lords had to alternate their place of residence between the national capital (Edo) and their local capital. The lord's wives and children had to remain in Edo all the time. Normally, the lord and some of his retainers spent one year in the capital and one year in the provinces. In effect, the families were hostages in Edo to encourage the lord's loyalty to the Tokugawa, and his frequent absences from the local capital prevented the creation of a rival local power base. The resulting movements of people from the local castle towns to the national capital and back played an important role in the development of roads, inns, restaurants, and everything connected with travel.

The Tokugawa political system not only fostered commercialization, but left scope for the crystallization of a fairly self-contained local government in the fiefs, with considerable autonomy. Behind the protective boundaries of local *han* autonomy, a lord (*daimyo*) could, if he wished, develop new initiatives and programs. He could innovate without fear that these innovations would be immediately attacked and undermined by the central government, unless such innovations directly threatened central rule. That is, the centralized feudalism of Japan permitted the rise of fiefs that could serve as pacesetters for economic, institutional, and technological progress.[10]

Chinese experience of the seventeenth and eighteenth centuries presents a marked contrast to some of these Japanese patterns. Given the differences in geography and government administration, there were no castle towns, no *sankin kotai* system, and the urban population was much smaller. It has been estimated that only 4 percent of China's population lived in cities around 1900.[11] Even allowing for shortcomings and incomparabilities in the data, this presents a sharp contrast to the above-mentioned 22 percent for mid-eighteenth-century Japan.

All this suggests that there were some very important factors differentiating pre-modern China and Japan. Under the impact of much greater urbanization and lower-cost transport, agriculture was probably more highly commercialized in Japan than in China.[12] Chinese governmental institutions did not encourage or permit the rise of independent power centers, except by default, during periods of dynastic decline and disintegration. In Japan literacy was significantly higher and the people were historically conditioned to borrow technology, art, architecture, and other cultural practices from abroad.[13] In contrast, literacy was not only lower in China but it seems that there was a pronounced and built-in resistance to borrowing ideas, technology, and institutions from abroad. To this list of differences must be added at least one other factor, namely, that imperialism came to the shores of China earlier than to Japan. Moreover, China's humiliation and defeat in the Opium War of 1840 was a much more forceful opening of the country than the entry of Admiral Perry's fleet into Yokohama harbor in 1858.

This highly sketchy and shorthand analysis suggests that in a number of crucial respects Japan was better equipped to embark on a process of economic development in the 1860s and 1870s than China. In retrospect, while there were many similarities between the two economies, the lower transport costs, greater commercialization, higher literacy, greater readiness to innovate, and stronger government in Japan, which was less constrained by incursions into its sovereignty, can be cited as some of the salient factors pointing to this conclusion.

China as an underdeveloped area

Having been left behind by the industrialization process in Western and Northern Europe, in Japan, and later in the Soviet Union, China on the eve of the Communist takeover (around 1945 to 1950) was, compared to these, a low-income country. It had experienced some industrial development and modernization in the twentieth century. Nevertheless it was poor. But was it also underdeveloped? This question can be addressed more meaningfully if we first have some understanding of the typical traits of an underdeveloped economy. We can then assess the extent to which these traits prevailed in the traditional Chinese economy.

The characteristics of an underdeveloped economy

The term *underdeveloped* is a relative concept. It implies that in terms of certain criteria an economy is less developed than those of a number of other countries.

Undoubtedly the most commonly used measure for ranking countries on the world development scale is per capita income, or per capita product. Theoretically, all countries in the world could be ranged along a development scale, with countries such as the United States, West Germany, Sweden, and Switzerland being at the top with a per capita product of around $6,600 to $8,300 in 1974 and countries such as China and India closer to the bottom with per capita products of less than $100 or $200 a year. Figures such as these must of course be handled with a great deal of caution. First of all, statistics for underdeveloped countries tend to be more or less unreliable. Secondly, per capita income figures based on conversion into dollars of national income figures derived in terms of domestic prices and domestic currency are not really comparable. The purchasing power of $100 will be vastly different in China than in the United States. This sum will purchase a much larger quantity of necessities in the former as compared to the latter. The same may not hold for luxuries; on the contrary in some cases, such as refrigerators, automobiles, and other consumer durables, the opposite may be the case.

Nevertheless, as a shorthand measure and as an approximation of reality, per capita income does reasonably well. This is borne out by the fact that it is quite highly correlated with a number of other measures that are conceptually less ambiguous but also less comprehensive. Such measures include estimates of calories per capita, or the protein and fat contents of diets in different countries. They also include such indicators as housing space per capita, infant mortality, and the number of telephones, physicians, and hospital beds per thousand. The precise ranking of countries may vary depending on which measure is used. However, countries that rank high or low by one standard tend to be similarly ranked by other standards.

The kind of technology used might serve as another way of characterizing an underdeveloped country. Such an economy may be expected to rely principally on pre-modern and pre-industrial methods of production. It is likely to apply traditional methods in agriculture, relying on biological (e.g., organic manure) rather than chemical (e.g., chemical fertilizer, insecticides, and pesticides) or mechanical (e.g., tractors or other kinds of farm machinery) inputs. Similarly, it implies the use of handicraft rather than mechanical methods of production in manufacturing.

Pre-industrial and non-mechanical methods of operation also typically prevail in transportation. As a result, transportation costs tend to be high, particularly over long distances. This presented especially serious problems in areas that were primarily dependent on overland transport before the introduction of the railroad. Typically, highways and roads tend to be very poor in pre-modern economies and may frequently be virtually impassable during certain periods of the year, while transportation by humans or by animals over foot or mountain paths restricts the quantity of goods that can be shipped and the distance over which these shipments can travel. These limitations are not only physical but also economic. The quantity of goods that can be shipped over long distances is also constrained because this form of transportation tends to be very high-cost per ton-mile.

Given pre-industrial methods of production and transportation, the productivity of labor will be low and the cost of transport high. This means that labor requirements in agriculture will be high. This large labor force will consume most of what it produces, leaving only a small surplus for sale. At the same time the high cost of transport will limit the possibilities for regional specialization. Thus small surplus and limited specialization mutually reinforce each other in limiting the extent of the market.

Low labor productivity based on pre-modern technology and limited specialization yields low per capita income. Correspondingly, with pre-modern patterns of living, consumption needs and standards also tend to be low. Therefore, the purchasing power to buy manufactured consumer goods will also be low. This, combined with limited farm surpluses for sale, places serious constraints on the growth of cities. In turn, with limited surpluses for sale, the cash income of the rural population and thus its power to purchase urban manufactures will also be limited.

Essentially it is in this sense that one can speak of underdeveloped countries being poor because they are poor and being technically backward because they are backward. We witness here a pattern of circularity which, if modern economic growth is to take place, must be broken into at one point or another.

China's economic backwardness

To what extent does this model of an underdeveloped country fit the Chinese case prior to 1900? By that time Western and Northern Europe and North America had experienced their respective industrial revolutions and had traveled some distance on the industrialization path. In relation to these areas China was quite underdeveloped in terms of the criteria suggested in the preceding discussion. By that time Japan had launched its industrialization drive and was clearly pulling ahead of China, although the gap between these two economies was not yet as wide as it was to become in later decades.

However, in relation to other underdeveloped countries in Asia and Africa, the Chinese economy of the nineteenth century can be considered advanced by pre-modern standards. This applies to both the prevailing level of technology and to the degree of commercialization in agriculture.

Actually, the term *pre-modern*, when applied to technology, is much too broad and vague a concept. Literally interpreted it could cover a whole spectrum of technologies, ranging from a stone hoe or a wooden plow to a steel plow that is animal-drawn. As far as China is concerned, its peasantry has gradually learned to carefully husband human and animal manure and in this way continuously replenish soil fertility through the centuries. Similarly the traditional Chinese state, through its imperial administration and local authorities, started to develop an irrigation and canal network a long time ago. In sharp contrast, manure was converted into dung cakes and used for fuel in India and irrigation works were much less well developed there. Therefore, the intensity of land use and crop yields per acre have traditionally been much lower in India than in China.

This contrast is brought into even sharper relief if we compare China with large parts of eighteenth- or nineteenth-century Africa and some parts of Southeast Asia where much more primitive forms of agriculture prevailed. In many areas these forms involved a moving pattern of agricultural production based on slash-and-burn techniques. That is, the original or primeval vegetation would be cut down and burned with the remaining ashes serving as a source of supplementary fertility to the soil. This enriched soil could produce fairly high yields initially but these would begin to diminish rapidly within a few years, at which point the population unit would move to a new location and cut down the forest and other vegetation there and thus start all over again.

Just as with technology, the degree of commercialization in agriculture – and hence the extent of household or village self-sufficiency – varies a great deal among pre-modern economies. Therefore, in this respect too China was more advanced than many underdeveloped countries prior to the twentieth century. As noted above, this conclusion does not hold for pre-industrial Europe and Japan but applies to the rest of Asia and most of Africa.

Pre-modern Chinese society was complex, with a highly organized market system and a hierarchy of local, intermediate, and inter-regional markets. Clearly, a closed, totally self-subsistence model does not fit the typical Chinese farm household. On the contrary, perhaps as much as 30 to 40 percent of the agricultural produce was marketed, with the bulk of this produce sold to other farmers within a limited region a few miles in diameter. At the same time, probably only about 7 or 8 percent of all farm output entered into long-distance trade.[14]

Given the high cost of traditional modes of transport, high-priced goods lent themselves much more readily to shipment over great distances. It is not surprising therefore that cotton, cotton textiles, silk, salt, sugar, beancake, tea, and tobacco were some of the most important goods entering inter-regional trade in China. On land routes the high cost of transport effectively eliminated low-priced, bulky goods such as grain from long-distance trade. The national as compared to the local grain trade was therefore primarily dependent on water transport, which was well developed in South China with its extensive network of rivers and canals. On these waterways grain could be shipped by junk at relatively low cost. This is in sharp contrast to the North, which was much less endowed with waterways and thus much more dependent on overland transport. This factor, combined with marked harvest fluctuations due to wide annual weather variations, has historically rendered grain supplies in the North much more precarious than in the South. The grain-supply problem was particularly acute for Peking, the largest population center in pre-nineteenth-century China. In order to solve this problem, the Mongols built a 1,000-mile-long canal (the Grand Canal) from the Yangtze River to Peking. This canal served as the main supply route to Peking until the advent of safe and efficient ocean and railway transport six centuries later.[15]

To sum up, pre-nineteenth century Chinese society was complex and multi-layered, with possibly about thirty cities of 100,000 or more. These cities had to be supplied with food by farm households who in turn purchased salt, sugar, cotton and at times cotton textiles, metal for fashioning tools and utensils, and some other products. In addition, the rural gentry purchased some luxury items such as tea, silk, and precious metals. Therefore, this was an economy characterized by a certain degree of rural–urban specialization coupled with some specialization in agriculture, dictated by variations in soil and climatic conditions. However, the degree of specialization was far from uniform throughout the country; some areas close to cities and on main transport routes were reasonably commercialized while others were largely self-sufficient.

Granting that the Chinese economy was fairly advanced by pre-modern and pre-industrial standards prior to the twentieth century, in what sense could it be considered underdeveloped in terms of the criteria outlined above? As may be seen from Tables 1-1 and 1-2, even as late as the 1930s it was still a preponderantly rural and agrarian economy. It seems that prior to the Sino-Japanese War (1937) about 60 percent of China's gross domestic product (GDP) was derived from agriculture (most underdeveloped countries fall within a 40 to 60 percent range). Moreover the economy as a whole – in contrast to particular localities or regions (e.g., Shanghai or Manchuria) – apparently did not experience marked structural changes. Manufacturing

Table 1-1. *China's gross domestic product for selected years in 1957 prices (in percent)*

	1914–18	1933	1952	1957
Manufacturing[a]	17.6	19.8	26.2	31.8
Agriculture	61.8	59.2	47.9	45.9
Services	20.7	21.0	25.9	22.3
Gross domestic product	100.0	100.0	100.0	100.0

[a]Includes transportation.
Source: D. H. Perkins, "Growth and Changing Structure of China's Twentieth Century Economy," in D. H. Perkins, ed., *China's Modern Economy in Historical Perspective*, Stanford, Calif., 1975, Table 1, p. 117.

Table 1-2. *Inter-sectoral composition of national product in Mainland China, 1933 and 1952 (in percent)*

	1933		1952	
Sector	1933 prices	1952 prices	1933 prices	1952 prices
Agriculture	65.0	57.0	56.0	48.0
Modern sectors	14.3	17.4	22.7	30.9
Industry, mining, and utilities	3.4	6.6	6.2	11.5
Transport	1.4	1.8	2.5	2.9
Trade	6.0	6.0	6.0	10.2
Finance	0.7	0.6	2.4	1.8
Government administration	2.8	2.4	5.6	4.5
Construction	1.1	1.7	1.8	2.5
Traditional sectors	14.4	15.2	12.9	13.1
Handicraft	7.0	7.4	6.5	6.6
Transport	4.1	4.4	3.6	3.7
Trade	3.3	3.4	2.8	2.8
Other	5.2	8.7	6.6	5.5

Source: T. C. Liu and K. C. Yeh, *The Economy of the Chinese Mainland: National Income and Economic Development*, 1933–1959, Princeton, N.J., 1965.

contributed less than 20 percent to GDP and the modern sector of industry generated only about 3 to 7 percent of the product in 1933. Traditional handicraft methods of production outweighed modern industrial manufactures in importance. This was even more the case in respect to traditional as compared to modern transport. As a result, less than one-fifth of the total product was generated in the modern sectors while the traditional sectors contributed about four-fifths of the national product in 1933.

Moreover, per capita product was low and more or less constant. Perkins estimates it was 113 yuan during World War I and around 123 yuan in 1933, all in terms of 1957 prices.[16] This rise in per capita GDP is so small that it lies well within the probable margins of error, given the uncertainties surrounding both the GDP and population estimates. In any case this is roughly equivalent to $50 at official rates of exchange, which of course greatly understate the purchasing power of this amount in China. This dollar estimate also overstates the difference between the U.S. and Chinese product per capita.

A high degree of population pressure on arable land resources is another trait that China shares with some other pre-modern economies, notably India and Tokugawa Japan. However, there were many underdeveloped areas that were fairly sparsely populated in the nineteenth century. This would certainly apply to parts of Southeast Asia, Africa, and the Middle East.

China's economic position can perhaps be most clearly demonstrated by the simple fact that the country's agriculture feeds today approximately one-quarter of the world population on seven percent of the globe's cultivated land. The pressure of population on arable land resources is further illustrated by the fact that acreage sown to crops in China is only seventy percent of that in the United States, but it must provide for three to four times as many people. This adverse population–food resource balance is perhaps the most important single fact conditioning and shaping China's economic development in the recent past and at present.

The population–food resource balance in traditional China

What factors have contributed to the rise of such a large population and what problems does this present from a development point of view? Much of China's demographic and economic history is obscure, only partially known and only partially understood. While the traditional bureaucratic Chinese empire has generated rich dynastic histories and a great wealth of historical documentation, the material contained therein does not withstand the tests of modern statistical evidence too well. These historical records are replete with population data which were collected for tax and labor-service purposes, but often these data-gathering activities were of a formalistic and ritualistic character without too much relation to reality. Nevertheless, on the basis of continuing research into these problems certain tentative conclusions can be suggested.[17]

It seems that there was very little net increase in population for a period of 1400 years between the Han and Ming dynasties. This does not mean that population was static. There were periods of population growth alternating with periods of population decline under the impact of war, civil war, and famine. Malthusian checks during this period apparently were prominent. Economic activity may have been characterized by a more or less circular-flow-type pattern, with very little if any economic growth.

On the same tentative basis it seems that between 1368 (i.e., the advent of the Ming dynasty) and the present – a period of about 600 years – China's population may have risen 8 to 10 times, from between 65 and 80 million to between 750 and 800 million. During the same period cultivated acreage apparently increased only fourfold. Between the early Ming and about 1800, population may have increased six times. These figures imply a doubling in yield per unit of land area on the assumption that farm production per head remained more or less stationary.

This relatively rapid (in terms of pre-modern conditions) rate of population growth was largely made possible by prolonged periods of peace and order between the early Ming and the late eighteenth or early nineteenth century, interrupted only once by major civil disorder during the transition from the Ming to the Ch'ing dynasty. Population growth apparently was most rapid in the eighteenth century, which was a period of singular peace and stability in China. While for 400 years as a whole (between 1400 and 1800) the average rate of population growth may have been 0.4 to 0.5 percent a year, during the eighteenth century alone this rate may have risen closer to 1 percent a year. It is uncertain whether this general expansion of the population and economy was accompanied by increases in per capita income and product. At present the evidence seems to be against it. It rather seems that these centuries witnessed both a gradual expansion in the economy (in its GDP) and in population, with per capita product and the average standard of living remaining more or less the same.

While in the eighteenth century population growth seems to have accelerated somewhat, the opposite was the case for the highly disturbed nineteenth century. The most outstanding event of this century for China was the Taiping Rebellion, which was very costly in terms of lives. According to some estimates about 20 million people were killed and the indirect population losses were very considerable indeed. Thus the data in Table 1-3 indicate a population decline of possibly as much as 60 million. However, beginning in the 1860s population rose once more, although at an unknown rate. If population was indeed 450 million around 1850 and about 700 million around 1960, this

Table 1-3. *Population estimates for China, 1400–1967 (in millions)*[a]

Year	Population	Year	Population
1400	65–80	1893	385 (±25)
1600	120–200	1913	430 (±25)
1770	270 (±25)	1933	500 (±25)
1850	410 (±25)	1957	647 (±25)
1873	350 (±25)	1967	700–750

[a]Figures in brackets represent the estimated range in the margins of error.

Sources: Dwight H. Perkins, *Six Centuries of Agricultural Development in China* (1368–1967), Chicago, 1969, Table II.1, p. 16. Figure for 1967 not given in Perkins's table but used repeatedly in Chinese Communist sources.

would mean a 55 percent rise over 110 years, which is a considerably slower rate of growth than during the preceding 400 years. Most of this new growth apparently took place in the twentieth century.

Present indications suggest that during the last century increases in cultivated area may have lagged behind increases in population, so that land per capita declined.[18] In general, there are many signs of rising population pressure on arable land resources and a general contraction in the availability of cultivable land.

In this connection it might be instructive to compare rice yields in contemporary China with those of Meiji Japan as well as contemporary Japan and contemporary India. If we take China's rice yield per acre in 1957 as a base (i.e., China in 1957 is equal to 100) Japan's yields were 94 for a five-year average for 1868 to 1882, those for contemporary Japan were 170 based on a ten-year average for 1953 to 1962, and those for contemporary India based on a ten-year average for the same period were 50.[19] This means that rice yields in pre-modern Japan were roughly at the same level as in pre-modern Chinese agriculture in the 1950s, while rice yields in India were only about one-half of the Chinese level. This difference is largely due to the fact that rice culture in China is much more intensive, with a much higher rate of double cropping, much more widespread irrigation, and much greater applications of organic fertilizer.

However, the other side of this coin is that China had by the late 1950s probably pushed these practices to such a point that further yield increases with traditional methods would become increasingly difficult and slow. If yields in China were to be increased significantly, injections of new types of inputs such as chemical fertilizer would be required. This is precisely what was done in Japan and in large part accounts for the doubling of rice yields between the 1880s and 1960.

Unfortunately, the demographic pressures on the Chinese economy were badly aggravated by developments after 1949. The Communist takeover in 1949 and the consolidation of the new regime's power position in the course of that year and in 1950 marked the end of a long period of war and civil war on the Chinese mainland. The cessation of this long period of conflict coupled with the establishment of political unity, law, and order over the whole country led to a marked reduction in death rates, even without the injection of new public health measures. Superimposed on this were a series of public health programs developed in the course of the 1950s. Under the combined impact of these two developments, rates of natural increase in China were stepped up considerably, so that for most of the Communist period population growth has fluctuated between a 1.5 and 2.5 percent rate. The only break in this trend may have occurred during the crisis years of 1960 to 1962 when the rates may have been lower, although it is unclear how much lower.

While it is uncertain what the average rate of population increase was in the first half of the twentieth century in China, it almost certainly must have been less than 1 percent a year. Thus conceivably within a relatively short time the rate of population growth in China may have been stepped up from somewhere around 0.5–1.0 percent per year to 2 or more percent per year. In a sense, with the advent of the Communist regime, Chinese society seems to have entered the stage of demographic transition or population explosion experienced in Europe in the nineteenth century. Like the other underdeveloped countries, but in contrast with nineteenth-century Europe, this process of demographic transition was compressed into a much shorter period and, therefore, the force of the explosion was correspondingly greater and its impact more far-reaching. Clearly, the disequilibrium among various sectors of the economy and the whole system of social and economic organization is very different if a transition from a low to a high rate of population growth is spread out over a period of 50 or 100 years than if it is compressed into a period of 5, 10, or 20 years.

In China, as in other underdeveloped countries, the restoration of peace and order combined with the spread of modern public health technology led to a rapid decline in death rates, while birth rates at best declined quite slowly. As a result, while Chinese society was characterized by high birth rates and high death rates before 1949, by the 1950s birth rates may have been declining quite slowly while death rates were falling rapidly. Lowering birth rates in China will be a long-range process, even with the most energetic population-control programs. However, more will be said about this below, when we discuss population policies in China.

This population explosion aggravated the pressures on the country's food supply and on its agriculture. With population growth rates of 0.5 to 1.0 percent in the past, per capita food supply and average food consumption levels could be maintained with relatively slow increases in farm production. However, when population growth rates doubled or perhaps even quadrupled within a relatively short period of time, this meant that the total food supply and hence yield per acre had to be increased rapidly as well.

This posed some difficult dilemmas for the policy makers in the People's Republic. At what pace could and should new technology be introduced in agriculture to accelerate its growth? How much investment would be required to bring about a rapid technological change in farming? What would be the implications of such an investment for resource allocation in the economy as a whole? Most particularly, what would be the implications of high rates of agricultural investment for the rates of industrial growth?

In a very fundamental sense, in the 1950s the Chinese Communist leadership attempted to bypass these population–food supply dilemmas by relying on organizational measures as a means of increasing agricultural output. They expected that the dilemmas posed could be resolved through institutional transformations of agriculture. Specifically, it was hoped that through agricultural collectivization large-scale methods of production could be introduced which then would yield increases in farm output. Similarly, it was anticipated that collectivization and the abolition of boundary strips between individual land holdings would increase the supply of cultivable land that could be brought under a plow. Finally, it was hoped that organizational changes would foster labor mobilization, with the increasing applications of this labor to be used for raising the intensity of land use.

In effect, it was thought that increasing input applications based on traditional technology could raise agricultural output sufficiently to meet the simultaneous demands of industrialization and a growing population. These attempts to increase agricultural output through organizational measures and primary reliance on traditional inputs reached their culmination point during the Great Leap Forward of 1958 and 1959. It was only the breakdown and economic crisis resulting from the Great Leap that finally forced the policy makers to face up to the necessity of introducing modern industrial inputs, principally chemical fertilizer, as a means of stepping up yield per acre and agricultural production in China in the 1960s. This too is a subject that we will return to in greater detail in later chapters.

To sum up this phase of our discussion on the economic heritage, the Chinese Communists inherited a preponderantly agrarian economy subject to acute population pressure. This population pressure was bound to be aggravated once peace, order, and unity were restored in the country, public health measures were introduced, and their application stepped up. Thus agrarian backwardness on the one hand and demographic pressure on the other were among the fundamental facts of China's economic heritage that the new Communist leadership had to confront and with which it had to deal. As indicated above, these leaders tried to bypass the problem in the first decade of their rule but began to confront it forcefully in the 1960s. These twin factors of agrarian backwardness and demographic pressure have profoundly conditioned the character of China's economic development and its economic policies since 1949.

Economic development in pre-Communist China

The rise of a modern factory industry

China's modern industrial development can be dated from 1895. Prior to that date, there was very little factory industry anywhere in China, even in Manchuria. The Treaty of Shimonoseki, concluded in 1895 after the defeat of China by Japan, permitted Japanese residents and Japanese enterprises to establish factories in the treaty ports (so-called because they were open to foreign trade, foreign residence, and gave special concessions to foreigners by international treaty). Through the operation of the "most-favored-nation" treaty clause, these privileges were automatically extended to the nationals of other countries with whom China had trade relations.[20]

As a result, foreign-owned factories began to be established in various cities, most notably in Shanghai, and in fact the bulk of modern industries were initially foreign-operated. However, these foreign enterprises provided a training ground for Chinese technicians and managers, who gradually accumulated capital and then developed manufacturing enterprises of their own. Thus by 1933 Chinese-owned factories produced close to an estimated 70 percent of total modern industrial output.[21]

The patterns of industrial development in Manchuria and China proper were markedly different. Economic expansion in Manchuria is a clear case of colonial frontier development with empty lands and a few people. Its growth was initially based on a mutually interacting process of land settlement, sustained rise in agricultural production, railroad development, and foreign trade expansion. The basic investments in railroads, port facilities, and foreign trade were predominantly foreign – Russian in North Manchuria and Japanese in the South.

Closely associated with this phase of agricultural and transport development was the growth of food-processing industries. Following World War I mineral resources began to be intensively exploited, and we see the rapid rise of coal mining and the beginnings of pig iron production and oil shale mining. However, industrial development accelerated after 1931, and particularly after 1936, when the region became the puppet state of Manchukuo under Japanese tutelage.[22] This was a period of heavy-industry growth, with the construction of steel plants and the expansion of chemical and engineering industries.

Manchuria's industrial development was primarily state-led and state-subsidized, largely based on Japanese capital and entrepreneurship. However, the engineering plants attached to the steel mills and coal fields in Manchuria created a pool of trained Chinese mechanics, machinists, and metal workers that supplied entrepreneurs and skilled workers to the private engineering sector. Moreover when the Japanese were forced to abandon Manchuria in 1945, they left behind a sizable industrial plant, a highly developed transport network, and a large pool of skilled manpower.

In marked contrast, industrial development in China proper was largely market-led, at first primarily based on foreign capital and enterprise, which during and after World War I was more and more displaced by Chinese firms. The Chinese government financed and subsidized some enterprises, but in many ways government was more of a retarding than a facilitating factor, with the possible exception of the 1928 to 1937 period. Chinese governments of the Republican period (1911–1949) hampered development through their failure to unify the country, to control warlordism, or to bring an end to civil conflict.

In spite of these handicaps, the treaty ports of China proper witnessed a rapid growth of consumer-goods and lighter producer-goods industries. This became possible because these treaty ports provided a certain measure of stability within the larger setting of instability. However, even so, it could not have been accomplished without the ingenuity and skills of Chinese entrepreneurs. The Ta-lung Machinery Works established in Shanghai in 1902 provides a good case in point. They started as a small shipbuilding repair shop and gradually grew into a large engineering enterprise.[23] By 1937 they occupied a modern plant equipped with over 500 machine tools and operated by 1300 workers. But the most important branch of manufacture that emerged, as shown in Table 1-4, was textiles. This too is an industry in which Chinese enterprise gradually grew from small beginnings, yet in the later stages of its development encompassed a number of large firms that competed very effectively with Japanese owned and operated textile mills in China. As a matter of fact amidst an aggressive expansion by Japanese textile firms during the inter-war period, the Chinese sector of the industry maintained and to some extent even expanded its output share.[24]

Under the impact of these developments in Manchuria and in the treaty ports, industrial growth in Republican China was quite rapid by international standards. For the Republican period as a whole, that is, 1912 to 1949, the average annual rate of industrial growth was 5.5 percent, which is above the long-term historical rate for the United States. If we eliminate World War II and the immediate post-war period – which was one of disruption and decline – and confine our measures to 1912 to 1936, the average rate of industrial growth jumps to 9.2 percent. This is a rate that was exceeded in the pre-war period only by the Soviet Union from 1928 to 1937.

In the post–World War II period, several countries grew very rapidly in-

Table 1-4. *Composition of modern industry product in China, 1933 (in percent)*

Industry	Net product	Gross product
Textiles	20.9	22.0
Food processing	5.2	6.8
Tobacco manufactures	4.0	11.2
Metal products	4.1	3.7
Machinery	0.7	1.2
Paper	1.1	0.6
Chemical	3.8	3.6
Mining	30.0	19.9
Utilities	21.7	14.4
Other	8.5	16.6
Total	100.0	100.0

Sources: For net product: Ou Pao-san, *Chung-kuo kuo-min so-te,* Shanghai, 1947, I, 54 and Table 2. For gross product: T. C. Liu and K. C. Yeh, *The Economy of the Chinese Mainland: National Income and Economic Development,* 1933–1959, Princeton, N.J., 1965, Tables F-1, F-4, H-1, and H-4.

dustrially, among them Pakistan and Japan, with their average annual rates ranging from 10 to 20 percent. However, by long-term historical standards these post–World War II rates must be considered exceptional. Abstracting from them, we must consider the growth of Chinese industrial output remarkably speedy. This conclusion is in no way contradicted by the fact that this growth started from a small base and thus, at least in its early stages, would necessarily be rapid if measured in percentage terms. On the one hand, the same would hold for the early phases of industrial growth in all countries, and yet these high rates did not prevail there. On the other hand, the rate of industrial growth in China continued to be high even at later stages when the total modern factory establishment was no longer so tiny. Thus the annual rate of industrial growth averaged 8.3 percent for 1923 to 1936, which still represents a rapid tempo of expansion.[25]

Yet even after decades of quite rapid industrial growth, modern industrial production in 1933 still constituted only about 3 to 7 percent of GDP, according to the data in Table 1-2. In effect this was a case of the rapid industrial growth of a small sector in a pre-industrial economy.

As mentioned above, for most of the period under consideration here, China's industrial development was dominated by consumer-goods manufactures, at least in the 1930s. If we define industry broadly, so as to include mining and public utilities, then the latter two follow consumer goods in that order of importance. In contrast, investment-goods industries were still of relatively minor importance. However, this situation did change by the 1940s, for which we unfortunately have no corresponding product composition. This shift between the 1930s and 1940s is but another reflection of the industrial developments in Manchuria and North China under Japanese occupation.

The economic history of textile manufactures in China provides a fascinating insight into the dynamics of industrial development in a less developed country. It represents a classic illustration of the impact of industrialization on an economy through market-extension and import-substitution effects. The first phase in the economic history of this industry may be dated prior to 1895, when China was an increasing importer of cotton textiles, with imported manufactured cotton yarn gradually displacing domestic handicraft yarn. This clear demonstration of demand for the manufactured product greatly reduced the risk of starting industrial cotton yarn spinning at home. Consequently, this market-demonstration effect became a significant factor in encouraging the development of industrial cotton yarn spinning in China.

As domestic textile factory production grew, it gradually began to compete with imported yarn manufactures. During this whole period, China was a net exporter of raw cotton and a net importer of cotton textiles. This was essentially the situation until 1910. However the situation changed between 1910 and 1920, that is during World War I, when China became a net importer of raw cotton while cotton yarn imports were halved and cotton cloth exports were begun. In effect, as the domestic textile industry expanded, its raw cotton requirements grew to the point that it could consume all the domestically produced cotton and then needed some additional raw materials which had to be imported from other countries. The industry expanded very rapidly during World War I, largely because China was more or less cut off from the rest of the world due to the diversion of foreign shipping to war-time tasks. As a result, textile factories located in China were forced to satisfy a much larger share of domestic demand. After a short post-war depression, the expansion of the cotton textile industry continued in the 1920s and the second phase reached its culmination in 1928 when China became a net exporter of cotton yarn, while yarn imports shrank to almost negligible proportions. At the same time, under the stimulus of rising raw cotton demand, domestic raw cotton production expanded to the point that it more or less could satisfy the needs of the cotton textile industry. As a result, raw cotton exports and imports were more or less in balance. This marked the consummation of what may be termed the cotton yarn cycle.

The evolution of the cotton cloth branch of the textile industry marks a second phase in the economic history of the industry. Between 1890 and 1920 cotton piece goods represented the largest single group of imports into China. Yet, handicraft weaving of cotton cloth continued to compete successfully with the imported product during this period, partly due to the fact that handicraft weavers could substitute the cheaper factory-made yarn – both imported and domestically manufactured – for the handicraft yarn. This was one of the factors contributing to a decline in handicraft spinning, while handicraft weaving was holding its own for a much longer period of time.[26] At the same time factory weaving was continuously expanding. After 1920, the import share of piece goods declined in relative importance, although they still maintained their absolute level. By 1930, the absolute import levels began to decline as well. This branch of the textile industry continued its growth after 1949 – so much so that by 1955, China became a large net exporter of cotton cloth. This represents the consummation of the second cycle – the cotton cloth cycle – in the development of the industry.

The third and final phase can be traced in terms of textile-manufacturing equipment. As the industry grew, its demand for textile machinery naturally grew as well. This demand was initially satisfied through textile machinery

imports. However, the very presence of this demand stimulated the rise of a domestic textile equipment industry which then, particularly after 1949, began to displace imports. This final phase reached its culmination point in the 1960s, when China actually became an exporter of textile machinery.

Thus we see in the evolution of this industry a very clear pattern, which starts with the opening of a market for manufactures by importers. The very existence of this market stimulates the rise of a domestic industry, which grows partly through import displacement and partly through expansion of a total demand for the product. The very expansion of one branch of this industry, through the operation of forward and backward linkages, leads to the growth of associated industries. Thus we can trace a continuous link between the imports of cotton yarn and the rise of a domestic cotton yarn factory industry. This industry, through the operation of forward linkage, stimulated the growth of a cotton cloth factory industry. Both the rise of yarn and cloth manufactures, in turn, through the operation of backward linkage effects, stimulated the rise and expansion of a textile machinery industry.

Structural change

Despite these strides in industrial development, the Chinese economy of the 1930s was still dominated by pre-modern activities, as shown by the data in Table 1-2. However, the modernization process continued after 1933, to some extent with accelerated force. This produced some further and rather significant changes in economic structure between 1933 and 1949. To assess these changes one would naturally want to compare the structures of GDP in these two years and preferably even in some of the intervening years. Unfortunately, however, there are no national income estimates for any of the intervening years and therefore we have to base our comparisons on 1952. This may not represent too serious a problem, because the new Chinese government's energies were focused on rehabilitating and restoring existing industrial capacity between 1949 and 1952. Therefore, while some structural changes took place in these first years of Communism, in many ways the GDP composition of 1952 reflects that of the immediate pre-Communist years.

What this comparison shows is that the relative position of agriculture, in terms of current prices, declined between 1933 and 1952 from somewhere around 60 percent to less than 50 percent. On the other hand, the weight of modern industry, construction, modern transport, and communication increased very appreciably. Part of this increase is apparent and part real. It is real in the sense that there was a genuine expansion in the size of the industrial sector between 1933 and 1949 in Manchuria, North China, and Shanghai largely under the impact of Japanese-led entrepreneurship and investment during World War II. This was paralleled by some additional railroad development and also some expansion of a few other modern sectors as well.

In part, however, the increased share of industry in GDP reflects changes in price structure. It is apparent that between 1933 and 1952 industrial product prices increased relatively faster than agricultural prices. This, in turn, reflects a change in the demand–supply relationships, in the scarcity relationships, of agricultural as compared to industrial products. It suggests that the demand for industrial goods relative to their supply increased faster than in the case of agricultural products, so that the value of industrial goods rose more rapidly than the scarcity value of agricultural goods. Moreover, by 1952, prices were to some extent regulated as a matter of government policy. Therefore, the lower agricultural prices were at least in part an expression of conscious policy designed to manipulate the price terms of trade in favor of the non-agricultural sectors of the economy.

However, even the 1952 GDP demonstrates that the Chinese economy was still highly underdeveloped, with about half of the product generated in agriculture. At the same time, Table 1-2 clearly illustrates that the Chinese economy was not stagnating since changes in structure and composition did in fact occur. It definitely shows that industry, at least, was growing in relative importance between 1933 and 1952.

Actually, industrial and transport development followed a divergent course during different periods. In Japanese-occupied areas output increased until some time in the early 1940s. It then declined, as it did in all unoccupied China during the war. With the end of hostilities in 1945 it gradually recovered but then, as the civil war gained momentum, production and transport were disrupted again. However, with the promulgation of the People's Republic in 1949 and the return of peace and order, economic recovery was very rapid. In this recovery major emphasis was placed upon restoration of industry and transport. Therefore, due to all these developments, it is not surprising that the industrial sector loomed larger in 1952 than in 1933.

At the same time, total GDP did not rise significantly and product per capita may even have declined. Therefore, while the Chinese economy may have experienced some structural change during this period, these two decades of war and civil war did not permit any significant growth of the economy as a whole.

The state of the economy in 1949

Having examined, however briefly, some of the basic structural characteristics of the Chinese economy that constituted part of the legacy left by the past, let us now explore some of the immediate and short-run difficulties and tasks that faced the Chinese Communists when they came to power. In 1949, the Chinese economy was inflation-torn, war-disrupted, and fragmented. To a greater or lesser extent these characteristics were mutually inter-related.

This economy suffered greatly from the Sino-Japanese War (1937–1945) and from the civil war accompanying and then following it right up to 1949. Industrial production was sharply curtailed, the transport and distribution system profoundly disrupted, and agricultural output declined as well. China's heavy industry, which was still in its infancy, undoubtedly received the sharpest blow. It was not only war-disrupted but, following the Japanese surrender in 1945, Russian troops occupied Manchuria and selectively dismantled industrial installations, carrying them off to the Soviet Union. Only the more modern and up-to-date equipment was carried off; the oldest and most obsolete machinery was left in place. Careful international surveys show that about 50 percent of Manchuria's industrial capacity was dismantled.[27] This affected steel plants, power plants, mining equipment, machinery plants, and similar types of enterprises.

Undoubtedly the Soviets had several different motivations for this action. They did not expect a Communist victory in China for a long time. Therefore, they wanted to weaken Manchuria as a heavy-industry base and economic base for a possible military attack on the Soviet Union, either by a resurgent Japan sometime in the future or by what appeared to them then as a re-emerging and strong Nationalist China. Moreover, Russia itself had been devastated and its industrial capacity drastically curtailed by the war, so the Soviets eagerly seized upon any opportunity that could help them restore their own economy and industrial capacity.

According to official Chinese Communist estimates, under the impact of war devastation, heavy-industry output in China was at about 30 percent of the previous peak level in 1949; consumer-goods output was at approximately 70 percent of the previous peak, as indeed was agricultural production.[28] Not only was production disrupted but transport and trade were sharply curtailed, so that even the shrunken quantity of goods produced could be distributed only with great difficulty.

This shrinking production combined with constantly rising government expenditures fueled the flames of inflation and hyper-inflation. These expenditures were largely financed by deficits "covered" by new note issues. This in turn led to a continuous expansion of the money supply and a rise in the demand for goods and services not matched by increases in production. This was a classic demand-pull inflation, with aggregate demand constantly outrunning aggregate supply.

To a considerable degree the inflation and hyper-inflation was self-reinforcing in that in and of itself it contributed to the further decline in production and disruption of distribution. With money rapidly losing its value in 1948 and 1949 in particular, workers were beginning to be paid daily in large bundles of paper currency. They then rushed out of the factories and various other enterprises to convert this money into goods as quickly as possible before it completely lost its purchasing power. This naturally contributed to considerable absenteeism, a decline in morale, and the lowering of labor productivity in general. Amidst these conditions there was a general flight from money into goods and a gradual reversion of the economy to barter.

This process was accelerated by the disruption of transport and trade. This, in turn, hampered the movement of goods over great distances and contributed to the fragmentation of the national market. Under the impact of these developments money was losing its purchasing power. It was also losing its function as a store of value and a medium of exchange. Thus, exchange became a direct commodity exchange, an exchange of goods without the intervention of money.

The legacy of the past

The key question I tried to address in this introductory chapter is how well was China equipped for the task of modern economic growth. What distinguishes modern from pre-modern economic growth? Simon Kuznets, in his important study on modern economic growth, defines the former as a sustained and continuous growth in population, national product, and product per capita.[29] It seems that the Chinese economy was growing in absolute size since the fourteenth century, of course with periodic interruptions. This process, involving a rise in total national product and population, apparently continued until 1952. However, based on the present state of our knowledge, it did not involve a sustained rise in per capita product.[30] Therefore, in this literal sense at least, one could say that *the economy of traditional and pre-Communist China did not experience modern economic growth.*

However, as indicated earlier in this chapter, China's twentieth-century economy did experience significant change and modernization, which helped pave the way for sustained increases in per capita product since 1952. At the same time, there were certain features of the traditional economic system that could be considered favorable to economic modernization and growth.

The economy inherited by the People's Republic was a preponderantly agrarian one, relying largely on pre-industrial methods of production in agriculture. However, by pre-modern standards Chinese farm practices were quite advanced and highly sophisticated. Nevertheless, the pressure of population on the land under cultivation was quite severe and there were definite indications that continuing growth of farm production based largely on increasing yield per acre would become more and more difficult within the framework of traditional technology.

This rural-based system of traditional China supported a highly organized and complex society with an imperial government, a bureaucracy in which access and advancement was to a considerable extent based on merit rather than inherited status, a merchant class, a local literati-gentry, and a large peasantry. It was a society with a relatively high degree of social mobility. Moreover, China had a long history as a cultural and political entity with a single written language. Therefore it was a society with strong elements of cohesion – in sharp contrast to India or Indonesia, for example, with their variety of ethnic, racial, and linguistic backgrounds.

A strong tradition of unity, cohesion, and stability – even if interrupted by periods of dynastic decline and dissolution – could be viewed as both a potentially facilitating and retarding element from a development point of view. It may be considered as facilitating in the sense that a strong and developmentally oriented regime could draw on this tradition to mobilize the people and get them committed to the pursuit of national goals. Such a regime could also build on the considerable organizational and management capacities exhibited by the traditional Chinese state, at least during periods of dynastic vigor and by the standards of a pre-modern society and polity. At the same time, the relatively stable and highly integrated system of traditional China with its conservative Confucian political elite could and did present strong barriers to technical and institutional innovation. The attitudes and policies of this elite throughout the second half of the nineteenth century greatly hindered China's development.

The economy of traditional China combined subsistence and market elements. Rural areas close to major administrative centers and main communication arteries were closely involved in a market network. On the other hand, more remote regions and places with no ready transport access except overland may have been only marginally involved with the market. The economic system of traditional China was characterized by a complex hierarchy of local, intermediate, and regional markets. Most of the transactions were largely of a local character, with some long-distance trade taking place. Such a marketing tradition can be of potential importance in the sense that a peasant household involved in the market – even if only locally – may be more open to new influences, innovation, and specialization. This may be particularly important once conditions change with the construction of a railway line, the opening of steamship traffic, or some other major change in the market conditions facing the peasant household.

Such changes began toward the end of the nineteenth century with railway building, the opening of waterways to steamship lines, and the rise of modern sectors in industry, transport, and domestic and foreign trade. Depending on time and place, these modern sectors both displaced and complemented traditional modes of production and economic organization. As noted above, the importation and domestic manufacture of factory yarn gradually displaced handicraft yarn. However, at the same time, the availability of cheaper factory yarn reinvigorated handicraft weaving until it too was eventually displaced by factory cloth manufacture. Similarly, modern banking could build on a tradition of native banks. The combination of these two forms of bank organization survived and they developed side by side right through the inter-war period.

The rise of modern sectors in transport, industry, banking, and trade created a sizable modern plant capacity, rail network, and a range of other facilities without which it is most doubtful that a major industrialization drive could have been launched after 1952. The People's Republic inherited from the past about 15,000 miles of railway, of which approximately 6,000 were in Manchuria and about 9,000 in China proper. It also inherited a modern textile industry with close to 6 million spindles and 60,000 looms, an iron and steel industry producing close to 2 million tons of pig iron and a million tons of steel, and an electric power industry generating close to 6 billion kilowatt-hours of electricity. On balance, it was a small industrial sector in relation to the size of the country, but in absolute terms it was not so small and it certainly provided an important foundation to build on.

The growth of the modern sectors in the twentieth century not only left a legacy of production and transport facilities but a pool of scientific and engineering manpower, a pool of skilled workers, and a trained labor force which, although small, nevertheless constituted a most essential nucleus for further development. The past also produced a pool of experienced entrepreneurs and businessmen who could occupy various technical and management roles in state economic organs and in the nationalized enterprises. Last but not least, the People's Republic inherited from the past a hardworking, disciplined, frugal people who formed a pool of human resources very well equipped to embark on the task of industrialization and modernization – given a strong and dynamic political leadership capable of motivating them to pursue collective and national goals.

2

Development strategies and policies in contemporary China

Economic objectives and goals

The immediate task facing the Chinese Communists in 1949 was to restore and rehabilitate a war-disrupted, inflation-torn, fragmented economy. Given the legacy of the past with its economic backwardness and population pressure, what were the objectives of industrialization in China, and what were generally the long-run economic objectives of the new regime? This is the broad issue to be addressed first in this chapter. The instruments and appeals used to motivate workers, cadres, managers, and peasants to pursue and implement these objectives will then be considered. The relative importance assigned to these appeals and the character of the incentives mix was changed from time to time as indeed was the priority allotted to different – and at times competing – objectives. These shifts in priorities and incentives produced policy changes and differing development strategies that are analyzed in the second half of this chapter.

If we examine the post-war experience of most underdeveloped countries we find that the urge for development derives from two closely inter-related sources. On the one hand, this urge is powered by a desire to reduce international inequalities and gradually close the standard of living gap between highly developed and low-income economies. On the other hand, the development urge derives from a felt need to close the economic, military, and political power gap between the more industrialized and less developed countries. In a very real sense, we are witnessing the operation of a powerful international and all-pervasive "demonstration effect." As underdeveloped countries have come into contact with technically more advanced economies through international trade, war, or colonialism, they have become increasingly conscious of the fact that there is a close link between levels of industrialization on the one hand and standards of living and/or standards of power on the other.

In the underdeveloped countries, the development urge is of course most strongly felt by the political and educated elite, who have traveled abroad or have had close contacts with foreign nationals, foreign cultures, and the possibilities opened up by the development process. It is this elite, then, that in varying degrees becomes the carrier of this urge to raise standards of living, to develop and to assert a sense of national dignity, national independence, and self-reliance.

The urge for industrialization in underdeveloped countries is greatly reinforced by an entirely different kind of consideration as well, that is, population pressure. As standards of public health are raised and death rates are reduced in the newly emerging nations, the rates of natural increase rise. Given the fact that in many underdeveloped areas, particularly in Asia, population pressures are acute even before this acceleration in rates of population growth occurs, some means to alleviate these pressures and create new employment opportunities must be found. These demographic pressures further underline the need to modernize agriculture and simultaneously develop the industrial sectors of the economy. The latter can provide new employment opportunities, while the former supplies the foodstuffs and raw material needs of a growing population and a rapidly growing urban labor force.

It is very difficult to think of a single developing economy in which the urge for economic growth and modernization can be categorized as purely welfare- or purely power-oriented. Typically we are dealing with a mixture of goals and objectives, but the character of the mixture may vary from country to country, with the relative weight given to the welfare component as compared to the power component differing from society to society. The differences do not revolve so much around ultimate objectives as around the relative priority assigned to these various objectives and the methods by which and the paths through which they may be attained.

There is no doubt that, in the case of China, while there is a great concern to assure a minimum standard of living, the need to develop industry as a basis of national defense looms quite large. This approach is, of course, not unique to China; it characterized development objectives in the Soviet Union, in Japan before World War II, and in some other countries as well.

Maoism and the character of economic objectives in contemporary China

However one might wish to define China's economic objectives, these cannot be really understood unless one examines and analyzes Mao Tse-tung's concepts of a good society and his image of the human ideal. In doing so one must remember that not all these objectives are accorded the same priority and that the relative emphasis placed on them changes, depending on circumstances. Therefore, just as with Lenin, it is not always easy to differentiate short-range considerations and long-range commitments in Mao's thought. All this is further complicated by the fact that not only did the situation facing the Chinese revolution and the Communist Party change radically between 1920 and 1970, but Mao's own views and perceptions changed during these five decades. Nevertheless, there are certain pre-dispositions and tendencies that appeared in Yenan (1937–1945) or even earlier, during the Great Leap, and again during the Cultural Revolution. In many respects these constitute the core of the Maoist outlook that we will concentrate on here, at the same time realizing that some elements of this outlook were de-emphasized during some periods.

An analysis of Mao's writings, speeches, articles, and editorials, as well as those of his close associates, reveals his ideal of communist man and of the way opened for the development and transformation of society and economy by the particular characteristics of communist man. Similarly, they reveal Mao's *vision* of a future industrialized, socialist society.

Possibly one of the most interesting characteristics of Maoism is its overwhelming stress on man. Man is the most precious thing. "Of all the things in the world, *people are the most precious*. As long as there are people, every kind of miracle can be performed under the leadership of the Communist Party."[1] Actually, what Mao meant is that man is *potentially* most precious or, more specifically, that man being malleable, he can be energized and committed and his potential mobilized provided that he is properly organized and indoctrinated by the Chinese Communist Party. Coupled with this stress on man is an almost messianic quality, a conviction that almost all men may be saved, although salvation is enormously difficult and backsliding is an ever-present danger. This danger can only be countered by vigilance, continuous indoctrination, and periodic "rectification" movements.

This communist man, once properly imbued, indoctrinated, and committed, can become a fountain of tremendous energy and consciousness that can conquer nature and overcome virtually all obstacles. "The more it is possible for men to carry out a conscious revolution in their own social relationships, the more they increase their power in the combat with nature, the more they can really command as by magic the latent productive forces, making them appear everywhere and develop rapidly."[2] The same theme was reiterated by Mao in 1955 when he said, ". . . People consider impossible things which could be done if they exerted themselves." [3] Another outstanding characteristic of communist man, or perhaps one should say of model communist man, is his capacity for total self-denial. For instance, A. S. Chen, in an analysis of forty-eight stories published in China during the first half of 1960, found in them two pre-occupations about work: first, the sacrifice of sleep for the sake of work, particularly for carrying out scientific experiments and pursuing inventions; and second, a complete imperviousness to weather conditions. Thus these stories in effect tended to glorify man's dedication to work and his ability and willingness to overcome natural limitations and to subordinate his bodily needs and personal comforts to the tasks of socialist construction.[4] The same theme of self-denial is stressed much more explicitly and repeatedly in one of the basic party documents drafted by Liu Shao-ch'i, "On the Training of a Communist Party Member." In it Liu stresses that "the individual interests of the Party member are subordinate to the interests of the Party, which means subordinate to the interests of class and national liberation, of Communism and of social progress. The test of a Communist Party member's loyalty to the Party and to the task of the revolution and Communism is his ability, regardless of the situation, to subordinate his individual interests unconditionally and absolutely to those of the Party." This is given added emphasis in Ch'en Yun's directive on "How to Be a Communist Party Member." He points out that "every Communist Party member should not only have an unwavering faith in the realization of Communism, but also be resolved to fight to the very end, undaunted by either sacrifices or hardships, for the liberation of the working class, the Chinese nation, and the Chinese people." At the same time "Communist Party members are fighters for a Communist *mission* under the leadership of the Party. Thus the interests of a Party member are identical with those of the nation, the people, and the Party. Every Party member should give his unlimited devotion to the nation, to the revolution, to our class, and to the Party, *subordinating individual interests* to those of the nation, the revolution, our class, and the Party."[5]

Another essential ingredient of communist man is his initiative and inventiveness, his willingness to experiment, to innovate, to try out new things. This is another one of the very important themes found by Chen in her studies of the Chinese stories published in the early 1960s. These stories convey the impression that an ordinary factory worker or young technician without research training and sometimes even without much formal scientific education can, by sheer determination and long hours of persistent work and study, come up with inventions that can make an immediate contribution to production. Similarly, in agriculture innovative efforts can overcome limitations imposed by weather, soil conditions, water supply, etc.

In this view creativity, inventions, innovation, and skill acquisition can be forged and induced from right thoughts. "*To learn flying* well one must first be adept in the control of one's feelings, and *struggle against certain incorrect ideological trends.* To do so one needs strong will power . . . Thus the excellent will power possessed by the proletarian fighter makes it easier for him to become an outstanding flyer." [6] This grows out of the conviction that if ". . . political work is done well this will be manifested in doing technical work well."[7]

Very significant operational and policy consequences follow from this vision of communist man possessed with these particular attributes of self-denial, total commitment, energy, struggle, initiative, and inventiveness. The stress on "men over machines" or "men over weapons" or "better red than expert" logically follows from the above vision of communist man. This does not mean that Mao necessarily believed that man in Chinese Communist society actually conforms to this ideal. It merely means that he was convinced that, given certain conditions, man *can* approximate the ideal and the model spelled out above. Furthermore, a careful analysis of the writings and directives of the 1950s and 1960s will show that at least as far as the top leadership is concerned, "red" and "expert," "men" and "machines," and "men" and "weapons" are not as sharp dichotomies and dualities as they are at times interpreted to be in different writings on Chinese Communist ideology, polity, society, and economy. In the short run, these are viewed by the leadership as possible substitutes. Under certain conditions, and most pronouncedly during the Great Leap, ideological commitment, mass mobilization, and organization were viewed as possible substitutes for expertness, professionalism, and the availability of capital equipment.

However, it was all along recognized that in the longer run professionalism, technological progress, advanced weapons, and complex machinery were necessary for continuing economic growth and an effective defense establishment. In this longer run, expertness was, and probably still is, viewed as an integral part of redness; that is, part of being "red" is to be inventive and innovative, and to seek scientific training and education sufficient to enable one to carry out innovations either of a simple or a more complex character, depending on one's role in the economy. Conversely, even a scientist or an expert who has all the necessary qualifications will not be innovative and inventive unless he is imbued with a spirit of boldness, zeal, and ideological commitment.

In Mao's and the Chinese Communist's view, all these qualities are necessary to realize the vision of a powerful, industrialized China that is beginning to catch up in terms of economic progress and growing national power with the Soviet Union and the countries of the West.

The accents on man, consciousness, the human will, the role of policy and organization, and the primacy of politics represent Leninist elements in Maoism. However, these elements were given much greater emphasis by Mao and seem to play a much more central role in his cosmology than in Lenin's. This strong streak of voluntarism can be viewed as an outgrowth of China's backwardness and lack of the classical Marxist pre-conditions for revolution. It reflects a recognition that revolutions must be willed and organized rather than expected to arise more or less spontaneously out of conditions of economic and social disintegration or crisis.

In this cosmology, industrialization plays a double role and is derived from two different wellsprings: Marxism and nationalism. On the one hand, the revolution re-creates the Marxist evolutionary path through rapid industrialization. Thus, through rapid industrialization a proletariat is developed and strengthened so that the end result of the process conforms to the Marxist schema of a proletarian dictatorship. On the other hand, industrialization serves as a prime means and necessary condition for attaining military and economic power. It provides the only road to great-power status in the modern world.

However, the objective of development is not only the attainment of great-power status or a rising standard of living but the perpetuation of a socialist society in which status and income differences are greatly narrowed. Mao was strongly committed to breaking down the barriers between mental and manual labor. He was concerned about division of labor, role differentiation, and income disparities becoming so pronounced that they produce wide status differences that would continuously undermine egalitarian values and the socialist system as a whole. These concerns were expressed by Mao on a number of occasions, as illustrated by the following quotations: "In regard to the management of enterprises under ownership by all the people we have adopted such measures as . . . the integration of workers and technicians, participation of cadres in manual labor, participation of workers in management . . ." In a similar vein, "scientific inventions do not necessarily come from highly educated people. At present, many university professors do not have inventions. On the contrary, many ordinary workers have them. We, of course, are not negating the difference between an engineer and a worker. We are not trying to do away with engineers. But there really is a problem here. In history it is always people with a low level of culture who triumphed over people with a high level of culture."[8]

Precisely for these reasons "if cadres do not participate in labor they inevitably must become divorced from the laboring masses and revisionism must inevitably arise . . . We must simplify and have some cadres go down to be tempered in labor, to be tempered in class struggle."[9]

Instruments and appeals for implementing these objectives

Given the regime's commitment to industrialization and status equalization, the question arises as to how this is to be done. How are resources to be mobilized, how are factors of production to be mobilized, and how are these factors to be used and allocated between competing needs and competing requirements? Rapid economic growth may require a higher rate of input mobilization, which can be accomplished in several ways: by bringing new workers into the labor force, by increasing the hours worked, and/or by raising the rate of saving and investment. Alternatively, the same objective can be accomplished by raising the efficiency of the labor force already utilized and of the capital already invested.

How is this to be done? In principle, the regime has three types of appeals or instruments available for resource mobilization and resource allocation. These could be categorized as *coercive, normative,* and *remunerative.*[10] In this particular context, *coercive* is intended to mean no more than involuntary, to be contrasted with the other two appeals, which involve voluntary commitment on the part of the participants and actors in the system. Coercion may in fact encompass a wide range of measures, ranging from bureaucratic methods – based on orders passed down through the governmental and planning apparatus – of allocating labor, capital, raw materials, and other inputs, to actual reliance on physical terror as a means of inducing people to do certain things they are not prepared to do voluntarily. In effect, it includes instruments ranging from those that involve telling people what to do to forcing people into doing certain things they do not want to do.

Normative appeals are designed to bring out the sense of idealism on the part of the actors in the system. This involves a sense of commitment to and an identity with system values. These system values in turn might be based either on nationalism, patriotism, and/or communist ideals. They may entail a better and clearer understanding of the meaning and purposes of the work effort by the various strata of the population. Normative appeals may also be based on peer approval, recognition, prestige, and the personal satisfactions derived therefrom.[11] In all these cases, people would not have to be told what to do, but would volunteer to do certain things or perform certain tasks in the economy that need to be done.

Remunerative appeals, as the term implies, are based on material incentives. In this case, the human actors in the system, the system participants, are supposed to be motivated by expectations of material rewards and thus perform different tasks in the economy either in response to or in expectation of such rewards. This implies a pattern of allocation based on a differentiated wage, salary, and price structure as the principal mechanism for directing resources to the various sectors of the economy. These same instruments simultaneously determine costs of production and thus also serve as a basis for choosing among alternative production techniques.

In analyzing these three types of instruments, it is important to note that only the last, that is, the remunerative, represents economic instruments, while the coercive and normative approaches involve the use of non-economic appeals for resource allocation. The importance and operation of these different types of appeals and instruments could perhaps best be illustrated by exploring their role in three alternative economic-system models.

The first model would be a *pure market economy* in which (1) resource allocation is governed by households, that is, consumers' preferences; (2) the allocation process takes place through the price mechanism; and (3) this process is based on material incentives used to implement the resource-allocation mix based on consumers' preferences. The second model could be considered as that of *market socialism,* in which (1) all enterprises and means of production are publicly owned; (2) planners' preferences prevail; but (3) the actual allocation of resources is still left to the price system so that planners' decisions concerning the resource-allocation mix are implemented through the market mechanism; and (4) this implementation still is based on material incentives and on highly differentiated rewards. The third model could most appropriately be designated a *bureaucratic resource-allocation or command-economy system.* This system would be based on (1) planners' preferences with (2) resources allocated by a process of physical planning, that is, by the allocation of commodities and factors of production not through the price mechanism, not through the market, but through administrative, bureaucratic means. This implies that the allocative process must be based on coercive and/or normative appeals.

What does it mean for a system to be based on consumers' preferences as compared to planners' preferences? A pure market economy will be based on *consumer autonomy* so that consumers have completely free and unrestricted choice to buy goods and services in accord with their own tastes and preferences; that is, they are free to allocate their household incomes without any restrictions between the goods and services available on the market. Moreover, these tastes and preferences will then govern the resource-allocation mix because in a market system these consumer preferences will be transmitted through the price mechanism to the producers. That is, in such a system, prices serve as signaling devices to indicate to enterprises the structure of consumers' tastes and preferences.

On the basis of these price signals, enterprises will make decisions of what to produce and in what quantities. In turn, these signals will ultimately also determine the character of their investment decisions. Similarly, the technical choices that producers will make will also be based on these messages in the sense that given the state of technology, relative factor prices will govern the factor mix to be used in the production process. For instance, if producers have a wide range of choice as to the techniques open to them under circumstances when the price of labor is relatively low, and that of capital is relatively high, they would tend, other things being equal, to use more labor-intensive methods to produce the range of goods desired by the consumer, and vice versa.

The market socialist system can also be viewed as a price-planning system. In pure form, this is in effect Oskar Lange's system, as developed in his prewar essay on *The Economics of Socialism.*[12] In contrast to the pure market economy, in this system planners are expected to decide what the desired rate of saving and investment should be. They also decide what the desired income distribution should be. Given consumer tastes and preferences, planners set – through a process of trial and error – interest rates and taxes in such a way as to attain these investment and income-distribution goals. That is, planners rely on fiscal and monetary management on the one hand and the price mechanism on the other to achieve their objectives. However, since the detailed and specific resource-allocation process takes place through the market mechanism, the appeals and instruments used must necessarily be remunerative, just as in the pure market economy. In real life, this system is to some extent approximated in Yugoslavia.

The third model differs from the first in that it is based on planners' rather than consumers' preferences. It differs from the second in that it no longer relies on the price and market mechanism to translate these preferences into an actual production mix, but instead resorts to physical planning, that is, to direct and administrative allocation of goods, services, and factors of production. In such a system, then, the planners would have to articulate a very detailed bill (list) of the final (consumer and capital) goods and services they desired. They would then have to decide, on the basis of the technological choices open to them, how much land, labor, capital, raw materials, various kinds of technical skill, and managerial inputs were required to produce this desired final bill of goods and services. Presumably these decisions would be based on certain technical norms or technical coefficients indicating what the unit labor and other factor requirements were for producing particular goods and services.

Having decided on the desired bill of goods and services and on the quantity and quality of factor inputs necessary to produce them, these factors then would be allocated to the desired uses through direct orders, by commands transmitted through administrative channels. Thus, in a sense this can be characterized as a *pure command economy*. The commands in turn may be based either on coercive and/or normative appeals. That is, factors, particularly labor, may be directed to particular sectors, localities, and production units on the basis of appeals to patriotism or to communist values without any resort to differentiated rewards. Alternatively and under certain circumstances, factors, particularly labor, may actually be forced to submit themselves involuntarily to certain types of work in certain localities and under certain conditions.

In fact, it is very difficult to envisage this kind of an economic system as a living reality. Except for a small primitive tribal economy, virtually any society would have a network of economic activities so complex that it would be difficult, if not impossible, for planners to define a bill of goods in physical terms with sufficient specificity to make the system operational. It would be extremely difficult to define in sufficient detail even the initial bill of goods and services and the initial composition of factor inputs. To make the necessary changes and adjustments in view of changing circumstances would be even more difficult. Such a system would necessarily be extremely cumbersome and inefficient. This inefficiency would be the more serious, the more complex and larger the economy.

In this pure command economy the relative reliance placed on normative versus coercive appeals would depend in large degree on the convergence of the preference and value systems of planners and households. The more divergent these preferences, the greater reliance might need to be placed on coercive instruments. However, if household and planners' preferences are not too far apart, normative appeals might succeed in shaping household preferences and altering them to bring them more in conformity with those of planners, thus rendering the use of coercive instruments unnecessary or creating a situation where only minimum reliance will need to be placed on them.

From Mao's point of view, an ideal system would probably be a command economy in which normative appeals would be so effective that the actors in the system would internalize, that is, adopt, the values and preference scales of the planners. Thus people would voluntarily commit themselves to go places and undertake tasks desired by the top policy makers without demanding special rewards in return for performing them. Moreover, they would be prepared to do this not only occasionally but on a continuing and sustained basis. This, in turn, would seem to be workable only if one could envisage the transformation of the human actors in the system into model communist men of the type outlined in the preceding section. One of the attributes linked to this ideal is an ethic of hard work and an ascetic personality, a personality that we often associate with the Protestant ethic. With such attributes, saving in the economy can be stepped up much more easily, just as Max Weber and R. H. Tawney argued earlier.[13] In their view these values, incorporated in the Protestant ethic, had contributed to the process of capital accumulation under capitalism. It should be stressed that Mao did not necessarily believe that people in general, and the Chinese in particular, start with these qualities, but that under certain conditions they are capable of acting in these particular ways, as shown above.

Central to Mao's outlook is the notion that the commitment, determination, and capacities of model communist man can only be attained through the infusion of a proper ideology. This ideology must first be adopted and internalized by the top leadership, then transmitted in its "correct," "true," and "pure" form to sub-leadership groups and to the cadres, who in turn must then transmit it to the masses of the people. According to Mao "our comrades must understand that we do not study Marxism-Leninism because it is pleasing to the eye, or because it has some mystical value, like the doctrines of the Taoist priests who ascend Mao Shan to learn how to subdue devils and evil spirits. *Marxism-Leninism* has no beauty, nor has it any mystical value. *It is only extremely useful.*" The crucial importance of ideas is further underlined by his conviction that "*once the correct ideas* characteristic of the advanced class *are grasped by the masses, these ideas turn into a material force which changes society and changes the world.*"[14] All this implies that if these "correct ideas" are combined with good organization, a high rate of resource mobilization can be attained. This can then also yield a high rate of resource utilization and a high degree of efficiency in the use of the resources mobilized.

There is no doubt that if the Maoist ideal could indeed be achieved, the complexities of the economic development problem would be greatly alleviated, not only for China, but for other underdeveloped countries as well. In these terms the problems ultimately raised by Mao's vision are several-fold. Can human beings indeed be made to behave in these particular ways, in large numbers and over long periods of time? Can effective methods indeed be developed so that the goal structure of the leadership and of the actors in the system is brought into harmony, based on the preference systems of the leaders? Third, even if normative appeals can approximate the vision of ideal or model communist man, can this in fact yield or assure a high degree of efficiency in resource utilization? Is there not a trade-off between a higher rate of resource mobilization and an efficient utilization of those resources? To put this question more concretely, can one expect the labor force to work long hours while its size is augmented and the hours worked are extended, without impairment of efficiency and a decline in labor productivity? The same considerations may apply to the application of masses of labor to land or to capital in the form of productive plants. Massing of such labor beyond a certain point may yield diminishing returns and may thus lead to a decline in the productivity not only of labor, but of land and capital as well.

Another way of saying the same thing is that a newly emerging nation carried by a wave of enthusiasm born out of its newly won sense of identity, sense of nationalism, and sense of self-reliance, can under certain conditions mobilize its people and tap its latent energies to perform a whole variety of developmental tasks. Up to a certain point, this can yield increases in output and in gross national product perhaps without the commitment of any new technical or skill inputs. However, the mobilization of such latent energies and previously untapped resources is essentially a once-for-all phenomenon that can perhaps yield a discrete and once-for-all jump in the level of output. To convert this into a continuous pattern of economic growth requires not only resource mobilization but the systematic adoption of new technology as well.

Economic policy issues

Once economic objectives are fairly well defined and appropriate means are found to motivate workers, peasants, and cadres in the pursuit of these ends, concrete and specific policies must be formulated to serve as guides for day-to-day direction of economic activity. Viewed from the vantage point of the early 1970s and the evidence uncovered during the Cultural Revolution (1966 to 1968), it is clear that the views of the Chinese Communist leaders differed as to the importance of different objectives and the priority to be assigned to them, the reliance to be placed on normative as compared to material appeals, and what economic policies would best translate goals into operational plans. In essence, these policy differences, tracing back to at least 1954–1955, revolved around two basic issues: the desired or feasible rate and character of economic growth and the role of the market or of centralized versus decentralized patterns of decision making in allocating resources.

These two overarching issues can perhaps best be explored by breaking them down into five concrete sets of economic policy problems. These may be considered as, first, the role of material incentives in allocating resources; second, the desired rate of investment; third, the desired pattern of investment; fourth, the role of professionalism and technical know-how in the production process and in economic management; and fifth, population policies.

The first of these can in turn be broken down into several sub-issues. The most important of these is the role of prices and wages as allocators. Ultimately, this goes back to the problem posed above, relating to the degree to which resources within the economy are to be allocated through physical planning or through price planning. One option open to the planners is to confine themselves to the definition of broad, aggregative, national income and investment targets, and then use indirect controls, that is, monetary and fiscal measures, to affect and shape levels of economic activity. This would leave the bulk of the allocative process to the autonomous actions of households and enterprises. This option is ruled out almost by definition for a centrally managed system such as that which prevailed in China.

The opposite course would be to allocate resources in strictly physical terms, in terms of quantities of inputs and outputs required, measured in tons or yards, etc., coupled with the allocation and distribution of these resources through command or through administrative, bureaucratic action. An intermediate possibility is some mixture of these two extremes. Thus the planners might define the production targets in physical terms and the inputs required to meet these targets could also be outlined in physical terms, but the actual movement of resources and the actual allocative process could take place through the price mechanism or through the bureaucratic mechanism; that is, once the decisions have been made, the planners could rely upon material incentives, upon income incentives, as a means of getting labor and other resources to the enterprises, sectors, and localities desired, or they could merely rely on administrative orders. It is really in this realm that most of the policy disputes concerning material incentives played themselves out in Communist China. The problem at issue is the role of income incentives as a means of motivating the actors in the system to behave in ways that are congruent with the planners' preferences. In essence the question to be faced is how important are prices and wages as motivators for actions by enterprises and households, or can alternative means of motivating these actors be relied upon?

Policy disputes concerning the role of material incentives are closely linked to another range of issues: namely, the role of markets in allocating goods, services, and factors, most particularly the role of commodity and labor markets in resource allocation. This in turn raises the question of what kind of markets; should these markets be free, partially controlled, or fully controlled? Should peasant households and collectives have the right to sell agricultural produce directly to the consumer, or to state enterprises, at uncontrolled prices or should all agricultural produce be subject to strict controls? The same applies to the operation of the labor market. Should wages be fixed, or should they be allowed to move more or less freely in response to changes in demand–supply relationships in particular places and in particular industries?

A third sub-issue relating to material incentives is the scope of the private plots in agriculture. These private plots constitute a very important source of supplementary income for the farm population. However, there is a competition for resources, particularly labor and also some organic fertilizer, between the private plots and the collectives. This creates some serious dilemmas. Elimination or curtailment of the private plot may have serious dis-incentive effects and may lead to marked contraction in livestock and vegetable production. On the other hand, if private plots are given a free rein, grain production in the collective may suffer because of inadequate labor or other inputs absorbed by the private plots.

A fourth sub-issue revolves around the question of what wage system should prevail in the economy. Broadly speaking, the question is whether a more or less egalitarian or a highly differentiated wage structure should prevail, that is, whether and to what extent should it be adjusted to the differing skill and productivity levels of different groups of workers. For instance, this issue came sharply to the fore after the organization of the communes in 1958. In the heyday of commune organization, attempts were made to introduce a supply system of wage payments. Under this system, payments in kind would be fixed according to need, rather than according to the worker's contribution to the production process. This, of course, had very strong counter-incentive effects, since reward would not be related to effort or to contribution. It was a system that did not prevail very long, since it ran into many difficulties almost from the outset and thus had to be abandoned.

Nevertheless, the pre-dispositions of the leadership had a marked effect on China's wage and salary structure. It seems to be more egalitarian than those of many less developed countries and of the Soviet Union. This is contrary to what one might expect, given China's much greater backwardness. To the extent that technical, managerial, scientific, and engineering skills are likely to be relatively much scarcer in an underdeveloped economy such as that of China, as compared to an economy such as that of the Soviet Union, one would expect in the absence of countervailing policy pressures a wide spread in the wage structure of the former relative to the latter. In fact, the opposite seems to be the case inasmuch as the wage span between the highly skilled and the masses of the unskilled appears wider in Russia than in China.[15]

A second general complex of policy issues that the Chinese Communist leadership had to face relates to the desired rate of investment. This, in turn, is but one aspect of a more general question concerning the desired or targeted rate of growth and the pace at which the development effort should be pushed. To the extent that investment in China would have to be preponderantly financed out of the country's own resources, a high rate of investment automatically requires a high rate of domestic saving. Given the fact that the savings rate in old China was fairly low, the transition to a high rate necessarily required more rapid increases in the level of saving than in GNP. At the same time as output rose, total consumption increased as well, although less rapidly than GNP. This left considerable scope for increases in the standard of living of large segments of the population who benefited not only from a rise in GNP but from a redistribution of income from the rich to the poor.

In the long run consumption could be kept in check (at least in the sense of lagging behind the rate of growth of GNP) much more easily if reliance on material incentives were minimized while normative and coercive appeals were used for motivating actors in the system. Thus, the rate of investment issue is intimately linked to the incentives problem. As a matter of fact, there is a certain amount of circumstantial evidence to suggest that those leadership groups who advocated more liberal and more cautious economic policies favored both a lower rate of investment and greater reliance on material incentives.

The rate of investment issue is also closely inter-related with the pattern of investment. This is the case in the sense that in a closed economy, that is, an economy in which there is no international trade (a hypothetical case only partially applicable to the Chinese situation), a high rate of investment necessarily must imply sizable allocations of resources to the investment-goods industries themselves. At the same time, since in a high-investment economy consumption is to be kept in check, the share of investment channeled into consumer-goods industries will also necessarily be relatively low. This further complicates the problem of relying on material incentives as the prime motivators in the system, since reliance on these incentives yields differentiated rewards and increases in purchasing power for wide groups in the population. By the same token, inflationary pressures are bound to be produced if money incomes grow rapidly with expanding investment but are not matched by corresponding expansion in consumer-goods production.

A most crucial policy issue cutting across all those mentioned above is the ever-present controversy best dramatized by the slogan that pits "Red" versus "Expert." The issue revolves around the kinds of qualifications and attributes required for a high level of performance in the economy. In this respect, too, policy has shifted from time to time. There were periods when the primary emphasis was on "better Red than Expert." At other times the opposite course was followed, that is, that of "better Expert than Red," and yet at times the focus of policy was on the need for individuals in management and technical positions who were both "Red" *and* "Expert." The central issue here is that of professionalism. In its essence, the question posed is whether and to what extent ideological commitment and reliability can make up for lack of technical expertise, technical know-how, and professional training.

As indicated above, there is a great deal of evidence to suggest that Mao's own biases ran in the direction of placing preponderant emphasis on the essentiality of ideological commitment as an absolute prerequisite for effective performance in the Communist system, including the economic system. However, there were others in the top leadership who did not consider ideological commitment primary, but stressed technical competence as a sufficient condition for effective performance. This controversy was clearly evident during the Great Leap and it has played a prominent role in the Cultural Revolution. It undoubtedly is one of the issues that stood between Mao and Liu Shao-ch'i. The issue of professionalism was also very important in the field of military policy. If anything, it was perhaps even more important than in the economy. It would be fair to say that it was really Mao's experience in military affairs that conditioned his attitude toward economic policies. Mao's and the Chinese Communist leaders' experiences during the twenty-five years of civil war preceding their successful conquest of the mainland taught them to place great reliance on guerrilla warfare and on people's war techniques. This means functioning in relatively small units, living off the land, operating with only light weapons so as to have a great deal of mobility, and working not with professionally trained forces but with a civilian army that is strongly imbued with revolutionary zeal. This type of army proved to be highly effective during the civil war and did indeed lead to a Communist victory. Why could not the same attributes that produced this victory also produce victory in the field of economic development?

This attitude was most pronounced during the Great Leap, but was not confined to it, as illustrated by an editorial in *Red Flag* on September 1, 1958.

> In the course of their advance the working people have put forward these slogans which are full of revolutionary spirit: *Get organized along military lines, do things the way battle duties are carried out* and live collective lives. "Get organized along military lines" of course does not mean that they are really organized into military barracks, nor does it mean that they give themselves the titles of generals, colonels, and lieutenants. *It simply means that the swift expansion of agriculture demands that they should greatly strengthen their organization, act* more quickly and *with greater discipline* and efficiency, *so that, like* factory workers and *armymen, they can be deployed* with greater freedom and on a large scale.[16]

There is a great deal of evidence to suggest that Mao looked upon economic development as the conquest of a series of obstacles, obstacles that could be stormed and overcome by zeal, dedication, and commitment. It seems that Mao and many of his colleagues in the top leadership did not fully appreciate the fact that the kinds of qualities required to engineer a civil war and a communist revolution may be quite different from those needed to manage a growing economic, social, and political system, particularly one that is trying to launch a country on the path to modernization, to an industrial and technical revolution.

In retrospect it is quite clear that there were differing schools of thought on these issues in China. These differences were apparently confronted in 1955 in relation to agricultural policy, most particularly the pace of collectivization. There were apparently many who advocated a go-slow policy, lest peasant resistance lead to the kind of agricultural disaster that accompanied Soviet collectivization between 1928 and 1932. However, Mao's decision to foster rapid collectivization prevailed without the disastrous consequences that were feared.

In general, many of the planners, economists, and technocrats were preoccupied with technical considerations and requirements, the need for technical skills, material incentives, and more or less balanced growth with proper attention paid to complementarities and inter-relations between different sectors of the economy. These same groups tended to favor a greater scope for the market mechanism, private plots, population control policies, and generally a less ideological approach to economic policy problems and economic management. At all the crucial policy turns, such as those relating to collectivization, the Great Leap, the Agriculture First Policy, and the Cultural Revolution, these counselors of caution were locked in debate with the more political and radical elements identified with Mao.

In an even more fundamental sense the policy struggles revolved around what priorities to assign different development objectives. Was it more important to accelerate economic growth, industrialization, and gain in great-power status even if this were to be pursued along a technocratic path, with wide income, role, and status differentiation? Or was it essential for China to assign very high priority to narrowing income and status differences between the country and the city, between the educated and the masses, between mental and manual labor, between managers and workers, and between intellectuals, students, cadres, and the peasants? Mao's predilections were to stress the pursuit of rapid industrialization without sacrificing the latter objectives. In the 1950s he apparently placed greater emphasis on the former, but particularly since the 1960s his emphasis would have been more on the latter priorities.

In a sense, the question of the appropriate population policies to be followed is more or less separate from the issues discussed above. This is not to deny that there are very definite relationships between demographic variables and investment rates and patterns. However, these relationships are less direct than those between material incentives and investment variables. Thus rapid population growth obviously increases the pressure on the household consumption sector of the economy. It becomes more difficult to keep aggregate consumption in check under these circumstances. At the same time, it also forces greater allocations to hospitals, schools, and types of investment that are less directly or less immediately productive. Similarly, high rates of population growth, if based on high birth rates, tend to yield a young population with a high dependency ratio based on a high ratio of children below the age of fifteen as compared to the population in the age groups capable of performing productive work.

Even though population policy may be less directly related to the economic policy problems treated above, there was apparently a close correlation in the attitudes of many Chinese policy makers toward these problems. On the whole, those groups of policy makers who favored greater reliance on material incentives, lower investment rates, and patterns of investment which are less exclusively heavy-industry oriented also tended to pay greater attention to population and demographic problems. Thus, it was these policy makers in China who advocated some form of population control, some form of family planning, and the adoption of a series of measures designed to slow the rate of population growth.

Actually, population policy in China went through a number of phases. Initially, it was ignored as a problem and any mention of it was attacked on ideological and doctrinaire grounds. All concern with population was regarded as Malthusianism and as such was viewed as a manifestation of imperialism. However, beginning in 1954 one can detect a subtle change in official attitudes. Circumstantial evidence suggests that the Chinese leadership may have been surprised at the results of the 1953 census, revealing a considerably larger population than officially estimated up to that time. This apparently led to some concern and a cautious discussion of the problem, which was gradually stepped up to the point that by 1956 and 1957 it resulted in a large birth control campaign. Carried out as a mass campaign for maternal and child health care, it involved the distribution of contraceptives, educational materials, films, posters, and repeated exhortations designed to foster birth control.

As relentlessly as the campaign was pursued, it was called off quite suddenly in late 1957 and 1958. This was coupled with leadership pronouncements that population was to be treated as an asset rather than a liability; that rising population meant the labor force – and hence the number of producers – would be increasing. However, this attitude was sharply modified under the impact of the agricultural and food crisis of the early 1960s. Since then Chinese policy makers have been fully committed to the introduction and implementation of comprehensive family planning programs both in the city and throughout the countryside. For over a decade this has been Chinese policy, and it is carried out through a combination of means.

The implementation of this policy involves late marriage, free distribution of contraceptive supplies and information, and the institution in hospitals of abortion and family-planning clinics. Last but not least, all this is coupled with far-reaching peer pressures and persuasion to limit urban families to two children and rural families to three. In the absence of published birth rate data it is difficult to assess the effectiveness of these programs. However, what evidence we have suggests that the programs have probably been quite effective in the cities. At the same time, Chou En-lai and other Chinese leaders often stated that the programs have not yet fully penetrated the countryside and probably have been less effective there.

Economic development strategies in contemporary China

The interaction of objectives, appeals, and policies crystallized into overall development strategies, each with a different set of priorities and emphases relating to incentives, rates and patterns of investment, the role of professionalism, and population policies. In these terms, Chinese policy makers and planners have pursued three alternative development strategies since 1949: A Stalinist strategy during the First Five-Year Plan period, 1953–1957; the Great Leap strategy between 1958 and 1960; and an "Agriculture First" strategy since 1961. The first was preceded by a period of economic recovery from war devastation and the laying of the foundations for the organization of a new economic system. This had to be done before any long-term development strategies could be pursued.

The Stalinist strategy

It was more or less natural for the Chinese to consider the Soviet experience as a basis for emulation when the People's Republic was founded in 1949. China and the Soviet Union were not only linked ideologically but by a bond of amity and alliance as well. More importantly, the Soviet Union had successfully pioneered a socialist path to economic growth. During the period of its first two five-year plans it had achieved rapid industrialization, speedy economic growth, and marked structural transformation in its economy. Furthermore, it had successfully withstood the Nazi onslaught, defended itself against invasion, and finally played a major role in the Allied victory in World War II. Therefore, it was not surprising that the Chinese Communists more or less adopted many features of the Soviet economic system and pattern of economic organization. It was also natural that they should under these circumstances emulate the Soviets in the type of development strategy to be used as a basis for economic planning and development.

The Stalinist strategy could be broken down into the following seven objectives. First, overriding commitment to achieving a high rate of economic growth more or less year by year or at least over an average of five years. Second, particular concentration upon industrial progress. Third, a heavy-industry-oriented pattern of industrialization and economic growth. Fourth, a high rate of saving and investment so as to attain the first three objectives. Fifth, industrialization at the expense of agriculture. Sixth, institutional transformation in agriculture and other sectors of the economy, and seventh, a bias toward capital-intensive methods in the choice of industrial production technology. At least to some degree, China's economic development encompassed all these elements within the framework of the First Five-Year Plan.

The overriding commitment to a high rate of growth coupled with a heavy-industry-oriented pattern of development was a logical concomitant of China's urge to catch up with the Soviet Union and the industrial West. Chairman Mao indicated in 1958 that "we shall catch up with Britain in about fifteen years." He then went on to point out that "if we are to have drive, *if we are to see to it that the Western World is left far behind*, do we not have to rid ourselves of bourgeois ideology?"[17] Thus, the commitment to rapid economic growth is infused with a sense of impatience and a drive to close the industrial, military, and political power gap between China and the other powers as quickly as possible.

To sustain this high growth rate and heavy-industry-oriented pattern of development required a high rate of investment. To attain this objective, saving was institutionalized by building into the very fiber of the economic system automatic mechanisms for raising and maintaining a high savings rate. This then was one of the prime purposes of the institutional transformation in the economy, most particularly nationalization and socialization.

In these terms, one of the purposes of collectivization was to facilitate the imposition of a high rate of involuntary saving on agriculture, either through increasing taxes and/or through manipulating price relations between agricultural and non-agricultural goods in such a way that the farming sector was forced to sell "cheap" and buy "dear." These price manipulations enabled the state trading companies to earn large monopoly profits, which were then paid into the government budget and became a source for financing investment and other government expenditures. At the same time, nationalization of the non-agricultural sectors provided a means through which all net earnings of government enterprises were automatically placed at the disposal of the government and became sources of budgetary revenue. In this way institutionalized means were provided to assure a high rate of saving both out of agriculture and out of the non-farm sectors of the economy.

There is a further consideration which prompted Chinese policy makers to push for institutional transformation in agriculture. It was hoped that agricultural reorganization, collectivization, and various forms of producer cooperation would not only assure a greater degree of state control over farm income and farm produce but that it would also provide a prime means for increasing agricultural output. In effect, it was hoped that the organization and restructuring of farm institutions and production forms could substitute for increasing industrial inputs in agriculture.

Specifically, it was thought that collectivization and even earlier forms of producer cooperation would capture certain economies of scale that could greatly contribute to increases in farm output without diverting investment resources from industry to agriculture. Traditional cultivating units in China were not only small, but fragmented. In many parts of China the basic unit of peasant cultivation was not a land holding concentrated in one location. Instead, it was more often than not divided into several parcels that were physically separated from each other by distances ranging up to several miles. This meant that a great deal of labor and draft livestock effort was wasted in traveling from parcel to parcel. It also meant that frequently each individual parcel was so small that livestock and even simple tools and implements could not be efficiently utilized. Collectivization, of course, would lead to consolidation of these different parcels. It would also mean that the strips dividing the different parcels and land holdings could be eliminated, so that some additional land would be gained for cultivation.

To the extent that agricultural production did indeed increase between 1952 and 1958, undoubtedly one of the significant sources of this rise could be found in these organizational gains. However, these were clearly once-for-all advances. Moreover, they could provide only limited increases in agricultural production, insufficient in and of themselves to keep up with continued and rapid population growth and also provide a margin for increases in per capita food supply availabilities.

Another hoped-for gain from this agricultural reorganization was in the field of technical innovation. It was felt that collectives led by party cadres with more or less advanced levels of consciousness, and possibly even some technical knowledge, could provide a better basis for breaking the crust of tradition than could have been the case in a private land-holding agriculture. That is, collectivization would, in and of itself, represent a sharp break with tradition. It would shake up the pre-existing pattern of mores and therefore could open up the farm village to new influences and the flow of new ideas. This receptiveness could then be reinforced by the cadres, who would themselves be an important source of these innovating ideas.

In fact, it is unclear to what extent innovation really took hold in the Chinese countryside in the 1950s and whether it was an important source for increases in agricultural production. There were several factors that militated against it. First, collectivization had strong counter-incentive effects, particularly to the extent that it was coupled with increasing farm collections that must have been unpalatable to the farm population. Second, the potential benefits that could flow from an innovation were to a greater or lesser extent counter-balanced by highly centralized patterns of management, through which the same set of recommendations for innovation might be disseminated over vast areas regardless of differing soil, climate, and other growing conditions. Thus attempts at innovation may have been, to some extent at least, defeated by the bureaucratized methods of introducing these into the countryside. For instance, in the mid-1950s, the production of the double-wheeled, double-bladed plow was greatly expanded and its adoption all over China vigorously pushed. However, while this plow helped to improve farm practices in some areas it was unsuited to most of South China.

In terms of its effects, the Stalinist strategy represented a pattern of industrialization at the expense of agriculture. At the least, it was at the cost of agricultural investment and sluggish rates of agricultural progress. In order to maintain a high rate of saving for financing increasing investments, consumption had to be kept in check in the cities and the countryside. At the same time only a small share of savings thus extracted was pumped back into farming, as evidenced by the fact that agriculture was kept on a short investment ration. Keeping consumption in check need not mean that there was no rise in the rural standard of living. It seems that grain retentions per capita did not decline in the countryside in the 1950s; they may even have marginally risen.[18] However, with a marked redistribution of income during land reform and collectivization, even a stable average per capita standard could lead to a rise for the bulk of the farm population.

Closely inter-related with the heavy-industry-oriented pattern of development was a bias toward capital-intensive methods of industrial technology. This was in part due to the fact that, for certain branches of industry, the production coefficients may be relatively fixed and there may be considerable economies of scale. This, for instance, is particularly true for steel production. The most up-to-date, technically advanced, efficient steel mills are the large, integrated ones. In this case, gains in efficiency resulting from size and consequent cost reductions may be so great as to more than counter-balance the fact that in a country such as China capital is relatively scarce and therefore quite dear, while labor is relatively abundant and therefore quite cheap.

This consideration may have been reinforced by the fact that, during the First Five-Year Plan period, China imported most of its capital equipment from the Soviet Union, which was industrially more advanced and itself subject to a capital-intensive bias in its processes of production. Since the Soviet Union is economically and industrially more advanced than China, this capital-intensive bias may have been more justified from an economic point of view there than would be true for a much more labor-abundant and underdeveloped economy such as that of China. Finally, the capital-intensive bias was undoubtedly reinforced by certain non-economic, psychological, and prestige factors, which placed a great premium upon large showy projects that could stand as outstanding symbols of industrial progress both for the population at home and for projecting an image of a powerful and rapidly industrializing China abroad.

The pursuit of a Stalinist development model was combined with a considerable emphasis on professionalism and expertise in technical and enterprise management, in planning, and in other activities. Moreover, as compared to later periods, material incentives as a means of motivating the labor force to greater and better effort were upgraded.

The Great Leap as a development strategy

As will be shown below, the Stalinist strategy of the First Five-Year Plan did result in rapid economic growth in China and most particularly led to impressive gains in industrialization. However, agricultural expansion was sluggish. These markedly divergent growth paths of industry and agriculture contributed to increasing dis-proportionalities, bottlenecks, and more or less severe strains in the economy, which became particularly marked by 1956 and 1957. These strains showed up in the form of tight urban food supplies on the one hand and agricultural raw material shortages for industry on the other.

Rapid industrialization was accompanied by rapid urbanization, as the industrial demand for labor grew and as rapid expansion in the cities provided added employment opportunities as well as a focus of attraction for the more or less depressed countryside. Thus it is officially estimated that between 1952 and 1957 urban population increased by close to 30 percent, while rural population increased by only 9 percent.[19] This rapid city growth placed an increasing burden on urban food supplies. The situation was aggravated by the fact that agricultural collections did not seem to have kept pace with the rise in urban population.

Despite collectivization and vigorous attempts to increase collections in the countryside, grain procurement fluctuated year by year partly in response to changing harvest conditions, but did not show a significant upward trend during the First Five-Year Plan period. As a result, per capita food supplies in the cities began to decline by 1956 and 1957. Similarly, growth in cotton production did not keep pace with the rate of expansion in the cotton textile industry, so that textile mills had to repeatedly operate below capacity due to raw cotton shortages. At times this gap in raw material supply was filled by cotton imports which, of course, absorbed precious foreign exchange that could otherwise have been used for importing more capital goods for the expansion of heavy industry.

For all these reasons, as the Chinese leadership began to think about the Second Five-Year Plan, which was to be launched in 1958, it felt the need to rethink the basic development model and development strategy on which the First Five-Year Plan was based. Chinese leaders began to clearly recognize by 1956 (as evidenced by some of the speeches during the Eighth Congress of the Chinese Communist Party) that the Soviet development model was not too well suited to Chinese conditions. Chairman Mao expressed these concerns in early 1958 as follows:

> In the period following the liberation of the whole country (from 1950 to 1957), dogmatism made its appearance both in economic and in cultural and educational work. . . . In economic work dogmatism primarily manifested itself in heavy industry, planning, banking and statistics, especially in heavy industry and planning. *Since we didn't understand these things and had absolutely no experience, all we could do in our ignorance was to import foreign methods.* Our statistical work was practically a copy of Soviet work . . . The same applied to our public health work, with the result that I couldn't have eggs or chicken soup for three years because an article appeared in the Soviet Union which said that one shouldn't eat them. Later they said one could eat them. It didn't matter whether the article was correct or not, the Chinese listened all the same and respectfully obeyed. In short, the Soviet Union was tops . . .[20]

Toward the late 1950s Chinese planners and policy makers became increasingly convinced that something had to be done about agriculture. Thus, it was considered essential to find some means to increase the pace of agricultural development. Initially, there was no clear agreement as to how this should be done. Agricultural policy makers were apparently agreed that if farm production was to be raised, two inputs were absolutely critical: fertilizer and water, that is, extension of the irrigated land area. However, disagreements developed in 1957 as to whether these inputs were to be provided in their modern or traditional forms; that is, would chemical fertilizer have to be supplied or would increasing applications of organic manure do as well. Similarly, would traditional labor-intensive irrigation projects do the job or was there need for modern irrigation equipment, power pumps, and other industrial inputs?

The problem was greatly complicated by the fact that planners and policy makers were most reluctant to divert state investment resources from industry, transport, defense, and other high-priority non-agricultural sectors. As a result, the advocates of traditional inputs won the day. The emphasis shifted to mobilization of labor in the countryside and the use of this labor to collect every ounce of human and animal excrement and apply it to farm land. This labor-intensive mass mobilization approach was also to be used in extending the irrigated land area.

Thus the Great Leap could perhaps be characterized as a Nurkse-Eckaus type strategy of economic development. While there is no evidence that Chinese economists and planners read the works of these two American economists, their formulations of the development problem seem to have been adopted – in a somewhat distorted and extreme form – by mainland policy makers. Thus Ragnar Nurkse's insight that surplus labor in underdeveloped countries could be converted into capital became a key assumption of the Great Leap.[21] Similarly, R. S. Eckaus's ideas concerning output maximization through the simultaneous pursuit of dual sets of technologies seem to bear a close kinship to the "walking on two legs" associated with the Great Leap.[22]

It would, however, be misleading to conclude from this that the Great Leap was a carefully designed and thought-out strategy. The contrary was the case. In fact it was a huge campaign, a movement, which developed an internal dynamic of its own based on a number of different but converging motivations. In retrospect these considerations and measures combined to reflect a definite approach and attitude to the development process, which can be characterized as a strategy.

The central objective of the Great Leap was officially defined as "simultaneous development of agriculture and industry."[23] This was to be achieved through two principal means: (1) by mass mobilization of underemployed surplus labor in agriculture and (2) by much greater reliance on production processes based on technological dualism. It was felt that if the surplus labor in the countryside could be mobilized for large-scale, highly labor-intensive projects designed to reclaim and irrigate land and to institute flood control, great gains in agricultural output could be obtained. In this way, labor would be converted into capital, and the investment potential inherent in surplus labor would be utilized without requiring much equipment or capital to start with. It was hoped that this mobilized labor could continue living in villages and travel to the mass projects from the village so that no additional housing would be needed, nor would special arrangements have to be made for food supply since these workers could be fed by their own farm households. In this way, the productive capacity of agriculture could be significantly augmented with virtually no additional cost.

A second aspect of this strategy was that the surplus labor could not only be utilized for irrigation, flood control, and reclamation, but also for expanding small-scale industrial production in the countryside. This was based on the expectation that industrial production itself could be significantly increased by consciously relying on a dual set of technologies. In those industrial branches in which technical coefficients (e.g., capital–labor ratios) were relatively fixed and where economies of scale were very significant, primary reliance would be placed on capital-intensive and large-scale methods of production. On the other hand, in industries where technical coefficients were less fixed and where there was a wider choice of possible production techniques, greater reliance would be placed on labor-intensive and small-scale methods of production. In official Great Leap terminology, this technological dualism was characterized as "walking on two legs." Furthermore, the concept of dualism was carried several steps beyond the pure choice of techniques.

In effect, it was envisaged that the whole economy might be divided into two broad sectors, one modern and one traditional. The modern sector would be preponderantly characterized by more capital-intensive and large-scale methods of production, while the traditional sector would be dominated by more labor-intensive and small-scale methods. At the same time, each sector would be more or less self-sufficient. The modern sector would become virtually an *input–input* economy rather than an *input–output* economy. It would be an *input–input* economy in the sense that every attempt would be made to minimize the leakages from the modern sector to the traditional sector, while the intermediate and final goods produced by the modern sector would be plowed back into the further expansion of that sector and/or would be exported. These exports, in turn, would then earn foreign exchange, which would be used to import capital goods for further expansion of plant and for a growing extension of the modern sector.

In contrast, the traditional sector would be pushed into involuntary autarky, with small-scale industries providing for all the consumption, production, and investment needs of this sector. Therefore, it was this conception of the economic process that prompted the leadership to encourage the construction of backyard steel furnaces, small-scale chemical fertilizer plants, and small-scale electric power plants in the heyday of the Great Leap. Thus, the traditional sector would provide for itself without relying on the output of the modern sector. However, this traditional sector would export food supplies and agricultural raw materials to the modern industrial sector without expecting any payment in return. This would be in the nature of an unrequited flow on tax account. In this way the pace of growth in the modern sector would be accelerated while, at the same time, mass mobilization of labor and its application to reclamation, flood control, and irrigation projects would greatly improve agricultural productivity and thus accelerate the growth in agriculture as well.

The Great Leap and the Great Crisis

As will be shown in later chapters, the Great Leap led to a Great Crisis. In part this was because the bumper harvest of 1958 was followed by several very unfavorable weather years, contributing to unusually poor harvests in 1959, 1960, and 1961. However, the depressed agricultural conditions of 1959–1962 and the great economic crisis of 1960–1962 must be ascribed to many other factors as well. There were many grievous misconceptions associated with the Great Leap and there were a host of technical, planning, and organizational errors committed in its implementation.

The Great Leap bore particularly the stamp of an evolving Maoist vision – much more so than the Stalinist strategy preceding it. Mao saw in the Great Leap an opportunity to fully emancipate China from reliance on the Soviet Union, and more importantly, to break out of the vicious circle of backwardness through a discrete leap, through a supreme effort, through a once-for-all mobilization effort designed to tap all the energies and latent capacities of the Chinese people. The hope was that one vast supreme effort could push China significantly upward in terms of its stage of development and thus launch the country on a path of more or less automatic and self-sustaining growth.

Thus the Great Leap was not only infused with a spirit of self-reliance, but also with an overpowering sense of impatience, an urge to catch up and to begin really closing the gap between the industrialized countries of the West and the Soviet Union on the one hand, and China on the other. For this and a number of other reasons, the Great Leap was based on a set of unrealistic expectations. In part, these reflected the convictions and the wishful thinking of the top leadership, but in part they were consciously manipulated by the leadership as a means of exhorting the populace and of arousing and mobilizing its spirit for maximum effort. Thus, to some extent, these unrealistic expectations served as one of the elements in the normative appeals being utilized as a prime instrument for mobilizing the population to an all-out effort.

In spite of these exaggerated and unrealistic expectations, the essential concepts underlying the Great Leap strategy undoubtedly had a certain amount of economic validity. That is, judicious application of underemployed labor to agricultural investment projects using preponderantly labor-intensive methods, coupled with expansion of small-scale labor-intensive industries and the reliance on technological dualism as a significant element in a development strategy can separately or in combination represent crucial elements of a development plan in a densely populated underdeveloped country. Therefore, the failure of the Great Leap was not primarily a failure in conception but a failure born of unrealistic expectations on the one hand, and inadequate and technically deficient implementation on the other.

These failures led to the very acute agricultural and food crisis that characterized the Chinese economy between 1960 and 1962. The marked contraction in agricultural production gradually spilled over into other sectors of the economy, that is, into industrial production, transport, and trade. In ways more fully discussed in later chapters, the agricultural crisis assumed such critical proportions that the Chinese were finally forced to begin large-scale imports of grain in early 1961 as a means of averting a serious famine.

Under the impact of these traumatic developments, the leadership finally recognized that there was no shortcut to agricultural development. Apparently it gradually came to the realization that solid agricultural development required large-scale application of industrial inputs and most particularly chemical fertilizer. Coupled with this was the realization that organization in and of itself could not serve as a substitute for these technical inputs. Moreover, that even if institutional transformation and reorganization succeeded in stepping up the rate of traditional input application [e.g., labor, organic fertilizer (animal and human manure)] this could not lead to significant agricultural expansion, since traditional Chinese agriculture was operating within the range of sharply diminishing returns. These, in turn, could be overcome only by significant technical rather than organizational transformation. Viewed in this perspective, the Great Leap tried to use essentially the same techniques for expanding agricultural production as were used during the collectivization period. Only the institutional forms were new, and the rate of traditional input application was more intense. In a sense, the Great Leap represented a last desperate attempt to bypass the agricultural problem and to avoid facing up to the necessity of channeling modern technical inputs into agriculture.

The "Agriculture First" strategy

Once the problem was clearly recognized, the elements of a solution were self-evident. Thus, the lessons of these disastrous experiences were finally translated into a new and altered development strategy which began to crystallize in 1961 and was publicly announced and began to be fully implemented in 1962.

The official slogan of the strategy was that economic development must be based on the principle that "agriculture is the foundation and industry is the leading factor." As stated, this slogan is full of ambiguity. It could either be read as assigning highest priority to agricultural development, or its opposite of still giving highest priority to industrial development. It is probable that this ambiguity was deliberate, in order to provide the regime with maximum flexibility in case it wished to change the order of priorities. However, the Chinese leaders in 1961 and 1962 went well beyond just sloganeering. Chou En-lai, in a speech before the National People's Congress in 1962, spelled out that planning and investment priorities were to be changed, with agriculture assigned first place, consumer-goods industry coming next, and investment-goods industries relegated to the lowest priority.

This represented a sharp break with the past since, up to 1960, the official priorities were precisely the reverse, with investment-goods industries first, consumer-goods manufactures second, and agriculture last. These new priorities were reinforced by a host of additional measures that gave them credibility. Thus, management, production planning, and income distribution within the communes were decentralized, with small production teams becoming the primary resource-allocation units. Agricultural taxation was eased and the price relationships between agricultural and industrial products improved in favor of agriculture. Most significantly, chemical fertilizer production and imports were greatly stepped up and the manufacture of certain small types of agricultural equipment was significantly increased. For instance, starting in 1962, small power pumps for irrigation were installed on a considerable scale in the Chinese countryside and much more electric power was allocated to the rural sector.

This new approach involved a strong commitment to the *technical transformation of agriculture.* The communiqué of the Tenth Plenum summarized these decisions as follows:

> It is necessary to mobilize and concentrate the strength of the whole Party and the whole nation in an active way to *give agriculture* and the collective economy of the people's communes *every possible material, technical and financial aid* as well as aid in the field of leadership and personnel, and to *bring about the technical transformation of agriculture,* stage by stage in a manner suited to local conditions.[24]

Within the framework of the "Agriculture First" strategy, most of these industrial inputs were concentrated in areas of "high and stable yields," where natural conditions were most favorable for immediate increases in agricultural output. Such areas reduced the risk of crop failure and maximized the returns from the increasing flow of industrially produced inputs. Under the impact of this policy, the predominantly rice-growing areas of south and central China were assigned highest priority for state investment in agriculture. According to one estimate, this process of rapid technological change encompassed 20 percent of China's cultivated area (about 25 million hectares) in the 1960s.[25]

The "Agriculture First" strategy was based on three essential ingredients. First, a reordering of the planning priorities, which meant significant expansion in those branches of industry that "support" agriculture, that is, provide important industrial inputs for agriculture. This was coupled with a significant increase in the rate of application of these modern inputs to farming. Second, an initial and temporary decrease in the rate of investment as compared to the Great Leap period and even as compared to the latter part of the First Five-Year Plan period. Third, greater reliance was placed on material incentives and rewards as a means of motivating farmers and workers in agriculture as well as in the non-agricultural sectors of the system. Thus, while the Great Leap placed preponderant reliance on normative appeals, with coercive appeals lurking in the background, a shift to the "Agriculture First" strategy brought with it a marked upgrading in the importance of remunerative appeals and a downgrading in the importance of ideological exhortation as an instrument for motivating the actors in the system.

A strategy that places greater reliance on material incentives more or less automatically tends to lead to a widening in the scope of the market. At the same time, it assigns an increasingly important role to the price-and-wage mechanism in the allocation of goods and factors among different sectors and different localities in the economy. Thus, it is not surprising that since 1962 private plots in the communes have been fully restored and wider scope has been provided for the operation of these plots and for the placement of farm produce in free markets.

Present indications are that there have been no radical departures from the basic outlines of this strategy, even during and since the Cultural Revolution, although the methods of implementation and some of the points of emphasis have changed. Agricultural development continued to be assigned a high priority, coupled with a "balanced growth" approach as a guiding principle of industrial development. Thus great attention was paid to complementary relationships between different economic sectors and, within industry, between different branches. A central objective of economic policy since 1960 or 1961, over and above agricultural development, has been "self-reliance."

In effect this meant emancipation from economic and military dependence on the Soviet Union.

The combined operational consequences of the "Agriculture First" and self-reliance policies were a larger allocation of investment and other resources to agriculture in the form of chemical fertilizer, irrigation pumps, other types of farm equipment, and rural electrification. To make this possible, domestic chemical fertilizer production was expanded, chemical fertilizer imports were stepped up, the farm equipment industry grew, petroleum extraction and refining was greatly extended to eliminate China's dependence on imports in this sector of great military significance, and defense production was greatly stepped up.

In the early 1960s, this policy was pursued with considerable reliance on material incentives in agriculture and industry. This gave rise to what Chinese sources referred to as "the development of capitalist tendencies in the countryside" and "economism" or "revisionism" in other sectors of the economy. There was a growing concern on Mao's part that the widening of the private sector's scope in the countryside, coupled with greater reliance on the market and on the price-and-wage mechanism, would lead to greater income differentiation and class stratification. These concerns undoubtedly played an important role in the decision to launch the Cultural Revolution.

The Cultural Revolution left the basic allocative priorities in the economy more or less intact. But it tried to infuse a spirit and a work ethic that would permit the pursuit of the same objectives by reducing the role of remunerative appeals (material incentives) and stepping up the importance of normative appeals (adherence to Maoist values). If anything, the importance of agriculture and of a rural value orientation ("learn from the peasants") was underlined by the Cultural Revolution, but at the same time the scope of private plots was more strictly curbed than before 1964 or 1965. Similarly, wage and income differentials were not checked, but tremendous pressures were exerted to reduce these differentials and to break down the barriers imposed by rank, role, or function in the system of economic management or indeed in the other functional fields as well, such as the army and the government administrative apparatus. During 1975 these pressures for narrowing wage, income, and status differences surfaced in the campaign to strengthen the dictatorship of the proletariat and to attack "bourgeois rights."

As one studies the evolution of economic policy in China between 1949 and 1975 one is struck by the shifts in development strategies, allocative priorities, the character of economic policies, and the methods of implementing economic programs. However, amidst these discontinuities there are very significant elements of continuity. Thus the tension between material incentives and ideological appeals has been a source of continuing policy conflict certainly from the early 1950s on. In actual fact, throughout the economic history of the People's Republic both elements have been present with cyclical changes occurring periodically in the relative importance of the first versus the second. The same can be said about the "Red" versus "Expert" controversies.

Going beyond this, each of the development strategies adopted had lasting effects. Even when one was abandoned, elements of it survived and were incorporated in the strategy succeeding it. For instance, labor-intensive mass irrigation, flood control, and reclamation projects were of considerable importance during the First Five-Year Plan period. They gained enormously in importance, to the point of being central, during the Great Leap, but they did not disappear thereafter. The same applies to small-scale industry, handicrafts, and rural industries. These were assigned very great importance during the Great Leap, to the point that their development was pushed irrespective of technical considerations, feasibility, or cost. With the collapse of the Great Leap, many of these projects were abandoned, but not all. A certain number survived; they were rationalized, placed on a sounder technical and economic basis, and have played a significant role in China's industrial development since. Quite a few of these projects have been revived since the Cultural Revolution within the context of a renewed emphasis on the development of rural industries. Thus, the "walking on two legs" strategy brought to the fore in a highly exaggerated, distorted, irrational form has never been fully abandoned; rather it has been rationalized and more recently given greater emphasis, but in a highly measured form.

Conclusions

This chapter and the preceding one are in a sense introductory. They set the stage for the subsequent analysis of China's road to industrialization. The pattern of economic change in approximately the last hundred years was explored in Chapter 1. In it I tried to show how the past left a legacy of backwardness, political barriers to economic growth, and acute problems on the one hand, and certain pre-dispositions facilitating development on the other. Both of these have shaped China's evolution since 1949. However, the economic path pursued by the People's Republic was not only influenced by the past but by the determination of China's new leaders to transform the country into a modern, industrialized, powerful socialist state. The objectives, policies, and instruments guiding this transformation were analyzed in this chapter.

In pursuing their development objectives, Chinese Communist leaders preferred to rely on normative appeals – such as patriotism and working for the good of the society as a whole – rather than material incentives. At the same time they realized that at the present stage of China's development, material incentives still play an important role in motivating workers, peasants, and cadres. However it is essential to keep the operation of these incentives within well-defined bounds, lest they lead to a widening of income and status differences and thus undermine socialist values.

A similar set of issues had to be confronted in facing up to the role of professionalism and technical competence in production and management. To preserve socialist values, ideological commitment must have primacy. Yet it was also recognized that the imperatives of industrialization demand a certain level of professionalism. This necessarily posed some dilemmas, leading to the emphasis on "redness" by some leaders at certain times, while at other times the reverse was the case with the need for "expertise" upgraded.

In moving forward to create both a socialist and a modern, industrialized, powerful state, planners and policy makers also had to decide what pace of advance the system could sustain and what rate and pattern of investment would assure the highest rate of growth while improving the distribution of income. This in turn required a whole series of corollary decisions concerning priorities assigned to agricultural development and within agriculture to food versus industrial crops. Correspondingly, the rate at which basic raw materials, investment-goods, and consumer-goods production should advance required another series of decisions. The approaches to economic development thus formulated were embodied in broad strategies that were analyzed and appraised in this chapter.

Each of these strategies had its own particular characteristics. The First Five-Year Plan was crystallized within the context of a close Sino-Soviet military and political alliance. This factor, combined with the Soviet record of rapid economic growth, induced the Chinese to emulate the Soviet model. However, gradually it became clear that this model was not too well adapted to China's resource endowments and realities. This recognition produced a shift in strategy designed to capitalize on China's resources, principally labor, accelerate the overall rate of growth, and break the development bottlenecks imposed by the relatively slow pace of advance in agriculture. As this strategy turned abortive for reasons outlined above, it too was abandoned. Certain of its elements were then embodied in the "Agriculture First" strategy, the principal hallmark of which has been the much higher priority assigned to the development of agriculture and those industries that supply inputs to it. Broadly speaking, these strategic shifts illustrate the willingness of leaders and planners to experiment, innovate, and learn from mistakes.

3

Property relations and patterns of economic organization in China

Given the development strategies and economic policies described in the preceding chapter, how were these implemented? What institutional devices and forms of economic organization were developed to provide state organs with the degree of central control required to translate policies into operational programs? These are the questions to be examined in this chapter. First the changing system of property relations will be described, then the forms of enterprise organization in agriculture and industry will be analyzed.

The system of property relations

The vast revolution that encompassed China was reflected in far-reaching changes in property relations, patterns of economic organization, and income distribution. In the process, the Party – through its cadres and the army – mobilized popular support to dispossess the dominant property-owning classes in the countryside and the cities through a series of major campaigns. This shift in ownership from the private sector to the state and collectivized sector was to give the government primary and virtually exclusive control over the allocation of resources, and that was one of its principal purposes in economic terms. This transfer was closely associated with a redistribution of income from the private to the public sector on the one hand and within the private household sector from the rich to the poor on the other.

Four different forms of ownership have been present in China since 1949. These four forms are: (1) state, public, or government ownership of enterprises and of the means of production or, as stated in official terminology, "ownership by the people as a whole"; (2) joint public–private ownership of the means of production; (3) private ownership; and (4) cooperative ownership. While all four of these forms have been present, their relative importance has differed from time to time and from sector to sector. Therefore, perhaps the best way of examining ownership patterns in China is to assess the comparative weight of each of these forms in the principal branches of the economy.

Ownership patterns in agriculture

In agriculture, only three forms of ownership can be found, namely state, cooperative, and private. State farms are not of major importance in China. Actually, they have been significantly less important than in the Soviet Union. The contribution of state farms to total agricultural production is quite modest, as evidenced by the fact that by the end of the First Five-Year Plan period (1957) less than 1 percent of the cultivated land area was encompassed by these farms. Their importance grew somewhat in later years. In 1964 state farms under the Ministry of State Farms and Land Reclamation encompassed not more than 4 percent of the country's cultivated area and less of its total sown area, since their multiple-cropping ratio was below the country-wide average. They produced about 1 percent of the country's grain output.[1] To these must be added state farms operated by the Army's Production and Construction Corps and farms coming under several of the other ministries.

State farms have been an important instrument for the reclamation of waste land, especially in the borderlands. Linked to this is their function of resettling Chinese from densely populated provinces in the sparsely populated regions where the earlier inhabitants belong mainly to minority nationalities. In this sense, state farms play a political and strategic as well as an economic role. In China proper, that is, in the inner provinces, they perform an important function as models for emulation and as experimental farms that introduce new methods of cultivation and production.

Private farming in China has undergone a marked transformation, as evidenced by the progress of collectivization shown in Table 3-1. Private land ownership is closely intertwined with the evolution of agricultural policy as a whole. Thus, when the Communists came to power, they embarked upon land reform. This process of redistribution was of course quite different in

Table 3-1. *Share of land area collectively cultivated or managed*

1953	0.6
1954 (at end of fall harvest)	3.0
1954 (year end)	14.0
1955	64.0
1956	90.0

Sources: State Statistical Bureau, *Communiqués on the Results and Implementation of the National Economic Plan* in 1954, 1955, and 1956, Peking, 1955, 1956, and 1957 respectively.

areas that were tenant-cultivated as contrasted with those that were owner-operated. Thus, in South China, where tenancy was most prevalent, land reform meant the transfer of ownership titles from landlords to tenant cultivators. In owner-operated areas it involved redistribution of land; that is, taking away some land from those peasants who had a relatively large holding and giving it to those who had very tiny holdings or who were landless laborers. During this initial period, private ownership of land was by far the dominant form in agriculture. State farms and producer cooperatives were at the time still quite experimental in character.

Between 1949 and 1952, about 45 percent of the farm land was redistributed to about 60 to 70 percent of the peasant households in China. On the average, the farm area thus gained by the peasantry was about one-third of an acre per capita. At the same time some forms of producer cooperation were beginning to be introduced even before 1952. In general, almost as soon as land reform was completed, and land titles were transferred, some movement for producer cooperation was inaugurated. From a Chinese Communist point of view, land reform served two principal purposes. On the one hand, it eliminated the economic and political power base of the landlord class, and thus broke the control of landlords over the countryside. This was considered by the Chinese Communist Party as a necessary prerequisite for gaining access to the peasantry and for consolidating the regime's control over the countryside. At the same time, through land reform land rents were appropriated by the state and were thus in effect nationalized. This was evidenced by the fact that the new agricultural tax in kind absorbed about two-thirds of the former land rent in the tenant-cultivated areas, which instead of being paid to landlords was now being paid to the state.[2] In owner-operated areas, the tax in kind can be viewed as the equivalent of an imputed land rent.

The Chinese Communists were anxious to embark upon some form of producer cooperation as soon as land reform was completed for a number of reasons. From their point of view, land reform constituted a necessary evil, a detour on the road to collectivization. This detour was necessary for tactical political reasons. The economic and political power position of the landlord class would have been effectively broken by immediate collectivization. Similarly, the land rent could have been nationalized perhaps even more quickly and effectively through collectivization, yet they instituted land reform.

In order to understand this detour, one must bear in mind that in 1949 and 1950, the regime was still consolidating its newly gained power. There probably was no other single measure that could have been more calculated to gain as large a measure of good will from the peasantry. Correspondingly, once land reform was completed, and the regime had fully consolidated its power and its levers of political and military control, it was anxious to push ahead with collectivization before the peasantry had an opportunity to consolidate its newly won gains. That is, the Chinese Communists knew that if they left the newly formed private land holdings to their own devices, the most enterprising peasant households might prosper and gradually accumulate wealth. This, in turn, would give them both a capacity and an inducement to resist the regime's incursions into economic and rural life. This, of course, had been the case in the Soviet Union in the early 1920s when Lenin launched the so-called New Economic Policy (NEP), which greatly strengthened the economic and political power position of the "kulak" class.

All these factors, combined with certain economic considerations, prompted the regime to push for some form of producer cooperation immediately upon the completion of land reform. Since the average land holding resulting from land reform was quite small (about 2.5 acres), there were strong economic grounds for combining several small farms into one producer unit.[3] Considerable economies of scale could be gained by enlarging the basic land management units and pooling labor, livestock, and other farm inputs. Moreover, a certain amount of land could be gained if it were possible to abolish the strips between different land parcels; that is, if the necessity for boundaries between land holdings were obviated. With these considerations in mind, the Chinese Communists developed certain transitional forms of producer cooperation designed to gradually but relentlessly lead the Chinese peasant onto the collectivization road. This process dominated the period from 1952 to 1955, although in some areas it was initiated and completed earlier.

The most rudimentary form of producer cooperation was represented by the so-called *ad hoc mutual aid teams.* These were small units, from six to seven households, that would pool their labor at harvest time; that is, in effect neighbors would be helping each other harvest their crop. This was a practice followed in many places in China on an informal basis many times in the past. It did not involve any long-term producer cooperation or permanent pooling of resources. However, once such an ad hoc team was established for harvesting, Communist cadres in the countryside would strongly encourage peasants to convert these into *three-season mutual aid teams.* They involved an organic extension of the ad hoc arrangements, being still confined to the pooling of labor, but now not only during harvesting time but also during sowing and cultivating time. This necessarily involved a closer bond of cooperation between the peasant households. The next step was the all-year-round or *permanent mutual aid team*. In a *permanent mutual aid team*, land, labor, and tools would all be pooled, but ownership would still be vested in each case in the individual peasant households.

In the APCs (*agricultural producers' cooperative*) *of the less advanced type*, the annual net product would be divided after the agricultural tax in kind was paid and after a certain amount was set aside for an investment fund. The rest was divided into a land share and a labor share. The land share was distributed according to the amount of land each peasant household brought into the APC, while the labor share was allotted according to the amount of work each household had contributed to the total production process. Gradually the land share was whittled down and at the point where an APC no longer made any payments on land, so that incomes were based on labor contributions only, it became an APC *of the more advanced type*, or what we would call a collective.

This process of transition was compressed into a period of four to five years, from about 1952 to 1956. When the big collectivization drive was launched in mid-1955, it really meant the conversion of all the mutual aid teams and the less advanced APCs into APCs of the more advanced type, as shown in Table 3-2. In this process, not only were the forms altered but the basic size of the unit was changed. Since the *mutual aid teams* were units of 6 to 7 households, there would be several such teams in a small village. The less advanced APCs, on the other hand, were units of about 30 to 50 households, based on the amalgamation of several teams frequently encompassed by a small village. In contrast, the collectives, or the APCs of the most advanced type, comprised 200 to 300 households and thus might be based on a large village or on a cluster of small villages incorporating a number of APCs of the less advanced type.

When collectivization was instituted, farmers were permitted to retain a small garden-sized parcel of land for their own use, usually referred to as a *private plot*. This parcel of land, adjacent to the homestead, would be used for raising livestock, particularly poultry and pigs, and for growing vegetables and occasionally some other crops. Private plots could not occupy more than 5 percent of the village's cultivated land area. The produce from the private plots could be disposed of by the peasants in so-called free rural markets, subject to minimal restrictions as to price, quantity sold, and other terms of sale.

These private plots, both in the APCs and later in the communes, played an economic role quite dis-proportionate to their size. Given the system of rewards in the collectives and communes, a peasant household's income depended on the state of the harvest and the size of the labor force. These two

Table 3-2. *Share of peasant households in different types of ownership units in Chinese agriculture, 1950–1959 (in percent)*

Year	Mutual aid teams	Agricultural producer cooperatives: Lower stage	Agricultural producer cooperatives: Higher stage	Communes
1950	10.7	negl.	negl.	none
1951	19.2	negl.	negl.	none
1952	39.9	0.1	negl.	none
1953	39.3	0.2	negl.	none
1954	58.3	1.9	negl.	none
1955				
(end of autumn)	50.7	14.2	0.03	none
(year end)	32.7	63.3	4.0	none
1956				
(end of January)	19.7	49.6	30.7	none
(end of July)	7.6	29.0	63.4	none
(year end)	3.7	8.5	87.8	none
1957	none	negl.	93.5	none
1958	none	none	negl.	99.1
1959	none	none	negl.	99.0

Sources: Percentages derived by author on the basis of number of households in Chen Nai-ruenn, *Chinese Economic Statistics*, Chicago, 1967, pp. 370, 371; A. L. Erisman, "China: Agricultural Development, 1949–1971," in *People's Republic of China, An Economic Assessment*, Joint Economic Committee, U.S. Congress, May 1972; State Statistical Bureau, *Ten Great Years*, Peking, 1960, pp. 34, 43.

combined determined the actual value of a standard labor day. However, since these were subject to marked annual variation, the private plots assumed a very significant role as a source of stability and income security. Since the produce from the private plots could be sold more or less freely, this constituted a very important source of cash income for the peasant household. Thus, it has been estimated that about 20 to 30 percent of total farm household income was derived from them.[4] Although in most years they were not to exceed 5 percent of the cultivated land area per capita in a village, 83 percent of the hogs raised in China could be found on private plots in July 1956.[5] Similarly, private plots were major producers of fruits and vegetables. As a result they played a decisive role in the country's fat and protein production, thereby making a most important contribution to the improvement of the diet and the maintenance of nutritional quality. Moreover, given their role in pig and poultry production, private plots became the principal source of organic fertilizer production. As a result, they emerged as a very important fertilizer base for all of Chinese agriculture, including its collectivized sector. This situation was modified somewhat in the 1960s as pig production was expanded in the collectivized sector.

Private plots, however, performed their economic role by competing with the collectivized sector for labor and organic fertilizer, that is, manure. Not surprisingly, the peasant was anxious to devote much of his and his family's labor to this plot at the expense of his labor input in the collective. This had been a perpetual problem in Soviet agriculture and was now a problem in Chinese agriculture as well. There were also frequent disputes between the peasant households and the collectives as to the quantities of organic fertilizer to be turned over to the collective and the terms on which this was to be done.

This competition for resources contributed to increasing pressures for the abolition of private plots. No wonder that these plots were swept away – at least temporarily – by the Great Leap hurricane and the drive for communization in 1958. As a result, for a year or two, all remnants of private property disappeared in Chinese agriculture with most adverse effects on pig, poultry, and vegetable production, coupled with a decline in the supply of manure and other organic soil nutrients. As these negative effects became more widely recognized and at the same time communization in general encountered growing difficulties, communes began to be decentralized rather haltingly in 1959, while concurrently private plots were also reintroduced in some areas.

Communes were very large agricultural production units, with about 4,550 households on the average during the "high tide" of communization in late 1958, and a total population of 20,000 to 30,000. However, there was a wide variation in size, ranging from an average of 1,400 households in Kweichow province to 9,800 in Kwangtung province. In the neighborhood of large cities some communes were even larger, with as many as 11,000 households. Gradually, this average size was reduced somewhat, but the commune has remained a large unit up to the present time, although its internal form of organization and functions have changed.

These communes were formed through an amalgamation of perhaps twenty to thirty collectives or APCs *of the more advanced type*, which in most cases coincided with an administrative unit, the *hsiang* (more or less corresponding to a township) or in some cases the *ch'u* (district, a unit above the *hsiang*). Within the commune there were three, and sometimes four, levels of organization: the *commune* center, the *production brigade,* and the *production team.*[6] The brigade more or less corresponds to the former collectives (APCs of the more advanced type), while the team is more or less based on the smaller APCs of the less advanced type. In some areas, where four levels of organization were introduced, the large brigade and the small brigade would correspond to the former APCs of the more and less advanced types, respectively, while the team would be based on the former mutual aid teams. The precise form of organization varied depending on the size of the communes, the basic pattern of village settlement, topography, and the type of agriculture practiced.

Initially, all ownership functions were vested in the commune center; that is, the commune appropriated the land holdings, tools, farm equipment, livestock, and all other assets. However, as communes ran into difficulties in 1959 and 1960, these ownership functions were gradually transferred downward, first to the production brigade and then to the team. With the onset of the acute food crisis in 1960–1961, the process of downward transfer in ownership was greatly accelerated and private plots were once more officially and programmatically sanctioned. As the communes were decentralized and responsibility gradually transferred to the production teams, apparently, in at least a few areas, there was a virtual reversion to private farming. It seems that these farm households were permitted to make their own production decisions as long as they met their tax and other delivery obligations to the team and through the team to the communes.

This led to what Mao and others referred to as the development of "capitalist tendencies in the countryside," which became a source of great concern since they represented a serious potential threat to the basic character of the whole economic, social, and political system. This concern was undoubtedly reflected in Mao's determination to reverse the process through the Cultural Revolution (1966–1968).

As a result, although private plots were not abolished again, the 5 percent limit was more strictly enforced as of that time. This then means that since 1961 the same three forms of ownership – cooperative, public, and private – that prevailed before the Great Leap were reinstituted and have prevailed up to the present. During and since the Cultural Revolution private plots have been eliminated in some communes. While average commune size decreased and their number increased between 1958 and 1963, since then they have been gradually enlarged, so that their number declined from about 75,000 to 50,000 within ten years. In some cases, production brigades have become the basic units of production and accounting, which results in the automatic elimination of private plots. There is some evidence that these changes represent not only localized responses to special situations but the beginnings of a trend that may gradually spread to the rest of the country, since it seems to be encouraged by the authorities as a matter of policy.

One of the most significant features of this radical transformation in landholding patterns was the apparent absence of large-scale, organized, mass resistance by the peasantry like that encountered in the Soviet Union between 1928 and 1932. Worry about possible peasant resistance to collectivization figured quite prominently in the policy and political discussions of the top leaders in 1955. Some advocated a policy of caution and gradualism, which was overruled by Mao. His judgment seems to have been vindicated at the time in the sense that collectivization did not lead to violence, resistance, or a drastic decline in farm production. However, once the leadership decided to go beyond collectivization and launch communization it did run into peasant resistance, although non-violent and passive, which forced a reconsideration of the whole pattern of commune organization.

Ownership patterns in the traditional sectors

Property relations in small-scale industry and handicrafts, in native transport, and in native trade bore many points of resemblance with those encountered in agriculture. Basically, we find two types of ownership forms in these sectors; namely, private and cooperative. Until about 1955, private ownership

Table 3-3. *Changing forms of ownership in handicraft industries, 1952–1956 (percentage distribution based on numbers of persons engaged)*

Year	Cooperative handicrafts	Individual handicrafts
1952	3.1	96.9
1953	3.9	96.1
1954	13.6	86.4
1955	26.9	73.1
1956	91.7	8.3

Source: State Statistical Bureau, *Ten Great Years,* Peking, 1960, p. 36.

was predominant in handicrafts, small-scale industry, native transport, and native trade, as shown in Table 3-3. With the general collectivization and nationalization drive launched in mid-1955, many of these small enterprises and individual handicraft establishments were merged into cooperatives so that since then this form has been predominant in all these sectors. However, the private form has not completely died out. Thus, some individual peddlers and handicraftsmen can still be found in China working on their own account up to the present day.

Ownership patterns in the modern sectors

A quite different system of property relations prevails in large-scale industry, modern transport, modern trade, banking, and modern services. The Communists inherited from the Nationalists a sizable public-enterprise sector in industry, transport, and banking. For instance, about one-third of industrial output was produced by enterprises that had been confiscated by the Nationalist government as Japanese assets at the end of World War II. Plants thus expropriated at the time of the Japanese surrender operated as public enterprises under the auspices of the National Resources Commission. Railroads had been operated as government enterprises even before the war, and several of the largest banks were also within the purview of the government sector. This provided the new regime with a government-enterprise base which could be used for competing with the private firms in these branches of the economy.

Up to 1952, private enterprise was still of major importance in large-scale industry and modern trade. In modern transport and modern banking, government ownership was already prevalent by 1952. Between 1952 and 1955, a combination of economic pressures and economic inducements was used to enlarge the scope and size of the government sector at the expense of the private sector. Then, in mid-1955, a large-scale nationalization drive was launched, the purpose of which was to convert all the remaining private enterprises in these various modern sectors into joint public–private enterprises. These were really organized as corporations in which the capital assets and the shares would be held both by private owners and government organs. Thus, by the end of 1956, only two kinds of ownership patterns could be found in these branches of the economy, as shown in Table 3-4. The two prevailing forms were government or public ownership, which was by far dominant, and joint public–private ownership.

Table 3-4. *Socialization of industrial enterprises (excluding handicrafts), 1949–1956 (percentage distribution based on gross output value)*

Year	Government enterprises	Joint public–private enterprises	Private enterprises under some form of government control	Private enterprises free of control
1949	34.7	2.0	7.5	55.8
1950	45.3	2.9	14.9	36.9
1951	45.9	4.0	21.4	28.7
1952	56.0	5.0	21.9	17.1
1953	57.5	5.7	22.8	14.0
1954	62.8	12.3	19.6	5.3
1955	67.7	16.1	13.2	3.0
1956	67.5	32.5	–	–

Source: State Statistical Bureau, *Ten Great Years*, Peking, 1960, p. 38.

In these joint public–private enterprises, private shareholders receive a dividend that cannot exceed a certain percentage rate of return on the assets. This rate of return was first fixed at 5 percent and then reduced to 3.5 percent. As a result, some remnants of private capitalists could still be found in China, particularly in Shanghai, as of the mid-1960s. There were reported to be around a quarter of a million ex-capitalist recipients of dividends at that time.[7] However these almost certainly lost their status during the Cultural Revolution, when this form of enterprise probably disappeared.

It is striking that nationalization of private enterprise in China was carried out not by decree but by relentless high-pressure gradualism. Thus industrial, trading, banking, and other types of enterprises were not nationalized from one day to the next by legal decree. Instead, as in agriculture, a combination of economic pressures and inducements was used. Thus government enterprises would sell their products well below market prices, incurring temporary losses, in order to bankrupt private firms. The state would levy heavy fines on private enterprises for tax evasion and other infractions. At the same time, government organs would enter into guaranteed sales agreements with private firms, thus providing an assured market for their products and/or secure sources of raw material supply. Between 1949 and 1953, these were the dominant methods used to enlarge the scope of the government-enterprise sector and to bring private enterprise under some form of government control (see Table 3-4). However, between 1954 and 1956, the socialization process was accelerated through government purchase of private-enterprise shares.

Enterprise organization in China

Organization of agricultural production

As is evident from the preceding section, production organization in Chinese agriculture has undergone many changes and transformations since 1949. In the early years, the dominant form of organization was a small owner-operated farm on which the peasant household produced pretty much what it had always produced in the past, subject to certain new constraints. The most important of these were the agricultural tax in kind and the compulsory purchase quotas imposed by the government authorities. Both of these compelled the peasant household to surrender a certain fixed quantity of its annual produce to the government, with the former to be turned over to the government organs and the latter to be sold to the state trading companies at fixed prices.

These obligatory delivery quotas and prices undoubtedly affected the farmer's production decisions. However, with the gradual collectivization of production, the farm household lost much of its autonomy in production decisions anyway. For instance, except for small private plots, decisions concerning land use – how much land is to be allocated to what crops – were no longer made by individual households but by the management organ of the collective as a whole.

Organization of collectives An *agricultural producers' cooperative* (APC) *of the advanced type* was usually managed by an administrative committee which was supposed to be elected by the members' conference, whose policies it was expected to carry out. Theoretically, this committee appointed the director of the collective. In fact, he was usually assigned by higher-level organs and his selection was merely ratified by the elected administrative committee. Under the jurisdiction of the administrative or management committee and its executive, that is, the director or manager, were placed various departments or sub-committees, each responsible for a special task such as grain production, livestock production, various other types of subsidiary products, finance, and so on.

Decision making and resource management in the APCs was carried out at three levels: the APC center, the production brigades, and the production teams. The APC center served as the basic tax-paying and compulsory delivery unit. However, specific land- and labor-allocation decisions were made by the production brigades, which in turn delegated certain production tasks to the teams.

For the most part, APCs were autonomous production units only loosely and indirectly linked to national agricultural plans. In the early 1950s, the state relied on such instruments as price and procurement policy as a means of achieving its agricultural production goals. However, in 1956, when collectivization was completed, an attempt was made to introduce planning in agriculture with physical output and sown area targets set and enforced by central planning organs. But these attempts at centralized and detailed production planning in agriculture broke down and thus had to be abandoned. As a result, while national agricultural plans continued to be formulated, purchase and agricultural tax quotas and price policy were used once more as the state's principal methods of control over APCs and later communes as well.

The APC (the collective) was linked to the rest of the economy through the deliveries and purchases it made to and from other units in and out of agriculture. Each APC had to pay an agricultural tax levied on its land holding as a ratio of "normal" or "standard" yield per acre. This "standard" yield, in turn, was based on the average yield of the principal crop or crops over a period of several years in the recent past. For the most part these taxes were paid in kind. In addition, each APC had to deliver to the state certain quantities of grain and other products at fixed prices.

All farm products falling within the purview of the "unified purchase and supply" system were subject to these compulsory deliveries. This highly regulated system of distribution was introduced for the principal food grains in November of 1953 and was gradually extended to include sweet potatoes, soybeans, oilseeds, sugarcane, tea, cotton and other plant fibers, tobacco, sheep wool, silk cocoons, cattle hides, and live hogs. For these items minimum per capita consumption levels were estimated in each APC. The compulsory delivery quotas were then fixed for several years in advance; they represented the residual after allowances for the peasants' own consumption and taxes were deducted from "normal" output. If the APC produced over and above its own consumption needs and its tax cum delivery obligations, it could dispose of the rest freely. In fact, state trading companies would often claim a prior right of purchase over these "above-quota" sales, which however were bought by them at "above-quota" prices as well. Products that were not encompassed by the "unified purchase and supply" system were not subject to fixed delivery quotas but could be sold in desired amounts to state trading organs or private households for their own consumption at regulated, but not fixed, prices.

APCs usually maintained accounts in the local branches of the People's

Bank. Thus the proceeds from the sale of these agricultural products would be deposited in these accounts. By the same token, the bank accounts would be drawn upon to purchase production requisites such as chemical fertilizer, insecticides, pesticides, farm equipment, or other items needed for agricultural production. Thus the sales and purchases of the APCs as such, as distinct from those of their members, would usually not involve cash transactions, but rather the crediting and debiting of bank accounts.

The sales of produce, whether on compulsory delivery or other accounts, combined with the retained farm output constituted the total annual revenue of the APCs. There were four kinds of claims against this revenue: the tax in kind, the reserve fund, the welfare or collective consumption fund, and the labor-income fund. The first three of these were set aside first and the labor-income fund was treated as a residual. The reserve fund was used for financing investments and purchases of production requisites. The welfare fund was applied to financing communal consumption needs. The labor-income fund was distributed among the membership according to the work performed by them during the agricultural year. This work performance, in turn, was based on certain *labor norms*. Each type of job had a defined norm denoting a certain quantity of work done of a certain quality. Each norm carried a certain number of *work points* and ten such points constituted a *standard labor day*. Each household's income was then based on the number of standard labor days contributed.

The size of the labor-income fund and hence of farm household income was subject to a high degree of uncertainty year by year. This income could not be forecast because, even if the tax in kind and the compulsory delivery quotas were fixed, the harvests were subject to large annual fluctuations. Therefore the precise monetary or physical crop value of a standard labor day could not be set in advance.

The problem was further aggravated by the fact that in the over-populated cooperatives managers did not hesitate to use as much labor as possible, both for current production and for large-scale capital projects. Since the number of standard labor days worked determined each worker's and therefore each household's claim on the total annual net earnings (in kind and in cash), an expansion in employment and thus in the total number of standard labor days worked diminished the value of each labor day unless the increase in employment was matched by at least a proportionate rise in farm output. Such decline in the unit value of a standard labor day could in turn have considerable dis-incentive effects.

Generally, while collectivization brought with it certain economies of scale in production, it also produced some serious management problems which were greatly aggravated when the size of the basic production unit was enormously expanded to commune size. By its very nature, agricultural production entails decentralized, on-the-spot decision making. Also, workers in a large farm organization are spread out so that discipline and control may be difficult to enforce. However, perhaps one of the most intractable problems was the acute shortage of rural management personnel, particularly accountants. Keeping track of the labor norms and the days worked by different members of the cooperatives was a fairly complex accounting task. Inadequacy of accounting led to many disputes and dis-satisfaction in the countryside.[8]

Organization of communes The communes constituted an essential and integral element of the Great Leap launched in 1958. Inasmuch as one of the most crucial elements of the Great Leap was mobilization of labor and its allocation, an institutional instrument had to be found to perform this administrative and allocative function at the local level. The collectives were too small to serve as management units for large mass-labor projects employing several thousand workers.

In many cases the boundaries of a commune coincided with a *hsiang* (township). Thus the commune assumed a multiplicity of functions. It became the unit of local (*hsiang*) government, the local militia unit, and the local political party unit. At the same time it took charge of all local economic planning functions. Concretely this meant that the commune was called upon to allocate all local resources of land, labor, and capital between the competing needs of crop production, animal husbandry, local industry, and mass-capital projects.

The highest governing organ of a commune was supposed to be a congress of all its members. This congress was composed of representatives of production teams and brigades as well as delegates of various functional and social groups, such as youth and women. The congress elected an administrative committee that included the director and deputy director of the commune. However, in practice these directors and their deputies were selected by higher-level organs, with the congress in effect ratifying this choice. This administrative committee can be regarded as the top management organ of the commune. Since the Cultural Revolution this function has been performed by the revolutionary committees of the communes, with a chairman and one or more vice-chairmen performing the key management roles. Under the revolutionary committee there are a number of departments taking charge of different aspects of commune activities, such as grain production, livestock production, forestry, local industries, finance, etc.

From an economic decision-making point of view, in their initial form communes were highly centralized units of local management. Actually, as seen from the top, from the vantage point of the central government in Peking, communization involved far-reaching decentralization inasmuch as many decision-making functions were delegated by higher-level economic organs to the local commune level. In contrast, looked at from the standpoint of a peasant household or a former collective of 200 to 300 households, communization – with the attendant assumption of economic-planning and resource-allocation responsibilities by the commune – represented far-reaching centralization of economic management.

In 1958, as the commune center emerged as the critical decision-making and management unit, ownership of the means of production including land was being vested in it, as were decisions concerning land-use patterns, labor allocation, allocation of other means of production, income distribution, and tax payments. In the course of 1959, some of these functions were transferred to the production brigade. As agricultural difficulties continued unabated and even became aggravated, ownership as well as resource-allocation and income-distribution functions were delegated as far down as the production team. Finally, in some localities, apparently in the early 1960s, this went so far that production teams sub-contracted certain definite agricultural production tasks to individual farm households. These in effect entered into a contract to make certain definite deliveries to the team, leaving the household free to allocate its resources beyond fixed deliveries in any way it wished. It is unclear how widespread this practice actually became at the time. In any case, since 1961 and 1962 the critical decision-making unit once more has been the production team, that is, more or less the same unit as in the mid-1950s.

Why these shifts, first toward centralization and then decentralization within the communes? Basically they were symptoms in a continuous quest to reconcile conflicting considerations of political and economic control on the one hand with efficiency on the other. Concentrating resource-allocative decisions in the commune center was designed to assure maximum control, innovation, and work effort in the countryside. However it became quickly apparent that this control brought with it such marked reduction in efficiency that it contributed to a decline in farm production. Once this was clearly understood, allocative and distributive functions were moved down to the team level. That is, detailed production decisions were delegated to smaller units in which soil and weather conditions were more uniform than in a large commune spread over thousands of acres. These small units could also respond quickly to changing and unforeseen circumstances without having to wait for messages to move up and down the commune bureaucracy.

In assessing the evolution of the communes, it must be remembered that they never assumed the extreme form of centralized organization that may have originally been intended or that was originally reported in the world press. Except in a few isolated instances, communes never involved the actual uprooting of villages with physical dismantling of houses and buildings in these villages, construction of new dormitories out of the bricks of the dismantled houses, separation of husbands and wives in different dormitories, and separation of children from parents. If this uprooting may have been the original intention of some of the Chinese Communist leaders, the few experiments with it apparently ran into so many difficulties and so much passive resistance that it was never implemented on a mass scale. However, there are two features of the communal system that were widely, but not universally, implemented and were of great importance. These were the communal mess halls and the changed system of labor rewards in the communes. These mess halls were probably designed as instruments of social control and as a means of checking food consumption in the communes. They were also supposed to release a great deal of family labor, particularly the labor of housewives, for production tasks. Communal mess halls undoubtedly achieved the latter objective, but it is very doubtful that they did serve as a means of keeping consumption in check. There seems to be some evidence to the contrary, inasmuch as apparently in 1958 much food was wasted in the mess halls so that perhaps more was consumed than would have been the case if food consumption had remained under the control of the individual farm household.

The other important change introduced by the communes in the early stages of their organization also proved to be counter-productive. This involved attempts at changing the wage-payment system in the countryside. One of the slogans of the communes was "reward according to need." As a result, many communes instituted a supply system of wage payments that entailed payments in kind. Under this system, each family was supposed to obtain the same necessities of life, such as food and clothing, regardless of its labor input. Some communes went to the extreme of paying all their wages in kind. Yet others retained a money-wage system, while most combined the wage and supply systems. Not surprisingly, the supply system had very strong dis-incentive effects, in the sense that it rewarded equally all households regardless of the quality of their work, the skills they brought to the production tasks, and the effort extended in the production process. Therefore, in the course of 1959 and particularly in 1960, most communes were forced to abandon the supply system and gradually revert back to the original wage system.

In retrospect, when the communes were launched in 1958 they played a major economic management role. Under the impact of the agricultural difficulties and the economic crisis resulting therefrom this role was sharply curtailed and the communes became local administrative and government organs. At the same time, some of the most radical innovations, such as the communal mess halls and the supply system of wage payments, seem to have gradually disappeared.

Therefore the long-term effect of the commune movement was to create a new and strengthened administrative and governmental unit, below the *hsien* (county) level. This unit performs some very important economic functions, such as tax collection, supervision of the compulsory farm procurement quotas, innovation, experimentation, diffusion of new cropping systems, and the management of the local rural industries. It also plays a major role in the improvement of human resources in the rural areas through the provision of greatly expanded health and educational services. At the same time it serves as the marketing center for the villages within the commune area and it supervises the supply and marketing cooperatives. However, it has played no direct role in farm production since 1961.

Forms of economic organization and management in the Chinese countryside have been characterized by reasonable stability since 1961. Seen from the vantage point of the early 1970s, the basic social unit is still the farm family household. This household usually owns the house in which its members live and the private plot surrounding it. The same peasant household supplies labor to the production team which allocates it – along with other resources collectively owned by the team, such as farm tools, machinery, etc. – between various farm production tasks. Sometimes a team may also operate small-scale industrial and handicraft enterprises drawing on local peasant labor. More frequently, such enterprises are operated by the production brigade or the commune.

The team is also the basic tax-assessment unit and it is responsible for meeting the quotas for the compulsory delivery of grain and other products to state trading companies at fixed prices. The production team administers the work-point accounting and allotment schemes originally developed by the APCs; these serve as the basis for the distribution of income among member households. In respect to all these functions, the brigade plays a supervisory role. It has to approve the allocative and income distribution decisions made by the teams under its control. The brigade is the lowest level at which Party institutions are organized. In addition to a Party branch, the brigade operates a political "enemy school," a militia company or battalion, primary schools, a medical station, and some brigade-run industries.[9]

Organization of industrial enterprises

As indicated above, the nationalization of industrial firms was virtually completed in 1956. Since then and until the Cultural Revolution, all enterprises were either public or joint public–private. However, from a policy, operational, and management point of view there was no difference between these two forms. The only distinguishing feature of the second was that the former private owners or shareholders theoretically retained part ownership in the joint enterprises. This did not entitle them to any participation in the management, but they received a fixed return on their invested capital. However this practice did not survive the Cultural Revolution, so that the public-enterprise form of organization now applies to all modern industry in China.

Forms of enterprise organization and management have been subject to considerable instability since 1956, reflecting repeated policy changes following a cyclical pattern. These forms exhibit a complex pattern of continuity and change, which has characterized the contemporary Chinese economic system since its birth. This pattern could be seen in agriculture and is just as evident in industry, with some elements persisting and others being transformed. The new forms thus continually emerging represent a shifting amalgam of stable and innovative characteristics.

These cyclical changes are most pronounced in respect to the role of politics and the Communist Party in the management of the industrial firm. Thus, roughly between 1952 and 1955, the Party was somewhat in the background; from 1956 to 1958 it began to play a more important policy role, leaving the actual day-to-day operations to management and technical personnel. The Great Leap placed politics in command and with it the Party assumed responsibility not only for policy direction but for management, thus in many cases virtually displacing or closely controlling and directing the firm's executives and engineers. With the collapse of the Great Leap and the onset of the Great Crisis in 1960 or 1961, the importance of technical and managerial considerations was recognized once again. However, management remained subordinated to the Party, with the latter providing policy and ideological direction and the former being responsible for factory operations under the overall direction of the enterprise Party committee or branch.

The relationship between the enterprise Party committee and the operational management of the firm was thus roughly similar just before the Great Leap (1955/56–1957/58), during the Great Crisis and its aftermath (1961–1966), and following the Cultural Revolution (1969 to the present). However, the Cultural Revolution led to an extreme politicization of all organizations and institutions in China, including the Communist Party itself. As a result, industrial enterprises were disrupted, economic accounting was thrown to the winds, and executives were attacked and frequently reduced to impotence.

This fluctuating role of politics affected all aspects of enterprise policy and operations, such as the status of management, the role of technicians versus party cadres, the role of economic accounting, the character of enterprise plans and targets, the criteria for enterprise performance, the role of material incentives and thus the character of the wage and bonus system, and a number of other features of industrial firm operations. However, it is possible that the actual changes in factory organization and management were not as pervasive as might appear at first sight. Thus one would presuppose – although this is far from certain – that the less essential branches of industry may have been more affected than the high-priority branches. This would mean that when "politics was placed in command" and the importance of technical and economic management downgraded, perhaps greater care was taken to assure continuity and minimize disruption in investment-goods as compared to consumer-goods industries, in defense-related versus strictly civilian branches, and in large enterprises of national importance as compared to relatively smaller and more localized enterprises.

A factory can be viewed as an organization designed to combine various types of labor, capital, and techniques in order to produce certain goods. Alternatively, a factory can be regarded as a network of human organization and a basic unit of political organization and indoctrination. Implicit in the Maoist vision described in Chapter 2 is a system in which men, transformed through ideological zeal and commitment, have internalized revolutionary values. These values enable them to work hard in an environment of human solidarity, performing a variety of roles and in this way advancing production and achieving technological progress. Thus revolutionary values are maintained and perpetuated and industrialization simultaneously pursued. The two mutually reinforce each other and in a sense become welded together. They become not mutually competitive but complementary or perhaps even identical pursuits.

This vision rests on several key assumptions. First, that workers, technicians, engineers, and managers can be expected to work hard and with maximum skill and efficiency while obtaining wages and salaries that differentiate rather narrowly between varying degrees of skill and effort. Second, that rapid increases in labor productivity, given strong motivation, can be attained without a great deal of specialization and role differentiation. A prerequisite for the validation of these assumptions is proper indoctrination of the workers in an environment of human solidarity. This is the central task of the Party cadres and the Party committees in the industrial firm.

Some Chinese Communist leaders and policy makers apparently considered these objectives and assumptions utopian, and therefore advocated policies that would place greater stress on material incentives and on income and role differentiation to attain industrialization objectives. Mao himself recognized that it would take some time before the masses would be transformed and their thoughts remolded to the point that these assumptions held and his vision could be realized. He understood that the path to his objective would not be a straight one; it would have to be interrupted by periodic tactical retreats and deviations. It seems that during these periods of retreat he countenanced the counsel of the skeptics and thus permitted economic and technical considerations to be more or less dominant for a time. However, when he sensed that there was a danger for these practices to become frozen in a mold he pushed to once more place "politics in command." Thus the zigzag and fluctuating course of management policies and practices in China largely reflects the mutually interacting relationships of the political forces within the Party (i.e., of Mao and his actual or potential opposition) and the actual course of the economy. The pattern evolving under the impact of these fluctuating policies will be explored in greater detail below in relation to certain specific features of industrial-enterprise organization.

The status of the industrial enterprise The public-sector industrial firm in China is largely patterned on the Soviet model. Specifically, this means that each enterprise is a legal entity: it can sue and be sued and can enter into contractual relations with other firms. It is autonomous financially, being an independent accounting and accountability unit. Therefore each enterprise has to keep a set of books, develop its accounts on a profit-and-loss basis, and account for its performance to higher-level organs. This does not mean, however, that profitability or profit maximization is the sole or even principal criterion of enterprise performance, as will be shown below. On the contrary, a public-sector firm can continue to operate even if it incurs continuing losses. The capital assets of an enterprise are the property of the state or its subordinate organs. It follows from this that the net earnings of these enterprises should accrue to the state, more specifically to the central government budget or to the budgets of subordinate governmental units.

In actual fact, during the First Five-Year Plan period, when the whole system of economic and fiscal management was quite centralized, public-sector enterprises of some size or significance came under the jurisdiction of central government ministries. This meant that they exercised supervisory responsibilities over these enterprises and appointed key management personnel. Correspondingly, net earnings were paid into the central government budget and grants for fixed-capital investment were extended to the enterprises from central budgetary allocations. However, after the decentralization decrees of late 1957 and particularly since the Great Leap a large number of enterprises were transferred from central to provincial and municipal government jurisdiction.

It seems that in the 1960s substantially less than 10 percent of industrial enterprises were directly subordinate to central ministries or their organs, but the enterprises under these ministries accounted for substantially more than 10 percent of total industrial output value and employment.[10] Generally, enterprises producing for the defense sector, engaged in the production of critical industrial materials, or oriented to the national or international market are most likely to fall under central ministerial direction.

Character of enterprise management: politics versus profits, or production in command Up to the Eighth Party Congress in 1956, the Soviet management model was dominant in Chinese industry. This meant that one-man management was official policy. However, the chief executive shared certain management functions with the enterprise Party and trade union committee.

One-man management on the Soviet pattern meant that each firm was headed by a director, who performed the role of a chief executive. The enterprise was operating on the basis of certain annual targets, the fulfillment of which was the personal responsibility of the director. He shared this responsibility with two key executives, who more often than not bore the title of deputy director or vice-director. These were the chief engineer, technical director, or production manager; and the chief accountant or comptroller. Since for the most part fulfillment of production targets tended to outweigh financial concerns at the time, it is not surprising that the first of these posts was usually more important than the second.

The Communist Party committee in each enterprise was headed by a secretary and a deputy secretary. The party unit performed partly a checking and inspecting function and partly an innovative one. It also served as a unit of political and social control. Thus it was responsible for checking on abuses of power, tendencies toward corruption, nepotism, and so on. The committee also bore primary responsibility for the indoctrination of the workers and employees in the enterprise and for their ideological health. The committee and its secretary and deputy secretary thus performed a fairly clearly defined range of functions that did not entail participating in the management and operation of the enterprise or even defining policy directions for the enterprise, except in the spheres clearly falling within the Party's purview.

Trade unions perform no collective bargaining functions in China and never have since the birth of the People's Republic. They are thus as in so many other respects quite different from their American counterparts. The function of trade unions in China is twofold. On the one hand, they are supposed to protect the health, safety, and welfare of workers in the enterprises, a function performed by unions in other countries as well. This may entail organization, administration, and utilization of clinics, mess halls, dormitories, and educational, recreational, and cultural facilities. They also administer employee insurance and other welfare funds on behalf of the state. On the other hand, they are supposed to reduce the rate of absenteeism and the turnover rate in the enterprise. Moreover, they are expected to assist in maintaining and raising labor productivity, labor efforts, and labor morale. The principal responsibility of trade unions is to create conditions that are conducive to hard work and increasing labor productivity. In a sense even the maintenance of health, safety, and welfare measures is oriented to this purpose. In performing these roles, the trade union in an enterprise is usually under the control of the Party committee, if not in theory then in fact. It seems that trade unions, like a number of other mass organizations, fell victim to the Cultural Revolution. However, they were revived in 1973.

One-man management was officially abandoned at the Eighth Party Congress in 1956. As the Chinese began to question the applicability of the whole Soviet development strategy, this was naturally also reflected in the sphere of industrial management. This process of questioning may have been reinforced by the fact that a certain process of decentralization coupled with some modifications in the Stalinist command system as a whole was also initiated in the Soviet Union around the same time.

While up to 1956 the enterprise director was a chief executive more or less independent of the Party committee in the guidance of the enterprise's internal affairs, he now had to share the direction of the firm with it. In a certain sense a division of labor was worked out; the cadres assumed control of policy and the directors retained operational responsibility under the leadership of the Party committee. As a result, the director became more of a technician.

Up to 1956, general policy guidance was handed down by the central industrial ministries to the enterprises. It was the director's responsibility to translate these ministerial guidelines into an enterprise plan and program still subject to the approval of higher-level organs. However, after 1956 this job of translation was assumed by the enterprise Party committee, which in a sense began to play a role somewhat equivalent to the board of directors in an American corporation. Close ministerial control and policy direction was part and parcel of a highly centralized command system. It was thus natural that as the process of decentralization was gradually getting under way some of these functions would devolve from the ministries to the enterprise Party committees. Therefore, in a sense decentralization and politicization of economic management were closely associated in China.

The process of decentralization and sharing economic management functions reached its culmination during the Great Leap. Now "politics was truly in command." While prior to 1956 enterprise Party committees were more or less subordinate to the director of the enterprise, this was now totally reversed to the point that decision-making powers were concentrated in the hands of the cadres. They assumed control and direction of all phases of enterprise operations, in many cases virtually eliminating the whole management function. This was the heydey of the mass line, when the latent genius of the masses was to be tapped and their spontaneous initiative mobilized. This meant that the policy decisions made by the Party committees would be carried out by production teams led by Party cadres. Production teams were to devise their own means of implementing the policies and targets decided upon by the Party committees. As part and parcel of this process, all distinctions between managers and workers were to be erased.

The spirit and substance of the Great Leap can be viewed as a strong reaction to the First Five-Year Plan development strategy, particularly as it was practiced up to 1956. That strategy embodied a highly technocratic approach to economic development, with great stress on professionalism in production and management. It pointed to the advantages of specialization and division of labor and was for its sake prepared to countenance considerable role, income, and status differentiation. It also entailed a relatively cautious development approach which paid considerable attention to complementarities, input–output relations, and technical requirements in production and enterprise management.

This approach was necessarily at variance with Maoist values. Therefore the Great Leap can be seen as an attempt to accelerate the development process through a non-technocratic, mobilization approach. But it can also be perceived as a deliberate attempt to break up the crust of bureaucratization and "new class" stratification that was in danger of crystallizing under the impact of First Five-Year Plan practices. Relying on the mobilization approach, it was natural for the Chinese Communist leadership to draw on its civil war experience and be influenced by it. Thus industrial management was more or less modeled on guerrilla warfare. Party cadres who had taken control of the enterprises began to act like combat leaders. The production team was regarded somewhat like a guerrilla unit. It strictly obeyed general policy guidelines, but was completely free to exercise its own initiative in implementing these policies and thus operating the factories. As in the civil war, the premium was upon improvisation rather than routinization as a way of coping with a rapidly changing situation.

Not surprisingly, this approach to management contributed to the collapse of the Great Leap. However, the failure of the Great Leap was most pronounced in agriculture, where management and technical errors in the operation of the communes on the one hand and in the large mass-mobilization projects on the other contributed to a sharp curtailment in farm output. The fall in industrial production was in turn largely a consequence of the repeated harvest failures, even though technical and management errors in the industrial sector itself contributed to the depressed state of manufacture in 1960 to 1962.

Under the impact of the Great Crisis, the Great Leap approach was abandoned, and the Eighth Party Congress practices were reintroduced. That is, managers, engineers, and technicians once more assumed operational responsibilities for the enterprise under the general guidance and supervision of the Party committee, just as in 1956 to 1958. Particularly up to 1964, technical, economic, and efficiency considerations were more and more pushed to the foreground. The emphasis was much more on "expertness" than on "redness." The extreme degree of decentralization characteristic of the Great Leap was modified so that, beginning in 1961, ministries reacquired some of their power, but not to the extent prevalent before 1957. Party-dominated provincial and district governments still retained much of their economic power, but not to the same degree as during the Great Leap.

In this new situation, factory managers were given much greater operational autonomy than at any time before and a much more flexible management system was introduced. This was evidenced by a reduction in the number of plan targets the enterprise had to fulfill (this reduction was actually instituted in 1958), by less stress on detailed output plans, and greater emphasis on profits as an enterprise performance indicator, as will be spelled out further below.

This process began to be reversed in 1964, when political departments were gradually introduced in all branches of economic administration. The reversal became complete with the launching of the Cultural Revolution. In its most overt and active form, this movement extended from about mid-1966 to mid-1968. It marked the height of politicization in all walks of life, except agriculture, since 1949. The situation was greatly aggravated by the fact that the Communist Party apparatus itself was one of the butts of attack, so that in many enterprises Party committees were disorganized. There was no organ to impose discipline, and many different Red Guard factions were vying for power and control in the factories.

There are many indications that cost accounting, economic accounting, accountability, and profits as an enterprise success indicator were anathema to many Red Guard groups during the Cultural Revolution. To them they were all identified with Liu Shao-ch'i, who in his approach to management supposedly placed profits instead of politics in command. All control and accounting was regarded as "strangling and suppression" of the creative energies and initiative of the workers. This was coupled with a conviction that production can go on without a plan and without accounting, and that, on the contrary, these stand in the way of expanding production. Instead of control, plan, and accounting, a "method of free operations" was introduced and management systems were eliminated as useless.[11]

It is difficult to determine how widespread these chaotic approaches became, that is, whether they were exceptional or typical. In any case, they were sufficiently widespread to cause concern once the Cultural Revolution was more or less terminated and efforts were initiated to gradually reintroduce many of the practices prevailing before 1966.

However, the Cultural Revolution did lead to some more lasting changes in enterprise organization. Since then, each enterprise, like all management organs in the government and the economy, is administered by a Revolutionary Committee. This committee is composed of representatives of workers, staff, party cadres, and some military. In effect, it performs the functions of both a management and a Communist Party committee. Frequently, and perhaps typically, the chairman of the Revolutionary Committee is also the Party secretary and one of the vice-chairmen is the chief engineer and another the chief accountant or comptroller. Another consequence of the Cultural Revolution may have been to give the workers in the enterprise a greater subjective sense of participation in the decision-making process. Whether from a strictly objective point of view this was in fact the case is very difficult to assess from this distance.

As one surveys this pattern of fluctuations it is important to bear in mind that the internal operations of a public enterprise and the role of management in it did not change as fundamentally as might appear at first sight. This means that out of a twenty-three-year period (1952–1975) about five years in all were profoundly disruptive, that is, the Great Leap and Cultural Revolution years. Each of these two overpowering movements left its mark. At the same time there were some strong built-in stabilizers in the process of industrial production and enterprise organization, which tended to rectify the anomalies produced by these overpowering movements.

The role of the enterprise in the planning process An industrial enterprise is both a contributor to and an object of the planning process in an economy such as that of China. In some aspects, the character of relationships between national economic planning and enterprise operations did not change very much, except during periods when annual planning in any meaningful sense almost disappeared during the Great Leap and the Cultural Revolution. It must also be added, and this cannot be emphasized sufficiently, that our understanding of Chinese enterprise operations is highly fragmentary. Much of our knowledge concerning these operations is based on a survey of thirty-eight industrial enterprises conducted by Barry Richman in China during May and June 1966, that is, just prior to the open launching of the Cultural Revolution.[12] This can be supplemented by studies of Chinese documentary sources containing highly scattered information, three earlier studies of China's economic system, and by reports from a number of observers who have visited China since 1972.[13]

On the basis of this scattered and highly tentative evidence, it seems that for most enterprises the basic operational plan is an annual one. Very rarely, if at all, does an enterprise operate on the basis of longer-term plans. On the other hand, within the framework of the annual enterprise plans there are quarterly, monthly, and even weekly ones. Fairly frequently the quarterly plan is the basic one.

Typically, the planning process starts with the central planning organs passing down preliminary targets, so-called control figures. These flow down the industrial hierarchy, where they are dis-aggregated, elaborated on, added to, and generally worked out in increasingly greater detail at each level, down to the enterprise and the individual shops in the factory. This is referred to as the "first down" stage. This is followed by the "first up" stage, which is frequently the last one, during which the process is reversed; that is, the detailed enterprise plans are aggregated, reconciled, coordinated, and rendered more or less consistent as they travel up the hierarchy. Once they reach the Center, the State Council calls planning meetings which are attended by representatives of provinces and municipalities as well as those from the various central government ministries most directly concerned. At these meetings production and consumption, that is, supply and demand, plans are compared and "balanced"; similarly, investment versus consumption plans are discussed. Following a reconciliation and decisions as to how to allocate investment funds among different regions and branches of the economy, the Planning Commission works out a final plan which has to be approved by the State Council, the Central Committee of the Party, and in a purely formal sense by the National People's Congress or its Standing Committee. It is then handed down in a final and more or less binding form. At times, if some issues remain unresolved, there may be for some parts of the plan a "second down" and thus a "second up" stage before the plan is finalized.

Since the Cultural Revolution this process is supposed to be reversed, at least officially and programmatically. That is, the initiative in the planning process is supposed to start at the bottom, at the shop floor level, so that the process begins with the "first up" and then is followed by the "first down," rather than the other way around. Thus preliminary targets and "control figures" are no longer supposed to be handed down from above. However, personal interviews with factory management personnel in 1972 and 1973 suggest that the old method (of first "down" and then "up") continues, although in a somewhat more informal and less institutionalized manner.

This complex, elaborate, highly bureaucratic process necessarily takes time. As a result, quite often an enterprise does not receive its final targets and plan until well after the planning year has started. Thus, according to Richman, the state plan was formally approved in February in 1953 and 1959, only around mid-year in 1954 and 1957, and in April in 1956 and 1960. Only a few of the enterprises he surveyed in 1966 had their plans approved before March, and some did not yet have them as of May and June. This was a much more serious problem during the First Five-Year Plan than in the 1960s. In effect, in the 1950s China operated under a *centralized command* system similar to the Soviet one. In the 1960s, on the other hand, this was perhaps more of a *decentralized command* economy. In the 1950s an enterprise was faced with a number of more or less binding targets it had to fulfill. In the 1960s, however, the number of targets handed down was smaller and the enterprise had somewhat greater flexibility in deciding what weight and importance to attach to the fulfillment of the different and at times mutually competing goals. Thus a Chinese industrial enterprise may have had greater control over its target mix in the 1960s than in the 1950s.

In its essential form this was a planning system clearly patterned on the Soviet one. This is not surprising, considering that national economic planning evolved in China in the early 1950s when Soviet influence and model emulation were most pronounced. But the spirit and substance of these plans changed considerably as Soviet influence waned. From an enterprise point of view, perhaps the most significant change was greater flexibility. This is underlined by the apparent fact that higher authorities had to approve annual plans only for a few broad targets, such as total output (either expressed in physical quantity and/or value terms), or total net earnings. These might be accompanied by quarterly breakdowns, but quite often higher authorities did not have to approve detailed quarterly and shorter-term plans.

An appreciation of the role of the enterprise in the planning process in the 1960s requires a clearer definition of the meaning of decentralization. It is absolutely essential to bear in mind that the intent of the decentralization measures was *not to delegate control* over resource allocation to lower-level organs or enterprises. On the contrary, the expectation was that through simplification of the target mix and some decentralization of government administration in the economic field, the efficiency and degree of control would be strengthened.

Centralization or decentralization are necessarily vague concepts unless they are more closely and operationally defined. The view of either process is crucially dependent on the vantage point from which it is approached. For instance, a transfer of a vast array of resource-allocation and control functions from the central to the provincial governments would represent a considerable degree of decentralization from the standpoint of the central authorities. On the other hand, from the standpoint of a county or other units of government below the provincial level, this may involve no change or conceivably even a greater degree of centralization than existed before. This would certainly be the case if the provincial government claimed for itself discretionary powers left earlier to lower-level jurisdictions. The same may apply in the relationships between a county and a commune, or a municipal government and a factory enterprise. That is, there may be a high degree of delegation from the center to the lowest levels of local government without any increase in the autonomy of a factory enterprise. On the other hand, under some conditions, decentralization could go so far that it would allow some greater exercise of autonomy even by the enterprise.

What is the situation of a state enterprise in China since the Cultural Revolution in this particular respect? As indicated earlier in this chapter, following the decentralization decrees of late 1957 and the Great Leap of 1958 to 1960, the overwhelming majority of enterprises were transferred from central ministerial administration to provincial and local administration. This can certainly be considered administrative decentralization. Did it also imply decentralization of control?

State enterprises in the 1960s and early 1970s seem to be under three types of jurisdiction or leadership: central, dual, and local. The largest and most important enterprises remained under central ministerial administration and control. Most enterprises, however, were placed under dual "leadership"; that is, for purposes of planning and resource allocation they remained under central control but administratively and politically they were placed under provincial or municipal jurisdiction. This means that local governments had a voice in the appointment of managerial personnel and the local party units were responsible for the party activities within the enterprise. The third category comprised mostly small- and medium-scale enterprises of preponderantly local significance, which were indeed under local (typically county) jurisdiction.

Regardless whether control over resource allocation was centralized or decentralized, Chinese national and enterprise plans were probably less "taut" in the 1960s than in the 1950s or than traditionally in the Soviet Union. At least in part this was imposed by economic conditions rather than by design. That is, in the early 1960s the "slackness" (lack of tautness) in the Chinese economy and in the industrial-enterprise system may have at least in part been due to the somewhat depressed state of the economy. Under the impact of the Great Crisis, the economy experienced considerable industrial unemployment and under-utilization of plant capacity. It would seem that just as full utilization of capacity was approached in 1965 or 1966, the Cultural Revolution led to another industrial decline; recovery from this setback apparently was attained by about 1969. Based on my visits to Chinese factories in December 1972 and January 1973 it seems that a certain measure of "slackness" characterized enterprise operations even amidst the new wave of expansion. For instance, in all the plants visited many workers were standing around more or less idle. In the Shenyang machine tool plant about one-third of the lathes were not in use. We were told that the annual output target was fulfilled by October and therefore the idle machines were being overhauled. One can legitimately speculate that while overhaul is important it is unlikely that it could be stretched out over such long periods if the targets were very taut. All of this was made explicit in a briefing at the Anshan Iron and Steel Corporation – the largest enterprise in China. The planning officials of this corporation told me in December 1972 that "in constructing the plan, the targets are fixed so that the plan can be over-fulfilled and enough room is left for the exercise of initiative by the masses. *Targets should not be too tight.*"

It seems that "lack of tautness" and flexibility may thus have been deliberately built into the planning process. This is evidenced by the marked emphasis placed on the accumulation of reserve stocks, both of raw materials and foodstuffs. The accumulation of these reserves was also facilitated by the introduction of less ambitious output targets, so that inputs were not as tightly stretched in relation to output requirements, as was the case during the First Five-Year Plan period.

Indicators of enterprise performance Stated in most general terms, the central objective of policy makers in an economic system is to secure the maximum possible increase in production from a given combination of inputs such as land, labor, capital, and raw materials; or conversely to minimize the bundle of inputs necessary to produce a certain quantity of a commodity or a service. Accordingly an industrial enterprise in China operates on the basis of multiple targets, some of which require maximization and others minimization. Prior to November 1957, that is, before the promulgation of the decentralization decrees, enterprises were faced with twelve mandatory targets relating to output, profit rate, technical progress, and labor productivity (all calling for maximization) on the one hand, and cost reduction – including keeping wage bill, number of workers and employees, and raw material consumed in check – on the other hand. However, in actual practice during this period the truly key objective, which served as the principal basis for gauging enterprise performance, was gross production value expressed in 1952 factory prices.

After 1957, the number of mandatory targets was markedly reduced. It is reasonably clear that during most of the subsequent period each industrial enterprise had some targets that it had to fulfill. Following the promulgation of the decentralization decrees, the following four were kept as mandatory: output of major products, total number of employees and workers, total wage bill, and total profit. However, it is far from certain that in actual practice there was any uniform set of targets equally applied to all industrial branches and firms in the 1960s. It seems that marketable output (value of manufactures ready for sale, expressed in current prices) replaced gross output value as a major indicator during the 1960s. Moreover, some index of profitability (usually in relation to sales or costs) emerged as a significant measure of enterprise performance in the 1960s. However, based on my own observations in China, it seems that at least since the Cultural Revolution, output of major products measured in physical terms has emerged as the most widely used indicator of enterprise performance.

For instance, we were told by the planning officials of the Anshan Iron and Steel Corporation that they were operating on the basis of six major target categories, listed in their order of importance: the output of major products stated in tonnage terms, the value of sales, product quality specifying how much is to be produced of each commodity of a certain grade or quality, the supply of raw materials, fuels, etc., required by the plant, and the cost reductions and profits expected (both stated in value terms).

The function of enterprise targets and success indicators is several-fold. On the one hand they serve as a means of controlling the activities of an enterprise and checking on its performance. On the other hand they serve as a means of channeling enterprise activities into patterns of resource allocation designed by the national planning authorities. They may thus provide planners with a series of instruments through which their resource-allocative decisions can be implemented and through which consistency and coordination between individual enterprise activities can be established.

In striving for plan fulfillment and the achievement of micro-economic equilibrium, one of the most critical and difficult problems facing planning authorities is how to devise enterprise success indicators in a way such that goals pursued by the enterprise will as fully as possible coincide with planners' intentions, preferences, and objectives. As shown in Soviet and East European practice, this is a most difficult task. For instance, if the highest-priority target for an enterprise relates to maximizing gross output value, if the targets thus defined are very demanding, and if the pressure is strong to fulfill or overfulfill these ambitious targets, then the enterprise, in order to protect itself against repeated failure, will tend to act in certain rather clearly predictable ways. It will tend to hoard labor and raw materials to make sure that its own production flow will remain uninterrupted. That is, it will try to minimize the possibility of supply bottlenecks developing which might then slow down and reduce output. At the same time, it will try to raise its gross output value to the maximum. One of the easiest ways of accomplishing this is to raise the cost of labor and materials purchased. Since a gross output value index is based on the total factory sales value of the good produced, it involves double counting of goods produced by other enterprises and purchased as material inputs by this enterprise. Thus gross output value can be most easily raised by increasing the degree of double counting.

Moreover, under these conditions enterprises will tend to substitute quantity for quality. This is well illustrated by the following complaint from the

Worker's Daily in 1955: "Factory manager Chao demanded that Inspector Li certify rejects to enable the plant to meet its output quota. Li refused. Chao then appointed Li assistant shop chief and ordered him to see that the plan was fulfilled. Li immediately changed his tune and demanded that the rejects be certified, but another conscientious inspector refused to give in and Chao's plan failed."[14]

Clearly, these practices are very wasteful and thus from an aggregate resource-allocation and social point of view quite undesirable. There are several ways the planners can guard themselves against these practices; that is, by specifying the maximum permissible employment and the quantities of raw materials that can be purchased by the enterprises. In fact, enterprises are typically handed such minimization targets. However, in actual practice the pressure for maximizing output tends to be much greater than for minimizing input. This amounts to saying that planners are so anxious to assure increases in total production coupled with rapidly rising output of particular high-priority products that they are prepared to sacrifice efficiency and countenance social waste. In this case, the production process may still be considered sub-optimal, but so to speak by semi-conscious design rather than by default. To the extent that this is the case, divergence between enterprise goals and performance on the one hand and planners' objectives on the other is reduced.

Similar problems must be faced if the highest-priority enterprise target is some physical measure of output specified in terms of stated quantities of certain products. Unless these are spelled out in enormous detail as to length, width, weight, quality, etc., an enterprise will be tempted to produce an assortment of goods that will most easily assure target fulfillment. For example, in a textile factory, cloth production targets may be stated in terms of length (e.g., yards or meters). A factory may then strive to over-fulfill its target by producing a greater total annual yardage than planned but much narrower than anticpated or than usable given the purposes for which it was required.

These practices are quite common in all socialist countries, including China. In China, however, they were apparently more prevalent in the 1950s than in the 1960s, since it was during the earlier period that such preponderant emphasis was placed on output targets. Yet even then the pressures for plan fulfillment and over-fulfillment were perhaps not quite as marked as in the Soviet Union. Thus failure to fulfill plans did not expose the enterprise to as strong sanctions or penalties as was the case in Russia; correspondingly, plan fulfillment or over-fulfillment did not lead to as large bonuses for the enterprise or its management.

Profit can serve as a reasonably good guide of enterprise performance when production costs and prices of goods and services produced are reasonably adequate indicators of the relative scarcities characterizing the economy. They will perform this function to the extent that they express, at least approximately, the relationships between goods and services demanded and the producers' capacity to supply them. Thus profits as indicators of enterprise performance and even more of efficient allocation of resources can be meaningful only to the extent that costs and prices are meaningful.

However, in a command economy such as the Chinese, most prices are administered rather than market-determined. This, of course, is not unique to the Chinese economy. Administered pricing is a widespread practice in all economies, capitalist or socialist. However, it is much more widespread and pervasive in command than in market systems. Moreover, since it is less likely that a commodity or firm will enjoy a complete monopoly position in a market system, ultimately even administered prices are subject to a market test in capitalist economies. Therefore, the extent of arbitrariness in pricing is likely to be significantly less in market than in command systems. For this very reason profits tend to be more reliable guides of enterprise performance in capitalist than in command economies. Nevertheless, even in these, profits may serve as a reasonably good guide of enterprise performance *within* each industrial branch, as long as all firms *within* an industry purchase labor, raw materials, and other inputs at the same prices.

In fact, this is how profits have probably been used by the planners in China. If the prices fixed happen to reflect planners' preferences reasonably adequately, profit targets may reduce the need for drawing up a long and detailed list of physical output and input targets. At the same time, the urge for profits will exert pressure on the firm to reduce costs and thus utilize its inputs more efficiently. This still leaves open the question of how consistency and efficiency are to be attained in the allocation of resources at the micro-level (enterprise) and macro-level (sectoral or economy-wide). It seems that the primary objective is to assure consistency, thus assigning efficiency much lower priority. To the extent that this is the case, the burden on the planning process is greatly eased, since the first is a much less demanding requirement than the second. Consistency or complementarity between inputs and outputs, in turn, is apparently attained through a variety of devices to be more fully spelled out below and in the next chapter.

An additional problem facing enterprises in China is that while they may be assigned several targets simultaneously, at times no clear indication is given as to which of these is accorded highest priority. The problem can become acute if the different targets are mutually competitive rather than reinforcing. For instance, in the 1960s an enterprise in China might have been handed four more or less mandatory plans: a profits plan, an output plan for certain major products, an employment plan specifying the maximum permissible size of the labor force, and a wage plan indicating the total wage bill that could not be exceeded. If these plans have considerable slack built into them, then the enterprise will be in a comfortable position and should have no serious difficulties fulfilling its output and profit plans.

However, if the labor force and wage-bill maximum allowed is low in relation to the output targets, then the enterprise may face a hard choice. It must find some means of hiring additional labor in order to fulfill the output plans. In this case it may also need to exceed its wage bill, particularly if labor is short, and there is some possibility that profits may be reduced. This was typically the situation in the case of "taut" planning, when all targets were based on extremely "tight" norms; that is, the planners tended to define the targets on the basis of the lowest possible input per unit of output or vice versa. As indicated above, this practice was less prevalent in the 1960s than in the 1950s.

This analysis suggests that success indicators may serve reasonably well as intruments for checking and assessing the performance of enterprises operating under similar conditions. They may be much more useful in comparing the performance of enterprises in the same industry located within a single region than firms drawn at random from different localities and industrial branches. They may thus provide some crude measure of efficiency for enterprises operating under roughly similar constraints and input conditions. However, they are much more ambiguous as indicators of goal congruence between planners' and enterprises' objectives. Precisely for that reason they may be less than fully effective in implementing the resource-allocation mix desired or targeted by the planners.

Enterprise transactions: sales An industrial enterprise in China sells its output to other enterprises or, in the case of consumer goods, to state trading companies, which then distribute these to retail outlets. These sales are based on contracts entered into by both parties subject to the approval of the appropriate ministerial, provincial, or municipal organs. Such approvals are essential, particularly for certain critical raw materials, intermediate products, many types of machinery and equipment, and consumer manufacturers that are considered essential necessities, such as cotton textiles. These products are for the most part subject to "unified distribution." This means that they cannot be bought and sold freely but can only be obtained on the basis of a government license. In effect, these products are subject to some form of rationing or quantitative supply planning.

For these commodities, administrative authorities designate what quantities of what commodity can be sold by one enterprise to another. Once the licenses have been granted for the purchase and sale of these products, the two enterprises engaged in the transaction conclude a contract which specifies in detail the quantities and types of products to be delivered, the prices at which these are to be shipped, and the delivery schedules indicating dates of shipment, the manner of payment, and any other particulars concerning the transaction. This highly centralized pattern of administrative allocation is widespread for all of the more important raw materials, intermediate products, and essential consumer goods.

The prices at which these products are sold are not set by the enterprises themselves. In the case of goods of national importance that are subject to "unified distribution," prices are as a rule fixed by the state planning authorities jointly with the relevant industrial ministries. Otherwise they may be fixed by provincial or municipal authorities subject to central approval or coordination. In either of the two situations, the enterprise itself participates in the price-setting process, sometimes with a major and at other times a minor voice. Payments between government enterprises do not usually involve an exchange of cash, but rather take place through the crediting and debiting of the bank accounts of the enterprises concerned, very much as in other economic systems. These accounts are periodically cleared, usually once a year, at which time the net debits or net credits of the two enterprises are calculated and final payments made accordingly, again generally in the form of bank deposits.

Enterprise transactions: purchases of inputs To produce its output an enterprise must obtain the necessary inputs, that is, a work force of adequate skill, size, and quality, the required raw materials, fixed and working capital, and management personnel. How does the industrial enterprise in China procure these inputs?

Manpower allocation Each enterprise is assigned a labor plan, which specifies the average number of employees during the year, the total number of employees at the end of the year, and the wage bill. Within the framework of this plan, each enterprise has the authority to hire labor. However, it must do so within certain constraints. Industrial wages in China are defined on the basis of an eight-grade classification, with each grade denoting a certain level of skill and responsibility. The income spread among these grades was roughly three-to-one in the 1950s following the wage reform of 1956. Within the framework of this wage system, in the 1950s an enterprise could theoretically go out and hire unskilled workers without restrictions. However, if they wanted to recruit workers from other cities or other parts of the country, a very serious barrier to labor mobility was the housing shortage in most cities and industrial centers of China. Thus, workers might have been reluctant to move and come to the enterprise unless they could be assured of housing. Moreover, all inhabitants who wanted to leave a particular city or locality had to obtain a permit from the local authorities. Similarly, upon arrival they needed a permit to stay in the city. Such a permit was a prerequisite to obtaining a ration card for the worker and his family. As a result, there were even then a number of serious barriers to labor mobility in China.

Whatever freedom of movement may have existed in the 1950s may have been abrogated in the 1960s. At least since the Cultural Revolution there is no free labor market in China and all labor is assigned administratively. The constraints on free labor mobility are further underlined by the fact that periodically large numbers of workers and other types of personnel are sent down from the cities to the countryside (*hsia fang*). The latest such mass exodus took place after the Cultural Revolution. A number of complex economic and political motivations seem to dictate these moves. In part, they may be designed to check the hoarding of surplus labor in the factories and the cities, thus reducing urban unemployment and underemployment. In part, they may represent an attempt to alleviate the food supply pressures in the cities; in some circumstances it may perhaps be easier to bring the population to the sources of food supply than to raise the rate of food procurement in the countryside and incur the costs of long transport hauls. Almost certainly these considerations are reinforced by ideological ones. *Hsia fang* serves as one of the means through which the barriers between urban and rural labor on the one hand and mental and manual on the other are to be removed. In some cases, this provided a means for removing a large number of displaced, restless, potentially troublesome Red Guard groups from the cities and channeling their energies into non-political and productive tasks. Workers, government officials, and cadres sent down from the cities might in many cases also serve to strengthen the accounting, management, and political capabilities of the communes, production brigades, and teams in agriculture.

The movement of high-grade scientific and technical personnel was perhaps subject to the greatest restraint. On the whole, these could not be hired but had to be allocated by central or local governmental authorities, somewhat like scarce raw materials.

The pool of managerial manpower suited to direct large-scale industrial enterprises was quite limited in China. The pool was further depleted in 1949 when many went to Taiwan and Hong Kong. Moreover, due to their conditioning and the kind of environment they were used to working in, the chief executives of large enterprises were not always suited to perform similar roles amidst the new conditions existing after 1949. Neither was the old type of working proprietor, who may have kept the accounts in his head, equal to the changed situation. New and more complex forms of organization demanded new and more specialized skills.

Under these circumstances key management personnel were drawn initially from several different sources. Many, especially in joint state–private enterprises, were recruited from the ranks of former owners and salaried managers who continued to be employed after their businesses had undergone "socialist transformation." Others were demobilized army officers, civil war veterans, and cadres; these cadres often filled the posts of enterprise Party secretaries. In time, managerial personnel were trained in educational institutions and in the factories themselves. Frequently, factory workers were promoted to be enterprise directors, heads of workshops, or in charge of some other management tasks. In the 1950s enterprise management in China was also greatly strengthened by the presence of Russian advisors and technicians. Some of these performed temporary management functions in the complete plant (turnkey) projects which constituted such a crucial element of industrialization in China during the First Five-Year Plan period.

Turnkey projects were large industrial installations or complexes that were designed in Russia. Their equipment and machinery was manufactured there, and they were then transported *in toto* to China, where they were installed by Soviet engineers and technicians, who operated the newly built plants until the Chinese were ready to take over. In many cases some Soviet technicians stayed behind as advisors. This practice and thus this source of enterprise-management assistance ceased when all Soviet advisors were withdrawn from China in 1960.

Management salaries in China are relatively lower than in the United States, the Soviet Union, or some other countries. In his survey of thirty-eight plants, Richman found that the highest-paid member of the management team in a Chinese enterprise in 1966 tended to draw a salary about two to three times as high as the average factory worker's wage in the enterprise. This, of course, may be somewhat misleading since both workers and managers obtain some services in kind, which if taken into account might increase the managers' total relative income. It is unclear, however, whether this would substantially change the outcome.

On my visits to Chinese factories in December 1972 and January 1973 I found that workers' wages ranged from 30 yuan to about 100 or 120 yuan a month. For technical and engineering personnel, salaries would usually start at about 50 to 80 yuan and go up to 150 or 200 yuan a month. Under some circumstances they could go up to 300 or 400 yuan.

Moreover, unlike the Soviet Union, managers in China do not usually receive bonuses for plan fulfillment or over-fulfillment. Middle-level management and technical personnel are eligible for such bonuses, as is the enterprise as a whole. In the latter case the proceeds are for enterprise welfare, and recreational or other special projects. On the other hand, at least prior to the Cultural Revolution, various perquisites went with high management positions, such as housing, cars, servants, and vacations at special resorts. However, these were apparently associated with positions held rather than fulfillment of plan goals.

One may draw several implications from the fact that material reward for managers in China was relatively more modest than in other countries and was much less tied to plan fulfillment than in other socialist economies. One would thus expect that the enterprise manager in China would not feel quite so strongly and personally the pressure to fulfill and over-fulfill plans. He is neither exposed to the same personal penalties nor rewards as his counterpart in the Soviet Union. In the 1960s, he also shared management responsibility with the Party secretary, the enterprise Party committee, and his deputies. He is probably also less motivated by material gain and is possibly more spurred on by psychic incentives, prestige, symbols of special recognition, a general feeling of contributing to national advancement and to the ideals of the society, etc. Alternatively, it would of course be possible that this lack of personal pressure militates against top-notch management performance. What little evidence we have does not support this hypothesis. That does not mean that enterprise management in China is uniformly of top quality. Probably the contrary is the case. But this is more likely to be due to deficiencies in managers' technical backgrounds, training, and the constraints under which they have to operate, rather than to a lack of incentives.

Raw materials allocation An industrial enterprise purchases its material inputs – fuel, electric power, and raw materials – from other industrial enterprises or from trading corporations. As indicated above, a certain number of raw materials and producers' goods are subject to rationing or "unified distribution." Those of greatest importance, for example, coal, steel, cement, etc., are allocated centrally, while others may be allocated by provincial or local governments. After an enterprise knows what its annual output plan will be and what its resource-allocation limits are for a given year or for a shorter period, it will try to procure the materials and equipment required from the producing enterprises on the basis of an approved "ration" or "license." In cases where an enterprise is only a small consumer of certain "licensed" materials or machinery, it will purchase these from a trading corporation under the jurisdiction of the Ministry of Commerce rather than from producing enterprises. The same practice would be followed by all firms, regardless of size of purchase, for all "unlicensed" commodities.

Inter-enterprise and trading-corporation purchases of materials and equipment are based on contracts of the type referred to above. In order to facilitate the "unified distribution" of these inputs, the Chinese have developed a number of devices designed to supplement, support, and facilitate the national control of key material inputs and local control of others.

The most important of these devices are the *supply and sales order conferences*, also known as materials-allocation conferences. At these conferences, detailed commodity-supply and sales relationships, specifications, delivery dates, and other contractual details are worked out between the producing and consuming enterprises. These conferences are usually organized along commodity or branch-of-industry lines. For centrally allocated commodities of major and strategic importance, they are typically jointly sponsored by the state planning organs, the materials-allocation agencies, and the ministry in charge of that industrial branch.[15] "Apparently all of the industrial ministries involved in the production of important producer goods are sponsors of national order conferences at least once a year."[16] The participants typically include not only the sponsoring agencies, but also representatives of the ministries that are the principal purchasers of the commodity to be produced and the principal suppliers of its material inputs. Lower-level provincial and municipal organs from the same types of bodies will also be represented, particularly from areas in which major producers or suppliers may be located. Finally, leading mangement personnel from all the more important producing enterprises, their suppliers, and sellers participate in these meetings.

All the ministries involved in the production of important producer goods sponsor such conferences at least once or twice a year. Such conferences are also quite frequently held at the provincial level and in large industrial centers like Shanghai.

At these various conferences, the authorities with jurisdiction over a particular industry, factory, or type of economic activity are concerned with general problems of consistency and balance between demand and supply in the allocation of materials, with the formalization of inter-enterprise contracts, and the issuance of special-allocation certificates. These give industrial organizations the legal right to receive stipulated types and quantities of the allocated goods. The materials-allocation agencies, on the other hand, handle various details in relation to the contractual arrangements. They also control the implementation of these contracts.

At least two other institutional devices for facilitating materials allocation were introduced in the 1960s. A relatively continuous type of commodity exhibition has been set up to provide a market for commodities not needed by various enterprises or commerical organizations but potentially useful to others. At these exhibitions, sellers can get cash, credits, or other commodities in exchange. Buyers can purchase the items on the spot without applying for allocation certificates to various governmental authorities. A similar and closely related innovation is the commodity banks set up in some cities for metals, equipment, minor machinery, components and parts, and some industrial materials. Enterprises can deposit or withdraw commodities from these "banks." When they deposit certain items they can either obtain others or maintain a line of credit with the "bank."

All these institutions clearly perform a clearinghouse, barter, quasi-market, and coordinating function in the field of materials- and equipment-allocation. Thus they introduce a great deal of flexibility into the planning process and enterprise operations. The national and local order conferences greatly speed up the materials-allocation licensing and contracting process by bringing all the principals in the various transactions face to face. This saves time and greatly enhances the probability that goods sold will more closely approximate the needs of the customers in terms of quality, specifications, delivery schedules, etc. Moreover, in case they do not, enterprises can turn to the exhibitions and commodity banks to bail them out of an unanticipated situation or unforeseen difficulty.

Supply of capital An enterprise obtains its initial fixed- and working-capital fund in the form of a grant from the government budget. The fixed-capital allocation is financed out of the "capital construction" category of expenditure, while working capital comes out of the "economic construction" item. The first is set aside for all fixed-capital outlays, including housing, schools, defense installations, etc. The second relates to all government outlays for the economy, both capital and other expenditures. Thus these two categories overlap in part. In the 1950s most of the capital allocations came out of the central government budget. However, following the decentralization of fiscal and industrial management, only enterprises controlled by central government organs are completely financed in this way. Others obtain their capital grants in part from the governmental authority under whose jurisdiction they fall. The central government grants were channeled to the enterprises through the People's Bank of Construction of China, later reorganized as a Basic Construction Finance Division of the Ministry of Finance.

The initial capital grant finances the cost of constructing the plant, installing the equipment, and placing the plant in operational condition. If at some later point the plant wishes to expand and such expansion requires additional investments of fixed capital, it will again have to obtain these from the appropriate government budget. The budget grants also supply working capital that is constantly and regularly needed to carry out a normal rate of enterprise activities. Any additional working-capital requirements for the purchase of raw materials, labor, and other inputs have to be financed through short-term loans from the banks. The banks charge interest on these credits, supposedly for servicing and administering the loan. The enterprise is not in a position to finance its own working-capital requirements since it pays the bulk of its earnings above costs into the government treasury.

Enterprise transactions: net earnings This brief survey of how an enterprise handles the sales of its products and how it procures its inputs would be incomplete without some indication of what happens to the differential between these two, that is, net earnings or net losses. Profits are of course a function of the prices at which goods and services are sold and the costs of inputs consumed in the process of production. However, as shown above, a Chinese enterprise cannot autonomously determine the prices of goods it sells or of inputs it buys. Some of the principles governing price and cost determination will be analyzed more fully in the next chapter. Regardless of the process by which profits are calculated, how are they disposed of?

Since in principle all industrial enterprises in China are either public or joint public–private, their net earnings naturally accrue to the owners. In the case of the joint enterprises a portion of the earnings is paid out – or at least was paid out until the Cultural Revolution – to the former owners or shareholders in the form of a fixed dividend. The remainder is treated the same way as public-enterprise earnings, that is, it is paid into the government budget.

Before doing so however, all enterprises are permitted to retain a small share of their profits under their own control to be used for certain clearly specified purposes, for example, bonus payments to workers, certain collective welfare projects, etc. Regulations concerning the precise share to be retained and the conditions of its use have changed from time to time.

Following deduction of this small retained-earnings share, all enterprise profits were paid into the central government budget, since all enterprises of any significance were under national control until 1957. However, following decentralization, only those enterprises that remained under ministerial control continued to transfer all their earnings to the central government. The others divided their profits between local and national governments on a 20:80 basis. However, since the central government continued to exercise firm control over local expenditures even after the decentralization of fiscal management, changes in revenue-sharing arrangements did not significantly augment local budgetary autonomy.[17]

Conclusions

As this brief survey of economic organization shows, Chinese leaders and managers evolved a system which more or less crystallized between 1955 and 1958. The institutional structure and the economic system has not changed substantially since. In form this system bears a distinct family resemblance to the Soviet system, with one important exception. The commune institution, both in its original conception and the way it has evolved, has no precise counterpart in the Soviet Union. But below the commune level, property relations and the patterns of collectivization are quite similar.

However these forms of economic organization are infused with significantly different spirit, style, and economic policies in China than in Russia. Undoubtedly this reflects differences in the cultural and historical backgrounds of the people, the stages of economic development, the circumstances under which they gained power, and the international environment in which they find themselves. That is, the very existence of the Soviet Union has created an entirely different situation for the Chinese from that which faced the Soviets in 1917.

While basic institutions in the People's Republic have been reasonably stable, economic policies have fluctuated in response to the shifting priorities of political leaders including Mao, changing leadership coalitions, and changes in the economic and political conditions facing the country. The Chinese leadership was almost certainly unified in its determination to convert China into a modern, powerful socialist state in the foreseeable future. However what weight, what priority, to assign the pursuit of socialist values was probably less clear. It is probable that not all leaders were equally committed to the reduction of status and income differences. They also did not always agree on what might be the most appropriate means to attain these ends.

Shifting management policies in agriculture and industry therefore reflected differences concerning the most appropriate means to be used to attain these ends. They also reflected a continuing quest to reconcile the conflicting requirements of control at the central level and operational efficiency at the local administrative and enterprise levels. Shifting jurisdictions of ownership and control from central ministries in Peking to the provinces, counties, and municipalities reflect this quest. The same applies to the shifts within agriculture from the commune center to the production team. Similarly, the changing number and character of legally binding targets assigned to industrial enterprises reflect shifts in the degree of enterprise autonomy tolerated or fostered by higher-level organs.

4

The resource-allocating system

The general planning framework

The primary task of an economic system is to develop institutions and means through which the tastes and preferences of decision makers can be translated into a specific mix of goods and services produced. This requires decision-making mechanisms for what is to be produced and in what quantities, how it is to be produced and distributed, and to whom. However, economic systems differ in terms of who makes the decisions and how they are made. They also function within vastly differing historical contexts, cultural and political settings, and stages of economic development. All these variables will affect the character of demand for goods and services and the technical and production capacity of the economy to satisfy it.

Some of the issues relating to the environmental setting of the economic system, such as technical backwardness and political and ideological setting, were dealt with in the first two chapters. Therefore in this chapter the means by which decisions concerning resource allocation are made, who makes them, and how they are implemented will be analyzed.

Three hypothetical economic-system models were outlined in broad-brush terms in Chapter 2 (see pp. 38–40). Somewhat the same ground will be covered here, but from a more specific and operational point of view, especially as it relates to resource allocation in particular sectors. As far as China, or indeed any living socialist system, is concerned only two of these three hypothetical models are applicable: those based on physical and on price planning. In fact, as will be shown below, in China resources are allocated both through the bureaucratic command system and through the market mechanism. In the latter case, prices and the market are typically used as devices to implement non-market-determined decisions by planners. Policy makers may, for instance, decide to increase steel production by 10 percent within a year regardless of cost and price considerations. They may then implement this decision by allocating specific numbers of additional workers, certain quantities of raw materials, fuels, and other inputs to the steel industry; alternatively, they may choose to fulfill this target through indirect means by raising wages and prices in the steel industry in order to attract additional resources to it. Bearing this context in mind, the pattern and approach to resource allocation will be explored first in agriculture and then in industry.

Before proceeding with this sectoral approach, let us briefly explore what kind of overall planning framework was instituted in China. The Chinese adopted a five-year plan from the Soviets. The First Five-Year Plan was formally launched in 1953 after the Chinese economy recovered from the shock waves of war and civil war. Yet it seems that the economy actually was operating on the basis of annual plans until mid-1955, for reasons to be brought out in Chapter 6. Therefore the First Five-Year Plan in effect became a two-and-a-half-year plan (mid-1955 to end of 1957). Preliminary targets for the Second Five-Year Plan (1958–1962) were announced by Chou En-lai at the Eighth Party Congress.[1] This plan, however, was swallowed up by the tempo and turbulence of the Great Leap and the Great Crisis following it when economic change was dominated by short-run exigencies rather than the systematic, longer-run considerations embodied in a five-year plan.

There was no third five-year plan even formally on the books between 1963 and 1965, when the economy was recovering from the depression of the early 1960s. Following a three-year hiatus, the Third Five-Year Plan was promulgated (1966–1970). However, the Cultural Revolution was launched during the first year of its operation and caused considerable disruption in the urban sector of the economy in 1967 and 1968. It is therefore unlikely that long-term planning was possible during this period. There are occasional references in the Chinese press to a Fourth Five-Year Plan (1971–1975), and it was mentioned in Chou En-lai's Report on the Work of the Government delivered at the Fourth National People's Congress in January 1975.

In this report, Premier Chou indicated that at the Third National People's Congress the development of China's national economy was envisaged in two stages, beginning from the Third Five-Year Plan:

> The first stage is to *build an independent and relatively comprehensive industrial and economic system* in 15 years, that is *before* 1980; the second stage is to accomplish the *comprehensive modernization of agriculture, industry, national defense and science and technology before the end of the century*, so that our national economy will be advancing in the front ranks of the world. . . . With this objective in mind, the *State Council will draw up a long-range ten-year plan, five-year plans and annual plans.*[2]

This statement clearly implies that the Fourth Five-Year Plan is to be followed by a fifth, which will run from 1976 to 1980. It also suggests that these five-year plans are embedded in longer-range perspective plans of ten to fifteen years.

These perspective plans are not entirely new in Chinese planning practice. A Twelve-Year Plan for Agricultural Development and one for the Development of Science were announced in 1956 to span the 1956–1967 period.[3] These perspective plans indicate directions and long-range projections of change rather than operational commitments. At the same time, there are some activities that require long-range planning horizons. This certainly would be the case for science education, manpower training, and educational planning in general, where the gestation period and lead-time are long.

Nevertheless, after all is said and done, since its inception the Chinese economy has undoubtedly been operating on the basis of annual and sub-annual plans. A detailed operational plan prevailed until the end of 1957. The other five-year plans were overtaken by events so that they could not be implemented. Possibly since 1970, with the return to economic stability, five-year plans may have become more meaningful. In the absence of any information concerning the substance of these plans it is difficult to ascertain this.

The distribution and pricing of farm products in China

In an underdeveloped, agrarian, but industrializing economy such as the Chinese, what role does agriculture play in the economic development process? What is the character of agricultural policy and what are its objectives? To understand the pattern and system of resource allocation in China, these questions must first be answered.

The agricultural sector is expected to first of all provide for the food-consumption needs of the population. Since population is growing, these needs are constantly rising. Rising demand for food is reinforced, however, by an urge for an increasing standard of living and thus growing per capita consumption on the part of all elements of the population. Rapid industrialization requires increasing transfers of farm produce to the non-agricultural sector. Given the urge for a rising standard of living and the propensity to devote some share of rising incomes to food consumption, strong dis-incentive effects may result unless this demand is at least partially satisfied.

Some farm products serve both human and industrial needs, while others are preponderantly channeled into one or the other. In any case, several industrial branches critically depend on agricultural raw materials; this is the case for cotton textiles, flour milling, brewing, cigarette manufacture, other branches of food processing, the leather industry, and some others. Rising employment and incomes lead to a growing demand for the products of these industries and therefore for agricultural raw materials. A certain portion of farm output must be set aside for reserves, to protect the economy against the sharp annual fluctuations in the quality of the harvest. Provision must also be made for meeting the food-supply needs of the military forces. At the same time, a certain share of agricultural output must be channeled into export markets since these exports serve to finance China's imports of machinery, industrial materials, and more recently grain and fertilizer as well.

Agricultural policy in China faced two key tasks: to find means for raising output and for allocating it among these competing claims. Obviously, these two tasks are closely inter-related since the problem of competing claims is much more acute and the choices are much harder if output is stationary or slowly rising than if it is rapidly expanding. However, for the sake of analytical clarity, these two issues will be separated and agricultural production policies will be discussed first and distribution policies second.

It would be fair to say that the planners were interested in increasing total farm output and in affecting its composition. To accomplish this they had to use different methods at different periods. Before collectivization, particularly before the introduction of compulsory purchase quotas for grain and other major products (i.e., before 1953), the market and private trade still played quite an important role in agriculture. Farmers disposed of the marketed portion of their produce in four principal ways. First, they had to surrender a certain share each year as a tax which was paid mostly in kind. The remainder was sold either to government trading companies, private traders, or by the peasants themselves at periodic rural markets. To control the produce markets and assure themselves of the government's and urban sector's needs, state trading companies were the heaviest buyers. They used advance-purchase contract arrangements to guarantee that they would command the quantities required.

These purchase contracts were usually concluded early in the growing season and involved a sizable down payment by the trading company. They thus provided the peasant with a source of ready credit free of interest charges. From the planners' point of view, major state participation in the market enabled them to exert considerable power in it and thus compete with the private traders, gradually reducing their influence and economic role. Once the state succeeded in dominating the farm-produce markets, it could use its position to influence production in agriculture by adjusting the relative prices at which it would buy individual products.

State trading companies also dominated the sales of consumer goods and production requisites to farmers. To the extent that they raised the purchase prices of farm products in general and/or lowered the prices of goods sold to farmers, they contributed to improving farm incomes and thus providing material incentives for an expansion of agricultural production. In effect, then, during this period planners had no choice but to use price planning as their principal or even virtually sole tool in stimulating growth in farm output.

This approach was particularly effective in influencing the allocation of land and other resources between different crops. For instance, in these early years planning authorities were very anxious to expand the production of cotton to provide an adequate and assured source of raw material supply to the rapidly expanding cotton textile industry. With this in mind, the price at which state trading companies would purchase raw cotton was raised in relation to rice and wheat. Since there was still substantial inflation in 1950 and 1951, the prices would often be quoted in terms of cotton–grain ratios. Between 1950 and 1952, this ratio was raised by 15 to 30 percent. Cotton growers were also favored from time to time with special credits or particularly favorable terms for the purchase of fertilizer or other production requisites.[4]

As a result, the area sown to cotton increased quite rapidly and substantially between 1950 and 1956, in any case much more so than grain. Since the opportunities to extend the total area under cultivation were quite limited, there was severe competition for land between grain and cotton. Competition for land was aggravated by the fact that grain production was a bulwark of the whole economy. This created some acute dilemmas for agricultural planners, which they tried to resolve first by raising the relative prices of cotton between 1950 and 1952, then lowering them, only to raise them again. This, in turn, led to fluctuations in cotton acreage, suggesting that peasants were quite responsive to price incentives.

Therefore, one can conclude that price and income stimulation proved to be fairly effective devices for increasing and planning the production of farm outputs. Yet continued pursuit of this course placed planners before some growing dilemmas. Following initial agricultural recovery from war devastation, the demand for food and agricultural raw materials was rising under the impact of industrialization. The launching of the First Five-Year Plan in 1953 led to a 40 percent rise in fixed capital investment that year. This resulted in a marked rise in urban employment and income. It also resulted in a growing demand for the import of capital goods, which had to be financed by increasing farm exports.

In the face of this situation, economic policy makers had several possible choices. They could slow down the rate of investment and industrial growth and in this way ease the demand pressure on farm products. This, however, would run strongly counter to their commitments and objectives. They could allocate a much larger share of investment resources to the expansion of modern agricultural inputs, for example, chemical fertilizer application and farm equipment, thereby raising farm output. But this too would lead to a slowing down in the expansion of high-priority industries such as steel, coal, electric power, cement, and engineering. Finally, they could use price-planning tools and reliance on the market to accelerate the growth of farm output. However, to do this would probably have required very sizable increases in the prices at which state trading companies would purchase farm products. With their larger incomes, farmers would then be in a position to purchase chemical fertilizer, farm equipment, and other modern inputs. The output of these industries was small and industrial planners were not prepared to assign the required investment and other resources to these branches of manufacture.

Therefore, attempts by farmers to use increased incomes to procure modern industrial inputs would turn out to be abortive. On the other hand, to the extent that increased farm incomes would be used to raise their own consumption of farm products and industrial goods, this would mean a transfer of resources from saving and investment to consumption. In sum, resort to price planning as the principal device for raising farm output would mean placing in the hands of the peasantry a vast pool of purchasing power and hence potential access to resources on a vast scale, which they were likely to use in ways that would run counter to the planners' preferences. Therefore, this course too had to be ruled out.

Under these circumstances the only path left open was increased mobilization of traditional inputs, resorting to a combination of political controls, ideological appeals, and material incentives to achieve this objective. The key instruments for the pursuit of this approach were gradual collectivization (in part to achieve this greater control), introduction of compulsory purchase quotas at fixed prices, guarantee of small private plots to peasant households, and continued access to free rural markets at which private-plot products could be sold. In effect, administrative devices for the allocation of agricultural products were being combined with price planning.

Given the vital role of grains as the staple food of China and of cotton as one of the key industrial raw materials, these were naturally the crops on which the state organs concentrated most of their attention. Precisely because of this, they received the bulk of the rural cadres' attention as well. The concentration on grain and cotton was reinforced by the farm procurement system. The emphasis on procurement guarantees for cotton and grain contributed to the built-in contradictions between physical and price planning in agriculture. Thus, from time to time government authorities manipulated the purchase prices of individual farm products, soybeans or oilseeds for example, in order to encourage output increases. However, unless this was coupled with an easing of the grain and cotton collection pressures, state cadres in the countryside would feel compelled to ignore the price signals, lest the expansion of other crops diminish the resources available for grain and cotton production.

Sensing that they did not have the administrative capability for detailed production planning in agriculture, central government policy makers tried to use price policy – price planning – to induce marginal output shifts in individual crops grown by collectives. These measures were more or less successful only in affecting the grain–cotton output ratios. They were much less successful in bringing about shifts from grain and cotton combined to other crops.

On the other hand, in some other respects price and market planning turned out to be more effective. As seen by economic planners at the top, private plots combined with free rural markets had certain allocative and incentive effects. They were a secure and possibly expanding source of supply for pigs, poultry and their products, and vegetables, all of which represent very important qualitative additions to the Chinese diet. They were also a major source of organic fertilizer (manure) for both the private and collectivized sector of agriculture. From this point of view the collective had a real stake in the development of private-plot farming up to a point. Moreover, the private plot and free rural market represented a source of strong positive incentives for the farm household. Provided that it did not divert the farmer's attention too much from his obligations to the collective, the small private sector in Chinese agriculture may have made it much easier for the peasant to reconcile himself to collectivization and to cooperate with it.

Just as collectivized forms of production have been a pervasive feature of Chinese agriculture since 1955–1956, so have compulsory purchase quotas at fixed prices been the principal avenue for marketing farm produce since late 1953. In both cases the detailed regulations and some of the features of the system were changed from time to time. But in its essentials the institution remained unchanged. "Unified purchase" of grain was introduced in November 1953 soon after that year's harvest was gathered. The practice was then extended to cotton in September 1954 and to soybeans, oilseeds, peanuts, sugar cane, and a few other crops thereafter.

The system thus introduced had certain crucial characteristics. Both the quantities to be sold to the state and the price at which they were to be sold were fixed. Quantities were determined on the basis of an "average," "normal," or "standard" yield concept. Seed and peasant consumption requirements were calculated and deducted from the "normal" production. The residual was then treated as marketable output. The bulk of this residual would then be considered as the quota to be sold to the state at official farm procurement prices. The precise practice in this respect varied from time to time and place to place. As may be seen from Table 4-1, at least until 1956–1957 the state did not buy up all the marketable output. Between 1953 and 1956, it left about 5 to 10 percent to be disposed of by the APCs themselves in rural markets. This practice ceased in 1957. There are indications

Table 4-1. *Marketing of food grains, 1950–1959*[a]

Year	Agricultural tax (in billions of catties of "fine grain")[b]	Total state procurement (tax and state purchases, in billions of catties of "trade grain")[c]	Total procurements (tax, state purchases, and free market, in billions of catties of "trade grain")
1950–51	35.34	–	65.18
1951–52	43.74	57.07	78.77
1952–53	38.80	63.19	77.28
1953–54	35.10	83.00	89.87
1954–55	38.00	90.27	93.57
1955–56	38.00	85.99	91.93
1956–57	36.80	83.43	91.98
1957–58	36.00	96.00	96.00
1958–59	–	111.30	111.30

[a]"Grains" in Chinese procurement practice include all cereals, potatoes (mostly sweet potatoes) in terms of grain equivalents measured at a 4:1 ratio, and soybeans. More generally, in other contexts, soybeans are often excluded.

[b]"Fine grain" is calculated by converting all grains, on the basis of appropriate equivalents, into the processed form of the principal grain of each region; the resulting conversion in this case tends to be around 76 to 78 percent of the original weight.

[c]"Trade grain" includes rice and millet in their processed form and all other grains at their original unprocessed weight; the resulting conversion tends to be around 83–86 percent of original weight.

Sources: David Denny, "Rural Policies and Their Influence on the Rate of Marketing of Food Grain," unpublished paper based on his doctoral dissertation, *Rural Policies and the Distribution of Agricultural Products in China,* University of Michigan, 1971; and Dwight Perkins, *Market Control and Planning in Communist China,* Cambridge, Mass., 1966, Table 4, p. 44.

that it was reinstated under the impact of the agricultural crisis in the early 1960s.

State procurement quotas were fixed for several years in advance. This was supposed to serve as an incentive device. The quota was not supposed to be changed, barring exceptional circumstances, so that when "normal" yields were exceeded the producer could retain the excess or sell it at prevailing market prices either to the state trading corporations or in rural markets. This was supposed to encourage the producer to increase farm production, knowing that he would be able to keep the additional output and dispose of it freely. Unfortunately this policy was not always followed in practice, so that the desired incentive effects were correspondingly weakened. Also, there were periods when rural markets were not permitted to function, in which cases the producers had to sell all their marketed output to the state. This, for instance, was the case from August 1957 to about November 1960, and explains why the last two years in Table 4-1 show 100 percent state procurement of grain.

The approach outlined above holds only for the grain surplus areas. Areas, particular localities, or households designated as grain-deficit would similarly define their "standard" yields and seed and food consumption requirements. Only in this case, instead of an excess there would be a deficit. This deficit was then covered by resales to these areas at fixed prices of grain collected in the surplus regions by the state trading organs. In effect, the deficit areas were assigned fixed grain rations. The importance attached to grain is also evidenced by the great lengths to which state organs went to gain dominance over the purchases of these crops. Thus by 1951–1952, state trading organs procured over 70 percent of the marketed grain output and a year later this rose to over 80 percent. However, the state had much less control over the marketing of other farm produce at the time, as evidenced by the fact that the corresponding shares for all agricultural and subsidiary products (including grain) were about 35 and 50 percent, respectively, in value terms.

Compulsory purchase of grain really grew out of the practice of "advance purchase" on contract prevailing prior to 1953. Therefore, it is not surprising that initially official farm procurement prices were fixed at the level at which state trading agencies had been buying farm products in the market on "advance purchase." It is doubtful whether these were "free" or in some sense "true" competitive market prices. Even before the "unified purchase" system was instituted, the state already dominated the grain market and established its unchallenged leadership in it. It is true that as long as producers could sell to private traders or to consumers directly in rural markets, the monopoly power of the state trading organs was far from absolute. However, by 1952 private traders operated under great handicaps; they were subject to a great variety of subtle pressures and were short of working capital, making it very difficult for them to compete with the giant state trading companies. On the other hand, direct sales by peasant households to consumers were certainly at best quite limited and on a relatively small scale, particularly for such bulky products as cereals, soybeans, etc.

That official state procurement prices for farm produce were below what might be considered market prices can be established more directly. First of all, they would not have been introduced if the state organs felt confident that they could increase their farm purchases at stable prices. Secondly, "above quota" produce disposed of in the market usually sold at perceptibly higher prices than those applied to the compulsory purchases. It was therefore generally recognized that compulsory purchases imposed on the peasantry a quasi-tax; it was not like the tax in kind for which they obtained no return, but it was a partial tax in that they had to sell their produce at prices below those they could have obtained in the absence of "unified purchase."

The rate of quasi-tax changed as official farm procurement prices changed and as the differential between the market price and the official price fluctuated. However, it would be misleading to consider the price differential as a measure of the quasi-tax. It is more probable that the differential over-states the tax element. Since the "free" market is small and all of the repressed, excess demand tends to be concentrated in this narrow market, prices in it were almost certainly above the levels at which they would have been if there had been no fixed purchase arrangements.

In general and as part and parcel of their agricultural development program, government organs more or less consistently increased farm procurement prices while raising the prices of industrial products sold in rural areas much more slowly. Thus since the Great Leap (1958) and up to 1974, farm procurement prices have risen by about 30 percent, while the prices of industrial goods purchased by farmers increased only about 13 percent. Thus the "parity" position of agriculture – the purchasing power of farm cash incomes – may have improved by more than 20 percent. During the same period, the agricultural tax burden declined from about 11 or 12 percent of total grain output to about 5 or 6 percent.[5] This policy was particularly pronounced in recent years, illustrated by an apparent decline in the cost of production requisites. In 1971 the price of chemical fertilizers was reduced by 10 percent and of farm equipment by almost 16 percent.[6] As will be shown further in Chapter 6, farm-output gains since 1963 can be largely ascribed to the gradual technical transformation of agriculture.[7] This technological progress was, in turn, greatly encouraged by the price policies pursued in the 1960s and 1970s.

What about the combined impact of these physical- and price-planning measures on farm marketings? Unfortunately, the impact of this agricultural expansion on the procurement of farm produce in the 1960s and 1970s cannot be assessed in the absence of data on farm marketings for this period. One would naturally expect these to rise as output increased, but at what rate this occurred is impossible to say. In any case, the procurement system was decentralized, in keeping with the decentralization of the economic management system as a whole. While up to late 1957 purchase quotas were apparently set centrally for district and county (*hsien*) units, it seems that since the Great Leap these responsibilities were transferred to the provinces. State organs were then only concerned with the net surpluses and deficits of each province for the major agricultural products subject to "unified purchase." Their attention was concentrated on the net balances of each province and on inter-provincial transfers. This meant that lower-level administrative and procurement units were responsible to the provincial authorities and it was the latter who had to meet certain quotas set by the central authorities.

Resource allocation in the industrial sector

Industrial policy in China

The First Five-Year Plan Industrial policy reflected the same type of fluctuations and shifts that characterized all other aspects of the country's economic transformation. Both during the economic recovery (1949–1952) and the First Five-Year Plan (FFYP) period great emphasis was placed on industrial development on a wide front. That is, the growth of all branches of mining and manufacturing were to be pressed. However, highest priority was assigned to the development of basic materials-producing and investment-goods branches. This meant that greatest attention was paid to the development of the iron and steel, cement, electric power, petroleum, chemical, and engineering industries. This is illustrated by the fact that during the First Five-Year Plan period close to 90 percent of the investment funds earmarked for industrial construction were channeled into the expansion of these industries.[8]

A number of factors contributed to the high priority assigned by the Chinese to the development of heavy industry. From the outset, one of the very key objectives of the new leadership was to create "a comprehensive and independent industrial system," more or less on the Soviet model. Marx's virtual identification of economic development with the growth of heavy industry, coupled with the Soviet experience, represented pre-disposing influences driving the economy in this direction. However, more practical and immediate considerations greatly reinforced this initial bias. If China was going to develop a minimum and independent defense capability, it was essential to build and expand military production. This, in turn, required the development of certain basic industries, such as iron and steel and machine building, which serve as critical inputs for defense production and are required for a number of other industries as well.

Of course, China could import military hardware, iron and steel, machinery, etc., and export in return agricultural products and industrial consumer goods. In this way China would be exporting goods which could be produced at home at relatively low cost and importing relatively high-cost items. In fact, this is what was actually done in the 1950s, but it was done as a transitional measure designed to aid in the development of a "comprehensive" industrial system at home, which in time could become "independent."

Rapid economic development under Chinese conditions required a significant rise in the rate of fixed-capital investment. As a result, this rate rose from about 7 percent in the 1930s to about 20 percent in the mid-1950s.[9] Once this rate – quite high by any standard but particularly by the standards of most underdeveloped countries – was reached, it could not be raised much higher without apparently creating quite acute strains in the economy. To attain this rate, fixed-capital formation between 1949 and 1955 had to rise faster than GNP. Such an accelerated pace in investment growth led to a marked rise in the demand for investment goods. Unless this demand was to be totally met by imports, domestic production of capital goods had to be markedly increased; particularly so since domestic manufacturing capacity in the investment-goods branches was relatively much smaller than in consumer-goods production.

Interestingly enough, China's pursuit of a "comprehensive and independent industrial system" became one of the evolving sources of friction with the Soviet Union. Thus the very emulation of the Soviet path became a source of conflict between Russia and China. The Russians wanted to develop a large socialist commonwealth led by the Soviet Union. A number of instruments were to be used to accomplish this objective, including an international division of labor – a division that would assure economic dominance of the Soviet Union in this commonwealth. The Council for Mutual Economic Assistance (CMEA) was to serve as the organ for the implementation of this policy. In effect the Russians were advocates of economic integration for the socialist world, while the Chinese favored the development of an "independent industrial system" and wanted to utilize Soviet aid and trade for this purpose. The Soviets, on the other hand, may have wanted to use aid and trade to render the Chinese more dependent.

A letter from the Chinese Communist Party to the Soviet Party published in June 1963 (*Peking Review*), contains the following passage:

> If, proceeding only from its own partial interest, any socialist country unilaterally demands that other fraternal countries submit to its needs, and uses the pretext of opposing what they call "going it alone" and "nationalism" to *prevent other fraternal countries* applying the principle of *relying mainly on their own efforts* in their construction and *from developing their economy on the basis of independence,* or even goes the length of putting economic pressure on other fraternal countries – then these are *pure manifestations of national egoism.* Such economic cooperation must be based on the principle of complete equality, mutual benefit and comradely mutual assistance.
>
> *It would be great power chauvinism* to deny these basic principles and, *in the name of "international division of labor" or "specialization"* to *impose one's will on others,* infringe on the independence and sovereignty of fraternal countries or harm the interest of their people.

There are many more charges and counter-charges in the 1960s, as Sino-Soviet relations deteriorated and gradually approached an open break following the withdrawal of Russian technicians from China in mid-1960.

Closely linked to the heavy-industry-oriented pattern of development was the preponderant emphasis placed on the expansion of large-scale industry during the period of the First Five-Year Plan. This again was due in part to Soviet influence, with the large complete-plant imports to China representing the core of industrial investment and expansion during this period. It was reinforced by the fact that Soviet advisors were more familiar with and conditioned to large-scale and capital-intensive methods of production. Moreover, the Chinese planners' own initial biases probably also ran in this direction. Therefore it is not surprising that modern industrial output rose at a much faster rate than handicraft production between 1952 and 1957.[10]

Another guiding principle of Chinese industrial policy has been to bring about a marked shift in the prevailing pattern of industrial location. China's natural resources are well dispersed. In contrast, industrial development in the twentieth century has been heavily concentrated in the coastal provinces and most particularly in Northeast (Manchuria), North, and East China. A combination of relative political stability, a modern transport system, readily available agricultural and industrial raw materials, and large markets attracted foreign capital to these regions. As a result, on the eve of the deliberate industrialization drive of the First Five-Year Plan (i.e., in 1952), over two-thirds of China's industrial output was produced in the coastal provinces.

In the light of this, the First Five-Year Plan stated that:

> The geographical distribution of our new industrial capital construction must . . . follow the principle of appropriately distributing our industrial productive forces over various parts of the country, *locating industries close to sources of raw materials and fuel and areas of consumption*, and complying with the *need to strengthen national defense*, so as to change gradually the irrational distribution of industry and *develop the economy of backward areas*.

This quite explicit statement spells out four criteria for the location of industry: proximity to sources of raw materials, proximity to markets, security considerations, and a desire to narrow regional inequalities in income, employment, and sources of modernization.

Unfortunately, these guidelines are not as unambiguous as they appear at first sight. Security considerations and the urge to narrow regional differentials in stages of development dictated a relative shift to inland locations. On the other hand, population and thus markets were heavily concentrated in the coastal areas. Sources of raw materials, depending on the particular branch of manufacture, could be found in widely scattered locations. Certain locations could offer decisive cost advantages because of the good and cheap transport and the availability of extensive industrial services. Some of the latter considerations, not mentioned in the First Five-Year Plan statement, tended to favor the further expansion of existing industrial locations.

Because of these contradictory pulls, this policy was not consistently applied during these years. At first there was a strong push for regional shifts in industrial location, but then there is evidence of second thoughts. Nevertheless, the weight of new construction was heavily concentrated in the interior, with about 55 percent of industrial investment located there as compared to about 45 percent in the coastal areas. This shift was reflected in some slight regional redistribution of industrial output between 1952 and 1957 (68:32 vs. 64:36). However, it seems that this ratio did not change much thereafter, since approximately the same share of industrial output was produced in the coastal provinces in 1973 as in 1957.[11]

The Great Leap The industrial policy of the First Five-Year Plan produced increasing strains in the economy. Supply bottlenecks, raw materials shortages, and dis-proportionalities of all kinds surfaced with increasing frequency. Thus there were marked dis-proportionalities between agricultural and industrial growth, which led to urban food supply shortages on the one hand and shortfalls in agricultural raw materials for the textile and food-processing industries on the other. Similarly, the dis-proportionalities in the rate of growth of producer- and consumer-goods output contributed to marked inflationary pressure. For all these reasons the leadership was searching for an approach to industrial development that would maintain the pace of heavy-industry growth but alleviate the shortages, pressures, and strains that this had created in the past.

Therefore, the Great Leap was designed to step up farm production and accelerate the rate of growth of consumer-goods industries as well. In many respects it represented a sharp break with the industrial policies of the FFYP. While the latter focused preponderantly on the development of large-scale, modern, relatively capital-intensive methods of production, the Great Leap sought to tap new sources of growth by "walking on two legs." That is, modern and traditional, large-scale and small-scale, capital-intensive and labor-intensive methods were to be developed side by side. Unemployed and underemployed labor, both in the city and in the countryside, was to be mobilized and employed in small-scale plants which were to produce raw materials and consumer goods in short supply.

Unfortunately, the euphoria and the politicization of industrial management created a climate in which only too often technical considerations were thrown to the winds. Many of the new plants were not capable of turning out usable products. For instance, the backyard steel furnaces produced pig iron of such a high sulphur content that it had to be resmelted. Attempts were made to produce all kinds of semi-manufactures and finished goods in these small-scale plants irrespective of whether they lent themselves to this type of production. Frequently, even if they did, workers, peasants, or office employees launched a new plant without benefit of technical advice.

Naturally not all projects were of this character. In fact, the Great Leap did lead to a massive industrial advance – but at a tremendous cost. Industrial output grew at the expense of marked deterioration in product quality. The Great Leap was also very disruptive in its impact on economic institutions, factory organization and management, work morale, and incentive. At the outset there was tremendous enthusiasm and optimism, but frequent industrial breakdowns due to the technical deficiencies mentioned and the incredibly fast-paced growth gradually took their toll.

Readjustment and self-reliance As the Great Leap collapsed and first agricultural and then industrial production declined, a new policy of "readjustment, consolidation, reinforcement and improvement" was announced in 1962. However, this policy had in fact been initiated at least a year earlier. This new policy incorporated many of the lessons learned from the shortcomings of preceding industrial programs. Its central principles could be characterized as support of agriculture, self-reliance, balanced growth, and emphasis on technical and product quality. Broadly speaking these principles seem to have guided industrial policy throughout the 1960s, even through the Cultural Revolution, although the spirit and the way in which they were implemented changed somewhat.

Chinese planners and policy makers learned from their FFYP experience that under Chinese conditions agricultural development could not be neglected, lest it slow down or arrest industrial growth. This perception was acutely reinforced during the Great Crisis (1960–1962), when a sharp decline in farm output resulted in marked industrial contraction. They learned from the Great Leap that primary reliance on fuller utilization or mobilization of traditional inputs would not by itself yield substantial and sustained increases in agricultural production. Additional applications of traditional inputs were apparently subject to sharply diminishing returns, which could be overcome by rapid technological progress. Technological advance, in turn, was crucially dependent on new, modern, industrial inputs. Recognition of this fact was reflected in the industrial policy of the 1960s, which placed major emphasis on the development of the chemical fertilizer and farm equipment industry, particularly irrigation pumps and small tractors.

Self-reliance, that is, the creation of an independent industrial system, was already a central principle of industrial policy in the 1950s, as indicated above. In the 1950s, however, this was a policy defining the long-run direction of industrial development. It was felt that in order to make China independent in the future substantial capital goods and military imports were required, which had to be paid for by growing exports. As a result, foreign trade rose quite rapidly and grew faster than GNP, so that, in a sense, the Chinese economy was becoming more foreign-trade-oriented. Moreover, the direction of foreign trade reflected the country's "lean to one side" policy; the bulk of China's trade was with the Soviet Union and other socialist countries.

In contrast, self-reliance in the 1960s assumed much greater operational significance and immediate application. It meant a reduction in China's general dependence on foreign trade, but in particular it strongly encouraged markedly reduced dependence on the Soviet Union. This was reflected in the fact that, unlike the 1950s, in the 1960s foreign trade grew less rapidly than GNP, so that the Chinese economy was becoming more autarkic. At the same time, trade with the Soviet Union dwindled. Since the Chinese especially depended on the Soviets for their supply of industrial machinery and equipment, crude oil and petroleum products, and military deliveries, a prime object of policy in the 1960s was to render China as self-sufficient as possible in those fields – all of which touched on national survival and security. Therefore a very active program of geological exploration was launched, which led to the discovery of significant new oil deposits. As a result, China became self-sufficient in crude oil and most oil products and by the 1970s became a supplier of oil to other countries, notably Japan. Similarly, there was a marked expansion in certain branches of the machine-building industry, particularly those with direct or indirect defense application, and of course in defense industries.

The policy of "readjustment and consolidation" implied that much greater attention was to be paid to complementarities in industrial development, so that structural imbalances and dis-proportionalities would be avoided or at least minimized. At the same time, greater emphasis was to be placed on the maintenance of raw material reserves to alleviate bottlenecks. In general, the pace of industrial growth was slower in the 1960s than in the 1950s, partly by design and partly by default. Moreover, instead of pushing for an industrial advance on a broad front, the new policy implied a more selective and specifically targeted growth with chemical fertilizer, farm equipment, petroleum, and defense production as the high-priority branches. The more leisurely pace of growth facilitated the maintenance of a better balance between inputs and outputs. It also created an environment in which much greater attention could be paid to product quality and to higher standards of technical performance.

Industrial development was temporarily disrupted by the Cultural Revolution, but economic policies formulated earlier were not significantly altered. However, with the end of this political upheaval, Chinese policy makers apparently undertook a fundamental reassessment of their foreign and domestic policies. This involved a new look at their perception of the Soviet threat and a reexamination of relations with the United States. A possible downgrading of the Soviet threat coupled with a restoration of the Communist Party's primacy over the army led to a gradual curtailment in the power and influence of the People's Liberation Army (PLA). One might speculate that these were among the issues in contention between Lin Piao and his adversaries that led to his downfall in 1971.

However this may be, it seems that all these considerations led to a reduction in Chinese military outlays by an estimated 25 percent between 1971 and 1972.[12] The resources thus released were apparently channeled into a large new industrial expansion program, based on the importation of complete plant and technology on the one hand and increasing exports of oil on the other.[13] This involved a liberalization of the self-reliance concept to allow for a more open foreign trade orientation than prevailed in the 1960s. This new investment program provides for a sizable expansion of the transport sector and the foreign trade infra-structure, involving expansion and improvement of port facilities and shipping, construction of pipelines, and growth in China's commercial aviation.

At the same time steel, petro-chemical, chemical fertilizer, and electric-power generating plants are to be significantly extended. The last three were assigned a high priority in the 1960s as well. However, this big new push represents a marked acceleration of earlier programs. For instance, thirteen large-scale, highly capital-intensive, technologically most advanced chemical fertilizer plants are to be newly installed so that, in terms of nutrient content, China's nitrogenous fertilizer capacity will double by the end of the decade.[14] In contrast, expansion of steel production is a priority added in the 1970s. Extension of steel capacity was aggressively pursued in the 1950s. It receded in importance in the face of the economic crisis and under-utilized capacity in early 1960s. Later in the decade this was converted into an increasing shortage of steel – particularly rolled and high-quality steel – as the machinery and defense-producing branches of industry grew very rapidly. These shortages were met by sizable steel imports, mostly from Japan, and now will be filled at least in part through expansion of domestic production.

The role of rural industry in the 1960s This new wave of industrial expansion, based on significant increases in large-scale, capital-intensive methods of production, is combined with a continuing emphasis on the development of rural industries. Small-scale and handicraft methods of production were widely prevalent in China even before 1949. They were carried on in households, mostly in the countryside, and in workshops involving mostly handicraft activities, machine repair, and small-scale manufacture. These shops and small-scale establishments were amalgamated into cooperatives in the 1950s. However, they were somewhat neglected by the state planning authorities at the time, with the principal emphasis placed on the development of large industrial projects. They were isolated from centrally directed industrial development during the FFYP period.

This policy was completely reversed when, as part and parcel of the Great Leap, major emphasis was placed on the development of small-scale and rural industries. Within the framework of "walking on two legs," two alternative approaches to the role of these industries emerged. It was recognized that most industrial commodities could be produced in a variety of ways, based on alternative degrees of capital intensity. Thus the choice of technology ought to rest on the relative supplies and costs of land, labor, and capital in China. At the same time, it was perceived that national and industrial product could be greatly augmented through employment creation and labor absorption, based on the simultaneous development of large-scale and small-scale industry.[15] With this in mind, a vast number of new small-scale enterprises were launched with insufficient attention paid to technical feasibility and product quality. Therefore, the new industrial policy of "readjustment, consolidation, reinforcement, and improvement" required a far-reaching weeding-out process among these new small-scale projects. Many were closed and abandoned, others were reorganized. However, this did not mean a return to the FFYP policy of relative neglect. On the contrary, small-scale methods of industrial production were fostered throughout the 1960s, but on a more rational and discriminating basis, with much greater attention paid to cost and technical considerations and their integration into a broader planning framework.

However, the Great Leap not only emphasized employment absorption but self-reliance as well. This required the rise and expansion of rural industries relying principally on local sources of raw materials, labor, and capital to supply the industrial needs of the farm sector. While the "employment absorption" and "agriculture-supplying" aspects of rural industrial development were not necessarily contradictory, they were different and only partially overlapping. These issues did not fully crystallize during the helter-skelter days of the Great Leap, but they did come to the fore in the 1960s and again in the 1970s as rural industrial development was rationalized, placed on a firm footing, and actively fostered by the state authorities.

It seems that there gradually emerged a division of labor. Rural industries located in farming areas within municipal boundaries seem to be preponderantly oriented to manufacturing finished products for the urban market or components for large factories based on sub-contracting arrangements. On the other hand, industrial establishments further removed from the cities and, in any case, under *hsien* (county), commune, or brigade control primarily serve agriculture.

Rural industries in China are very diverse in terms of size, origin, age, and degree of technological sophistication. Some date back to Republican days, many are survivals of the Great Leap but often on a reorganized and much more efficient basis, and quite a few have been launched since the Cultural Revolution. It is estimated that rural industries employ about 10 to 17 million workers, comprising about half of the Chinese labor force engaged in manufacturing and mining. They may be producing 5 to 10 percent of the total gross industrial output. However, they play a major role in chemical fertilizer and cement production, contributing about 50 percent to the total production of these two key industries.[16] In addition to these, machine-building and farm processing plants are of major importance in the countryside. The former supply agriculture with a large portion of its farm equipment needs, pumps, small electric generators, and a variety of other types of machinery.

Rural industries also vary, depending on their level of ownership and administration. There seems to be a significant correlation between size, equipment, and technical sophistication on the one hand and the organizational level to which the plant belongs. For instance, in Lin Hsien there were sixty-five rural industrial plants in mid-1975, employing a total of 8500 workers with an annual gross output of 41 million yuan. Of these, *twenty* are state owned and county operated; they produced 60 *percent* of the county's industrial output. *Nineteen* plants are collectively owned by communes and production brigades but county-operated; they contributed *26 percent of the output*. *Twenty-six* plants are collectively owned *and* operated by communes and production brigades; they contributed *27 percent of the output*. The average work force per plant in these three categories was 210, 137, and 62, respectively.[17]

Thus, it is clear that these are not small-scale industries in the usual sense. Some of them are quite large, employing 500 to 800 workers, and are even fairly mechanized. The equipment comes in a variety of shapes and sizes, some old and some new. However these are not obsolete, broken-down plants, even though they are generally smaller, less mechanized, and technologically not as advanced as large urban factories. They are clearly based on the rationale that in a country with an underdeveloped and high-cost transport system many industrial plants must be scattered in the countryside to serve local markets and rely as much as possible on local inputs. Although this may raise the costs of production this might be more than counter-balanced by lower costs of transportation.

Industry-wide planning and management

The industrial planning system Industry was directed and managed under the "two-track" system which characterized all aspects of central control in China. Control was exercised along two parallel lines: through a Communist Party channel and a government administrative one, with horizontal links between the two at each level of government. Thus, after 1959 all the industrial and transport ministries came under the State Council Office of Industry and Communications, headed by a vice-premier. Parallel to it there was, at least until the Cultural Revolution, an Industry and Communications Political Department, an Industrial Work Department, and a Communications Work Department of the Chinese Communist Party's Central Committee. In general, the Party channel was responsible for broad policy direction and political indoctrination; it also played an important role as a watchdog to make sure that the policy line of the leadership was actually implemented. On the other hand, the administrative channel was responsible for implementation and day-to-day direction.

Under the impact of the Cultural Revolution, this "two-track" system apparently became blurred or even merged. That is, while the distinction between Party and government organs was maintained at all levels, their staffs were merged, except for the two top organs, that is, the Central Committee of the Chinese Communist Party and the State Council. The administrative structures of both the State Council and the Party were periodically reorganized. Therefore, from time to time new ministries were created through subdivisions of existing ones, and some ministries were consolidated. At any rate, under the State Council's Office of Industry and Communications there were in the mid-1960s seventeen ministries, each in charge of a different branch of industry. In a certain sense these ministries could be compared with holding companies or large, multi-divisional, multi-plant, corporations in the United States. Ministerial direction and control over an enterprise in China may be as close or in some cases even closer than that of corporate headquarters in the United States. Yet while in our system the corporation is the principal financial, juridical, and accounting unit, in China it is not the ministry but the individual enterprise that performs these functions.

Of the seventeen industrial ministries in the mid-1960s, three were concerned with consumer goods and fourteen dealt with producer goods. In a certain sense this could be viewed as an index of relative importance and concern as seen by the central government. One of the consumer-goods ministries dealt with the textile industry, the second was responsible for handicraft production, and the third was concerned with a wide variety of consumer manufactures. Eight of the producer-goods industries were in one or another branch of machine building. However, at least five of these were in defense production. The others directed the farm equipment, communications equipment, and general-engineering industries respectively. In addition, there were ministries for coal mining, petroleum extraction and refining, metallurgy, chemicals, and for building construction and building materials. The number of these ministries was reduced to eleven when the new State Council was appointed at the First Session of the Fourth National People's Congress in January 1975.[18]

Just as there was a "dual track" of Party and administrative direction, so there was within the administrative track itself dual control over enterprises: that exercised through the central government and that exerted through local government organs. The degree and scope of control exercised by the Party or government on the one hand and central versus local government on the other was subject to fluctuations reflecting changes in policy discussed in preceding sections and chapters. In part these fluctuations and policy shifts reflected a continuing search for an optimum pattern of control. Such an optimum would have to reconcile the conflicting considerations of central control and of flexibility in planning and plan implementation. Central control was desired to assure that the policy makers' goals would be faithfully implemented; flexibility was required so that planners, administrators, and enterprise managers could respond rapidly and make the necessary plan adjustments in the light of constantly changing circumstances. The latter suggested the need for considerable decision-making authority and autonomy in economic administration at lower levels of government and in the enterprises. It is therefore these conflicting considerations, and the search for an optimum associated with them, that first led in the Soviet Union and then in China to periodic shifts from centralization to decentralization of economic management.

As indicated above, decentralization can take two alternative, but not mutually exclusive, paths. It can lead to market or bureaucratic decentralization. In the first case, the authorities may transfer more or less responsibility for resource allocation and plan implementation to the price and market mechanism. This entails increasing the autonomy of individual enterprises. In the second case, central authorities may delegate more or less of the planning, plan implementation, and management functions to lower levels of administrative control. Thus, resource allocation and control are still bureaucratically directed, but the pattern of decision making is more dispersed, with more governmental organs involved. Under this second pattern of decentralization, enterprises may acquire more or lose some autonomy, depending on how tightly lower-level administrative organs choose to exercise their control.

In China, there were periodic changes in both these respects. In the first few years following the birth of the People's Republic, both market and bureaucratic decentralization prevailed. At that time, there was still a great deal of private enterprise in all sectors of the economy, including industry. These private firms were still attempting to maximize their profits within the constraints imposed upon them. Moreover, the governmental and planning apparatus was not yet geared up for full-scale and comprehensive management of the economy or of even the industrial sector. At the same time, state administration was carried on through six regional governments still reflecting the location of the principal armies and the formation of People's Governments in the areas newly occupied by the People's Liberation Army.

Each People's Government had complete authority over the industrial enterprises located in its respective area. It exercised this control through its own industrial ministries. As part and parcel of a gradual process of centralization, the People's Governments were replaced by Administrative Committees of the central government in 1953. At the same time the regional industrial ministries were replaced by much less autonomous or less powerful industrial bureaus. During the same period, as more and more enterprises were nationalized and/or as the central government apparatus was strengthened, the scope of the market was gradually confined. The objective was to construct a fairly centralized system of economic planning.

In 1953, when the regional People's Governments were abolished, public enterprises that had by then been nationalized were divided into central and local state enterprises. The former were to be the responsibility of the central ministries and the latter were to be controlled by provincial, municipal, or lower-level industrial bureaus. In 1954, that is, before the large-scale nationalization drive of 1955–1956, close to 60 percent of gross industrial output value (value of sales) was still produced by local state enterprises, private firms, and cooperatives. (This almost certainly over-states the relative importance of local, private, and cooperative enterprises. Given the fact that these tended to be smaller and less self-contained than the large enterprises under central government administration, the degree of double counting in their measure of gross output value is likely to be greater. Therefore, a value-added measure of output for these two groups of enterprises would probably show local enterprises to be less important.) Following nationalization and the organization of a number of new industrial ministries to take charge of these state enterprises, the degree of administrative centralization probably reached its zenith. Therefore, by 1956–1957, the relative importance of the local, state, and cooperative enterprises as compared to those under ministerial control was probably reversed.

Not surprisingly, this growing centralization was accompanied by increasing strains in economic management. Therefore, almost as soon as the new structure was completed in 1956, second thoughts were voiced about the wisdom of the course being pursued. This was particularly pronounced at the Eighth Party Congress held that year. It was increasingly realized that central management of a command system in such a vast economy was a most complex, if not heroic, task. For industry, and most particularly for factory industry, the job was relatively simpler since it was still a relatively small sector. There were about 15,000 public enterprises in industry in 1955, about 30,000 large- and medium-scale private and joint public–private firms, and an overall total (including small-scale) of approximately 125,000 firms. By late 1956, when the nationalization process was more or less completed, there may have been therefore 15,000 to 30,000 enterprises under direct state administration, some of which were controlled by local governments.[19] The bulk of these enterprises were concentrated in Northeast, North, and East China, which tended to facilitate state management.

On the other hand, considering the underdeveloped state of transport and communications and the scarcities in technical, engineering, accounting, planning, and management personnel at all levels (central and local government and enterprises), central management of even a sector this size would be fraught with many problems. The new system was tested in 1956, and exhibited severe strains. That year the development pace was greatly accelerated; state investment levels were raised from one year to the next by 60 percent, and other inputs were also greatly stepped up. As noted above, this rapid rate of acceleration created acute strains and shortages of all kinds. It is probable that, given the ambitious pace at which industry was being pushed, such strains were inevitable. Nevertheless, the centralized management system had to bear part of the blame.

Against this background a series of decrees was promulgated in November 1957 that provided for quite far-reaching decentralization of industrial and fiscal management. Domestic economic considerations may have been reinforced by the Soviet example of decentralization instituted earlier that year. However, the Chinese decentralization pattern differed markedly from its Soviet counterpart. While it led to a large-scale transfer of factory enterprises from ministerial to local (provincial and municipal) government control, industrial ministries were not abolished but retained certain responsibilities for planning in their industrial branch. This applied particularly to investment planning, new plant design, and stimulation of technological progress.

It seems that the essential features of this system have survived to the present day. During the Great Leap, as might be expected, decentralization was at times carried to excess. As a result, economic planning and coordination suffered. Therefore, during the period of "readjustment and consolidation" (1961–1965) some recentralization was required. The guiding slogan for these moves was the dictum "the whole country is a (single) chessboard," clearly implying that all economic measures are inter-related, and a move in one place, one sector, or one enterprise must be coordinated with all the others. The Cultural Revolution did not signal any change in centralization policy. However, it led to a great deal of disruption in government organs and in many enterprises, so that there may have been considerable decentralization by default.

Materials supply planning and allocation At the very heart of the industrial-planning process, regardless of whether it was bureaucratically centralized or decentralized, was the allocation of resources needed in industrial production, that is, raw materials, labor, and capital. This task can be, and in fact in most planned economies is, divided into two phases: current production planning, involving utilization of existing plant capacity; and investment planning, relating to decisions concerning future expansion of that capacity. In a relatively labor-abundant economy such as the Chinese, annual, operational planning largely revolves around the allocation of industrial materials that are relatively scarce, are utilized in a number of industries, and on which high-priority industries are critically dependent.

In China, as in the Soviet Union, such materials are subject to centralized allocation or so-called unified distribution. In effect, they are subject to rationing and can be obtained by industrial enterprises in two principal ways. Large enterprises can purchase these from the producing firms after obtaining approvals from the appropriate planning and ministerial organs. This is a clear case of physical planning based on material balances estimated by the central authorities. In contrast, small enterprises or small consumers of the particular material can purchase these from government trading corporations, thereby considerably reducing the planning and administrative burden of the allocative agencies. The number of items subject to "unified distribution" rose quite considerably during the FFYP. It was 28 in 1952, 96 the next year, 235 by 1956, and 417 by 1958. However, under the impact of decentralization in industrial management the number of items subject to centralized allocation was supposed to shrink to 132 by 1959 and probably has not risen significantly since. We have no precise information for subsequent years, but it seems that in 1972 it may have been between 100 and 200.[20] Also following decentralization, in provinces that were relatively self-sufficient in industrial materials the number of commodities subject to central control was typically markedly reduced. On the other hand, local planning organs and industrial bureaus operated a materials-allocation system at the provincial level.

While perhaps no more than 300 types of materials and equipment were subject to "unified distribution" in China at the peak of central management of the economy, the corresponding number was 1500 for the Soviet Union in the 1950s. This is not surprising, given the more advanced state of the Soviet economy, which means that the array and variety of goods produced is much greater, the economy more complex, and the different branches of industry more inter-dependent. Therefore, from one point of view the central planning and management task in the Soviet economy is a much more demanding one than in China. Planning and materials-allocation errors in a branch of Soviet industry may be expected to reverberate much more widely throughout the industrial sector, with possible effects on other sectors as well. However, planning and management capacity is also more advanced in the Soviet Union than in China. This is not only due to its much longer experience in managing a command economy, but again is in large part ascribable to the more developed state of the Soviet economy.

A highly industrialized and relatively more advanced economy is likely to generate information more quickly and more reliably (other things being equal), in part because of its more developed communications network. Also, the number of trained personnel equipped to handle planning, accounting, statistical, and economic management tasks is necessarily much greater in the Soviet Union as compared to China. On the other hand, as noted above, there are some counter-balancing factors. The number of commodities that needs to be centrally allocated in China is significantly smaller. Moreover, to reduce the planning burden, the Chinese have deliberately left a vast number of small enterprises outside the planning framework, letting them secure their input requirements through the market. These small firms may have accounted for one-third of the gross value of industrial output produced in the mid-1950s. This reduction in the planning burden automatically implied a reduction in the planners' scope of control, but almost certainly not in fields or areas that would be considered by them essential or of high priority. The Chinese also eased the administrative burden on the materials-allocation system by introducing some new distributive devices such as "supply and sales order conferences," "commodity banks," and some other exchange mechanisms (see pp. 104–109).

Why is materials allocation such a critical planning device in a command economy? Clearly, if the supply of these materials were abundant, there would be no need for "unified distribution." In that case distribution could be delegated to the market without incurring any serious risk that high-priority industries would be left without an adequate supply of raw materials. However, if industrial materials are reasonably scarce and competing demands are placed upon them, an entirely different situation is created. Under these circumstances market delegation may be expected to lead to rapid price increases generated by acute demand pressure. These pressures would be maximized under conditions of rapid industrial expansion, based on ambitious output targets, with greatest concern for fulfillment of the plan in certain high-priority sectors. For these high-priority sectors, the availability of the required raw material supply at the right time and in the right place might determine whether they can or cannot meet their targets.

Therefore, these industries would be compelled to bid for these resources, no matter what the price. Moreover, in an acute scarcity situation, even if they paid higher prices and bid in the market for more raw material, they could not be certain that it would not be bid away from them anyway. Thus physical command allocation of materials in a planning system is essentially a function of ambitious output targets and a very strong commitment to fulfill these in the high-priority sectors. If it works properly, an industrial firm producing high-priority items can be assured of the necessary supplies at fixed prices.

Planners determine the quantities of centrally allocated materials that need to be produced and/or imported by drawing up "material balances," which in turn are based on input–output "norms." This is a method first developed in the Soviet Union during the period of their First Five-Year Plan and then adopted by all socialist countries, including China. An input–output "norm" defines how much raw materials are required to produce a unit of output. For instance, it would specify how much coal, pig iron, and other materials are needed to produce a ton of steel at prevailing levels of technology. Naturally, at any one time there are likely to be a range of such "norms," with the most efficient and/or technologically advanced producer using less pig iron or coal or both to produce a ton of steel and the poorest producers using considerably more.

In drawing up the next annual plan, the planners may start by setting quite "tight" or relatively "loose" norms, depending on whether they decide to be guided by the practices of the most efficient or less efficient producers in the industry. "Tight" norms would put pressure on the enterprises to reduce costs and improve efficiency. On the other hand, there is always the possibility that the norms fixed by planners would be either unrealistic or so advanced that only a few producers could meet them. In that case, firms may be forced into a continuing struggle for materials. In contrast, if the norms were loose, the firms could quite easily meet their targets but there would be considerable risk that materials would be wasted.

In the planning process there is an inherent conflict between planning organs and enterprises. Planners have a strong interest in economizing on raw materials and in guaranteeing that output will be maximized per unit of raw material used. Enterprises, on the other hand, want to protect themselves against the risk of under-fulfilling the output plan and thus have a strong urge to hoard materials, which provides them with the best guarantee that their plan will be fulfilled. Hoarding and conflict between planners and producers are not phenomena confined to socialist economies. They were widely prevalent in all war-time economies, including that of the United States, and essentially for the same reasons: the overriding necessity of having the required quantities of certain types of products at the right place at the proper time.[21] For all these reasons, planners tended to set "tight" norms in the preliminary plans ("control figures") that were sent down ("first down") to the enterprises. The enterprises, on the other hand, did everything in their power to modify these and "loosen" them in the "first up" process. In this way, the process of drafting the annual plan entailed some tough bargaining, concerning input norms, between planning organs and enterprises. This bargaining necessarily takes time and may account in part for the fact that annual plans often were promulgated in final form only after the planning year started.

When all the enterprise norms are finalized, material balances can be finalized too. The latter are really separate balance sheets for each commodity. They compare total supply itemized by source with total requirements itemized by consuming sector and/or enterprise, as illustrated in Table 4-2.

The two sides of a material balance are supposed to be estimated separately. The supply side represents the planners' best estimate of what each plant may be capable of producing. Here too there is an inherent conflict between enterprises and planners, with the latter wishing to raise targets and the former desiring to reduce them. The demand side is based on the material-input norms estimated by planners to be feasible for enterprises which, for instance, may be consumers of steel. If the supply and demand sides balance, the con-

Table 4-2. *Hypothetical material balance for steel (in millions of metric tons)*

Source of supply	Quantity to be supplied	Consuming sector	Quantity required
Steel Complex No. 1	8.0	Iron and Steel Industry	3.0
Steel Complex No. 2	4.0	Plant No. 1	1.2
Steel Complex No. 3	3.0	Plant No. 2	0.6
Steel Complex No. 4	2.0	Plant No. 3	0.4
Steel Plant No. 5	1.0	Plant No. 4	0.3
		Plant No. 5	0.2
		Other	0.3
Miscellaneous small		Machine-building	9.0
steel plants	2.0	Plant No. 1	5.0
		Plant No. 2	3.0
		Other small plants	1.0
Total	20.0	Construction	5.0
		Other	3.0
		Total	20.0

sistency problem has been solved for this one commodity or industry. However, in the first instance there is no reason why the two sides should balance; on the contrary, the opposite may be presumed.[22]

If expected demand exceeds the anticipated supply, the planners can either raise the output targets for one or more of the steel-producing enterprises or cut down on steel consumption. To accomplish the latter, they could tighten the steel input norms of the consuming industries or allow these industries to reduce their output targets. Thus, for the hypothetical balance in Table 4-2, this might mean reducing the supply of steel made, for instance, available to the construction industry. The construction enterprises may in this way be induced to substitute other, perhaps less scarce, materials for steel. Alternatively, they might be pressed to tighten their input norms, that is, to leave their output targets unchanged and try to meet them without substituting other materials. If neither of these courses of action seems possible, planners might have to acquiesce in construction-target reductions.

In the opposite case, if supplies exceed anticipated demand, corresponding adjustments would be required. Either way, changes in the material balance for one commodity necessarily require adjustments in other balances as well. The greater the inter-dependence between different industrial branches, the more widely will change in one balance reverberate through the economy. In the example given in Table 4-2, if demand exceeds supply and the planners decide that therefore steel production targets will have to be increased, this will almost certainly raise the coal and pig iron requirements of the steel industry. Therefore, at the least, the material balances for coal and pig iron will be affected. In turn, this will affect the balances of those industries that supply material for coal and pig iron production, and so on. Therefore, this process requires several rounds of successive approximations until all balances become mutually consistent, at least on paper. At first sight, this appears to be an extremely awkward, cumbersome, time-consuming approach to materials-supply planning. However, with the advance of computer technology, it can be greatly speeded up and compressed.

Consistency at the planning level is, of course, no guarantee of consistency in the course of plan implementation. On the contrary, there are bound to be deviations from the plan; some norms may turn out to have been unrealistic or certain output targets may be too ambitious and cannot be fulfilled. These deviations from the plan arising in the process of its implementation disturb the more or less precarious consistency between materials supply and demand achieved during plan formulation. For this reason alone, it is essential to maintain flexibility in the planning system so that it will be in a position to cope with these disturbances and unforeseen contingencies. In the field of materials supply, *national supply and sales order conferences*, continuous *commodity exhibitions*, and *commodity banks* are examples of innovative institutional devices introduced in China to assure this kind of flexibility.

Allocation of high-grade manpower Undoubtedly the scarce production factors in China are land; certain types of industrial materials; capital; and technical, engineering, scientific, and really highly skilled manpower. These are the elements that constrain the pace of industrial development. Scarcity of high-grade manpower may possibly be considered the most critical of these in limiting development and technical progress in the long run.

Chinese planners and policy makers recognized this, more or less, depending on which policy phase was dominant at any one time. It was certainly realized during the FFYP period and during the early 1960s. Some tentative measure of this scarcity can be obtained by comparing the supply of such manpower available with some estimates of requirements. The total pool of scientific, engineering, and technical manpower in China was estimated at close to 600,000 in 1955.[23] Of these, about 350,000 were engineers and technicians; another 125,000 were medical workers; and the rest were scientists, doctors, science teachers in colleges and secondary schools, and some others. At the same time, potential need for this type of personnel was projected at about 6 million if development was to proceed along the lines then forecast for the first three five-year plans.

Therefore, just as with industrial materials, there was a marked imbalance between demand and supply – actual and potential. Leaving allocation of this manpower to the market would have almost certainly created even more acute demand pressures than was anticipated in the case of materials. High-grade engineers, for instance, would have been in a position to command a very high scarcity price. This could not be countenanced by the planners for several reasons. Just as with industrial materials, they wanted to be sure that the high-priority production sectors would be guaranteed their minimum manpower needs. They could not be sure that the market could provide it to them in the face of such an acute scarcity situation. However, such a course would have been ruled out on ideological grounds irrespective of its allocative merits. Letting scientists, engineers, and some others earn such premium wages would lead to precisely the kind of income, role, and status differentiation so contrary to Mao's value system. It would have necessarily led to the creation of a "new class."

Therefore, some kind of a physical-allocation system, some type of a rationing device, had to be devised for this type of manpower. In 1956 central organs were entrusted with planning the distribution of new graduates, with the Ministry of Higher Education being responsible for actual assignments. More experienced technical and scientific manpower came first under the jurisdiction of the State Council's Bureau of Experts and later, in the 1960s, under the Scientific and Technological Personnel Administrative Bureau.[24] It is unclear how effectively assignments to specific posts were enforced. There are repeated indications of resistance by graduates and others to taking jobs in remote places. It is similarly unclear how the manpower planners made their assignment decisions, what criteria were used for determining priorities, and what principles governed the rationing of scarce manpower. However this may have been done, this allocation process did not rely solely on administrative orders but was reinforced by psychic and material inducements during most periods. For instance, the authorities responsible for the assignment of new graduates conducted extensive discussion sessions to impress them with the importance of their new assignments. On the other hand, there would be special prestige inducements, housing, research facilities, and other emoluments made available to scientists and advanced research workers. This was the case even though the range of differentiation in income terms may have been smaller than in some other countries.

It is fairly clear that while rationing such high-grade manpower, the planners attacked the problem in two additional ways. In the short run, they alleviated the skilled manpower shortage through large-scale importation of scientific, technical, and management manpower from other socialist countries. About 11,000 Soviet scientists and technicians worked in China in the 1950s, half of them in industrial enterprises. At the same time, about 38,000 Chinese were trained in the Soviet Union; approximately half of these were workers, while the others included 7,500 students. This particular source of supplementary supply disappeared with the sudden removal of all Soviet technicians and advisers in 1960.

To close the gap between availabilities and requirements in the longer run, planners greatly broadened the educational pyramid and thus sharply accelerated the rate at which new scientific, technical, and engineering manpower was produced. This is illustrated by the fact that in the thirty-six years between 1912 and 1947, 211,000 students graduated from higher educational institutions. In sharp contrast, more than twice as many were graduated in the nine years between 1949 and 1958. There undoubtedly are some incomparabilities in these figures, and perhaps from a strictly academic point of view the rise in numbers may have involved some decline in quality. However, this is far from certain for the period before the Cultural Revolution.

Another way of gauging the growth in the supply of high-grade manpower is to examine the number of graduates from institutions of higher learning in China in various years. Thus while this number was less than 20,000 in 1949–1950, it rose tenfold to 200,000 by 1962–1963. It declined somewhat thereafter, but the total inventory of scientific, engineering, and technical personnel may be expected to have continued to grow. However, this expansion was interrupted by the Cultural Revolution, which led to the closing of virtually all institutions of higher learning and most middle schools. As a result, at least three but more probably five years of training were lost between 1966 and 1970 or 1971.

These institutions have been gradually reopened since 1969, but new curricula and new admission procedures are still in the process of crystallization. The total supply of this type of personnel may even have declined during the Cultural Revolution. Not only were very few new scientists, engineers, and technicians being trained, but many who were trained and working were dislodged from their places of work and sent to rural communes. They were sent to so-called May 7th Schools; some had to undergo "reform through labor," while others spent varying periods of time there more or less voluntarily in order to break down the barriers between manual and mental labor. Given the strong elitist tradition of Chinese intellectuals, one could argue that a certain degree of exposure to rural life and conditions may be beneficial from a social and ideological point of view for all groups concerned. On the other hand, to the extent that it takes people out of scientific laboratories, it is bound to have some disruptive effects on research and scientific progress, particularly under circumstances in which this type of manpower is particularly scarce.

In many fields, Chinese science policy since the Cultural Revolution seems to emphasize diffusion of existing knowledge, application and adaptation of scientific findings to production rather than fundamental research. Given China's stage of development, this type of a strategy may be highly rational in terms of a broad cost-benefit calculus. Thus, it may make a great deal of sense to let highly advanced countries bear the cost and burden of pushing forward the frontiers of science. However, such a policy cannot be pursued in all fields and not indefinitely by a large and rapidly developing country such as China. The dilemmas thus posed can perhaps most clearly be illustrated in reference to Chinese agriculture. An American delegation of plant scientists visiting China in the fall of 1974 found that farm extension work was very well developed and of high priority. This was in part helped by the fact that many agricultural scientists were transferred from the laboratories to the farms to conduct local experiments there. Nevertheless, these advances may have occurred at the expense of future-oriented scientific work. Thus it probably undermined – at least temporarily – China's ability to develop through fundamental agricultural research those new, higher-yielding farming systems on which its future progress will depend.[25]

Allocation of labor Unlike scientific and engineering manpower, unskilled and semi-skilled labor is a relatively abundant factor in China. As a matter of fact, at least until the mass labor-mobilization drive of the Great Leap, there was considerable open and/or disguised unemployment both in the countryside and the cities. Instead of a labor shortage, there was initially a labor absorption problem, due to an imbalance between the rate of growth of non-farm employment opportunities on the one hand and the rate of growth of population and the annual additions to the labor force on the other. In any case, this labor absorption problem seems to have gradually been dissipated, as the intensity of land use was greatly stepped up – based on increases in multiple cropping, inter-planting, and transplanting several other crops in addition to rice – and the scope of rural industrialization was extended from 1963 to the present.

In most underdeveloped countries subject to population pressure, there is a rural labor surplus. Typically, however, there may be certain costs associated with recruiting and disciplining such labor for industrial, urban employment. Such newly recruited labor is frequently characterized by a high rate of absenteeism and turnover, and quite low productivity. It seems that these problems were not too serious in China given workers' attitudes, including those drawn from rural areas. Nevertheless, the number of experienced industrial workers was not unlimited and their productivity is undoubtedly higher than that of new rural recruits. However, the cost of training new workers for unskilled or semi-skilled industrial tasks may also have been low. Therefore one can assume that while the supply of industrial labor was to some extent limited (i.e., the labor supply function was not infinitely elastic), it was not difficult to fill job vacancies in factories.

Labor allocation in China is planned and its movement is subject to control. As noted earlier, each enterprise had a labor plan specifying the maximum number of employees the firm could engage and an annual wage bill it could not exceed. During periods when there were strong pressures to fulfill or over-fulfill output plans, enterprises tended to employ more labor even if they had to exceed the labor plan. This, in turn, was made possible by lax enforcement of the regulations.

According to regulations prevailing since 1958, a factory or construction firm is not supposed to hire its labor directly but should apply to the local branch of the labor department. It is supposed to establish whether additional workers are needed and, depending on its findings, send the appropriate number to the factories. If the hiring of additional workers means exceeding the enterprise wage-bill allocation, short-term credits must be obtained from the banks to cover these additional outlays. The banks were charged with the job of enforcing financial discipline and curbing the proclivity of enterprises to use additional labor. In actual practice, controls were not very strictly enforced either by the labor bureaus or the banks. As a result, there was a great deal of labor hoarding and over-staffing in Chinese industrial enterprises.[26] Over-fulfillment of the labor plan was a very common tendency in Soviet industry as well during the initial Five-Year Plan period. However, given the acute shortage of labor, Soviet enterprises were fiercely competing for it. Lax enforcement of labor and financial controls led to bidding up the price of labor and to marked wage inflation. In China, in contrast, lax controls led to large increases in urban employment without sharp increases in wages. This again underlines the vast differences in the labor-supply situations in the two countries.

At least since the Cultural Revolution, labor in China has been subject to physical and administrative allocation. Most of the restraints on the movement of labor were designed to stem or even reverse the migration of workers from country to city. This phenomenon has been a hallmark of industrialization in all countries and is widespread in virtually all developing countries. In China, as elsewhere, it was propelled by a combination of "push and pull" forces. At times, conditions in the countryside were disrupted under the impact of rapid collectivization and communization, and these conditions may have encouraged migration to the cities, that is, "pushed" people into migration. At other times or concurrently, the "pull" of the cities induced many people to move. The greater attractiveness of the cities may have been due to higher wages, better working conditions, or better housing.

Regardless of what the roots of this movement were, the Chinese have probably instituted more vigorous efforts to stem this tide than any other country. To leave his rural domicile (collective, commune, production team) and place of work, a person has to obtain a permit from local authorities. At the other end, in the city, he has to obtain a permit to stay. Without such a permit he cannot get a ration card. Security or party units may be stationed at key points en route (e.g., bus or railroad stations) to persuade or order people to return to their farms and provide them with the means to do so. In the city, even if the new migrant obtains a permit to stay and a ration card, he or she still has to find housing. Actually the acute urban housing shortage constitutes not only a serious barrier to rural–urban migration but also to inter-urban and inter-enterprise mobility. Almost certainly, prospects of better housing were as potent an incentive for attracting labor to an enterprise as higher wages. However, there were certain restrictions to mobility at the enterprise level as well. Appropriate higher-level authorities (e.g., the provincial industry bureau, the industrial ministry, or an organ of the Ministry of Labor) were supposed to approve all transfers of personnel as well as the hiring of new workers.

In part because these regulations were not too strictly enforced, and in part because it was difficult to enforce them, the urban population grew very rapidly in spite of all attempts to stop rural migration. This trend was particularly pronounced during the Great Leap. As a result, the authorities resorted to a series of unprecedented moves, at least unprecedented in the history of modern economic growth and industrialization. Between 1959 and late 1963, urban population in China was reportedly reduced from 130 to 110 million, reflecting a more or less forced back-migration to the country, a "sending-down" (*hsia-fang*) process.[27] In general, most recent arrivals from the country were supposed to be sent back first, while those most fitted for factory work were to be retrained in the city. In practice this injunction was not always followed. This movement was repeated following the Cultural Revolution and has continued since. Each year a large number of urban youth are sent to the countryside upon graduation from middle school.

Over and above those that were permanently sent down, there were several different types of groups assigned or encouraged to go to the country more or less temporarily. These included party cadres, students, and Red Guard groups sent partly to help with the harvest, lend a hand in commune administration, participate in rural educational tasks, and generally alleviate the shortage of highly literate, skilled, educated manpower in the countryside. Some were "sent down" for varying periods to participate in "reform through labor" in and out of the "May 7th Schools."

Price and wage determination As in other sectors, in industry too physical and price planning were combined in allocating resources. As was shown above, physical planning played a dominant but not exclusive role in the allocation of industrial materials and manpower. Some of the materials were set aside for market distribution through the state trading companies. These trading organs sold them, in turn, at fixed prices to small enterprises or small consumers of particular items. The materials were not assigned to them, and they were free to purchase them or not as they wished. In making their decision to buy or not to buy, enterprises would be guided by several criteria: was the particular material absolutely essential to the production of the firm's output, could substitutes be found for these materials, and, if so, what were the relative prices of the substitutes? Clearly, then, the price of the material for the firms that were buying it in the market performed a definite allocative function; it played a role in determining how much of it would be used, and what the demand for it would be at prevailing prices. Presumably, if at these prices demand greatly exceeded supply, the state trading companies would adjust the price upward and vice versa. This then was in a sense an administered market price, fixed periodically through a process of trial and error and applicable to a narrow segment of the commodity market.

However prices might play at least a small, marginal role as allocators, even for those materials that were centrally distributed to enterprises. Given the fact that enterprises, particularly after decentralization and the Great Leap, were under considerable pressure to reduce costs and increase profits, they had a vested interest in obtaining an adequate or ample supply of materials, but at the lowest possible cost. Therefore, in production processes in which some materials were more or less substitutable, an enterprise might prefer more of a cheaper one. However, its flexibility was limited by the fact that it was assigned definite quantities of these materials. Nevertheless, in instances of this kind the enterprise might be induced to bargain with the planners for more of the relatively cheaper material and less of the more expensive one. Alternatively, the enterprise might try to trade some of its allocation of the more expensive material with other enterprises that were short of it, provided it could be sure to obtain some of the cheaper one in return. While this type of inter-enterprise barter was not permitted, it was definitely practiced, at least on a limited scale. In the 1960s, this practice was more or less institutionalized through the "commodity banks" referred to above.

Whatever limited allocative role prices played in materials distribution, how were these prices fixed? What were the principles of industrial price formation? A large number of government agencies were involved in the price-setting process in China and their relative roles changed frequently. In most general terms, prices of industrial materials were fixed by central planning organs in collaboration with the industrial ministries concerned. Following decentralization, local economic organs had some voice in setting the prices of items produced in factories under their jurisdiction. For industrial products not subject to "unified distribution," prices were set by the Ministry of Commerce in consultation with the planning organs and the relevant industrial ministry. In the 1960s, comparable local trading and industrial bureaus also played a significant role.

These various organs, separately or in combination, usually fixed three kinds of prices: ex-factory prices, wholesale prices, and retail prices. References can also be found to so-called allocation or transfer prices, but it is not clear how these differ from ex-factory or wholesale prices. We are here primarily concerned with the ex-factory price, that is, the price paid to the industrial producer. It includes four elements – costs of production, depreciation allowances, profits, and taxes paid at the factory. Wholesale prices are calculated on the basis of factory prices with costs, taxes, and profits of wholesale commercial organs, and transport costs added. Similarly, retail prices reflect the additional taxes, profits, and costs incurred at the retail level. Since prices of virtually all industrial products are fixed, government organs can, if they so desire, separate the links between factory, wholesale, and retail prices. They may (and at times have done so) change one without changing the others. For instance, they may want to reduce factory prices of certain products perhaps to put pressure on the enterprises in the particular industry to cut costs. At the same time, they may not want to encourage rising consumption of the now lower-priced (ex-factory) product and therefore decide to leave the wholesale and retail price untouched or possibly leave just the retail price alone. This can be done by simply changing the taxes and/or profit at the wholesale and/or retail level.

Costs of production in China are calculated on the basis of average costs for the industry as a whole. Since an enterprise obtains most of its fixed capital in the form of a free grant from the government budget, no interest rates are charged. Therefore, enterprise cost calculations do not allow for capital costs, except for the costs of short-term loans obtained from the banks. On the other hand, the costs of repair, plant maintenance, raw materials, electric power, fuel, and labor are included. Quite different considerations govern price setting, and therefore the tax and profit rate, in producer-goods as compared to consumer-goods markets. The principles governing the latter will be analyzed in the next chapter in the context of macro-economic policy and inflation control.

During the first few years in the life of the People's Republic, markets were more or less free and resources were preponderantly allocated through the price mechanism. Broadly speaking, this was true for the 1950–1952 period. At the time, producer-goods prices shot up both in absolute terms and relative to other prices. This was because Korean War requirements, combined with domestic industrial rehabilitation needs, stimulated a very brisk demand for producer goods. This rise in demand occurred at a time when China's industrial capacity was sharply curtailed by war devastation and by Soviet dismantling of plants in Manchuria. The supply situation was greatly aggravated by the imposition of the U.S. trade embargo and a general rise in world prices of raw materials and producer goods.

The Chinese then froze producer-goods prices at these high Korean War levels. Even after a reduction in 1955–1956, they remained quite high. Taxes levied on producer goods at the factory level were quite modest. These were so-called industrial and commercial taxes, roughly equivalent to a sales tax or to the Soviet turnover tax. High prices and relatively low taxes left room for high profits. Thus it has been estimated that in 1957, after the price reductions, the profit rate for heavy industry as a whole was 43 percent above average cost.[28]

It is naturally impossible to determine to what extent these prices represented true scarcity indicators. Given the relative scarcity of capital in China, high producer-goods prices would seem to be in accord with the country's factor endowments. This would have been a significant consideration if these prices had served a major role as allocators of producer goods. However, as indicated above, they performed a rather limited allocative or distributive function. Therefore, administrative rather than economic considerations were primarily responsible for the relatively high producer-goods prices. Average costs varied greatly among enterprises in a given industry. Some firms were technically much more backward than others and operated under relatively high-cost conditions. New enterprises and mines also usually operated at a high cost at first. As a result, if prices of producer goods had been set lower, a number of firms would have operated at a loss, thus requiring subsidies. Administration of such a vast system of subsidies would have, however, imposed an enormous bureaucratic burden on the Chinese planning organs, industrial ministries, and local industrial bureaus.

One could agree that, irrespective of how significant an allocative role these prices played, the Chinese pricing method may be economically more rational than that practiced in the Soviet Union. Setting prices of producer goods fairly high in relation to average cost for the industry may come closer to marginal-cost pricing than if these were fixed at, or barely above, average cost. Thus in this respect there was a very significant difference between Chinese and Soviet planning practice, even during the FFYP period. The Soviets set producer-goods prices relatively low, at approximately 3 to 5 percent above average cost for the industry. This resulted in a complex system of subsidies. At the same time it imparted a producer-goods bias to industrial production processes in the Soviet Union. Since such goods were relatively cheap, enterprises were encouraged to purchase them more than might have been the case otherwise. There are indications that this was not accidental, but reflected a capital-intensive bias of the Russian planners. Whether this was an economically rational course for the Soviet Union at the time of the first two five-year plans (1928–1937) is rather doubtful. Although the Soviet Union was relatively better endowed with capital in 1928 than China in 1952, capital was still a very scarce factor relative to labor. This suggests that a price policy designed to economize on capital and capital goods might have been more rational in economic terms.

The major disadvantage of the producer-goods price policy practiced in China was that it reduced the cost pressure on the industrial enterprise. Rising costs could for the most part be absorbed by squeezing profits. Another qualification that must be considered in assessing the picture presented is that prices of producer goods were not necessarily uniform in China. For instance, following the launching of the "Agriculture First" policy in 1961, prices of capital goods for agricultural use were repeatedly lowered.[29] This may have involved some subsidization of farm production in order to encourage investment and modernization in agriculture. Inter-sectoral price diversity was coupled with inter-regional price variation and a certain lack of consistency in price policy. Thus the prices of coal, electric power, and petroleum products, for instance, were fixed on a regional basis. In contrast, the price paid for chemical fertilizer by the final user was the same throughout the country.

The producer-goods pricing and distribution system prevailing in China, and to a greater or lesser extent in other socialist countries, bears certain points of resemblance to production controls instituted in many capitalist countries during World War II, including the United States. Under these circumstances, demand tends to outrun supply amidst full employment of resources, thereby possessing all the ingredients of a classic inflationary situation. To prevent open inflation, a combination of price controls and rationing of producer goods is instituted. Seen from this point of view, the systemic differences between an economy such as the Chinese and a war-time capitalist economy are more those of degree than of kind, although the differences in degree may in some respects be so marked as to represent differences in kind. Price controls, rationing, and quantitative allocations tend to be more pervasive in an economy such as the Chinese. Moreover, all enterprises are public rather than private.

If prices played a secondary role in the distribution of producer goods, they were even less important in the allocation of another scarce input – engineering, scientific, and managerial manpower. As we have seen, these categories of personnel were almost universally assigned to their jobs. Nevertheless, wages and salaries of high-grade manpower were during most periods quite highly differentiated. The spread in these was much greater than that of unskilled or semi-skilled workers, and the top of the range went considerably higher, particularly if one takes into account services in kind (housing, car, etc.).

The average industrial wage is quoted in most Chinese sources as about 60 yuan per month, which is also the figure conveyed to foreign visitors in recent years. At times averages ranging from 50 to 70 yuan are given. The typical monthly salary of a manager or chief engineer seems to be around 200 to 250 yuan; however for quite senior personnel this can go up to 300 to 400 yuan. Therefore the top of the engineering or management salary scale is three to six times the average blue collar wage; in relation to the bottom of this wage (30 yuan), it is a multiple of seven to thirteen, not counting the services in kind.

These salaries and other emoluments must have played an important role in inducing people in these categories to work harder and better, to move up the scale, and to distinguish themselves. To the extent that this was the case, differentiated wages and salaries did play a significant role in attracting personnel to certain types of jobs. This does not mean that non-material incentives, such as striving for prestige, power, or patriotic and ideological dedication may not have also played an important allocative role.

While wages and prices seem to have played a subsidiary role in the allocation of materials and high-grade manpower, they played a much more significant role in the distribution of skilled and semi-skilled labor and consumer goods, particularly in the 1950s. With this in mind, the character of the wage-and-price system and its role as an allocator will be analyzed in greater detail below.

Wage policy in China was directed toward three inter-related objectives: (1) to provide workers with incentives to work harder and attain higher skills, (2) to allocate the labor force between different occupations, industries, and regions, and (3) to maintain control over the total industrial wage bill to assure price stability. To implement this policy, the Ministry of Labor, in cooperation with the industrial ministries and (after decentralization) with the involvement of local industrial bureaus, established an eight-point wage classification differentiated by skill, experience, and performance. This classification was codified by the 1956 wage reform; however in some cases other classifications, relying on a twelve-point spread for instance, have been practiced.

As noted above (pp. 101–104, and the preceding section of this chapter), an industrial enterprise had more or less complete autonomy in setting the wages of individual workers, as long as these fell within the prescribed eight-point (or in some cases alternative) system, and provided that the total wage payments thus established did not exceed the wage-bill target. The latter were maxima not to be exceeded by the firm. They were designed to discourage the hoarding of labor and over-staffing; they were also supposed to help maintain price stability. If the total wage bill could be kept under control, then total worker purchasing power could be kept under control. It was felt that, in this way, it would be easier to establish an equilibrium between the demand for consumer goods and their supply. Wage-bill controls were thus designed to alleviate inflationary pressures in consumer-goods markets.

Although a fairly uniform wage system was established following the wage reform of 1956, in fact there were some inter-industry, inter-plant, and inter-regional differentials. Wages tended to be higher in heavy industry than in light, consumer-goods branches. They were also higher in Shanghai and Manchuria than in other major industrial centers. These differentials reflected the relative priority assigned to different branches of industry, and the experience and seniority of workers in the particular place. The money value of a particular wage grade varied from plant to plant and place to place. Therefore, the average wage in a plant or industry reflected a combination of any one of three elements: the money wage assigned to individual grades, the wage grades assigned to individual workers, and the experience, seniority, and performance of the workers in any one grade.

For instance, a high-priority enterprise in heavy industry might be assigned a wage-bill target higher than that of a lower-priority firm employing the same number of employees. In such a case, the heavy-industry firm would have greater flexibility in the precise money value attached to a wage grade and also in assigning workers to higher grades. As a result, this firm would have a competitive edge in attracting better trained and more experienced workers. In this way, wage differentials performed certain definite allocative functions. However, not all differentials were of this character; some reflected variations in the cost of living in different parts of the country and others were due to the peculiarities of the wage-fixing system. Thus often the money value of wage goods in the same locality might differ, depending on whether the particular enterprise was under central ministerial or local control. At times, these differentials were quite erratic and could not be readily explained on economic grounds.

As a result, workers of roughly equivalent skills and performing similar or identical tasks may be paid different wage rates. No wonder that on occasion such differentials have caused some difficulties and friction. For instance, an American delegation of engineers, economists, and sociologists visited China on a month-long study tour of small-scale rural industries. They repeatedly found that workers in county-operated plants were paid according to the standard industrial wage classification, with their average wages slightly below those of large-scale urban factories. At the same time, plants operated by communes based their wage payments on work points developed by agricultural production teams. As a result, workers in commune-run plants received lower wages for quite similar work than those employed in county-operated enterprises.

Not all wage payments in China were based on time rates (i.e., hourly, weekly, or monthly). On the contrary, piece rates were quite prevalent in the 1950s; they seem to have attained their greatest importance in 1956, when 42 percent of production workers in state enterprises were on piece rates.[30] This method of payment seems to have declined thereafter, both because it was difficult to administer and ran strongly counter to the egalitarian ethos of the Great Leap. The eight-grade wage structure crystallized in the course of the 1956 wage reform provided for about a 3:1 spread between the highest and lowest grade. Apprentices in the process of training would receive a below-grade remuneration for two to three years.

In recent years, industrial blue collar wages in China have ranged from about 30 yuan a month for a grade-one worker to 100 or 120 for the top grade. Occasionally, this may go as high as 150.[31] This represents an industrial wage span typical of many other countries, although somewhat narrower than that encountered in some less developed countries. However, this wage spread has been under periodic pressure in China. Thus in early 1975 a campaign was launched against "bourgeois rights," coupled with an attack on the eight-point wage scale. It expresses a strong and periodic concern by many leadership elements that such wide wage differentiation may lead the society away from the egalitarian ideal.

Although wages in modern capitalist economies are in part administered rather than purely competitive, there are functioning labor markets in these systems and wages do serve as allocators. In contrast, there is no free choice of occupations and no collective bargaining in China. During the FFYP period, wage differentiation seems to have played some allocative role in respect to skilled and semi-skilled industrial workers. However, at least since the Cultural Revolution, labor in China is assigned by government organs; it is allocated administratively rather than through a labor-market mechanism. Under these circumstances, wages primarily spur workers on to skill improvement, advancement, and harder work. The most significant role of wages may be to serve as an incentive for raising labor productivity.

It is quite clear that the wage system in China is an administered one. Thus wages are not formed through a free interplay of demand and supply forces in the labor market. However, there are not many economies in which they are actually determined in that way. In a number of countries wages are set by collective bargaining between large corporate entities and large unions. In many cases, arbitration procedures – either compulsory or voluntary – have been introduced. This does not mean that market forces play no role in the wage bargains arrived at in this way. What it implies is that this process does not yield pure competitive wages. The wages thus emerging represent an amalgam of: (1) demand and supply (market) forces, (2) government stabilization (anti-inflationary) policies, and (3) relative power (bargaining strength) of the worker versus employer sides in the bargaining process. Seen in this light, wage formation in China does not differ all that radically from that in other countries.

Investment planning Planning for economic development involves two distinct but inter-related processes: current operational planning, revolving around the utilization of existing plant capacity; and investment planning, concerned with the allocation of capital for the expansion and growth of plant capacity. Most of the analysis thus far in this chapter is related to the first problem; therefore we now turn to a consideration of the second.

Investment planning requires several kinds of decisions. First of all, what should be the rate of investment, that is, how much of the current ouptput should be saved, how much of current consumption should be sacrificed to increase future consumption? At what rate should this future consumption grow, and therefore how should the resources set aside (not consumed) out of current output be invested? What should be the future direction of development and therefore into what sectors, industrial branches, products, and facilities should investment be channeled? That is, what should investment priorities and the inter-sectoral pattern of investment be? What should be the locational pattern of industrial production, where should the new plants be located, and what weight should be given to the competing criteria in deciding new plant locations? Finally, the character of project design, the size of plants, technical specifications, and the technological level of new projects must be determined. Unfortunately, we know very little about how these decisions have been made in China in the past twenty years or so.

New industrial construction was generally divided into "above-norm" and "below-norm" projects. The precise definitions of these varied between different industrial branches and at different times. For the most part, projects requiring investments of 10 to 30 million yuan or more would be considered "above-norm." For most of the past twenty years, these projects remained under central government control and came within the purview of central planning organs. Following the decentralization of industrial and fiscal management in late 1957, and the reform of the planning system in late 1958, the upper limit of "below-norm" projects may have been raised – at least for a while – and local economic planning organs given greater control over these. However, the degree of local control was circumscribed by the fact that most of the investment was financed out of the central government budget. After the decentralization of fiscal management, 20 percent of the enterprise earnings were paid into local government budgets and enterprises were allowed to retain a slightly higher share of their earnings. However, this did not increase the scope of local-government-financed investment, since central budgetary authorities maintained firm control over all government outlays including those by the local government.[32] Although it did provide the enterprise with some marginal resources for capital projects, use of retained earnings for enterprise investment was illegal unless it was specifically approved by the appropriate planning organs.

It is not at all clear what criteria planners used in allocating capital. Apparently, through a process of trial and error, they discovered that under normal economic conditions and with the institutions prevailing in China the system could support a 20 to 25 percent rate of investment without undue strain. The problem of investment choice, that is, what the pattern of investment should be and what technologies to use, was more or less simplified during the FFYP period because of several factors. The broad direction of development was determined by the basic objectives of the new regime. One of these objectives was the creation of "a comprehensive and independent industrial system." The development of such a system required marked expansion of China's quite modest heavy-industry base. This was greatly reinforced by an urge to develop as rapidly as possible an independent defense capability (see pp. 120–123). Therefore it was a foregone conclusion that basic industries such as coal mining, electric-power generation, and steel, cement, and machinery production would be assigned high investment priorities.

Even if priorities were more or less clear, this did not resolve the issue of technical choice. Should the new industrial projects be large-scale or smaller-scale? Should they be designed for more capital-intensive or labor-intensive methods of production? Should they be based on some explicit or implicit notion of profitability or rate of return on the investment? Explicit consideration of a rate of return was excluded by ideological considerations, since according to Marxist theory capital is merely embodied labor and not a separate factor of production. Therefore, from a Marxist point of view, it is erroneous to think of rate of return on capital. In fact, Soviet planners have found it necessary to introduce implicit concepts of rate of return as a tool in investment design. However, indications are that Chinese planners did not consider this too important an issue. Part of the reason for this may have been that the issues of technical choice were pre-determined in the 1950s, so that the degree of freedom left to the planners may have been quite limited.

Choice was pre-determined by at least two kinds of considerations. First, for some of the basic industries, modern factory methods require production on a large scale. For instance in the case of steel, there are very far-reaching cost advantages to a large, integrated mill or a steel complex as compared to a number of smaller plants geographically separated and each producing part of the total process. Put another way, in some of these industries factor proportions and capital coefficients were relatively fixed, and thus the range of choice fairly limited. Second, there were 694 "above-norm" projects in the FFYP, of which 455 were to be completed during the first plan period, with the rest to be left for completion during the second plan period. At the very core of this FFYP program, which dominated the whole investment plan and especially the industrial investment plan, were 156 complete-plant imports (so-called turnkey projects) from the Soviet Union. As noted above, these projects were designed in the Soviet Union; the equipment for them was manufactured there, brought to China, and installed there by Russian engineers and technicians. This relieved Chinese planners of the need to worry about technical-choice issues.

The situation changed markedly when Soviet economic and technical assistance ceased and Russian engineers and advisers withdrew. Also during this period, the Chinese decided to accord a significantly higher priority to the development of small- and medium-scale industry. The direction of industrial development in the 1960s, and therefore the problem of inter-sectoral investment priorities, was fairly clearly defined by the "Agriculture First" and "self-reliance" policies. Thus it was clear that the chemical, farm equipment, oil extraction and refining, and machine-building industries would be accorded high investment priorities in the 1960s. However, to the extent that in certain branches of these industries factor proportions were not fixed, there was a range of choice as to size of plants to be built and technical processes to be designed. The issue of technical choice was now less pre-determined and therefore more complicated. Unfortunately it is far from clear how these problems were tackled in Chinese planning practice. Small- and medium-scale projects were recommended on the grounds that they required less capital investment, building materials, and machinery per unit of output; they could be constructed faster and thus brought more quickly into production; they would save in transport either from sources of raw material and/or shipment to markets; they would utilize more labor and therefore could absorb the underemployed or unemployed in the countryside.

These general principles could be translated into more or less operational criteria by comparing alternative designs for new industrial projects and assessing which best meets these various standards. The difficulty naturally arises from the fact that some projects will rank high by one standard and low by another and vice versa. Therefore, to rank alternative designs requires some kind of a weighting system for these different criteria, indicating what relative importance is to be attached to each so that some kind of aggregate preference index can be constructed. It is not clear whether Chinese planners used such a weighting system, and if so what importance was attached by them to the different criteria.

There is some evidence that the Chinese are conscious of a "payout" or "recoupment" period. Thus, one can find a number of statements in Chinese sources in effect amounting to "let's invest more in activity or plant X because the capital outlay can be returned to the state within *t* years." Similarly, both in written sources and in statements to visitors (most recently to the rural small-scale industries delegation), factory managers and cadres state that one of the advantages of small-scale plant construction is that the lag between the time such a project is started and fully operational is much shorter than for large plants. It is thus possible that some form of capital saving may serve as an important criterion in Chinese investment decisions and technical choices.[33]

Conclusions

As in so many other aspects of their societal evolution, Chinese leaders pursued somewhat different resource-allocation policies, both in agriculture and industry, in the 1960s than in the 1950s. The relative importance of different instruments used in the planning process and the role of planning itself shifted over time.

Long- and medium-range planning played a quite limited role. Planners and policy makers clearly had some long-run objectives in mind, which at times were incorporated in perspective plans such as the Twelve-Year Plan for Agricultural Development and a similar plan for the development of science. These, however, were not firm plans but projections, hopes or guides to direction of movement. Five-year plans, which were operational, particularly for investment planning, in other socialist economies, were much less operational in China. They were disrupted or overtaken either by sharp harvest fluctuations and/or marked policy shifts. Therefore, operational planning in China was largely confined to periods no longer than one year.

For a short period, that is, from about 1952 to 1957, the Chinese tried to more or less emulate the Soviet model and develop a centralized command-allocation system. Chinese planners gradually perceived that this system was not too well suited to Chinese conditions. As a result, under the impact of the Great Leap and its aftermath, there emerged a more decentralized command system. It was based on the bureaucratic delegation of many resource-allocating decisions to provincial and lower levels of administration, while maintaining central control over the most important of these decisions.

This meant that raw materials, high-grade manpower, labor, and capital were for the most part bureaucratically allocated in industry. Some materials, not subject to "unified distribution," or even if subject to it destined for distribution to small enterprises, could be allocated through the market, but at fixed prices. Prices, wages, and thus commodity and labor markets played a considerable role as long as there was a sizable private-enterprise sector in China. But since 1956 this form of allocation has dwindled for industrial goods and inputs.

The situation is somewhat different in agriculture. Due to the very size, geographic spread, and the vast number of production units, planning in agriculture has been less detailed. The principal instruments of resource allocation in agriculture were procurement planning on the one hand and allotments of production requisites on the other. These were based on a blend of physical and price-planning instruments, with prices and markets playing a somewhat larger role than in industry. This can be illustrated by the operation of the procurement system. To the extent that production teams obligate themselves to deliver certain fixed quotas, prices play no role. However, the procurement process is reinforced by price inducements, both through increases in the procurement price, and through payment of premium prices for the purchase of "above-quota" grain and other produce.

Similarly, production teams, brigades, and communes cannot go out and buy freely any desired quantities of electric generators, pumps, farm equipment, or chemical fertilizer. Since all these products are probably encompassed by materials-supply rationing, they can only be obtained on the basis of allotments. However, to the extent that their prices are lowered either absolutely and/or in relation to the sale prices for grain and other produce, demand pressures for them rise, which in turn might induce some increases in their production and distribution.

What role do prices and wages play under these circumstances? Prices and the market mechanism play a very important role in the distribution of pigs, chickens, and vegetables raised on private plots and sold through free rural markets. Prices also play an important role in distributing industrial products under the circumstances specified above. Finally, they do play a very important role in consumer-goods markets. They will affect what commodities and in what quantities consumers buy, except for the few rationed items for which the quantities that can be purchased are fixed. Prices will also affect the purchasing power and thus the consumption levels of both urban-worker and peasant households.

Wages similarly play a limited but not unimportant role. Although there is no free choice of occupations in China, earning potential and working conditions almost certainly play a role in attracting young entrants into the labor force to certain fields of endeavor. Wage differentials tend to attract workers from agriculture to industry, for instance, and even though there are formidable barriers to voluntary and unauthorized movements, not all demands and pressures can be resisted. Wages can also play a significant role in fostering skill acquisition, skill accumulation, harder work, and rising labor productivity. Finally, wage levels and structures have important income-distributive, purchasing-power, and standard of living effects to be further discussed in the next chapter, within the context of macro-economic stability.

5

The quest for economic stability

The historical roots

As shown in preceding chapters, the Chinese Communist leaders dedicated themselves to transforming China into a modern socialist state. They had certain images of what the broad contours of that future state might be. These images were shaped by their ideology and world view on the one hand and by the realities of China's economic backwardness on the other. Both the ideas and the economic realities were to a large extent the legacy of the past. Therefore, one of the key problems facing the new leaders was how to build an economic system best adapted to attain their goals and objectives given the conditions inherited from the past. These were the issues addressed in Chapters 3 and 4.

Having constructed this economic system, what were its performance characteristics? How effective a vehicle did it turn out to be in pursuing and implementing the new regime's objectives? It is clear from the preceding chapters that to attain their goals, Chinese leaders pursued a high investment–growth strategy of development. Such a strategy was bound to generate inflationary pressures. Yet, as will be shown here, these pressures were contained very effectively. How this was done and what factors contributed to this outcome will be examined in this chapter.

With worldwide inflation and deep recession characterizing the mid-1970s, we are much more concerned about economic stability than we were some years ago. Policy makers and economists rather complacently assumed that they had at their disposal effective instruments for controlling inflation and unemployment in market economies. Some even wondered whether the business cycle was perhaps obsolete, in spite of the fact that cyclical fluctuations in levels of economic activity and rates of economic growth have characterized capitalist development since the industrial revolution. These cycles were marked by fluctuations in output, employment, and prices, with alternating phases of inflation and deflation. Thus, the process of modern economic growth has been purchased in presently industrialized economies at considerable social cost, perhaps most dramatically illustrated by the Great Depression of the 1930s.

The elimination of these booms and busts has been a central concern of socialist movements since the time of Marx. This quest for stability was especially emphasized by the Chinese Communists, in light of the country's prolonged and extreme inflationary experience. Inflation in China has deep historical roots and far-reaching connotations.

According to some historians, in the Chinese experience inflation was closely associated with the dynastic cycle. Based on this hypothesis, the rule of Chinese dynasties tended to be characterized by alternating periods of vigor and decline.[1] During the rising and expanding phase, the central imperial government tended to be strong. This strong government, in turn, had firm control over the bureaucracy, and was in a position to broaden the tax base and curb the tax-farming proclivities of the bureaucracy. It could thus assure rising revenues for the imperial center, at the same time providing an opportunity to lighten the tax burden of an individual peasant household.

From this point of view, traditional Chinese society can be viewed as being composed of three strata: the imperial center, the bureaucracy, and the peasantry. During periods of strong government, the tax base would tend to expand, with a larger relative share of the revenue collected channeled into the imperial center. Correspondingly, the relative income share of the middle layer – the bureaucracy – would tend to shrink during this phase. As a result, the fiscal position of the imperial government would tend to be strong at these times.

On the other hand, periods of dynastic decline led to a weakening of the imperial government's control of the bureaucracy and a corresponding expansion in the role of this middle layer. This frequently produced two kinds of consequences. More and more land was amassed by the bureaucracy and gentry and was thus withdrawn from the tax rolls, so that the revenue base was narrowed. At the same time, a larger share of the revenue tended to be retained by the bureaucracy at the expense of the imperial center. With central government expenditure at best remaining more or less stable, shrinking revenues opened the way to deficit finance, which in pre-modern times typically took the form of debasement of the currency.

Therefore, in the eyes of the Chinese people, inflation traditionally stood as a symbol of governmental weakness. In a sense, it was another sign that the Mandate of Heaven was withdrawn from the rulers. For this very reason, the inflation and galloping hyper-inflation of 1937–1949 assumed a significance considerably beyond its economic costs. Correspondingly, it increased the determination of the new regime to avoid this inflationary experience at all costs and to strive for monetary and fiscal stability in China.

The war-time and post-war inflationary spiral

The most recent and perhaps far-reaching inflation experienced by the Chinese people was a child of war and weak government. It was a classic demand-pull inflation fueled by large government deficits, which in turn were financed by the printing press, that is, by the printing of new notes.

With the outbreak of the Sino-Japanese War in 1937, Chinese government expenditures – particularly military outlays – rose rapidly at a time when the tax base was shrinking. The Japanese gradually occupied all the coastal provinces, so that China was cut off from its industrial, most modern, and advanced economic sectors quite early in the war. These sectors and coastal regions of China contributed a large share of the tax and customs revenue to the central government. With this source of revenue cut off and expenditures rising, there was relatively little choice but to resort to deficit finance.

However, deficit finance was endemic to the Republic's finances from the time of the 1911 revolution to the outbreak of the war with Japan. During the 1930s, about 20 percent of the central government's expenditures were financed by deficits. During war time, these deficits rose to about 70 percent or more of total expenditures. Shrinking revenues resulted from contracting output on the one hand and the government's inability to significantly broaden the tax base on the other. Although a land tax in kind was introduced during the war, attempts to tax incomes and profits proved unsuccessful.[2]

Of course, government deficits are not in and of themselves inflationary, depending on how they are financed. Thus, if they are financed for instance by bond sales to households, they need not be inflationary, since these represent a form of personal saving and corresponding reductions in consumption outlays. On the other hand, the opposite will be the case if deficits are financed by bond sales to banks, through government loans from the central bank or direct note issue, since all these add to the money supply and the purchasing power of consumers through credit creation. Even with these conditions prevailing, deficit finance need not be inflationary if the economy is operating at less than full employment or if – particularly in a less developed country – an increasing share of output is brought to market and sold. Thus, rising total money purchasing power generated by an expanding money supply can be offset without necessarily aggravating inflationary pressures either by utilizing unemployed resources to expand production and/or by increasing the supply of goods and services brought to market.

This is because in essence a demand-pull inflation is but a symptom of an excess demand for goods and services in relation to the supplies available at stable prices. When the economy is operating at close to full capacity and available resources are fully utilized, it is not capable of quickly increasing the production of goods and services even if new purchasing power is suddenly injected into the money stream. Under these circumstances rising household incomes tend to chase a relatively fixed bundle of goods and services, with consumers competing with each other for this fixed bundle and thus bidding up prices.

Unfortunately, the Chinese Nationalist government was not capable of generating a sufficient degree of adherence or confidence from the public to market bonds to households on an appreciable scale. The different war-time bond issues were not purchased and repeatedly failed. Sizable amounts were raised only when the government resorted to compulsory bond levies, which at their peak in 1943 covered over 10 percent of the deficit. For the 1937 to 1945 period as a whole, only 5 percent of the cumulative deficit was financed through sales of bonds.

Even under the most favorable conditions, bond sales to the public amidst war-time conditions would not be sufficient to contain and fully control inflationary pressures. With rapidly rising government expenditures and growing deficits at a time when more and more resources are devoted to defense production and the accumulation of military inventories, money demand at the disposal of households is bound to rise more rapidly than consumer-goods supplies. This creates enormous upward pressures on prices, which are likely to be contained only by a whole combination of measures including price control and rationing. The Chinese Nationalist government did in fact introduce various measures of price control, beginning in 1938 and continuing through the war, but with very limited success.

This inflationary process was at first a relatively moderate one but gained momentum as the war progressed. This is evidenced by the fact that wholesale prices in Shanghai rose on the average by about 60 *percent* in *three years*, that is, between 1935 and 1938. However, in the subsequent year, that is, between June 1939 and June 1940, they more than *doubled* in Free China (i.e., in the areas under Chinese government control). They increased *two and a half times* in the following year and about *trebled* each year between 1941 and 1945.

As pointed out by S. H. Chou, at the end of World War II the price slump that had started before V-J Day continued in both Free China and the Japanese-occupied areas. The anticipated resumption of international trade and the flow of fresh supplies from the coast to the interior led not only to a reduction in the buying pressure on the market, but also to considerable dis-hoarding of commodities by speculators. This trend was reinforced by a rise in public confidence in the Nationalist government as a result of the war's end and the defeat of Japan.[3]

Unfortunately, price decline turned out to be a purely temporary phenomenon, and the situation began to deteriorate rapidly as the anti-Japanese struggle was converted into a civil war between Nationalist and Communist armies. As a result, the inflationary process began to gain momentum once more and finally degenerated into galloping hyper-inflation. This is most clearly dramatized by the fact that Shanghai wholesale prices rose *seven and a half million times between May 1946 and March 1949.*[4]

Inflationary effects

One might legitimately ask what are the economic, social, and political consequences of inflation. In what sense is inflation a problem?

In most general terms, inflation is likely to affect income distribution and the allocation of resources. As a rule, the burden of rising prices is borne unequally by different groups in the population. It tends to bear most heavily on those with fixed incomes, such as pensioners, welfare recipients, the unemployed, and other disadvantaged groups. Thus, it frequently hits hardest those least able to afford it. At the same time, profits tend to keep abreast or ahead of inflation, while wage and salary earners are not uniformly affected; some benefit, some may stay abreast, and yet others experience a decline in real incomes. The impact of inflation on wage and salary earners really depends on the institutional arrangements in the labor market on the one hand and the rapidity of price changes on the other. Thus, if wages and salaries are contractually fixed for certain periods of time, say a year or more, while prices rise rapidly and continuously, wages will tend to lag behind prices and consequently workers will experience losses in real income. On the other hand, if there are cost-of-living adjustments built into the wage bargains, wages are likely to keep pace with prices.

Sustained price rises also affect the balance between creditors and debtors. In an inflationary period, when money is losing its purchasing power, credits extended today can be repaid in cheaper money later to the benefit of debtors and the disadvantage of creditors. To guard against this risk, interest rates tend to rise during inflationary times. However, if price rises are continuous and rapid, it is unlikely that interest rates will increase sufficiently to compensate creditors for the loss of purchasing power.

For roughly similar reasons, rapid inflation may discourage voluntary, personal, household saving. Bank deposits may quite rapidly lose their value, as does cash in hand. Moreover, interest accruing on savings accounts usually does not go up rapidly enough to compensate savers for the decline in the "real value" of money.

On the other hand, inflation may represent a form of unintended, involuntary saving. Assuming that labor and other resources are fully employed, or that the mobility of labor and other factors of production is so restricted that they cannot be easily moved from place to place, investment and defense production can be increased only by bidding away resources from consumer-goods production. This competition for resources will mean a rise in wages, raw material prices, and money incomes. With these increased incomes, consumers will try to increase their consumer-goods purchases at a time when the production of these goods is not rising or only rising quite slowly. As a result, the competition of consumer households for a limited consumer-goods basket will start driving up the prices of these products.

The net result of this process will be that by the end of the year a larger share of the total output of goods and services, of the GNP, will have been allocated to investment and defense and a smaller share to consumption. Thus, the non-consumption share of GNP will have been increased and more of this GNP will in some sense have been set aside for "saving." However, this did not take the form of household saving and was not the result of a deliberate choice of consumers. It was rather the result of decisions by government authorities and producers who bid away resources from the consumer-goods sector. Therefore, increased saving or non-consumption was imposed, so to speak, on the consumers *ex post facto*.

Most of these effects were apparent in the Chinese inflation. In China this was to a large extent a profit inflation, which worked in favor of the recipients of profits at the expense of those receiving other income shares. The absence of effective tax measures made it impossible for the government to tax these profits. More often than not, these windfall profits were channeled into luxury consumption or invested in inventories, precious metals, and foreign currencies for hedging against inflation.

Hoarding of these inventories aggravated scarcities of consumer goods and raw materials and thus contributed to further price rises. Moreover, the channeling of profits into speculative rather than productive forms of investment contributed nothing to increasing production and to alleviating the scarcity of supplies on the market. Therefore, this particular form of profit inflation was self-reinforcing.

Money wages lagged behind rising commodity prices, so real wages declined. The lag was most serious for government employees and school teachers. The purchasing power of salaries in Chungking in 1943 was *one-tenth* of its 1937 level for civil servants and *one-sixth* for school teachers. At the same time, the real wages of industrial workers declined only by 30 percent and those of landless laborers by 40 percent. On the other hand, farmers' real incomes did not decline very much.[5]

It is thus quite clear that the Chinese inflation was markedly redistributive in its effects. A large share of the war costs was imposed through a spiraling inflation on a limited number of government employees, military personnel, school teachers, and recipients of rental and interest incomes, with virtually no regard for their ability to pay. In sharp contrast, a certain number of war profiteers accumulated enormous gains at the expense of the other income groups.

This redistribution of income and the unequal burden thus imposed necessarily demoralized underpaid teachers and government employees. This encouraged corruption of civil servants and forced them to find a variety of means for assuring their survival. No wonder China's inflationary experience weakened its whole social fabric and seriously undermined its structure of government.

A sustained and rapidly spiraling inflation not only redistributes income but sooner or later tends to disrupt the production of goods and services. Drastic declines in real wages may undermine work incentives and lead to profound social unrest. Furthermore, under a regime of runaway inflation, resources are bound to be mis-allocated; a significantly larger share of resources than might otherwise be the case tends to be channeled into hoarding and luxury consumption rather than expanding production of consumer necessities and manufacturing facilities in general.

In its final stages, the Chinese inflation was both a symptom of and a factor contributing to the total breakdown of the economy, as indeed has been the case with the classic hyper-inflations of post–World War II Germany, Greece, Hungary, and some other countries. Inflation was becoming so rampant and pervasive that people had to be paid daily in large bundles of paper. By 1948 and 1949 this paper was so rapidly losing its value that all wage and income recipients had to convert it immediately into purchases of goods before it became worthless. This of course meant that workers and employees would spend some time away from their jobs each day converting money into goods, with resulting absenteeism and loss of working time. Thus not only were many production hours lost but the whole organization and efficiency of the work process was markedly weakened.

This not only disrupted production but the distribution of goods and services as well. At a time when a currency becomes virtually worthless, so much so that people flee from money into goods, the economy tends to revert more and more to commodity barter. This was perhaps most clearly illustrated in post–World War II Germany when cartons of American cigarettes became a significant medium of exchange and a store of value, thus assuming some quasi-monetary functions. By late 1948 and early 1949, as the Nationalist regime was nearing its collapse, money in China lost all its functions. It no longer could serve as a store of value, as a medium of exchange, or as a standard or measure of value. According to some reports, which cannot be fully validated on the basis of the available data, the real value in terms of goods of the last two issues of Nationalist notes printed was less than the real cost of printing those notes.

The restoration of stability

The civil war between the Kuomintang and the People's Liberation Army, coming on the heels of the long Sino-Japanese war, left China in a state of devastation. Thus when the Chinese Communists assumed power in 1949, they inherited a war-torn, inflation-torn, fragmented economy. Industrial and agricultural production was sharply curtailed, much of the railroad stock was destroyed, and many rail lines were blown up. Therefore, the supply of commodities available for consumption and sale was drastically reduced, both because of the decline in production and the far-reaching disruption in the system of distribution.

Given the scarcity of consumer goods on the one hand and the large quantities of currency in circulation on the other, it took some time to dampen the inflationary flames. To do so not only required restoring production, transport, and distribution, but reorganizing the whole budgetary and banking system and bringing it under tight government control. However, the first order of business, a prerequisite for the restoration of the economy, was to terminate the civil war, consolidating the hold of the new regime and establishing peace, unity, and order.

The Chinese Communist troops entered Peking (The Northern Capital), the traditional symbol of *Chung Kuo* (The Middle Kingdom), on January 23,

1949. This was followed by the fall of Nanking (The Southern Capital), the seat of the Nationalist government, on April 23, 1949, and the capture of Shanghai on May 25. The People's Republic of China (PRC) was officially proclaimed on October 1, and less than two weeks later Canton was taken by the PLA. The last remnants of Nationalist troops were subdued in December and thus the process of uniting all of mainland China under the new regime was completed by the end of 1949.

As long as the civil war continued inflation was taking its toll, as evidenced by the fact that Shanghai wholesale prices rose on the average sixfold between July and December 1949. However, this galloping hyper-inflation was gradually brought under control. It was considerably slowed down in the following months and the spiral was broken in March 1950.[6] Under the impact of quite drastic deflationary policies, a temporary crisis ensued. Prices actually declined and this unforeseen depression was marked by bank failures, business bankruptcies, accumulation of unsold inventories in the cities, and large-scale urban unemployment. This trend was reversed with the outbreak of the Korean War, after which wholesale prices once more rose, so that by the end of the year they exceeded the March peak by about 30 percent. Thus 1950 was a year of marked price fluctuations, during which the new government gained increasing control over price formation, but did not yet fully attain this goal. However, price stability was essentially attained in 1951, with Shanghai wholesale prices rising by less than 20 percent in a twelve-month period. At the same time, raw material and producer-goods prices increased much more rapidly under the competing pressures of Korean War requirements and domestic reconstruction.

In summary, inflation continued rampant in 1949 but was greatly slowed down and was beginning to be brought under control in 1950. By 1951 price increases were comparatively mild, and by 1952 complete stability was established. Thus, inflationary flames that were lighted on the eve of the Sino-Japanese war, and spread progressively over a period of twelve years, were dampened and then doused within two to three years. How was this feat accomplished?

The first step consisted of currency conversion and unification. In 1948 and 1949 there were a number of currencies in circulation in China: those issued by Communist authorities in liberated areas, the Nationalist currencies, and foreign currencies such as silver dollars. Toward the end of 1948, the People's Bank of China was established and the new *jen-min-pi* (people's currency) was issued to replace some of the local currencies on a par basis. This new currency gradually replaced all others in circulation, at varying rates of conversion. This process of conversion and currency unification was more or less completed by the end of 1949. However, a separate currency – the Northeast yuan – continued to circulate in Manchuria until March 1951, when it too was converted into the *jen-min-pi*.[7]

At the same time, the attack on instability proceeded along two parallel lines, affecting both the supply and demand for goods and services. On the supply side, a series of measures was taken to restore agricultural and industrial production as quickly as possible and to reactivate the exchange and distribution of goods and services. On the demand side, stringent and quite orthodox fiscal and monetary measures were introduced, designed to curb increases in money purchasing power. This required balancing the government budget, restoring confidence in the monetary medium, and controlling money and credit.

Budget balancing involved curtailing government expenditure in early 1950 and a reorganization of the tax system based on increased rates of urban taxation. At the same time, fiscal management was greatly centralized, with many local government functions transferred to the central government. Beyond that, in effect, local and central government budgets were integrated into a unified national budget plan.

After the outbreak of the Korean War, government outlays began to increase once more under the impact of rising military expenditures. But in contrast with past regimes, the expanding outlays were financed by non-inflationary means. Not only was the tax base broadened, but tax administration and the efficiency of tax collection were greatly improved. As a result, revenues increased considerably. However, there was still a small deficit of about 10 percent of total expenditures – a remarkable achievement compared to the gaping deficits of preceding years. This deficit was not financed by note issues or bank borrowing, but was covered by bond sales and citizens' contributions fostered by patriotic campaigns; in this way deficits were offset by household saving and the transfer of funds from consumers to the government treasury. Given consumer-goods scarcities prevailing at the time, and the resulting imbalance between money demand and goods brought to market, excess purchasing power was in effect mopped up in this way. Thus, inflationary pressures were dampened and an equilibrium between consumer demand and supply was gradually reestablished.

In order to curb a rapid growth of demand, beyond the devastated production system's capacity to supply, it was not sufficient to reduce budget deficits. It was essential to dampen the credit inflation that helped to fuel the galloping expansion in money supply. Therefore, in accord with the series of stabilization moves of January to April 1950, the People's Bank began to pursue a tight, deflationary credit policy. In combination with other anti-inflationary devices, the bank gradually succeeded in curbing speculation and black market credit, and in controlling the interest rate. Monthly interest rates for loans to Shanghai traders rose from 24 to 30 percent in June 1949 to a peak of 70 to 80 percent in December, and then declined to 18 percent in April 1950 and 3 percent a year later.[8]

These figures illustrate once more a point brought out earlier in this chapter. In a period of rapid inflation, lenders charge high interest rates as a hedge against the risk that borrowers will repay the loans in money of much less value. Correspondingly, borrowers do not resist these high rates, knowing that the probability is high that they will be able to repay the loans in money that has in the meantime been greatly devalued.

Clearly, restoration of confidence in the monetary medium was a necessary pre-condition for reducing the interest rate. It was also necessary to activate other types of transactions in the economy. For instance, it would have been very difficult for the government to sell bonds to households if they feared that these would be amortized years later in valueless money. Similarly, the public would not deposit funds in banks, particularly in savings accounts, unless it could be assumed that these deposits would not be wiped out through devaluation. The same applies to wage and salary payments. When the monetary medium loses its purchasing power day by day, such payments cannot be fixed for a week or a month, lest the real wage dwindle to a fraction of its former level.

To obviate this problem, the Chinese government decided to guarantee the purchasing power of these transactions. Accordingly, wage and salary payments, bank deposits, and bond issues were expressed in commodity-basket values. These were termed *wage, parity deposit,* and *victory bond units* respectively. All these measures were designed to discourage the flight from money into goods and to foster the accumulation of savings and bank deposits.

These basket units were composed of necessities in certain fixed quantities. They typically included a food staple, cotton cloth, coal, and some vegetable oil. The precise composition of the basket might vary from region to region. The monetary value of each unit would be quoted once a week or once in ten days in each of the major cities. As a result, if someone, for instance, would make a bank deposit of so many JMP [*jen-min-pi* (people's currency)] at a certain date, he would translate this into commodity-basket units and in effect deposit that number of units. Then, if the depositor wanted to withdraw his account some months later, he would receive the money value of the basket units as of the time of withdrawal rather than the original date of deposit.

These fiscal and monetary controls attacked the inflationary spiral from the demand side, and were designed to mop up excess purchasing power. However, restoration of monetary and price stability required the assurance of adequate supplies to at least meet the dampened demand. In a sense, the success of the whole stabilization experiment depended upon the government's ability to guarantee the supply of consumers' necessities and the faith of the public in such a guarantee. This was clearly recognized by the Chinese Communists, as illustrated by the following statement of a Bank of China manager:

> The reserve for the issuance of JMP is not gold but the supplies under the control of the government in the liberated areas . . . The reserve is not kept in the vaults of the bank but is being continuously dumped on the market through the government-run trading companies. The duty of these companies is to stabilize the commodity prices, prevent sudden rises or declines, regulate supply and demand, and prevent speculative activities.[9]

During these early years, before commerce and industry were nationalized, state trading companies competed with private traders in buying up agricultural produce. It was their objective to dominate markets, to acquire sufficient market power to place them in a position to regulate the prices and supplies of foodstuffs. On the whole, they were quite successful in this undertaking, so that with the food supplies under their control they could engage in quite effective stabilization operations. They performed an initial distribution function, buying up surpluses and channeling them into cities and regions experiencing acute scarcities, into areas where prices of consumer goods were rising and where demand pressures were acute. In this way, they could contain speculative price rises and assure reasonable price stability.

The state trading network could perform this function only if the volume of goods entering distributive channels could be greatly expanded. This required not only improved organization of the distribution system and a recovery in production, but also restoration of the badly disrupted transport network. For this reason, rehabilitation and expansion of transport was one of the regime's high-priority targets. Therefore, a high proportion of government investment in 1950 and 1951 was devoted to railroad reconstruction. As a result, while less than half of China's total railway trackage was in operation in October 1949, all lines were restored by mid-1951 and the intensity of their use was greatly stepped up. At the same time, new railroad construction was vigorously pushed; for instance, the 320-mile-long Chungking–Chengtu railway – the roadbed for which was prepared by the Nationalist government before the war – was completed in 1952, thus bringing the Szechwan rice basin into closer proximity to East and North China.

The maintenance of stability

A striking feature of China's economic development since 1952 has been a remarkable degree of monetary, fiscal, and price stability. Based on officially published indices, *retail prices apparently rose at an average annual rate of 1.5 to 2.0 percent* between 1952 and 1957 or between 1952 and 1963. While no price indices have been published since 1963, it is unlikely that the average rate of price rise was higher than this in the later 1960s. Actually, one cannot rule out the possibility that urban retail prices may even have declined somewhat since 1965. There is at least one report that Shanghai retail prices dropped by 2.5 percent between 1965 and 1971.[10]

This suggests that once the inherited hyper-inflation was contained and brought under control by 1951 and 1952, stability was maintained despite rapidly rising demand generated by increasing investment and government expenditures. This stability was achieved by a combination of measures based on a high rate of involuntary saving, price controls, and rationing.

In the 1950s, as the economy recovered and developed, a rising share of GNP was channeled into non-consumption, principally into investment and military outlays. This meant that the labor force in the investment-goods and defense industries was increasing quite rapidly and that their total wage bill and money incomes were rising at a high rate. Therefore, a great deal of new purchasing power was generated in these industries, without a corresponding rise in the output of consumer goods and services available in markets for purchase by consumers.

This imbalance between money incomes and consumer-goods availabilities was most pronounced in 1953, 1956, and during the crisis years of 1960–1962. In 1953 and 1956 this was primarily due to large and sudden spurts in fixed-capital investment. In contrast, the imbalances of the early 1960s were occasioned by drastic shortfalls in supply, reflecting a succession of harvest failures and resulting shortages of foodstuffs and cotton textiles.

Rising investments and defense outlays were in large part offset by increasing saving, mostly by state enterprises that paid virtually all their profits into the government budget. This could be considered the equivalent of corporate saving in the United States, which principally comes out of undistributed profits and depreciation funds. In this respect the difference between a

Chinese and an American enterprise is that the former distributes no dividends, but channels almost all its earnings into non-consumption expenditure routed through the government budget. Given the far-reaching market power of public enterprises in China, they, in combination with state organs, can determine the prices at which they buy their raw materials and sell their finished products. Similarly, goods entering trade can be bought and sold at prices that assure large monopoly profits for the state trading companies.

Thus, through administered pricing, state organs and public enterprises can assure high profit margins for the latter, which then are converted into savings. Ultimately these savings are financed by producers and consumers, but not through their own individual choices and decisions. These savings are institutional rather than personal, involuntary rather than spontaneous, and imposed through the state-controlled price mechanism.

The other principal means of financing non-consumption expenditure in China is through the tax mechanism. The bulk of taxes is indirect, mostly sales and turnover taxes levied at the producer, at the wholesale, and at the retail level.

Involuntary savings have been the principal method of financing investment, defense, and other non-consumption expenditures in other socialist countries as well, particularly in the Soviet Union. However, there are quite far-reaching differences between the Soviet and Chinese approaches to this problem. The Soviets relied preponderantly on turnover taxes rather than state-enterprise profits as a means of raising government revenue for financing non-consumption. But this is a minor difference. Much more crucial is the fact that during the period of rapid industrialization, turnover taxation in Russia was coupled with rampant inflation. From 1928 to 1940, wage rates rose almost sixfold, consumer-goods prices in state and cooperative stores about twelvefold, consumer-goods prices in the collective farm markets more than twentyfold, and prices of basic industrial goods about two-and-a-half-fold.[11] In marked contrast, during a more or less comparable twelve-year period in China (1952–1964), wage rates rose by about 40 percent and retail prices by a modest 20 to 25 percent.[12]

How can one account for this sharply contrasting pattern of price behavior? The Soviets during the period of their first two or three five-year plans practiced highly "taut" planning. The whole planning process was based on overfull employment of resources, high rates of investment, and rapid rates of economic growth. With very ambitious targets facing production units, these units tended to hoard labor and raw materials to guard themselves against the risk of under-fulfilling the plan because of shortages of required inputs. This hoarding naturally aggravated the shortages. As a result, there was a great deal of competition for labor and continuing upward pressure on wages.

However, even more fundamentally, this forced-draft industrialization continuously produced an imbalance between demand and supply, between money income at the disposal of consumer households and the availability of consumer goods produced and brought to market. Amidst these conditions there were persistent and acute shortages of consumer goods. Not only was it necessary to introduce rationing from time to time, but often goods could not be bought even with ration coupons because they were sold out. Thus in addition to formal rationing, there was rationing through empty shelves and long queues in front of retail stores. To alleviate these symptoms of repressed inflation, Soviet authorities would from time to time permit quite substantial increases in prices.

These price increases were designed to clear the markets and restore equilibrium between consumer demand and consumer-goods availabilities at the higher prices. This market clearing through price increases was usually brought about by raising the turnover taxes on those commodities in particularly short supply.

How did the Chinese avoid the repetition of this experience? Part of the explanation lies in the differing resource endowments of Russia and China. To this must be added some marked differences in the character of economic planning in the two countries. China compared to Russia was and is a much more labor-abundant economy. When the People's Republic was founded there was considerable open unemployment in the Chinese cities and industrial centers and a great deal of underemployment in the rural areas. While there undoubtedly was underemployment in Russian agriculture too, the mass exodus from the country to the city following collectivization between 1928 and 1932 sharply reduced this potential labor reserve.

Unemployment in the Chinese cities persisted through most of the First Five-Year Plan period (1953–1957). Moreover, the urban labor force was augmented by a rapidly rising participation rate of women. Finally, there was the very large reservoir of labor in the countryside to draw upon. Therefore, China's labor supply was ample, even during the period of most rapid industrialization in the 1950s. Chinese industrial centers did not experience the sharp competition for labor so characteristic of Soviet industrialization. As a result, there was no comparably strong upward pressure on wages.

Rapid wage increases in China were also prevented by a much more far-reaching set of controls on labor mobility than existed in Russia. The labor market in China has been much less free, with much of labor assigned to its place of work. Also, to the extent that rationing was more pervasive in China than in Russia, workers could not move without authorization lest they lose their ration privileges and could not obtain housing in the place they moved to unless the move was authorized. Such barriers to movement existed in Russia too but were apparently less stringently enforced than in China. This does not mean that there were no violations of these rules, but probably much less in China than in Russia.

Therefore, competition for labor in China was much less pronounced than in Russia for two basic reasons: a greater abundance of labor, and much tighter controls on labor mobility. As a result, both the need and inducement to bid away labor from others and the ability to do so were lessened in China as compared to Russia.

In terms of money flows, as shown by Franklyn Holzman and others, the Soviet economy is segmented into cash and non-cash sectors.[13] Cash is used almost exclusively in transactions involving households. Enterprises and collective farms pay individuals wages in cash (peasants also receive payments in kind), and these individuals spend their cash buying back the products of enterprises producing consumer goods. In addition, workers pay farmers cash in the collective farm markets for surplus goods which the latter sell. In contrast, inter-enterprise transactions involve no cash payments, no circulating currency. All inter-enterprise payments and money flows take place by crediting and debiting the enterprise accounts in the state bank upon proof of delivery. Enterprises are allowed to draw cash out of these accounts only to meet payrolls.

The same general practices were adopted by the Chinese. Nevertheless, the currency in circulation and money incomes of households expanded much more rapidly in Russia than in China. This was largely due to the fact that forced-draft industrialization in Russia led to rapid expansion in the labor force and significant increases in wages, without corresponding increases in productivity during the pre–World War II period. Therefore, costs rose and the total wage bill expanded at a very marked rate. As a result, cost-push and demand-pull elements combined to produce an inflationary spiral with rising money incomes bidding for a rather slowly expanding basket of consumer goods.

In Russia, inflationary pressures were also seriously aggravated by the profound agricultural crisis engendered by the far-reaching collectivization campaign between 1928 and 1932. This led to a drastic decline in food production at a time when the Soviet regime, regardless of its human or social consequences, drove ahead with the industrialization drive unabated. As a result, urban and industrial employment and money income were rapidly rising at a time when food supplies brought to urban markets were sharply contracting.

China experienced an agricultural crisis of similar proportions in the aftermath of the Great Leap, between 1959–1960 and 1962. In contrast to the Soviet Union, however, this led to a marked industrial depression, a curtailment of urban employment, and a decline in money incomes. As a result, the decline in consumer-goods availabilities was at least to some extent matched by corresponding declines in household purchasing power. Thus, although there were acute food shortages, the inflationary pressures generated were much milder than during the more or less corresponding period in the Soviet Union.

In China, as noted earlier, the wage bill increased much more gradually, because both the non-agricultural labor force and wage rates rose much more slowly. Consequently, currency in circulation also expanded much more gradually. It was thus much easier to maintain equilibrium between disposable household income and consumer-goods availabilities. This does not mean, of course, that inflationary pressures were totally absent in China. But they were quite mild, as evidenced by the fact that both money wages and particularly retail prices rose quite slowly.

However, in a planned economy based on a network of direct controls such as the Chinese, an official retail price index may be an inadequate measure of inflationary pressure. The index may not be sufficiently representative of all consumer-goods prices, or may give undue weight to the prices of those goods that are rationed and subject to some form of price control. Therefore, an index of this kind could easily understate the rate of price increase. This probably was the case to some extent in China.

Beyond this, and more fundamentally, official price indices cannot measure the extent of repressed inflation, that is, excess demand and liquid purchasing power which cannot find an outlet due to a lack of goods to buy. At least for the First Five-Year Plan period, it is possible to derive estimates of this repressed inflation and thus of total inflationary pressure. These suggest that the average annual rate of inflationary pressure was about 3.5 percent, about equally attributable to open and repressed inflation, with each accounting for about half the rise.[14] However, this was not a smooth trend; rather, it was characterized by marked annual fluctuations. The increases measured in this way were quite pronounced in 1953 and 1956, with rates of increase of 14 and 11 percent respectively, followed in each case by a decline. Of course, as indicated earlier, these were the years when the pace of investment and industrialization was sharply accelerated.

Unfortunately, we do not have the data on which to base similar estimates for later years. However, we have some retail price indicators up to 1963 which suggest a rate of price increase of 1.5 percent a year.[15] Assuming that repressed inflation was at least as marked, one might surmise that the trend value for the rate of total inflation in China may have been around 3 to 4 percent up to 1963. If the retail price index, largely reflecting controlled price items, dropped between 1965 and the early 1970s, as suggested by some sources, then the rate of total inflation may have dropped as well. Given the fact that at least since 1952 this was a fairly rapidly growing high-investment economy, this can be considered quite a mild rate of inflation. As shown above, it demonstrates much more effective inflation control than in the Soviet Union; but it also compares favorably with the inflationary experience of post–World War II Western Europe and Japan, not to mention the persistent inflation in Latin America and many other underdeveloped countries.

The role of monetary management and the banking system

The principal objective of monetary policy in China is to foster economic growth and encourage the development of production and distribution on the one hand and assure monetary and price stability on the other. Therefore, the key task of this policy is to satisfy the transactional demand for money free of inflationary pressures. This means that the system must be provided with just the right amount of liquidity, so that production and distribution can be financed without interruption and without inflation. Thus, the role of money in an economy such as the Chinese is passive, permissive, and accommodating. Unlike in market economies, money is not an active or autonomous force in the system.

The implementation of these objectives is conditioned by the character of property relations and the organization of the economic system as a whole. These system characteristics define the channels through which and the ways in which money flows through the economy. Since 1956, when the socialization process was virtually completed, monetary flows in China went through four principal and closely inter-linked channels: the budget, the state enterprise sector, a collectivized sector (mostly in agriculture), and a household sector.

Budgetary revenues are derived from state-enterprise profits, various commodity and turnover taxes incorporated into the prices of goods and services, agricultural and other minor taxes, and at times proceeds from the sale of government bonds to citizens. Thus payments flow from all of the three other sectors into the budget. Correspondingly, budgetary expenditures are channeled into the state-enterprise and collectivized sectors for investments and some subsidies; into defense outlays for hardware and personnel; into buildings and facilities for collective consumption in health, education, and welfare; and into wage payments for government personnel. Therefore, money also flows in a reverse direction from the budget to all the other sectors.

At the other end of the spectrum, households receive wages, salaries, and other forms of income from public enterprises, collectives, and government bureaus. In turn, they make purchases at state retail stores and collective farm markets, thus channeling money flows into the public-enterprise and collectivized sectors. While households are suppliers of labor and consumers of goods and services, public-sector enterprises are producers of these goods and services and purchasers of labor, capital, and raw materials. Thus they pay wages that accrue as incomes to households, and purchase capital goods and raw materials from other enterprises and from agricultural collectives. They also purchase foodstuffs from the latter for sale to consumers. Therefore state enterprises channel money flows to other enterprises, to collectivized units, and to households. They also remit taxes and profits to the government budget. On the other hand they receive funds from the government budget for investment and related purposes, from households for the sale of consumer goods and services, from other enterprises for the sale of intermediate goods and services, and from collectives for the sale of both producer and consumer goods. Finally, collective units remit taxes to the government budget and make payments to state enterprises, for goods and services purchased, and to households for labor supplied. At the same time, they receive incomes from agricultural products sold to state enterprises and to households.

This is a highly schematic and over-simplified sketch of money flows in the Chinese economy. It omits foreign receipts and payments and does not take account of the role of the State Bank. International transactions constitute such a small proportion of the total, and through a variety of institutional devices they are so completely insulated from the mainstream of the economy, that we can ignore them for our present purposes. The same cannot be said of the banking sector.

As indicated in Chapter 3, all state enterprises finance new plant construction, plant expansion, and all capital projects out of government budgetary grants. When a new enterprise is started, an initial working-capital grant is also made. However, as the enterprise steps up its rate of capacity utilization and thus employs more labor and uses more raw materials, its working-capital requirements also rise. This additional working capital is financed by bank credit. Thus, enterprises and rural communes depend on the banking system to meet their short-term capital needs.

The recipients of these short-term credits had to pay a relatively low banking charge, which in the late 1950s ranged from about 5 to 7 percent a year.[16] This was viewed as a charge for banking services rendered rather than as an interest rate in our sense of that term. That is, it definitely was not a price for capital or a price at which the market for loanable funds would be cleared.

The absence of an interest rate in a banking system not based on reserve requirements meant that the economic constraints on bank credit expansion were quite weak. As a result, there were continuing and powerful pressures from the state-enterprise sector to increase credit. To the extent that enterprises could obtain short-term credit, they hoped they could hire additional labor and purchase more raw materials so that they could more easily fulfill their production plans. In contrast, the banking authorities were eager to minimize the credit at the disposal of enterprises. On the one hand, they were supposed to use their power to extend credit as a means of curbing the enterprises' proclivities to hoard inputs. That is, banks were expected to perform a plan-supervisory function. They were also naturally concerned about the inflationary implications of an expansion in bank credit.

However this was a rather unequal contest, in which for the most part the concern about credit expansion was subordinated to the more powerful pressures to increase production. In part this was due to the fact that the planning authorities knew they could curb enterprise appetites for more inputs through direct controls over labor and raw materials allocation. At the same time, they expected to control inflation and assure macro-economic equilibrium through rather stringent cash controls and ceilings on currency circulation.

In effect, once rampant inflation was brought under control and the economy became more or less fully socialized, the planners were not too concerned about an expansion in the aggregate money supply as long as its utilization could be confined to the state-enterprise sector. Much of the time an easy, rather than a tight, credit policy was followed in respect to state enterprises. To the extent that state enterprises used these credits for the purchase of industrial raw materials and other types of intermediate goods, payments were settled between enterprises through the debiting and crediting of the purchaser's and seller's bank accounts respectively. That is, all settlements were handled through a system of inter-enterprise clearings administered by the banking system.

However, the ever-present risk was that a greater or lesser share of these short-term credits would "leak" in the form of cash payments to the household sector for wage payments and to the collectivized sector for agricultural purchases. The liquid purchasing power under the control of households and collectives was much more difficult to control than bank deposits. Planners and various state organs could much more effectively regulate and control the spending of bank deposits by enterprises than the cash expenditures of households. The latter could and would be converted into a rising demand for consumer goods, with possible attendant inflationary pressures resulting therefrom.

Under these circumstances, the central task of monetary management became cash control rather than changing reserve requirements, manipulating the rediscount rate or having the central bank conduct open market operations, or varying the interest rate by private banks – instruments so familiar in private-enterprise market economies. The money managers in China were therefore very anxious to contain, reduce, and minimize the liquidity of the money supply and particularly cash in circulation.

With this in mind, a series of cash-control measures was instituted. Cash on hand for all state enterprises – including retail outlets – and government organs was limited to the minimum necessary for a maximum of three days. All currency above this minimum had to be converted daily into bank deposits. The total weekly, monthly, and annual wage bill that could be disbursed by an enterprise was similarly fixed. In drawing up the agricultural procurement plan, close attention was paid to the cash outlays resulting therefrom.

This cash-control policy was pursued along two parallel paths. On the one hand, it was designed to curb payments in cash; on the other it entailed a series of measures designed to absorb the liquid purchasing power floating around the economy. With this in mind, both urban and rural household saving and deposit formation were strongly fostered. At the same time, agricultural collectives were encouraged to accept payments in bank deposits rather than cash, drawing on these for the purchase of production requisites from state enterprises. The use of cash was to be limited to the payment of that portion of each farm household's annual income share that was to be paid in money rather than in kind. Finally, in the 1950s, and most particularly during the earlier part of that decade, periodic savings-bond and aid-Korea campaigns were conducted to mop up liquid purchasing power.

The key agent in administering this cash-control program was the People's Bank (PB). This is not really one of a number of banks but for all practical purposes the only bank in the country. It comprises a nationwide banking system under a single administration. Branches of the People's Bank are located all over China, both in cities and county seats. Sub-branches or offices are found in market towns, which usually also serve as the centers of commune administration. Below the commune level and in the villages there are rural credit cooperatives, which are closely directed by the People's Bank and in effect serve as its local units.

Of all the modern sectors in the Chinese economy, banking was the first to be nationalized. This process was essentially completed by 1952. Since then, the People's Bank of China has enjoyed a virtual monopoly position in the country's banking system. The only reason one might consider it virtual rather than total is that there were a few specialized banks, which however really functioned as divisions of the People's Bank and were administered by it. Thus the Bank of China served as the foreign-exchange division of the PB, engaged in financing foreign trade. It also served as the PB's representative abroad. The Joint Public–Private Bank was the end product of the merger of all the surviving private banks. Its principal function was to provide for the financial needs of the rapidly shrinking private sector. As almost all private enterprise became socialized by 1956, this bank lost its raison d'etre and disappeared.

In addition, there were two banks that functioned as fiscal agencies directly controlled by the Ministry of Finance. The Bank of Communications disbursed and managed the funds for capital-investment projects financed out of the state budget. It also handled the publicly owned shares of the joint public–private companies. It received dividends on these public shares and supervised the internal financial management of joint enterprises.

In 1954, when the Bank of Construction was founded, it took over the investment disbursement and management function. It was also charged with the operational supervision of all construction enterprises and units. Thus the Bank of Communications shrank in importance, and when the process of socialization was completed and the joint enterprises began to be treated in effect as public enterprises, it dwindled into insignificance. From time to time other specialized banks were formed, but most of them did not last very long.

Given its monopoly position, the PB necessarily performs a multiplicity of functions. It performs central banking, commercial banking, and plan-supervisory functions. As a central bank, it is the sole bank of issue. At the same time it serves as the government bank, in which nearly all cash held by the state organs is kept. As a commercial bank it serves as the "center of cash, credit and settlement." Thus the bank receives deposits from households, state enterprises, rural communes and their sub-units, and various types of cooperatives. It extends short-term loans to these various units, except households. The term "settlement" is roughly equivalent to our concept of bank clearings and refers to inter-enterprise non-cash settlement involving payments through bank account transfers.

All the indications available suggest that this banking system succeeded reasonably well in both its key objectives: to provide sufficient liquidity to enterprises to facilitate production and distribution, and at the same time control and contain the flow of cash held by the public. Indirect evidence for both these propositions is provided by some illustrative figures for the 1950s, the only period for which such data are available. These show that total bank deposits doubled between 1952 and 1957. At the same time enterprise deposits increased more gradually, except for 1956, when inflationary pressures were building up.

Personal (household) deposits were not only rising rapidly in volume but, more significantly, their share in the total money supply was increasing as well, from about 4 percent in 1950 and 7 percent in 1952 to close to 20 percent in 1957. Moreover, the proportion of time deposits as a percentage of total deposits rose from about 35 percent in 1952 to 65 percent in 1957, and the duration of these deposits lengthened as well; in urban areas, the average number of days a deposit was kept in the bank rose from about two months in 1952 to four months in 1956. The tendency toward increasing deposit formation is also borne out by the savings data for urban households. These suggest that personal deposits as a share of personal incomes increased from 6.5 percent in 1953 to almost 11 percent in 1957. This represented a most rapid rise in the marginal propensity to save; that is, the share of additional, incremental income saved went up in the urban areas from 20 percent between 1952 and 1953 to almost 70 percent between 1956 and 1957.[17] These data strongly suggest that, at least during the First Five-Year Plan period, the banking and monetary authorities were quite successful in mopping up a great deal of the liquid purchasing power at the disposal of households.

The role of fiscal management and the budgetary system

The budgetary and fiscal system of China was designed by the leaders of the People's Republic to serve as a prime instrument for mobilizing resources and allocating them in such a way as to foster industrialization and rapid economic development, while maintaining price stability. In this respect the broad macro-economic objectives of Chinese policy makers were quite similar to their counterparts in free-enterprise market economies, both in highly developed and less developed countries. The differences arise from the fact that in China, as in all socialist systems, due to the far-reaching nationalization of the economy, the scope of the budget is much larger and therefore its significance as an instrument of economic policy is even greater than in market economies.

As noted above under "The maintenance of stability," fiscal policy played a very important role in arresting hyper-inflation and in establishing economic and price stability in 1950–1951. The problem was attacked both from the revenue and expenditure side. The whole revenue system was revamped, the number of taxes was reduced, the tax system was simplified, and tax collection and tax administration were very much improved. As a result, the revenue base was greatly broadened. At the same time expenditures were brought under tight control. Consequently, deficits were drastically curtailed and for a number of years surpluses were generated. Moreover, the deficits were financed by non-inflationary means.

Unfortunately, there are no comparable data for the 1960s. However, one might surmise that it would be surprising if at least during the crisis years (1960–1962) some budget deficits had not been incurred. The same might have happened during the Cultural Revolution years (1966–1968). If so, it is not clear how these deficits were financed, since there were apparently no bond drives in the 1960s and no foreign credits. It is therefore possible that in a few years some resort to note issue became necessary.

Even if the Chinese may have been occasionally forced by circumstances to resort to deficit or perhaps even inflationary means of financing, it was almost certainly done reluctantly and only to a modest degree. Chinese planners were, and still are, strongly committed to orthodox finance and a most cautious and conservative fiscal policy. This was clearly enunciated on a number of occasions during a month-long visit to the People's Republic in December 1972. It was perhaps most explicitly stated by Fu Tse-hao, the Director of Budget Administration in the Ministry of Finance. He indicated that the basic and guiding principle of budget policy in China is to "*maintain equilibrium between revenue and expenditure with a small surplus*," a principle that must be followed at all levels of government. He added that a corollary of this policy is that note issue cannot be used to finance budget deficits.

The rapid expansion in the budget, as shown in Table 5-1, reflects three inter-related tendencies at work. The economy was developing speedily and GNP was rising; the scope of the budget was being enlarged as more and more branches of the economy were being nationalized; and budget administration was unified, that is, the national budget became increasingly consolidated for

Table 5-1. *Budget receipts and expenditures, 1950–1959 (in millions of current yuan)*

Year	Receipts[a]	Expenditures	Surplus or deficit[b]
1950	6,190	6,810	−620
1951	12,390	11,900	490
1952	17,370	16,790	580
1953	21,270	21,490	−220
1954	24,440	24,630	−190
1955	24,840	26,920	−2,080
1956	28,020	30,580	−2,560
1957	30,320	29,020	1,300
1958	41,060	40,960	100
1959	54,160	52,770	1,390

[a]Exclusive of credit receipts and state insurance revenue.
[b]Deficits are slightly over-stated and surpluses are somewhat under-stated to the extent that they do not take account of insurance incomes, which in Chinese budget practice are lumped together with proceeds from deficit finance.
Sources: State Statistical Bureau, *Ten Great Years*, Peking, 1960, pp. 21–24; and N. R. Chen, *Chinese Economic Statistics*, Chicago, 1967, Table 10. 1, p. 441 and Table 10.7, pp. 446–447.

all levels of government: central, provincial, and local. While GNP rose by about 36 percent between 1952 and 1957 and doubled between 1952 and 1959, budgetary receipts rose much faster. Therefore total revenues rose in relation to GNP from about 25 percent in 1952 to 31 percent in 1957 and 36 percent in 1959.[18] This 1959 ratio was very much affected by the extreme mobilization measures of the Great Leap and for that reason may be considered above normal. While no budget data were published for the 1960s, one might surmise that these ratios may have fluctuated between 35 and 40 percent in the last decade – still a high share by international standards.

The budget served as a means for mobilizing resources on a vast scale and bringing them under the government's control. This control was then to be utilized for allocating resources in accord with planning priorities so as to guide the economy in the direction desired by the policy makers. To achieve this control, the fiscal system and budget administration was being highly centralized. However, this led to considerable rigidities and inefficiencies, so that at the end of the 1950s fiscal management was decentralized. As Fu Tse-hao indicated to us, the prevailing policy was and still is for the central government "to provide unified leadership in budget administration while encouraging decentralized management." This meant that the Center defined the basic fiscal policy guidelines, formulated the consolidated national budget plan, set the rules and standards for budget administration, and administered the central government budget. This left local budget administration within the purview of local governments, subject to the guidelines of the national plan and the rules and standards centrally defined and applicable to all units of government.

By far the two principal means for resource mobilization were taxes and state-enterprise earnings. Both increased rapidly under the impact of economic recovery and development but, as the scope of the state-enterprise sector widened, profits rose faster than taxes. As indicated by the data in Table 5-2, taxes were the dominant revenue source in the initial years, while state-enterprise earnings were relatively unimportant. However throughout the 1950s profits gained in importance, so much so that they replaced taxes as the leading revenue producer by the end of the decade.

There were important shifts in tax revenues as well. From the outset, industrial and commercial taxes were more important than all other taxes. These were indirect taxes, levied on sales and turnover at the production, wholesale, and retail levels. Typically, tax rates would be quite low on raw materials, machinery, and other intermediate goods. They were highest on luxury or semi-luxury products, but quite low on necessities.

Initially, agricultural taxes were still quite important; they increased gradually until 1954 and then remained more or less at the same level. As a result, they declined markedly in relative importance. These were direct taxes levied

Table 5-2. *Principal sources of budget revenue, 1950–1959, 1970–1972 (in percent)*

Revenue sources	1950	1952	1957	1959	1970–72
Tax revenue	75.1	55.6	49.9	37.8	(36)
Industrial and commercial taxes	34.7	35.0	36.4	28.9	(30)
Agricultural tax	29.2	15.4	10.0	6.0	(6)
State-enterprise profits	13.3	26.5	36.6	52.7	(60)
All other revenue	11.6	17.9	13.5	9.5	(4)
Total	100.0	100.0	100.0	100.0	100.0

Source: Calculated from data in George N. Ecklund, *Financing the Chinese Government Budget*, 1950–59, Chicago, 1966, Table 1, p. 20; for 1972 based on interview with Fu Tse-hao, Peking, December 1972.

as a percentage of a "standard" or "normal" yield per acre of land. This was not a land tax since it was not levied on land values but on the income produced by land. Agricultural tax rates were fixed progressively, that is, rates on higher-income-yielding lands were higher for most years. However, during some periods the agricultural tax became more of a flat-rate proportional tax, collected in kind. It was primarily paid in grain, usually in the prinicpal crop produced in an area; occasionally, and particularly in areas specializing in industrial crops, it was paid in cash.

It seems that the trends in the composition of revenues begun in the 1950s continued into the 1960s. Thus state-enterprise profits apparently made further gains in relative importance, mostly at the expense of other revenue, which greatly diminished in importance. At the same time, total tax revenues and the principal kinds of taxes more or less maintained their relative importance.

The budget served not only as the principal means for mobilizing resources but as a powerful tool for allocating them so as to bring about industrialization, economic development, and a marked structural transformation in the economy. The extent to which and how rapidly this was achieved will be discussed in the next chapter. Here we want to analyze the composition of government expenditure and its impact on resource allocation. The budget can of course only affect the allocation of those resources that enter marketing channels and are not consumed right within the household that produces them. It may be roughly estimated that about 20 percent of China's GNP was "immobilized in this way" in the early 1970s, that is, cannot be moved or reallocated from place to place or sector to sector. If about 35 to 40 percent of GNP was encompassed by budget transactions, this means that about half of the mobilizable output of goods and services was reallocated through the budget.

The extent to which the budget was used as a vehicle for fostering economic development may be seen from the data in Table 5-3. In evaluating these data, certain definitions must be kept in mind. "Economic construction" refers to all outlays on economic activities; this includes expenditures on plant expansion, subsidies to enterprises and agricultural production units, and provision of working capital for these. The "national defense" item finances troop maintenance, that is, housing, food, military salaries, and similar outlays. Whether or not it also encompasses procurement of military hardware is not quite clear.

Therefore, national defense as listed in the budget may represent an underestimate. For instance, in 1959 possibly 20 to 25 percent of total government

Table 5-3. *Distribution of government budget expenditures, 1950–1959 (in percent)*

Expenditure category	1950	1952	1957	1959
Economic construction	25.5	45.4	51.4	59.0
Social, cultural, and educational outlays	11.1	13.6	16.0	11.1
National defense	41.5	26.0	19.0	10.9
Government administration	19.3	10.3	7.8	5.4
Other	2.6	4.7	5.8	13.6
Total in percent	100.0	100.0	100.0	100.0
Total in millions of yuan	6,810	16,790	29,020	52,770
Share of fixed-capital outlays appropriated in total government expenditure (percent)	(15.3)	(22.1)	(43.6)	(50.6)

Sources: These are all official data culled from State Statistical Bureau, *Ten Great Years,* Peking, 1960, pp. 23–24; and from N. R. Chen, *Chinese Economic Statistics,* Chicago, 1967, Tables 10.7 on pp. 446–447, 3.20 and 3.21 on p. 158. Data for the share of fixed-capital outlays in total budgetary expenditures were derived from official data on the assumption that these are equivalent to "within plan" investments in basic construction. In fact, these two concepts are not completely identical in Chinese practice, although the differences between the two are probably minor. "Within plan" investment figures had to be used, since data for budgetary appropriations on basic construction are available only for 1952 to 1957 and not for 1950 and 1959.

outlays may have been devoted to military expenditure, perhaps twice the amount officially listed. This is based on a crude estimate that the Chinese may have used about 10 percent of their GNP on financing the military establishment, including research and development for acquiring a nuclear capability. If this was the case, then probably economic construction outlays should be reduced accordingly.

However, even after these adjustments are made, the basic allocative trends illustrated by the budget are not altered very much. That is, the weight of economic development outlays was gaining in importance in the 1950s, while national defense and government administration declined in relative importance. These trends could not, of course, continue indefinitely. On the contrary, one might surmise that except for the highly disrupted Cultural Revolution period (1966–1968) and the crisis years (1960–1962), the composition of the budget was more or less stabilized. Economic development expenditure may have absorbed about 50 percent of the total budget; perhaps another 20 to 25 percent went into national defense, and 15 percent to health, education, and welfare.

Every one of these expenditure categories can be divided into two parts: capital outlays, that is, buildings, plant, and equipment; and operating expenses. Thus capital outlays cut across all these categories. As may also be seen from Table 5-3, the appropriations for these capital investments were rising particularly rapidly. Thus, while in 1950 they constituted about one-fifth of total government spending, at the end of that decade they absorbed well over one-half of the budget. This is but another illustration of the fact that the policy makers and planners were channeling an increasing share of the resources under their control into investment. It is therefore not surprising that the rate of fixed-capital investment (in relation to GNP) more than doubled in seven years, from less than 10 percent in 1952 to well over 20 percent in 1959. The sharp rise in investment thus became the principal means through which the rate of economic growth was accelerated and industrialization was pushed.

The great emphasis placed on industrial development is most clearly brought out by Table 5-4. Even in the early 1950s about 40 percent of the

Table 5-4. *Distribution of fixed capital invested by the state, 1952–1958 (in percent)*

Economic sector	1952	1955	1957	1958
Industry	38.8	46.2	52.3	64.8
Construction	2.1	3.9	3.3	1.0
Prospecting for natural resources	1.6	3.2	2.2	1.7
Agriculture, forestry, water management, and meteorology	13.8	6.7	8.6	9.9
Transport and communication	17.5	19.0	15.0	12.7
Trade	2.8	3.7	2.7	2.1
Culture, education, and research	6.4	6.3	6.7	2.3
Public health and welfare	1.3	1.1	0.9	0.4
Urban public utilities	3.9	2.4	2.8	2.2
Government administration	0.4	1.5	1.3	0.7
Other	11.4	6.9	4.2	2.2
Total in percent	100.0	100.0	100.0	100.0
Total in million yuan	4,360	9,300	13,830	26,700

Source: State Statistical Bureau, *Ten Great Years*, Peking, 1960, pp. 57–60.

state-investment total was directed to industrial development. By the time of the Great Leap (1958–1960), industry absorbed over two-thirds of total investment. In marked contrast, agriculture, which employed about 80 percent of the labor force, was allotted less than 10 percent of the state's capital outlays. However, there was a great deal of additional investment in agriculture by the APCs (agricultural production cooperatives), production teams, and communes. Therefore, an investment distribution that would take into account all forms of investment – state, private, and cooperative – would be less skewed in favor of industry.

Such estimates have in fact been made by Kang Chao for the First Five-Year Plan period. They indicate that almost a third of total investment resources, excluding housing, were channeled into agriculture in 1952 and almost a quarter in 1957. Correspondingly, industrial investments rose during the same years from about one-fifth of the total to well over one-third.[19]

While these total and state-investment figures are not fully comparable, it seems that government expenditures on "capital construction actually carried out" comprised about 53 percent of the total in 1952 and 66 percent in 1957. Well over half of the non-state investments were agricultural. Seen in this light, it seems that state planners kept agriculture on a low-investment ration for two reasons: they did genuinely accord it much lower priority than industry, but they also counted on the agricultural sector as being capable of generating a fair amount of self-investment. However, these two forms of investment are only partially inter-changeable or comparable. Most of the state's capital outlays were channeled into the purchase of modern inputs, such as farm equipment. In contrast, self-investment in agriculture more often than not involved the construction of buildings, facilities, and simple tools using local labor and local materials. Thus the developmental impact of the two forms of investment differs markedly, with the first likely to have a considerable modernizing effect with consequent rise in input productivity, while the second may yield some increases in output without any increases in productivity.

It is not surprising therefore to find that industrial expansion was most rapid from 1952 to 1957, with very high allotments of state investment, while agricultural development was most sluggish, even though total investments in it were not all that much lower than in industry. These relationships are brought into bold relief by the estimated average annual rates of growth in the two sectors cited in the next chapter – 16 to 18 percent for industry, and about 2 percent for agriculture during the 1952–1957 period.

The development priorities of state planners are clearly illustrated not only by their distribution of government investment between agriculture and industry, but also by the allotments made to the various branches within industry. These indicate that only 14 percent of the state's fixed-capital outlays were channeled into consumer-goods industries, while 86 percent went into investment-goods branches.[20]

Unfortunately, there are no similar data for the 1960s. However, the investment mix was almost certainly quite different, based on what we know about changes in Chinese economic policy. State investments in agriculture almost certainly went up, both in absolute and relative terms. Moreover, in contrast with the 1950s, a much larger share of investments self-financed by communes and lower-level units went to purchase modern inputs. Some basic industries, which received very high-priority attention in the 1950s, were accorded lower priority in the 1960s. This would apply to steel, coal, and perhaps electric-power generation. On the other hand, petroleum extraction and the chemical industry were assigned much higher priorities.

As this brief analysis suggests, China's budgetary system has served simultaneously three inter-related purposes; it was used as a powerful tool for mobilizing resources, for allocating them so as to promote economic development and the restructuring of the economy, and for containing inflationary pressures. It seems that, judged by these three criteria, fiscal policy and management was reasonably successful. Together with monetary policy, it contributed to the maintenance of quite remarkable price stability in a high-investment and rapidly industrializing economy. This was probably a much easier task in the 1960s, when the economy was growing more slowly, than in the 1950s and 1970s, when it was expanding more rapidly, investment rates were rising, and plant operations were approaching capacity limits.

Budget management was also quite successful in performing its allocating and plan-implementing function. The budget really served as the principal instrument through which leaders', policy makers', and planners' preferences could be imposed on the economy. Through its grants of fixed and working capital and through subsidies, the budget became a most potent tool for directing resources into the priority sectors in accord with these preferences.

Conclusions

The People's Republic of China must be given very high marks indeed for its record of price stability in the last twenty-five years. In an age of worldwide inflation this is no mean achievement. The explanation must be sought in the country's factor endowments, in the system of controls, and in the attitudes of the people.

Virtual wage stability could be maintained for long periods in large part because, fundamentally, this is a labor-abundant economy. As a result, rising urban and industrial labor requirements could to a considerable extent be met by absorbing the unemployed and underemployed in the cities and at the same time bringing large numbers of women into the labor force. This does not mean that there was no flow of labor from country to city, but, as was indicated, there was a reverse flow as well. At any rate, due to the relative abundance of labor there were apparently no marked upward pressures on the wage level. Wage increases were also prevented by the absence of collective bargaining and strong, independent trade unions. All of this was further reinforced by controls over wages and the movement of labor. Therefore, wage stability reflected not only a relatively abundant labor supply but also wage and market controls designed to regulate both the demand and supply of labor.

Wage stability eliminated a potential source of cost-push inflation. At the same time, it helped to control actual or potential increases in household money incomes and therefore in the purchasing power of consumers. Household consumption was also kept in bounds by containing "consumerism" and the material aspiration levels of workers, peasants, and cadres through education and Communist Party indoctrination.

Nevertheless, in a rapidly growing economy with a high rate of investment and expanding employment, the wage bill and total household incomes are bound to rise. This may be expected to induce inflationary pressures only if household purchasing power rises faster than consumer-goods availabilities. In fact, this has inevitably happened in China from time to time. These pressures were countered and controlled through a combination of price controls over a wide range of consumer goods, rationing of necessities, and measures designed to mop up liquid purchasing power. In the earlier years this led to periodic bond drives and savings campaigns, while in later years it was largely confined to encouraging household saving and increasing savings deposits. All these measures relating to households and retail markets were reinforced by controls over enterprises, in particular relating to the wage bill, cash flows, and credits.

6

Economic development and structural change

The setting

Chapters 5 to 8 deal with the different aspects of China's economic performance shaped by the factors discussed in the earlier parts of this book. In a fundamental sense, one could view China's economic development as a dialectic process based on a continuous confrontation and interplay between *scarcity* rooted in the country's economic backwardness and *ideology* shaping the new regime's goals and objectives. Scarcity and ideology were both, to a greater or lesser extent, conditioned by the legacy of the past explored in Chapter 1. At the same time, ideology and the aspirations arising therefrom influenced the development strategies examined in Chapter 2. All these then molded the system of economic organization described in the two subsequent chapters.

Expressed in Marxist terms, this development process could be considered the product of both the base and the superstructure, that is, the mode of production and the relations of production on the one hand, and of ideas, cultural style, motivation, and revolutionary will on the other. The effectiveness of these inputs from the past, from ideology, and from the system of economic organization can thus be expressed by measuring its impact on economic stability, on growth and structural change, on international economic relations, and on income distribution.

Within this analytical framework, the degree of economic stability attained in China was appraised in the preceding chapter. Therefore, here we will examine how rapidly the economy grew and some of its most significant growth characteristics. This appraisal will be based on an analysis of aggregate and per capita GNP trends and changes in GNP composition. However, any assessment of a country's economic performance based on GNP measures is necessarily fraught with problems and difficulties, which are briefly discussed below. Such measures also involve the utilization of a comparative yardstick, explicitly or implicitly. Thus whether a particular growth rate is slow or rapid can only be determined in relation to the experience of other countries. Yet a comparative analysis of the Chinese case is greatly complicated by the fact that we are dealing here with a country of unprecedented size in terms of population and one of the largest in terms of area. The implications of this fact for purposes of comparability are explored briefly in a subsequent section of this chapter. This is followed by a general overview of China's development since 1949 in order to set the stage for the subsequent analysis of sectoral and aggregate trends in the economy.

Limitations of the GNP measure and some of its implications

Total national product can be a significant indicator of an economy's capacity to deliver goods and services and to set aside resources for consumption, investment, and defense. If one wants to gauge the extent to which an economy is capable of sustaining a modern military establishment, one might be primarily interested in the total size of the industrial sector, the relative weight of that sector in the economy, and the character and structure of that sector. With the same purposes in mind, one would also be very interested in the composition of the national product, particularly the relative importance of agriculture and the traditional versus modern sectors in the economy. Similarly, one would be interested in the composition of the labor force: what share of the labor force is tied down to agriculture, as compared to the modern sectors of the economy. One would also want to know what the pattern of national expenditure is: what share of GNP can be set aside for investment and defense, and what portion is reallocable and not tied down – frozen or fixed – in the subsistence sector.

On the other hand, as an indicator of labor productivity or of the standard of living, a measure of per capita product or per capita consumption may be more appropriate. For a whole host of reasons, to be analyzed at the end of this chapter, differences in per capita product over time for a single economy are more useful and less ambiguous than international comparisons of such product at one point in time. In the latter case, one is necessarily forced to convert the national products of a number of countries as measured in their own prices and currencies to a common denominator, usually U.S. dollars. This leads to so many distortions that such figures have to be used with a great deal of caution. However, for a single national economy, trends in per capita product or income over time may fairly well approximate advances in labor productivity and/or standard of living. Yet even in this case there are certain problems. Long-term growth of a national economy encompasses such profound structural and technological changes that comparisons of per capita output over long periods may over-state the real growth in final output and final consumption. For instance, the American or British economies today are preponderantly urbanized, while in the eighteenth and even in the nineteenth centuries they were still dominantly agrarian. If people live in large urban centers they have to commute daily to and from work and the transport sector must correspondingly be expanded. The output value of the transport sector, net of material inputs, is entered in the national product and contributes to economic growth, but this does not necessarily mean that it represents a contribution to the satisfaction of final consumer wants. Nor does it mean that people who commute do it for pleasure or in order to satisfy their wants. In this case, transportation is in a certain sense an input, a means, yet it is counted in the national product as if it were an end. Moreover, these are not the only elements of incomparability between the national products of highly industrialized countries such as the United States or Britain, compared to their state 100 or 200 years ago.

Virtually all other measures of change in the standard of living, such as energy consumption, literacy, infant mortality, death rates, number of telephones per 1,000 population, standards of nutrition, housing space per capita, etc., can also be misleading, particularly if each is used as a separate indicator. Therefore, each measure has built into it certain biases, and on balance, probably per capita product is as comprehensive an indicator as we have at our disposal up to the present time and also probably less ambiguous, even though it is far from perfect.

Bearing these limitations in mind, an analysis of China's GNP and other performance indicators shows that rates and patterns of economic growth have been subject to marked fluctuations in the last twenty-five years. Thus we see two sharply contrasting decades, with the first (1949–1959) being aptly called the Ten Great Years.[1] The second decade, however, was characterized by less rapid advance.

These fluctuations may represent an interplay of harvest cycles and policy cycles. It appears that every few years favorable weather conditions resulted in good harvests. These good harvests tended to have a positive impact on the economy as a whole. In contrast, a succession of poor harvests such as occurred in 1959–1962 led to a marked depression in the economy as a whole. These harvest cycles were seemingly intertwined with policy cycles which represented alternating movements of mobilization, consolidation, and mobilization again. Favorable harvests tended to be followed by mobilization, while poor harvests usually led to consolidation, reduction in the rate of growth of investment, or even cutbacks in investment and other measures designed to ease the pressures on resource mobilization and utilization.

One could speculate that these economic fluctuations were an expression or symptom of a clash between scarcity and ideology – scarcity being rooted in China's economic and technological backwardness. This backward economy circumscribed the means: the resources available for industrialization and economic development. In contrast, ideology defined the goals: the objectives, the ends, and the demands for rapid economic change, fast-paced economic growth, and marked structural transformation. To pursue these goals, far-reaching resource mobilization was required. However, this mobilization repeatedly bumped up against capacity ceilings imposed by economic backwardness and scarcity.[2]

Comparability of China with other industrializing countries

The attempt at deliberate industrialization in China represents an unprecedented case in the history of modern economic growth, comparable only to India. All currently industrialized economies, except Japan, entered the stage of their respective industrial revolutions from a significantly higher per capita income base than China.

There are a number of underdeveloped countries, some in Asia, which are launching their industrialization drives from as low a per capita product base and in the face of at least as unfavorable initial conditions as those confronting China. However, except for India, there is no other national unit which now or in the past has encompassed such a vast population. Thus China has embarked on the road to industrialization in a country of unprecedented size. What then is the significance of size and what are its implications from an economic-development point of view?

In exploring this question, most economists have focused their attention on the advantages of size from the standpoint of growth. In this connection, two factors tend to be emphasized most frequently, economies of scale and resource endowments. It has been pointed out that, given two countries at roughly similar stages of development, size of market limitations would tend to be considerably less severe in the larger country with a larger population, than in the smaller country. Thus market size is more likely to suffice for the construction of at least a limited number of optimum-scale plants in the former as compared to the latter. For example, a fully integrated steel mill may find an internal market sufficient to absorb all its output more readily in China or in India than in a small African country. Advantages may also accrue to a country with a vast territory, since it may well encompass within its boundaries most of the mineral resources needed for modern economic growth. Of course, both sorts of advantage are fully operative only in closed economies. They may be less important the more freely the countries concerned are engaged in international trade.

Relatively less attention has been paid to the dis-advantages of size, which may be particularly pronounced for low-income, underdeveloped countries. These dis-advantages revolve largely around transport and communication barriers, and problems of administration and control imposed by a combination of territorial expanse, vast population, and geographic configuration. All these factors represent obstacles to ready access, and tend to hamper the flow of new goods, new techniques, new ideas, and generally the diffusion of innovating influences.

The transport and communication barriers also complicate the task of improving literacy and basic education. This further reinforces the barriers referred to above, which in turn may greatly reduce administrative, governmental, and bureaucratic capacity. As has often been pointed out, the traditional imperial administration of China could impose reasonably effective centralized control over the vastness of the mainland, but only because the functions or tasks over which it strove to exercise control and the degree of penetration it sought were quite limited. There is no question that the transport and communication network and technology at the disposal of the Chinese Communist regime was greatly improved as compared to imperial times. However, the degree of penetration and control desired and demanded by the new regime has very much increased as well. As a matter of fact, one could hypothesize that the degree of control initially sought may have been greater than the regime's administrative capacity to exercise it. This undoubtedly must have been a significant factor in the breakdown occasioned by the Great Leap and in the considerable weakening of centralized controls in China in the early 1960s.

One could ask whether size is indeed the crucial variable here. Suppose each Chinese province became an independent state, would this really make a difference and, if so, in what way? It certainly would not affect geographic access; that is, transport barriers, distance from the coast and from the main overseas shipping lanes, and the continental, inland character of the bulk of the mainland would not be affected. This might suggest that geography may be a more significant factor than size. However, size itself aggravates the access, diffusion, and learning problems in several ways. Communication lanes between the center and its parts are clearly lengthened in large as compared to small nation-states. It is more difficult to penetrate every area and every household in a large country with a vast population than would be the case in a smaller unit.

Size might affect development prospects in still another way. It is a well established fact that large countries tend to have small foreign-trade shares in relation to gross national product. This in part reflects the fact that in a large country the totality of external, relative to domestic, transactions tends to be small.[3] However, this too tends to curtail the diffusion of new influences, new techniques, new methods of production, and new goods in large countries, at least to the extent that foreign trade serves as a major avenue for the flow of these innovations. This certainly seems to be the case in China.

China's economic development: an overview, 1949–1974

The fluctuating pattern of development referred to above can be more clearly perceived by analyzing the different phases of development that the Chinese economy has traversed since 1949. One might divide this period of nearly a quarter century into the following ten phases: (1) Recovery and Rehabilitation (1949–1952); (2) Plan Preparation (1953–mid-1955); (3) Big Push (mid-1955–1956); (4) Retrenchment (1957); (5) Great Leap (1958–1960); Great Crisis (1960–1962); (7) Recovery from Crisis (1962–1966); (8) Cultural Revolution (1966–1968); (9) Recovery from Cultural Revolution (1968–1970); (10) New Wave of Expansion (1970–1974).

Recovery and Rehabilitation

As noted in Chapter 5, the Chinese Communists inherited a war-torn, inflation-torn, fragmented economy in 1949. They set themselves the goal of restoring this highly disrupted economy and putting it into working order within a period of three years. The new regime set about this task most energetically and with a great deal of effectiveness. On the one hand, it restored factories and railroads so as to increase production and to restore the capacity to move and distribute the goods produced. In order to contain the flames of inflation, it was essential to increase the supply of consumer goods. This required increasing food production, textile output, and other consumer necessities. It required distributing these goods equitably throughout the country. However, increasing supply was only one side of the coin. To restore economic stability, money demand and the galloping price rises had to be reduced. This was approached by reforming and unifying the fiscal and monetary systems, and fiscal and monetary management. All budgets – central, provincial, and local – were consolidated into a national budget plan and brought under a national budget administration. The whole system of tax administration was simplified; revenue collections were stepped up; and tax morale was significantly raised. Correspondingly, control over government expenditures was tightened, and, in this way, government deficits were markedly reduced.

In fact, the supply of goods moving into markets was fairly quickly stepped up, while money purchasing power and thus the demand for these goods was kept under close rein. To achieve this, not only were government deficits sharply curtailed, but rationing of consumer necessities and price controls were gradually introduced. Even if these controls were not fully standardized on a national basis and articulated in uniform regulations, they were in large part enforced by relying on the market power of state trading companies, who were gradually controlling an increasing share of total output moving into market channels. They were consciously using supplies under their control to relieve scarcities and thus reduce the pressures on the price level.

What is particularly remarkable about this period is that the rehabilitation of industrial plants, the recovery of agricultural productivity, and the gradual restoration of price stability were all achieved in spite of the fact that China had to wage a war in Korea. The Korean War clearly aggravated China's scarcity problem, since many consumer goods, particulary food and clothing, had to be diverted to the Korean front. However this was counter-balanced, at least to some extent, by the fact that the Korean War commanded large-scale national support and made it easier for the new regime to use patriotic appeals to mobilize resources. As a result, while the demand for goods was almost certainly increased beyond what it might have been, correspondingly, the capacity for resource mobilization was augmented as well.

Plan Preparation

The first three years were not only used to restore the economy, but also to establish and consolidate a network of new institutions that enabled the state and its organs to exercise increasing control over resource mobilization and allocation. That is, during this rehabilitation period, the new regime succeeded in capturing what Lenin had called "the commanding heights" in the economy and polity.

Against this background, the authorities felt that the country was ready for a drive to industrialization, rapid economic development, and marked structural transformation. With this in mind, the First Five-Year Plan was announced to begin on January 1, 1953. However, at that stage, the skeleton targets announced for the five-year period ahead were more in the nature of generalized projections or forecasts than fully elaborated and detailed plans. It seems that between January 1953 and mid-1955, the Chinese economy was at best operating on the basis of ad hoc and short-range plans, perhaps gradually easing into annual plans. It would be fair to say that the economy was not yet ready for detailed, comprehensive, national planning. A national statistical bureau was only founded in late 1952. Up to that time, provincial and local authorities kept statistical records, but without the benefit of a nation-wide standardized system of definitions and methods of collection and compilation. It was thus difficult to draw up comprehensive national plans until a reasonably adequate data base was developed. The same applied to systems of enterprise accounting. As shown in Chapter 3, as of 1953, a significant share of Chinese industry as well as other sectors was in private hands. Many private and public enterprises had no established tradition of keeping books and reliable sets of accounts. To the extent that a prime requisite of economic planning is planning at the enterprise level and enforcing plan performance at that level, standardized, comparable, reliable sets of accounts were essential.

A third major element that had to be taken care of before a long-range industrialization plan could be launched was Soviet aid. The Chinese were in the process of negotiating with the Soviet Union for the delivery of complete plants, which were to constitute the core of the First Five-Year Plan. These negotiations were not completed until the summer or fall of 1953 so that this, too, contributed to a delay in launching a full-fledged long-term plan.

This does not mean that the Chinese economy was marking time in the two-and-one-half-year period. On the contrary, it was a period of rapid advance in production and gradual transformation in institutions. The scope of both the state and the cooperative sector was continuously enlarged; agricultural production was raised, and industrial output was brought up to capacity levels. That is, most of the industrial growth during this period was based on fuller utilization of existing and rehabilitated facilities. Only to a small extent did it represent output of new plants, which were just beginning to be built.

The Big Push

In mid-1955, a detailed five-year plan was announced for the period 1953 to 1957. This meant that one-half of the period was already past and, therefore, in effect this was a two-and-a-half-year plan.

The announcement of the plan marked a sharp forward lurch right across the board, affecting all segments of the economic, political, and social system. It represented a very significant turning point in the economic history of the People's Republic of China. It marked a deliberate and significant acceleration in the pace of development. It was preceded by an extended debate – mostly behind the scenes – concerning development strategy and the desired pace of development. As shown in Chapter 2, this debate was resolved by Mao personally, who decided to launch a full-fledged collectivization drive and to complete the socialization and nationalization of the non-agricultural sectors. This acceleration was also evidenced by a 60 percent rise in government investment between 1955 and 1956.

These measures were undertaken following the very good 1955 harvest, which left the regime with room to maneuver and reduced the risk of failure. The new measures, and particulary increased capital investment coupled with greater mobilization of labor and raw materials, did indeed lead to a sharp rise in industrial production in 1956. However, 1956 was a mediocre weather year and, as a result, agricultural production declined somewhat. The rise in investment, the step-up in resource mobilization, and the full utilization of existing plant capacity resulting therefrom, combined with a decline in farm production, created strains, supply bottlenecks, and marked shortages throughout the system. This was reflected in marked inflationary pressures during 1956.

Retrenchment

To alleviate these pressures and relieve supply bottlenecks, the regime was forced to consolidate and retrench. State investment was cut back somewhat; the rate of resource mobilization was reduced in general; and the pressures on the farm sector were eased. This took several forms, all designed to improve farmer incentives and thus contribute once more to a rise in agricultural production. The scope for private plots was somewhat enlarged; the collectivization pressure was eased; and a series of decentralization decrees was promulgated toward the end of the year 1957, designed to provide for greater local autonomy in fiscal, monetary, and economic management. As a result, all sectors continued to expand, but at a slower pace.

This year marked the end of the First Five-Year Plan. These five years witnessed unusually rapid industrial development, coupled with rather sluggish agricultural growth. It also brought with it a significant acceleration in the rate of population growth, as compared to earlier decades. Population growth, coupled with rapid industrialization, led to a rural exodus and a process of rapid urbanization. At the end of the First Five-Year Plan period, the Chinese economy seemed clearly launched on a development path, but nevertheless, certain difficulties were quite apparent. These mostly revolved around the poor performance of agriculture, which in turn threatened to retard industrial growth and growth in the economy as a whole.

The First Five-Year Plan period also witnessed the complete institutional transformation of the Chinese economy, with agriculture fully collectivized except for small private plots and with all of the non-agricultural sectors nationalized. The Chinese economy emerged from this period with its systemic features quite well crystallized. In spite of many disturbances, changes, and campaigns since then, the basic contours of that system have not changed very much between then and now.

The Great Leap Forward

It seems that at the Eighth Party Congress in 1956, a thoroughgoing review of economic progress and industrialization during the First Five-Year Plan period took place. This was in preparation for drafting the outlines of the Second Five-Year Plan. The Chinese Communist leadership was apparently reasonably satisfied with the pace of industrial advance, but seriously concerned about the sluggish performance of agriculture. It became increasingly clear that agriculture might become a bottleneck sector, holding back the development of the economy as a whole.

In a preponderantly agrarian economy such as China's, agriculture plays a most strategic role from several points of view. At a minimum, farm production must be increased rapidly enough to keep pace with population growth. However, in a speedily industrializing economy, this is not enough. Industrialization necessarily brings with it urbanization and a rapid expansion of the industrial labor force. This may then be expected to bring with it a rising per capita demand for food, based on higher urban than rural incomes. This indeed happened in China as well, with urban population increasing by 30 percent between 1952 and 1957, while rural population rose by only 9 percent.[4]

In addition to supplying food, agriculture must provide many of the raw materials for industry. For instance, the fate of the textile industry will be crucially affected by the supply of raw cotton; the leather goods industry will depend on the availability of hides and skins; food processing, brewing, and tobacco manufacturers will all be dependent on agricultural supplies. Therefore the pace of advance in a wide range of consumer-goods manufactures will be crucially affected by the pace of agricultural development.

In addition, agriculture must generate export surpluses in order to earn the foreign exchange with which to finance the import of capital goods and certain kinds of industrial raw materials. In an agricultural country such as China, the bulk of exports will necessarily have to be farm products in raw or processed form. However, agriculture is not only a supplier of goods for domestic and export needs, but is also a supplier of production factors, such as labor and capital. A rapidly expanding industrial sector necessarily draws some of its labor force from the rural areas. Moreover, in one form or another, agriculture is called upon to save and finance a significant part of the investment for the expansion of industrial plant, transport, and other sectors as well.

Given these considerations, the Chinese Communist leadership was determined to step up the pace of growth in agriculture, while at the same time maintaining and even perhaps accelerating the pace of industrialization. As indicated in Chapter 2, Mao became convinced that both these tasks could be accomplished simultaneously through an all-out mobilization effort. It was therefore expected that the Great Leap would at the same time lead to a rapid expansion in agricultural production, in factory output, and in small-scale production.

In the short run, this did indeed happen. The year 1958, which marked the beginning of the Great Leap, happened to be a favorable weather year, so that both the spring and autumn harvests turned out to be very good. As a result, this large increment in agricultural output generated rapidly rising supplies of food and raw materials, both for domestic needs and for exports, which helped to accelerate industrial growth. In addition, the all-out mobilization of labor and capital contributed significantly to a large increase both in factory and small-scale industry output.

Unfortunately, this tremendous acceleration sowed the seeds of its own destruction. Communization, particularly in its initial forms, had profoundly disruptive effects in agriculture. It was disruptive of traditional institutions and farming patterns. This, combined with serious planning and technical errors, contributed to a drastic decline in farm production. Thus the poor 1959 harvest was not only due to bad weather, but also in part to the fact that economic planners and policy makers greatly over-estimated farm output. They may have concluded that in the face of these very high yields, the agricultural production required to cover all the needs spelled out above could perhaps be produced on a reduced acreage. It was apparently felt that low-yielding lands could be safely withdrawn from cultivation and turned over to pasture. Misjudgments based on inaccurate information were compounded by many technical failures in the construction of dams and irrigation projects, and a host of other planning errors.

As a result, agricultural output declined markedly in 1959. Poor weather, combined with the problems outlined above, produced a succession of three very bad harvests between 1959 and 1961. In industry, quantity was substituted for quality, so that while production in factories, small-scale plants, and mines increased dramatically indeed, some of the output was of such low quality that it could not be used. This, for instance, was the case for much of the pig iron and steel produced in the backyard furnaces. There were also numerous reports concerning the deterioration in the quality of coal mined.

Nevertheless, the momentum generated by all-out mobilization of labor, capital, and raw materials carried over into 1959, so that investment was maintained at a high level and industrial output also advanced appreciably, although at a somewhat slower rate than in 1958. Both exports and imports reached their peak levels in 1959, so that a downturn in agriculture was coupled with a continuing upswing in the non-agricultural sectors of the economy.

Although serious difficulties began to surface in 1959, they quite clearly engulfed the whole economy in 1960, particularly following the poor harvest of that year. There were increasing food supply problems and all the consumer-goods industries dependent upon agricultural raw materials suffered from acute supply shortages. By the end of the year, more and more sectors began to exhibit the symptoms of an economic downturn.

The Great Crisis

As a result, the Chinese economy entered into the throes of a deep depression. The decline in agricultural production was necessarily reflected in acute shortages of food supply, which became fully apparent only in 1960. This decline then spilled over into industry, particularly consumer-goods manufacture, which was gradually forced to curtail operations because of raw material shortages. As a result, these industries began to operate well below capacity. In the face of this, new plant expansion ceased and machinery and equipment orders by the consumer-goods sectors were correspondingly reduced.

Producers of investment goods were affected in several ways. First, the demand for their products was curtailed by agriculture and then by consumer-goods industries as well. All of this was further compounded by the fact that, due to a rapid deterioration in Sino-Soviet relations, the Soviet Union quite suddenly withdrew all its technicians and advisors from China in the late summer and early fall of 1960. This meant that a number of projects in the process of construction had to be suspended, particularly in the capital-goods sector. The decline in farm production and consumer-goods output also affected China's export capability and its capacity to finance capital-goods imports at a high level. This, in turn, reinforced the cumulative downturn of the investment-goods industries dependent on imported capital-goods components.

Under the impact of all these developments, China experienced a deep economic crisis between 1960 and 1962. The principal symptoms of this crisis were: very severe food shortages, bordering in some areas on famine; similarly acute shortages of textile cloth; and sharp reductions in foreign trade coupled with large-scale imports of grain. Furthermore, all this was accompanied by open urban unemployment.

Recovery from Crisis

Under the impact of these developments, the Chinese Communist leadership was forced to reexamine its policies and priorities. As shown in Chapter 2, agricultural development was assigned highest priority in 1961–1962. Communes were reorganized and material incentives for the farmers were greatly improved. At the same time industrial projects, suspended when the Soviet technicians were withdrawn, were completed during this recovery period, which extended from about 1962 to 1966. Also a number of new industrial projects were initiated based on the importation of complete plants (turnkey projects) from Western Europe and Japan. These were principally in the petro-chemical industries.

Economic recovery during this period was marked by a good harvest in 1962. From then until 1967, Chinese agriculture experienced continuous growth, year by year. This provided a favorable setting for the recovery of the non-agricultural sectors. The high priority assigned to agricultural development necessarily had certain implications for industrial policy as well. This period witnessed a rapid expansion of chemical fertilizer production, involving the construction and completion of both large-scale and small-scale plants. One of the interesting developments of this period was the marked growth of small- and medium-sized industry, based in the countryside and closely linked to agriculture. A similar development, although less far-reaching, took place in the farm equipment industry, but perhaps one of the most notable achievements was the far-reaching rural electrification program. This not only served to introduce lighting into peasant homes, but greatly improved water-resource management. With rural electrification, a network of pumping stations could be built with small generators, many of them manufacturered in small- and medium-scale plants in the countryside. These pumping stations went far in improving flood control, drainage, and the distribution of water for irrigation.

A second major guideline of economic policy during this period was "self-reliance." That is, the Chinese were pursuing a systematic import-substitution policy, trying to reduce their import dependence. This was of particular importance in those industries that were closely linked to national defense. In the past, China depended greatly upon the Soviet Union for the supply of crude oil and its products. It also looked to the Soviets for its supplies of modern and heavy military equipment and weapons. With the Sino-Soviet split, it became essential from a national defense point of view to step up petroleum and defense production. This led to very extensive geological explorations and the discovery of new oil fields, which then was reflected in rapidly rising oil production. At the same time, we witness a rapid growth of machinery output, which was essential for the provision of defense material.

During the Great Leap and the Great Crisis, there was a general deterioration in economic planning and management. Similarly, as indicated earlier, there was a substitution of quantity for quality. These tendencies were reversed during the recovery period. Greater attention was paid to efficiency, better management, more economic rationality, and better output quality.

The Cultural Revolution

This process of recovery and new development was interrupted in late 1966 by the Cultural Revolution. While the Cultural Revolution was primarily an ideological and political movement, it had certain economic consequences, many of them unintended. In the early stages of this almost cataclysmic movement, the leadership was anxious to keep the revolution out of the factories and the farms. It pretty well succeeded as far as the agricultural sector was concerned. The Cultural Revolution had very few disruptive effects in agriculture, as far as we can tell. However, unfortunately, this was not the case for industry, transport, and foreign trade. While many of the data for this period are unsatisfactory, it seems that transport was profoundly disrupted. A great deal of freight space was preempted for the movement of the Red Guards from the provinces to Peking, and from the capital to the provinces. This left large quantities of industrial raw materials and equipment standing on railroad sidings for extended periods. Raw material shortages resulting therefrom forced many factories to curtail their level of operations. In addition, at varying periods and in different places during 1967 and part of 1968, factional disputes led to work stoppages and even some armed struggles. Even when these did not occur, so much time was spent in revolutionary activities by workers that the time available for production was necessarily reduced.

The dip in industrial production, coupled with the disruption in transport, led to a decline in exports and imports in 1967 and 1968. The foreign-trade downturn was reinforced by occasional delays in China's ports due to work stoppages on the docks and the slower pace of loading and unloading ships.

Recovery from the Cultural Revolution

The disruptive effects of the Cultural Revolution were essentially of a short-run character. Therefore, by 1969, the Chinese economy was once more pointed in a forward direction. While the 1968 and 1969 harvests were below 1967 levels, this was probably due more to unfavorable weather conditions than the effects of the Cultural Revolution. However, 1970 was another very favorable harvest year, so that agricultural production, by this time, exceeded 1967 peak levels. In the meantime, industrial production was recovering rapidly from the Cultural Revolution downturn, and it also had, by 1970 and possibly even by 1969, exceeded earlier levels.

New Wave of Expansion

It seems that with recovery from the effects of the Cultural Revolution, the Chinese economy was once more carried forward by an expansionary momentum. Agricultural production had increased somewhat further beyond 1970 levels, but it is in industry and foreign trade that growth was most pronounced.

Given the preoccupations of the leadership and the cadres during the Cultural Revolution, long-range economic planning considerations were apparently pushed into the background between 1965 and 1970. However, following the fall of Lin Piao in 1971, there was a seemingly overall policy reassessment which led to a significant upgrading of economic development concerns in China. This was reflected in a number of government statements, culminating in Chou En-lai's report to the National People's Congress in January 1975. There are indications that this new emphasis led to a marked rise in investment. Another symptom of this new policy is the very large-scale orders placed by the Chinese for the importation of complete plants from Western Europe, Japan, and the United States. Deliveries on these projects started during 1974, and are to be completed within a three- to five-year period. This means that between 1977 and 1979 China's chemical fertilizer, rolled steel making, and in particular crude oil extracting and refining capacity will be very significantly augmented.

It may very well be that agricultural production has once more reached a plateau. If so, even simultaneous improvements in water-resource management and increasing applications of chemical fertilizer may not be sufficient to generate a rate of farm production growth sufficient to keep well ahead of the pace of population increase. If this is indeed the case, new technological breakthroughs will be required to launch Chinese agriculture on a new expansionary path. In fact, it seems that a whole new wave of innovations is being introduced in Chinese agriculture involving an extension of double and triple cropping, transplanting of wheat and even cotton, inter-cropping, and a whole variety of other practices. All these may involve significantly greater applications of chemical fertilizer, combined with the development of new strains and varieties. If this line of speculation is warranted, then the large number of chemical fertilizer plants being constructed may be viewed as an attempt to reach this new stage sometime in the latter part of the 1970s.

This new push in agriculture, most recently dramatized by a large national leadership conference held in Tachai, seems to be closely inter-related with the further development of rural industry, particularly county (*hsien*) administered medium-scale plants in fertilizer, farm equipment, and other agriculture-related industries.[5]

Agricultural development

As noted in Chapter 1, approximately one-quarter of the world's population lives in China and obtains its food supply from 7 percent of the world's cultivated land. The acreage sown to crops is 70 percent of the U.S. level, but this area has to support three to four times more people than inhabit the United States.

This indicates that the density of population in relation to the cultivated land area is very high in China. There is a high degree of population pressure on farmland. The character of Chinese agriculture, therefore, reflects this reality. Since so many people have to be supported on a limited acreage, Chinese agriculture must maximize the production of calories per acre. This means that it must concentrate on the production of high-energy-yielding products, primarily cereals. Therefore, it is not surprising that 80 percent of the total sown area is allocated to grain production – principally wheat, millet, and kaoliang in the North and rice in the South. Wheat and rice are the most important crops; they are grown in every province of China, although there is a greater concentration of wheat in the North and rice in the South. The regional differentiation is reinforced by the fact that northern agriculture is largely based on dry farming, while lands in the South are largely irrigated.

The strategic importance of grains in China's food supply is also reflected in the composition of the total agricultural product. In terms of gross output value, food crops contribute 65 percent. These figures of course vary somewhat from year to year, depending on the character of the harvest. Food crops may fluctuate between 60 and 70 percent, and grains alone may range between 50 and 60 percent of total gross output value.[6]

To produce the food needed to supply such a large population requires a highly intensive agriculture, with large applications of labor and material inputs and high yields per acre. To obtain these high yields a lot of labor has to be tied down in agriculture so that, in a certain sense, this is a preponderantly agrarian economy because it is preponderantly agrarian. To put it differently, as long as Chinese agriculture is based on essentially traditional and pre-modern technology, its labor requirements will be high.

There are many indications that in recent years the intensity of land use is being stepped up year by year through the extension of double cropping and inter-cropping. It is also clear that a major new movement is under way to emulate Tachai in the dry farming areas of North China. This means reclaiming and terracing the land (referred to by the Chinese as "farmland capital construction"), sinking tube wells, and constructing an irrigation network in North China.[7] All this involves large investments and capital projects to be constructed largely by new labor with very limited use of capital equipment. Therefore labor requirements are continuously increased in order to develop farm production based on a preponderantly land-saving and capital-saving technology. Under the impact of all these measures, definite labor shortages are beginning to develop in the Chinese countryside. This in turn increased the pressure to mechanize certain processes, to shorten the cultivating and harvesting time in the multiple-cropped areas, thus extending the growing season per crop and at the same time saving some labor.

One of the outstanding characteristics of Chinese agriculture is the relatively high yield per acre, as seen in the indexes for wheat and rice in Table 6-1. It is interesting to note that major rice-producing areas such as Thailand and Burma have significantly lower rice yields than China. The same applies to India, although this is to some extent compensated for by the fact that in recent years wheat yields seem to be marginally higher than in China. Only in contemporary Japan, Taiwan, and South Korea do yields significantly exceed Chinese levels in Asia. However, this required very intensive applications of chemical fertilizers and other modern inputs. Viewed in a long-term perspective, Chinese agriculture clearly faces a major challenge. At the minimum, it must find some means to maintain a rate of agricultural advance rapid enough to keep pace with population growth. Preferably, its development should be accelerated, so that it could provide a margin for rising farm production per capita. This raises certain fundamental problems of development strategy. If per capita agricultural supplies are to be raised, and at the same time, if agriculture is to meet other demands placed on it, should it be obtained through domestic production, or should China opt for an open economic posture, increasing its import dependence at least insofar as agricultural products is concerned? That is, should China pursue a policy of agricultural self-sufficiency, or should it perhaps step up an exchange of raw materials and consumer-goods manufactures for foodstuffs? This dilemma

Table 6-1. *Index of comparative wheat and rice yields in selected Asian countries and the United States*[a]

Country	Wheat	Rice
China	100	100
Burma	54	54
India	110	55
Indonesia	–	73
Japan	219	181
South Korea	200	149
Thailand	–	60
United States	185	163

[a]Based on average yields in kilograms per hectare for a three-year period (1971–1973).
Source: Derived from data in United Nations Food and Agriculture Organization, *Production Yearbook*, 1973, vol. 27, Rome, 1974, pp. 44–47.

may more easily be resolved in the future, if China does indeed raise its domestic petroleum production sufficiently to become a major oil exporter. This would permit China to earn a great deal of additional foreign exchange, which could then be utilized for purchases of agricultural products.

However, this certainly was not the policy pursued in the 1950s. At that time, the challenge posed to agriculture was to be largely met through ideology and organization. That is, it was hoped that agricultural self-sufficiency could be pursued and at the same time the domestic farm sector could meet the demands placed upon it, principally through the more efficient utilization of resources already available. It was hoped that the reorganization of agriculture, particularly collectivization, would capture the economies of scale and would give government and party organs much greater control over agriculture. These controls could be used to ensure fuller and better utilization of traditional inputs. As shown above, it was not until the collapse of the Great Leap and the onset of the Great Crisis that the Chinese Communist leadership realized that this approach was not good enough; that even with the indoctrination of the peasantry and the organizational transformation of the 1950s, ideology and organization combined with increasing applications of traditional inputs were bound to bump up against the reality of diminishing returns.

Against this background agricultural self-sufficiency was relaxed in the 1960s and China became a major importer of grain. However, even these sizable grain imports constituted only a marginal increment to the total Chinese food supply. Consequently, there was continuing pressure placed on Chinese agriculture to accelerate its rate of growth.

This acceleration was largely achieved through rural electrification and rapidly increasing applications of chemical fertilizer. Rural electrification provided the basis for a marked improvement in water-resource management, so that water and fertilizer combined with new strains and varieties – particularly in rice culture – fostered rising yields. Total chemical fertilizer supplies, both from domestic production and imports, increased dramatically from about 2 million tons in 1957 to almost 30 million tons in 1974, which would represent a fifteenfold rise in 17 years.[8] Roughly during the same period, electrical power consumption in agriculture rose almost four times, from about 1.5 billion kilowatt-hours in 1962 to 5.5 billion in 1971.[9] Land under irrigation was extended from about 30 to 40 percent of the cultivated area between 1957 and 1974. The number of small walking tractors in use has risen significantly along with other types of farm machinery, although the degree of farm mechanization in Chinese agriculture is still quite limited. Finally, farm incentives have improved significantly. The relative price position of farm products sold as compared to manufactured products purchased by the rural population has improved, and the agricultural tax burden has been lightened as gauged by the share of this tax in total farm crop production.

The impact of these measures can best be perceived through an analysis of the grain production data in Table 6-2. These suggest that grain output grew at a rate of about 2.2 percent during the First Five-Year Plan period, that is, between 1952 and 1957. It then rose very appreciably in 1958, only to collapse in 1959. It seems that under the impact of the crisis, grain production may have declined by 50 million tons, that is, by 25 percent between 1958 and 1960. By 1963, it had more or less recovered to 1957 levels and then resumed a continuous expansionary path until 1967. During this four-year period, grain production grew at the unusually rapid rate of almost 6 percent a year. However, this rate of increase has slowed down considerably since then, as illustrated by the fact that the average annual rate of growth was perceptibly

Table 6-2. *Grain production trends in China, 1952–1974 (in millions of metric tons)*[a]

Year	Production	Year	Production
1952	166	1965	205
		1966	220
1957	185	1967	230
1958	(200)	1968	(215)
1959	(165)	1969	(220)
1960	150	1970	240
1961	162	1971	246
1962	174	1972	240
1963	183	1973	250
1964	200	1974	259

[a]The 1952 figure is Chao's estimate; the 1958, 1959, 1964 to 1966, 1968, and 1969 data are U.S. government estimates; the data in parentheses are particularly uncertain. The figures for other years represent reconstructed official Chinese estimates.

Sources: Kang Chao, *Agricultural Production in Communist China, 1949–1965*, Madison, Wis., 1970, Table 8.15, p. 227; A. L. Erisman, "China: Agricultural Development, 1949–71," in *People's Republic of China: An Economic Assessment*, Joint Economic Committee, U.S. Congress, May 1972, Table 2, p. 121; D. H. Perkins, "Constraints Influencing China's Agricultural Performance," in *China: A Reassessment of the Economy*, Joint Economic Committee, U.S. Congress, July 1975, Table 1, p. 351.

less than 2 percent between 1967 and 1974. For the two decades (1952–1974) as a whole, the average rate of growth was just about 2 percent a year.

If in the next few years grain production does not rise much more rapidly than in the last few years, one might be inclined to speculate that chemical fertilizer applications as presently combined with other inputs must have entered the zone of diminishing returns in China. That is, when the applications accelerated markedly after 1963, their initial impact may have been very significant, but after a while their impact may have been gradually dissipated. The unusually rapid rate of growth in grain production between 1963 and 1967 may have been due to the fact that at one and the same time the fertilizer supply rose from about 6 to 18 million tons (in gross weight, it almost certainly increased less rapidly in terms of nutrient content), the efficiency of water management was improved greatly, the area under irrigation was extended, and last but not least the new rice varieties were diffused during this period. Subsequently fertilizer applications continued and the area under irrigation was further extended, but the once-for-all effects resulting from the earlier boost in the efficiency of water management and from the introduction of new varieties was largely dissipated. This suggests that the continuous development of new plant strains and varieties and large additional improvements in water management are essential if fertilizer response rates are to be maintained and yields are to be further raised.

In some respects, this pattern of performance is discouraging, in the sense that even with the quite far-reaching efforts in the 1960s, food production may have just barely kept pace with population growth for the Communist period as a whole. On the other hand, cotton production seems to have fared better, with a rise of about 95 percent between 1952 and 1974, as compared to a less than 60 percent increase for grain. However, other industrial and oil-bearing crops apparently fared worse than cotton. Therefore, industrial crops as a whole probably did not out-match the performance of grain. Based on qualitative indications, mostly from observations of visitors to China over a period of years and some fragmentary data, vegetable production and supply seem to have increased quite rapidly, more rapidly than grain production. At the same time, the pig population also rose fairly rapidly. According to necessarily tentative estimates, grain, vegetable, and pig production increased by 30, 60, and 40 percent respectively for the 1957–1970 period.[10]

The problem we face in analyzing long-term trends in agricultural production in China is lack of adequate information for the non-grain sector of farming. For this reason, it is very difficult to reconstruct and estimate the value of total agricultural production for the 1960s. Except for the 1950s, we have no continuous series for oil-bearing crops, industrial crops other than cotton, or livestock products. Nevertheless, from some scattered data in Chinese sources and based on certain assumptions, D. H. Perkins has reconstructed China's gross agricultural output value for 1957, 1964, 1970, and 1974, all in 1957 prices. On this basis it seems that total farm output grew at an annual rate of about 2.2 percent.[11] At the same time, grain production grew somewhat more slowly, at about 2 percent a year. However these differences are well within the possible margins of error. In any case they suggest that total farm output and grain production progressed at about the same pace.

Even though China's farm production may not have greatly outpaced population growth, its performance in the last two decades compares very favorably with past rates of growth. According to Perkins's studies, grain output rose at an average annual rate of about 0.7 percent between 1914–1918 and 1957.[12] In per capita terms, this meant that total farm production just about kept pace with population. This suggests that, while the rate of growth in farm production at least doubled in the People's Republic as compared to Republican China, so did population. The net result may be that there was no appreciable rise in farm output per capita since 1949, as there certainly was none before then.

At the same time, the performance of Chinese agriculture since 1949 compares favorably with that of a number of other countries. For instance, Japan is most frequently cited as a case in which agriculture has played a very crucial role in industrialization and modern economic growth since the Meiji Restoration (1868). Yet agricultural product in Japan did not grow any faster than in China. Between 1885 and 1917, a period of thirty-two years, it rose at an average annual rate of 1.8 percent. Between 1905 and 1936–1940, it rose at an average rate of 2.2 percent. Therefore, the pace of agricultural expansion in Japan before World War II was no more rapid than in China since 1952. However, since population growth in Japan was slower, the same rate of growth yielded a sustained rise in farm output per capita at an average annual rate of 0.5 to 1 percent. Moreover, Japan succeeded in accelerating its pace of agricultural advance after World War II, so that farm product growth rose to an average of 3 percent a year.[13] Similarly, Denmark is usually considered as an economy in which agricultural progress has played a very crucial role. Between 1870–1879 and 1930–1939 (exclusive of the abnormal war years of 1915–1920), agricultural product rose at an annual rate of 2 percent, the same as in China. In England, the home of the first industrial revolution, real product in agriculture, forestry, and fishing grew at an average annual rate of

1.2 to 1.5 percent during the first few decades of the nineteenth century. It rose to a peak of 1.8 percent per year in the middle of that century, but then declined, falling below 1 percent in the last decade.[14]

In India, agricultural growth rose faster than in China, that is, almost at 3 percent per year between 1952–1956 and 1970. Yet, since India's population also increased more rapidly than China's, on a per capita basis the performances of the two countries for roughly the same periods are very similar. Moreover, precisely because Indian yields were so much lower than China's, it was easier to raise them.[15]

All these data suggest that Chinese agricultural performance, viewed in a historical and comparative perspective, has been quite impressive. Nevertheless, it has not succeeded in generating a decisive margin of per capita growth. To meet this challenge, it will have to find a way to further accelerate agricultural development and/or reduce the pace of population growth. In this respect, the Japanese experience may be most instructive. Post–World War II Japan succeeded in raising its long-term agricultúral growth rate from 2 to 3 percent a year with unusually intensive efforts and very large-scale applications of modern industrial inputs. This is probably the maximum to which Chinese agriculture could realistically aspire, barring a quite major technological breakthrough. However, to attain this in a large country such as China may be a much more monumental task than was the case for Japan. On the other hand, if the Chinese were to succeed in coming even close to matching the post-war Japanese performance, they will have broken the historical vise in which the country has been held by the race between population and food supply. At the same time, if recent indications of a decline in China's population growth are validated, then the same result might conceivably be obtained even if the agricultural growth rate of the last two decades is increased only quite modestly.

Industrial development

China's modern industrial development can be dated from 1895, when the Treaty of Shimonoseki permitted the location of Japanese industrial enterprises in the treaty ports. Through the application of the most-favored-nation principle, this permission was extended to nationals of other countries.

Prior to that date, Chinese statesmen, under the aegis of the self-strengthening movement and impressed by the need for industrial development as a basis for military strength, did indeed establish some arsenals and a few scattered manufacturing establishments. However, factory industry did not become fully established in China until foreign enterprises led the way after 1895.

A market for industrial products was opened up through imports of foreign manufactures, particularly textiles. When it could be demonstrated that such a market existed, the risk of establishing factories on Chinese soil was greatly reduced. Although initially it was foreign enterprise and foreign investments that led the way, demonstration of their success induced Chinese entrepreneurs to follow suit.

Textile imports led to the development of a domestic cotton-spinning industry with both destructive and constructive effects from the standpoint of economic development. Competition from manufactured cotton yarn gradually undermined handicraft spinning, thereby seriously reducing this source of rural income. On the other hand, the introduction of cheaper manufactured yarn greatly strengthened the handicraft weaving of cloth, allowing handicraft weavers to compete effectively with imported cloth. Consequently, it was not until much later that factory production of cloth was extensively developed.[16]

The rise of a textile industry was paralleled by the growth of other branches of consumer-goods manufacture, such as the production of cigarettes, matches, paper, food processing, and so on. Gradually the beginnings of a modern producer-goods industry followed. Some modern coal mining methods were introduced. Machine repair shops and certain types of machine production were established, particularly in the 1920s and 1930s.[17] This development was particularly pronounced in Manchuria, where the expansion of an extensive railroad network created a demand for iron and steel, and locomotive and other machine repair. Mining, ferrous metallurgy and other heavy industries expanded rapidly in Manchuria, particularly during the inter-war period. This was made possible in large part by the import of capital and entrepreneurship, initially from Russia and then from Japan.

During the fifty-year period between 1895 and 1949, there thus developed a cadre of Chinese entrepreneurs, industrial managers, technicians, and at least a small pool of skilled industrial workers. Starting from this base, the new regime greatly accelerated the process of industrial growth coupled with far-reaching structural changes in Chinese industry. The early Communist period, as illustrated by the 1952 data in Table 6-3, still largely reflects the pre-war situation. Chinese industry was then dominated by textiles, food processing, and other consumer-goods manufactures which supplied well

Table 6-3. *Structural changes in Chinese industry, 1952–1974 (in constant 1952 prices)*

Sector	1952	1957	1965	1970	1974
Total industrial production	100	100	100	100	100
Producer goods	35	48	53	55	62
Consumer goods	65	52	47	45	38

Source: R. M. Field, "Civilian Industrial Production in the People's Republic of China, 1949–74," in *China: A Reassessment of the Economy,* Joint Economic Committee, U.S. Congress, 1975, Tables B-4 and B-7, pp. 168, 170.

over half of total industrial output. At the same time, machinery and basic industrial materials contributed only one-third of the total.

This structure was, however, rapidly and dramatically transformed under the impact of the new industrial policies. As a result, the relative share of consumer-goods industries shrank to around 40 percent by the early 1970s. During the same years the contribution of machinery output rose most rapidly, from about one-tenth in 1952 to more than one-fifth in the early 1970s. This means that the pace of machinery-output growth was twice as fast as that of total industrial production. Therefore, in terms of industrial structure, by the 1970s the Chinese economy bore many of the earmarks of a quite advanced economy. A systematic study of industrial evolution in presently developed economies shows that producer-goods sectors do not become predominant until an economy attains quite advanced stages of industrialization. Moreover, this would be associated with much higher levels of per capita income than prevail in China.[18]

However, in making these international comparisons of industrial structure, it is essential to bear in mind that a country embarking on the process of deliberate industrialization in the mid-twentieth century will necessarily develop a different industrial structure than a country that may have experienced its industrial revolution amidst laissez faire conditions in the nineteenth century. This may be partly due to the fact that twentieth-century technology is more capital intensive, and that a backward country industrializing this late is in a position to enjoy "the advantages of backwardness."[19] It can borrow quite advanced technology from abroad, thus saving itself the long process of research and development. These considerations must have been bolstered by the fact that a large country with China's resources and market size would tend to develop a machinery industry at an earlier stage of development than a small and preponderantly foreign-trade-oriented economy.

For these reasons, it would be surprising indeed if China's industrialization were merely to follow past patterns and replicate the path pioneered by economies that embarked upon this process a century or a century and a half ago. However, tendencies born out of technological progress and the latecomer position of the Chinese have been greatly reinforced by policies pursued since 1949. During the First Five-Year Plan period and the Great Leap, the Chinese were anxious to establish a broad industrial base, moving rapidly ahead particularly in the development of basic industries supplying materials such as iron and steel, coal, cement, and electrical power. This was coupled with the expansion of the machine-building industry in the 1950s. This pattern of development was fostered and reinforced by the close Sino-Soviet alliance, which had far-reaching implications for Chinese economic and industrial policy. First of all, the pattern of development in many respects reflected Soviet concepts and Soviet models. At the same time, it was heavily dependent upon the importation of large-scale, capital-intensive, complete factories from the Soviet Union. Finally, it meant that the Chinese military establishment was in large part dependent upon the import of weapons and matériel from the Soviet Union.

However, this situation changed radically following the Sino-Soviet split in 1960. As a result and under the impact of a "self-reliance" policy, the Chinese now had to reformulate their industrial policy. They had to rapidly expand their machine-building capacity, particularly those branches of machine building that produced for the defense sector. Secondly, they had to emancipate themselves from dependence on the Soviets as far as petroleum and its products were concerned. Therefore rapid growth of oil extraction and refining capacity was assigned high priority. In addition, the greater emphasis placed on agricultural development meant that certain branches of industry that supported agriculture, such as chemical fertilizer and farm equipment, required speedy expansion.

The impact of these policies is fairly clearly reflected in Table 6-4. It is apparent from this table that the production of certain basic materials, such as steel, coal, and cement, which expanded particularly rapidly in the 1950s, grew more slowly in the 1960s. On the other hand, the production of crude oil and chemical fertilizer production rose much faster, increasing tenfold in the 1960s. The major factor in the growth of oil output has been the opening of the Ta-ch'ing oil field, which began large-scale production in 1963. This was

Table 6-4. *Industrial production trends in China, 1952–1974*[a]

Product	Units	1952	1957	1959	1966	1973	1974
Crude steel	thousand metric tons	1,349	5,350	13,400	15,000	25,500	23,800
Crude oil	thousand metric tons	436	1,458	3,700	13,900	54,500	65,300
Coal	thousand metric tons	66,490	130,732	300,000	248,000	377,000	389,000
Cement	thousand metric tons	2,861	6,680	12,300	16,900	29,900	31,600
Chemical fertilizer	thousand metric tons	194	803	1,880	9,600	24,760	25,400[b]
Electric power	million kilowatt-hours	7,261	19,340	42,000	61,900[b]	124,800[b]	133,800[b]
Machine tools	units	13,734	28,297	35,000	50,000	80,000	n.a.
Tractors	units	–	–	9,400	46,138	133,263	n.a.
Motor vehicles	units		7,500	19,400	43,000	100,000	110,000
Freight cars	units	5,792	7,300	17,000	7,500	16,000	n.a.
Merchant vessels	LSD tons	6,100	46,400	64,500	19,800	161,700	n.a.
Bicycles	thousand units	80	806	1,479	2,044	4,859	n.a.
Cotton cloth	million linear meters	3,829	5,050	6,100	6,910[b]	8,660[b]	9,550[b]
Sugar	thousand metric tons	451	864	1,130	1,710	2,230	2,190
Paper	thousand metric tons	603	1,221	1,700	2,079[c]	n.a.	3,742[b]

[a]All data for the 1960s and 1970s are estimates compiled by R. M. Field (unless otherwise noted) in "Civilian Industrial Production in the People's Republic of China, 1949–74," in *China: A Reassessment of the Economy*, Joint Economic Committee, U.S. Congress, 1975, Tables B-1 to B-3, pp. 165–167; for some series, e.g., machine tools and merchant vessels, these may be under-estimates.
[b]These estimates are by T. R. Rawski, "China's Industrial Performance, 1949–73," paper submitted to the SSRC Conference on Quantitative Reassessment of Economic Indicators for the PRC, January 1975.
[c]These are Rawski's data, but for 1965 rather than 1966.

reinforced more recently by the drilling of newly discovered fields in North China, most notably in Takang and Shengli, and the beginnings of off-shore oil exploration and drilling in the Pohai Gulf. Since 1965, China has been essentially self-sufficient in crude oil and has produced a complete line of petroleum products, although it must still import additives for high-quality and specialized products. Since 1972 or 1973 China has become a net exporter of oil, with both its production and exports continuing to rise.

The growth in chemical fertilizer production was stimulated by the completion of a number of new factories, in part domestically produced and in part imported as complete turnkey projects from Western Europe in the early 1960s. However, in part it was made possible by the rapid development of chemical fertilizer production in medium-scale plants in rural areas. More recently, in 1973 and 1974, the Chinese have concluded large contracts for the importation of additional complete fertilizer plants from Western Europe, Japan, and the United States. When these plants are completed and become fully operational, China's nitrogenous fertilizer production capacity will be doubled in terms of nutrient content.

One of the striking features of Table 6-4 is the relatively slow development of cotton cloth production, at least as compared to all the other products listed. It is of course precisely this relatively slow growth of textile production that contributed to the decline in the share of light industry in total industrial output. This is but another illustration of the economic policies pursued in the last two decades. These fostered the rapid expansion of producer-goods industries and assigned much lower priority to the development of consumer-goods manufactures. The structural changes in Chinese industry resulting therefrom are clearly reflected in Table 6-3.

What has been the actual growth performance of Chinese industry under the impact of these industrial policies? The development of industry in China and its pattern of performance presents a sharp contrast to that of agriculture. Given some uncertainties surrounding the industrial production data, two alternative series are presented in Table 6-5, both valued in terms of 1952 yuan. The official index is based on the total gross production value culled from Chinese sources. In contrast, the Field series were compiled from physical output data for 42 commodities produced by 11 branches of industry. These commodity-production figures were then weighted in three stages to derive a value index.[20] Actually the differences between the two series are not large. The official series shows a somewhat faster rise for the 1952 to 1974 period. The two series diverge most for the Great Leap period, hence the sizable discrepancy for the 1952–1960 and 1960–1966 periods. Since the differences are

Table 6-5. *Average annual rates of growth of industrial production in China, 1952–1974 (in percent)*

Period	Field	Official Chinese series, reconstructed	Period	Field	Official Chinese series, reconstructed
1952–57	16.0	17.9	1960–66	4.0	0.2[a]
1952–60	18.0	23.1[a]	1960–74	6.0	5.2[a]
1952–66	12.0	12.7	1966–74	8.0	9.1
1952–74	11.0	11.4			
1957–66	10.0	9.0			
1957–74	9.0	9.5			

[a]Based on 1959 rather than 1960, since the official reconstructed series lack information for that year.
Source: R. M. Field, "Civilian Industrial Production in the People's Republic of China, 1949–74," in *China: A Reassessment of the Economy*, Joint Economic Committee, U.S. Congress, July 1975, Tables 1 and 2, pp. 149–150.

relatively small and the official reconstructed index is more broadly based, it may serve as a valid basis for an analysis of industrial production trends.

In any case, both series illustrate the slowdown in industrial growth in the 1960s as compared to the 1950s. In part this was due to the sharp decline in industrial production between 1966 and 1968. But it seems that the rates of growth for the 1950s were rather unique; the trend rates seem to have been between 8 and 10 percent rather than 16 to 18 percent a year. It is most interesting to note that these trend rates of industrial growth more or less correspond to those attained during the Republican Period. Thus the rate of growth for 1912–1914 to 1935–1937 was over 8 percent.[21]

Regardless of which series one uses, these are clearly high growth rates by international standards, although comparisons with other countries must be qualified by the fact that different methods of index construction used in different countries may affect the results. Bearing these qualifications in mind, Chinese industrial growth of the 1950s was comparable to the very high rates attained in the Soviet Union during the first two five-year plans, that is, between 1928 and 1937. Similarly, it was comparable to or possibly higher than those attained in post-war Japan. Industrial growth rates for the Soviet Union for 1928–1958 are estimated at about 10 percent a year; and for Japan, for 1890–1940, they are close to 8 percent a year. India, which launched its deliberate industrialization program roughly at the same time as China, experienced an average industrial growth rate of about 6 percent a year. Therefore, the Chinese experience compares favorably with these as well. This impression is reinforced if we compare Chinese performance with that of presently industrialized countries other than Japan. For instance, the industrial growth rate for the United States averaged around 4 to 4.5 percent for the century between 1860 and 1959. For Germany, the rate was similarly around 4 percent for the four or five decades preceding World War I. For France, it was 3 percent for the three decades preceding World War I, and 2 percent for a longer period stretching from around 1880 to 1940. The rates for Great Britain were below 5 percent for the early nineteenth century, but hovered around an average of 3 percent per year for later decades.[22]

While the new dramatic and most highly visible feature of China's industrialization has been the development of large-scale factory industry, this was coupled with the rapid expansion of rural industries, particularly since the Great Leap. Unfortunately an analysis of rural industrial development is greatly complicated by the paucity of the data available to us. It is compounded by the conceptual confusion resulting from the inter-changeable usage of three quite distinct terms, that is, *handicrafts*, *small-scale industry*, and *rural industry*. The definition of handicrafts is based on methods of production, of small-scale industry on size of plant (variously defined), and of rural industry on the location of plant in rural areas. These concepts often overlap in the sense that plants using non-mechanized methods of production (handicrafts) tend to be small in size and are frequently located in rural areas, but this certainly is not always the case.

In Chinese statistical practice a distinction is made between *individual handicrafts* and *handicraft factories*. The former refer to establishments using family labor or no more than three hired workers. Any handicraft enterprise with more than four hired workers is considered a handicraft factory. *Small-scale industrial enterprises* are those employing not more than 15 workers, or, if no mechanical power is used, more than 30 workers and employees.[23] In contrast, all enterprises owned and operated by counties (*hsien*) or sub-county units (e.g., communes or brigades) are defined as rural industry.

While these categories are clear and distinct, we have no continuous and comprehensive production series for these sub-sectors of industry. The data available indicate that in the 1930s handicrafts (embracing both individual handicrafts and handicraft factories) were a more important contributor to total manufacturing output than factory industry. This was reversed by 1952, and by 1957 only about one-fourth of industrial output (excluding mining and utilities) was produced in handicraft establishments.

There are no corresponding estimates for later periods.[24] Moreover, small-scale and rural industry expanded very rapidly at the height of the "backyard furnaces" movement during the Great Leap. A vast number of small-scale, labor-intensive enterprises was established in 1958 and 1959 in the cities and countryside. Many of these were set up without adequate attention to technical and economic considerations and the quality or usability of their product. As a result they did not survive for very long, but those that did were nationalized, began to grow, and were accorded increasing attention by the state organs in the course of the 1960s.

This whole development has been given a new boost and new emphasis since the Cultural Revolution. Thus the further and continuing expansion of small-scale industry on the one hand and of rural industry on the other has assumed a quite clearly defined role in China's overall development design. The role is essentially a twofold one. In part its origins can be traced to the "walking on two legs" strategy of the Great Leap, with its focus on alternative technologies and alternative methods applied to the production of a particular item. In these terms a range of industrial goods could be and indeed would be produced by more or less capital-intensive, more or less mechanized, or more or less large-scale methods of production. The particular method chosen would depend on the levels of skill and technology attained and the relative costs of labor and capital in different parts of China. The dominant consideration would be to find the best and least-cost (taking account of both direct and indirect costs, including transport cost) method of satisfying both producer and consumer demand for a particular commodity. This may mean that the same product would be produced both in small or medium-sized semi-mechanized factories and in large-scale, highly modern plants. In some cases the small, medium-sized, and large plants may be inter-related through subcontracting arrangements. Based on these, small plants may produce components that are assembled in the large factories. In effect, this leads to a more or less dualistic pattern of industrial development, in many ways akin to the industrialization path followed by Modern Japan.[25]

But this is only one of the vantage points from which this development was approached. Another and more prominent approach in China, particularly since the Cultural Revolution, stresses the role of rural industry in supporting the development and modernization of agriculture and the countryside as a whole. This has led to the establishment and growth of rural-based coal mining and chemical fertilizer, cement, farm machinery, steel, and power-generating plants. These are designed to meet locally agriculture's demand for producer goods. These industries can draw on locally supplied raw materials, on resources that have meager alternative employment opportunities (especially unskilled labor underemployed during certain seasons), and can lead to substantial savings in transport cost. They also play a major role in introducing new techniques and new methods of production into the countryside. Last but not least, they lead to local control over many local economic tasks and thereby lessen the burden on central administrative resources.

Under the impact of this rural industrial development, almost all simple farm tools, a substantial portion of basic farm machinery, and virtually all machine repair is supplied by local plants. As of 1974, 44 percent of China's chemical fertilizer (in terms of weight) was produced by such plants, as compared to 6 percent in 1960. More than half the country's cement is similarly produced. The 30 percent of coal extracted from local mines is mostly used for local industry, cooking, and heating in the countryside. Rural plants produce 15 percent of China's steel output, all of which is used in rural industry and construction.[26]

These rural plants are not necessarily small. The more important ones are county-operated state enterprises, frequently employing several hundred workers and relying on factory methods of production. However, their average size – both in terms of employment and output – is smaller, and they are less mechanized, using less advanced technology, than their counterparts in urban areas. More importantly, they play a crucial role in an integrated approach to agricultural and rural development. By providing locally produced inputs, thereby economizing on transport costs in a vast sub-continent with still quite inadequate overland communication, these rural industries foster agricultural modernization and increases in farm production. In addition, they encourage rural industry as a whole, expose elements of the peasantry to the industrial way of life, and serve to narrow the psychological and technical distance between both the city and the country and between the industrial workers and the peasantry.

Rates of growth and change in the economy

In preceding sections, the course of agricultural and industrial development was explored. Based on that analysis and on detailed national-product estimates for the 1950s, the growth performance of the economy as a whole will be assessed in this section.

This task is greatly complicated by the fact that there are no detailed and reasonably reliable national product estimates at our disposal for the period after 1957. Therefore, a variety of quite crude methods must be used to reconstruct GNP for the 1957 to 1974 period. The task is further complicated because there is no full agreement among students of the Chinese economy concerning the industrial and agricultural production growth rates. Most specialists use the official grain production series as a basis for estimating agricultural product. However, there are some who do not attach a high degree of credibility to these series, and therefore use output figures which are adjusted downward. Similarly, for industrial production, some investigators base their estimates on the official gross industrial production value data, while others use adjusted estimates which yield lower rates of growth. Therefore, the discrepancies of GNP estimates for China reflect both differences in methods and differences in the basic output series used.

Consequently, it is not surprising that there are differences in the average annual rates of growth derived by T. C. Liu and K. C. Yeh on the one hand, and by the U.S. government, D. H. Perkins, Thomas Rawski, and me on the other.[27] Against this background, the data in Table 6-6 represent no more than a tentative attempt to reconstruct a more or less hypothetical series based on certain assumptions. The 1957 estimate can be regarded as reasonably firm, since there were fairly detailed and quite reliable data available for that year, and these were systematically and carefully marshaled by Liu and Yeh. For 1952 I made a downward adjustment in the Liu and Yeh estimates to take account of what appears to most students of the Chinese economy as an overstatement of farm production in their estimate for that year.

In contrast to the earlier estimates, the figures for 1958 to 1974 are very

Table 6-6. *Gross domestic product in China, 1952–1974 (hypothetical estimates in billions of 1952 yuan)*

Year	GDP	Year	GDP
1952	73.8	1966	165.6
1957	100.8	1968	151.8
1958	138.4	1969	179.2
1959	148.5	1970	209.6
1964	130.7	1974	272.9
1965	145.1		

Sources: Estimates for 1952 and 1957 based on T. C. Liu and K. C. Yeh, *The Economy of the Chinese Mainland*, Princeton, N.J., 1965, Table 8, p. 66, with the 1952 figure adjusted downward. For an explanation of this adjustment and for the basis of estimates for the other years, see text.

tentative, and based on partial indicators. They were derived on the assumption that agricultural production as a whole changed from year to year at the same rate as grain production, so that an index based on the data in Table 6-2 and applied to 1957 farm product value could represent movements in total farm product. Similarly, the official gross output value index in Table 6-5 was applied to the 1957 industrial product estimate to derive the series for subsequent years. The service sector was broken down into two sub-sectors. It was assumed that transport, trade, banking, and finance were closely inter-related with the production of goods. Therefore they could be expected to move at more or less the same rate as commodity production, that is, farm and industrial output combined. On the other hand, government administration, personal services, and residential rent were correlated with population growth, which was assumed to have grown at an average annual rate of 2 percent between 1957 and 1974.

The data in Table 6-6 clearly demonstrate not only fairly rapid rates of economic growth, but underline once more the fluctuating character of China's economic development. As may be seen from both Tables 6-6 and 6-7, national product rose at a fairly steady rate between 1952 and 1957. At that pace, GDP would have doubled in a decade. However, there was a spurt in economic growth during the Great Leap, as evidenced by a rise in GDP of over 20 percent between 1957 and 1959; but by 1960, the beginnings of economic decline are quite evident. Between 1959 – the peak – and 1961 – the trough – GNP fell by about 20 percent. It then began to recover, but did not return to the 1959 level until 1965. Moreover, as a result of these ups and downs, the doubling of the 1952 product was also attained only in 1965. The Cultural Revolution pulled the economy down again; but, this was a mild and temporary interruption in the growth trend of the latter 1960s. This is evidenced by the fact that by 1970, the 1966 peak was subtantially exceeded once more, and growth continued more or less unabated.

Assuming that the hypothetical reconstruction of GNP in Table 6-6 reflects fairly well the actual behavior of the Chinese economy, it seems that the average annual rate of growth for the period as a whole (1952–1974) was about 6 percent. It was somewhat above this rate during the First Five-Year Plan and substantially above it during the Great Leap. It was, however, below it for the 1959–1970, or even the 1959–1974, periods. It is thus quite clear that, as a result of the depression in the early 1960s and the dip during the Cultural Revolution years, the growth performance of the Chinese economy was poorer in the 1960s than in the 1950s. This again illustrates the contrast in the pace of economic advance in the second decade as compared to the first. Significantly lower growth rates were obtained by Liu and Yeh in their GNP estimates, as illustrated by the data in Table 6-7. According to these data, the rate of growth ranged between 2.6 and 3.3 percent for the 1957 to 1970 period, which would include the Great Leap, the Great Crisis, and the Cultural Revolution years. In contrast, my hypothetical projections in Table 6-6 yield a growth rate of close to 6 percent for the same period. These large discrepancies are due to the fact that Liu and Yeh credit Chinese agriculture with much slower advances since 1963 than most other investigators suggest. At the same time, they rely on an industrial production index compiled by Field some years ago, which he has since revised significantly upward. In essence our estimates are based on the assumption that official Chinese data are credible, while Liu and Yeh reject these.

Regardless of which estimates are used, there is no question that these represent a dramatic acceleration in economic growth, as compared to China's past. While we have no GNP estimates for any ten- or twenty-year span for Republican China (1911–1949) or for the nineteenth century, it is most improbable that the economy at that time expanded faster than 1 or a maximim of 2 percent per year. Similarly, compared to the growth pace of presently industrialized countries, China's performance in the last twenty or twenty-five years must be considered quite impressive. This is evidenced by the fact that the long-term growth rate of Great Britain for the nineteenth century was about 2.5 percent a year; for France, about 2 percent; for Germany, slightly below 3 percent; for Sweden, the United States, and Canada, between 3 and

Table 6-7. *Average annual rates of growth of gross domestic product in China, 1952–1974 (in percent per year in terms of 1952 prices)*

Period	Rate of growth	Period	Rate of growth
1952–57	6.4	1959–66	1.6
1952–59	10.5	1959–74	4.2
1952–66	6.0		
1952–74	6.2	1966–74	6.5
1957–59	22.0	1957–70	
1957–66	5.7	Liu–Yeh (high)	3.3
1957–74	6.0	Liu–Yeh (low)	2.6
		A. Eckstein	5.8

Sources: Table 6-6 and T. C. Liu and K. C. Yeh, "Chinese and Other Asian Economies, A Quantitative Evaluation," *The American Economic Review, Papers and Proceedings,* May 1973, Table 5, p. 222.

3.5 percent; and for Japan, about 4 percent. In contrast, China's growth performance is less impressive in comparison with the pace of development of a number of other Asian countries in the post-war period. For instance, for the 1957–1970 period, the average annual rate of economic growth was about 9 percent in Taiwan, 10 percent in Japan, 8 percent in Korea, and close to 9 percent in Thailand. In India, it was about 3.5 percent.[28]

What all these indicators suggest is that China's economy has advanced at a fairly rapid speed during the past two decades. The rate of growth in GNP was appreciably higher than in India (at least based on the estimates in Tables 6-6 and 6-7). The performance gap of these two countries is even greater when aggregate growth is translated into per capita terms. Thus, per capita product may have risen at an average rate of about 1 percent in India, as compared to about 4 percent in China. However the per capita estimates for China are subject to additional uncertainties arising from the lack of population data. The late Premier Chou and other Chinese officials have stated on several occasions in recent years that the average rate of population growth is around 2 percent a year. It fluctuated between 2 and 2.5 percent in the 1950s, a period for which population series were published. Since the early 1960s the Chinese have embarked on very active programs of population planning; therefore, one would expect growth rates to have declined. But in the absence of hard data it may be safest to proceed on the assumption that the rate of population increase averages about 2 percent per year for the 1950 to 1975 or the 1952 to 1974 period as a whole. In evaluating the comparative performance of these two economies, it must also be borne in mind that India was the beneficiary of large-scale foreign aid as well. Thus India has been a net importer, while China has become a net exporter, of capital. This may have changed

Table 6-8. *National product, population, and per capita product trends in China, 1952–1974*

Year	GDP (in billions of 1952 yuan)	Population (in millions)	Per capita product (in 1952 yuan, rounded)
1952	73.8	575	130
1957	100.8	630	160
1970	210.0	820	260
1974	272.9	880	310

Sources: GDP from Table 6-6; population estimated on the assumption that it grew at an average rate of 2 percent a year.

somewhat since 1972, when China began to incur intermediate-term credits for the purchase of complete plants. Even with these, there is no question that the attainment of sustained growth rates involved much heavier savings and investment burdens for the Chinese than for the Indian economy.

The uncertainties surrounding the population figures necessarily affect the results in Table 6-8. In the absence of any officially published figures, two different sets of estimates have emerged. The first, developed by John Aird, assumes that population growth rates dipped briefly under the impact of rising death rates during the agricultural crisis of the early 1960s, but then resumed their earlier rate of increase, so that their average annual growth has been about 2.2 percent a year since 1964. Leo Orleans, on the other hand, assumes gradually declining rates, which by the 1970s yield about a 1.5 percent rate of growth. As a result, Aird estimates population at about 910 million in 1974, while Orleans places it close to 840 million.[29]

The discrepancies are largely due to the fact that Orleans assumes that the vigorous and far-reaching birth control measures of the 1960s did lead to a decline in the birth rate, following earlier declines in the death rate, so much so, that rates of natural increase were reduced. On the other hand, those who project a continuation of the population growth rates of the 1950s assume that the birth control measures have not yet reached sufficiently large segments of the population to have a significant impact. The population figures in Table 6-8 are between these two estimates, based on the assumption that both birth rates and death rates have declined, but perhaps not as rapidly as Orleans suggests, and not in ways which would yield as sharp a decline in rates of natural increase.

The estimates in Table 6-8 suggest that per capita product in China may have risen from about 130 yuan in 1952 to more than 300 in 1974, in terms of 1952 prices. Another element of uncertainty is added in any attempt to translate these yuan figures into U.S. dollars. Clearly, different results would be obtained, depending on whether one converts at the official exchange rate or at some kind of a purchasing-power parity rate. The latter would be the more appropriate one, but to derive it would require much more detailed information than we have at our disposal. On the other hand, the former would yield per capita incomes of approximately $55 for 1952 and $130 for 1974, based on exchange rates prevailing in 1952. In terms of current (rather than 1952) Chinese prices at presently prevailing exchange rates, the 1974 GDP per capita would go up to about $190. These figures almost certainly understate the purchasing power of incomes in China, probably even in terms of an American consumption pattern.

Implications of the structural shifts in the Chinese economy

As noted repeatedly throughout this volume, aggregate and per capita growth was closely linked to marked structural changes in the Chinese economy. In many respects, China's whole development pattern has been unusual as compared to other low-income economies. Typically, underdeveloped countries tend to have the preponderant share of their labor force in agriculture (60 to 80 percent), with close to half (40 to 60 percent) of their national product derived from that sector. However, in all countries the process of economic development has brought with it significant shifts in these ratios, leading to a gradual decline in the share of agricultural product and the proportion of the labor force engaged in agriculture. This seems to hold equally true when comparing countries at differing stages of development at one point of time, as well as a single country over long periods of time. This is perhaps one of the few generalizations one can make about the process of economic development which seems to hold with no exception.

There are a number of complex factors that contribute to this result. In most general terms, these trends are rooted in technological progress on the one hand, and in the character of demand for goods and services on the other. That is, as incomes rise in the process of economic advance, a proportionately smaller share of these incomes tends to be spent on bare necessities, particularly foodstuffs, and a correspondingly larger share is spent on clothing, housing, and certain kinds of services. This means that the demand for agricultural goods rises less rapidly than that for other products. On the other hand, technological advance permits increasing quantities of food and agricultural raw materials to be produced by a relatively smaller labor force. As a result, labor can be released from agriculture to other sectors where consumer demand is rising so rapidly that their labor requirements are rising, even in the face of rapid technological progress.

Seen in these terms and as evidenced by the data in Table 6-9, China followed the typical pattern of an underdeveloped, low-income country up to about 1952. Thus, in 1933, it had a product structure like that of the most underdeveloped countries. This was still essentially the case in 1952, although to a somewhat lesser degree. However, by the 1970s, it seems that only one-quarter, or one-fifth, of China's GDP was derived from agriculture, and perhaps as much as one-half was derived from industry. This means that, in terms of farm product shares, China would be equivalent to a middle-developed country, as seen in the upper half of Table 6-9, while in terms of its

Table 6-9. *Sectoral shares of gross domestic product for groups of countries, about 1958, and for China, 1933–1974*[a]

Groups of countries in increasing order of GDP per capita[b]		A	I	S
I	$ 51.8	53.6	18.5	27.9
II	82.6	44.6	22.4	33.0
III	138.0	37.9	24.6	37.5
IV	221.0	32.3	29.4	38.3
V	360.0	22.5	35.2	42.3
VI	540.0	17.4	39.5	43.1
VII	864.0	11.8	52.9	35.3
VIII	1,382.0	9.2	50.2	40.6
China				
1933		57	16	27
1952		47	21	32
1957		39	31	30
1966		28	44	28
1974		20	54	26

[a]A refers to agriculture, including forestry and fishing; *I* includes factory and small-scale industry, handicrafts, public utilities, and construction; *S* encompasses transport, trade, government, and all other services.

[b]For each group, this is an average per capita GDP for six countries.

Sources: The upper half of the table is from Simon Kuznets, *Economic Growth of Nations*, Cambridge, Mass., 1971, Table 12, p. 104. The lower half is based on Table 6-6 and explanation in the text except for 1933, 1952, and 1957. These are derived from T. C. Liu and K. C. Yeh, *The Economy of the Chinese Mainland*, Princeton, N.J., 1965, Table 8.

industrial share, it would compare with that of the most highly developed countries.

This suggests that China's whole development pattern has been unusual as compared to other economies. A similar phenomenon was noted in our analysis of China's industrial structure. Producer-goods industries loomed very large, as compared to consumer goods, as was shown in Table 6-3. That is, industry occupies an unusually large share of total national product and, within industry, the producer-goods branches loom unusually large as compared to other countries at similar stages of development.

China's development pattern is unusual in an additional sense. Trends such as those observed in Table 6-9 are almost invariably paralleled by similar tendencies in labor-force composition. That is, such marked changes in product structure are almost invariably accompanied by slower but nevertheless quite perceptible changes in labor-force structure. However, in the Chinese case, there is no indication that the rural labor-force share of approximately 75 to 80 percent has diminished. There is, of course, always the possibility that these unusual patterns may be more statistical than real. We have virtually no data at our disposal concerning labor-force composition, and only some fragmentary indications of the rural population share. Chinese statements repeatedly refer to 80 percent of the population being agricultural or rural. If it is rural, then, to the extent that part of it is engaged in small-scale industry, handicrafts, transport, trade and other service occupations in the rural areas, the actual agricultural labor-force ratio must be less than that. However, even under the most extreme assumptions, it could not be less than 60 to 70 percent.

These unusually large differences in labor and product shares in part reflect pricing distortions. These shares are also likely to be distorted by the method used for deriving the service sector estimated for 1966 and 1974. Therefore the services contribution to GDP may very well be under-stated and that for industry over-stated for these years. This tendency is undoubtedly reinforced by the fact that 1952 prices tend to under-value farm output and over-value industrial product. Since that time, agricultural procurement prices have been gradually rising and industrial prices have declined. Therefore, in terms of 1970 prices or current 1974 prices, industrial shares in Table 6-9 would be lower and agricultural shares higher.[30] However, even these price-adjusted shares would still place China's national product composition much higher in the "Kuznets scale" than its average per capita income would warrant.

The anomaly suggested by the estimates in Table 6-9 is compounded by the fact that in agriculture the labor-force shares did not follow the declining trend in product shares. As a result, about 70 to 80 percent of the country's labor force produced only about 20 to 30 percent of the product, while the remaining 70 to 80 percent of GDP was contributed by no more than 20 to 30 percent of the labor employed. This large discrepancy can be accounted for in part by government policy and in part by China's factor endowments. In a land-short economy, a sustained rise in farm output can be obtained only by continuous increases in yields per acre. This, in turn, can only be accomplished by stepping up the intensity of land use, year by year. In a capital-scarce economy this calls for increasing applications of labor and other production requisites (e.g., chemical fertilizer) to the land. For this, as well as other reasons, government policy has deliberately been designed to stem the migration of labor from the country to the city. Moreover, from time to time, back-migration from urban to rural areas was strongly encouraged. As a result of all these tendencies, labor productivity differentials between agricultural and non-agricultural sectors have probably increased rather than decreased. In 1957, these differentials were already larger in China than for any other country for which we have GNP and labor-force estimates. If farm labor shares indeed have not changed significantly in the intervening years, and if the economy actually followed the path pictured in Tables 6-6, 6-7, and 6-9, then inter-sectoral labor productivity differentials must have increased rather than decreased. One would expect that sooner or later rising labor productivity would induce pressures for rising consumption. Therefore, if inter-sectoral labor productivity differentials are widening rather than narrowing, it may be more difficult to reduce the income and standard of living gap between country and city.

How was this rapid growth and marked structural transformation attained in China? The experience of modern economic growth since the industrial revolution in England indicates that the crucial ingredients of this process are based on the application of science to the methods of production, as represented by technical progress, combined with a growth in the labor force and a growth in the capital stock. However, economic expansion has not only been the result of increasing application of labor and capital, but also reflects significant improvements in the quality of that labor and that capital. There is no question that these tendencies are clearly observable in the Chinese case. Unfortunately, it is very difficult to quantify these inputs due to a lack of adequate data, and therefore it is virtually impossible to determine what share of China's economic growth can be ascribed simply to growth in labor and capital, and what portion to technological progress and the rising productivity of these factors of production.

What data we have suggest that the non-agricultural labor force increased by about 8 percent between 1952 and 1957. The total labor force increased at least as rapidly as that. If this was indeed the case, then during the First Five-Year Plan period, there was at most a quite modest change in the ratio of non-agricultural employment. Since the rate of industrial growth in the 1960s was less rapid than in the First Five-Year Plan period, while total labor-force growth probably did not slow down significantly, this too would reinforce the impression of no significant change in the labor-force ratios. It is therefore probable that the agricultural labor force may have risen just about at the same rate as total population, that is, somewhere between 1.5 and 2 percent a year. At the same time, the data in Table 6-2 indicate that agricultural production did not rise much faster than that. This means that average labor productivity in agriculture must have remained more or less stationary. On the other hand, labor productivity in industry – where product grew at an average annual rate of about 11 percent per year while labor force increased at perhaps not much more than a 2 percent rate – must have been rising at a very rapid rate, again suggesting an increasing divergence between agricultural and industrial product per worker.

This process of growth and structural transformation was decisively affected by an improvement in the quality of the non-agricultural labor force. Increasing literacy, rising levels of general education, and a rapidly expanding number of trained technical, scientific, and managerial personnel have almost certainly brought about a significant improvement in the quality of human resources and thus have contributed to the process of economic growth in China.

Another and most important aspect of this development was brought about by quite high rates of investment. This rate rose from about 11 percent in 1952 to about 20 percent in 1957, and a peak of 30 percent in 1958. It shrank drastically during the depression of the early 1960s, but has probably fluctuated between 20 and 25 percent since that time. These are quite high rates by the standards of all countries – developed or underdeveloped – although they are by no means unprecedented, even in other underdeveloped countries. This investment in fixed capital leading to the creation of new production capacity and of more modern mechanical methods of production constitutes an essential ingredient of modern economic growth. Much of technological progress, improved methods of production, and better techniques are embodied in the new capital constructed. That is, much of technological progress is embodied in this process of capital formation.

In sum, the rapid advance in industrial production and GNP reflects not only increasing applications of labor and capital resulting from continuously high investments. On the contrary, it also reflects a constant improvement in the quality of the human and capital resources, which then yield decisive increases in the productivity of both labor and capital.

7

The role of foreign trade in China's economic development

The gains from trade

As shown in the preceding chapter, China's economic growth since 1949 has been very impressive by the standards of China's past development and compared with the pace of expansion of presently industrialized countries in the nineteenth century. It has also been quite rapid, although not exceptional, in comparison with the post-war growth tempo of other underdeveloped countries. It is evident that in terms of two major criteria – stability, analyzed in Chapter 5, and growth, examined in Chapter 6 – the performance of the Chinese economy must be rated highly for the last quarter century.

Foreign trade has played a marginal but very significant role both in maintaining stability and in contributing to growth. Grain imports during the agricultural crisis years of the early 1960s helped to alleviate food shortages, particularly in the cities. Thereby they also helped to contain inflationary pressures, especially at that time, but since then as well. Imports of machinery, transport equipment, complete plants, and other capital goods fostered China's industrialization, modernization, and technological progress, and in this way contributed to China's economic growth. The course and changing structure of foreign trade can also serve as a very useful indicator of stability and growth in ways that will be explored in this chapter.

Before proceeding with this analysis, one needs to ask why do countries engage in international trade. Are there gains from trade? International trade clearly creates greater dependence on the rest of the world. Does it also yield substantial benefits and, if so, what are these?

Significant potential gains accrue to an economy that takes advantage of the international division of labor and specialization across national boundaries. These gains are rooted in the fact that certain types of goods can be bought more cheaply abroad than they can be produced at home, and vice versa. These cost differences arise from specialization on the one hand and differences in resource endowments and in the accumulation of man-made skills and machinery on the other.

Some individuals have greater ability for certain tasks than others. Even if all individuals had exactly the same natural abilities, specialization in a limited number of occupations would still be advantageous. In this way much greater skill can be acquired than if everyone produced everything for himself. There results an increase in skill and a saving of time when each individual is occupied in the production of a large number of one particular commodity instead of cooperating in the production of a small quantity of many various goods.[1]

Countries or regions, like individuals, are quite differently endowed with supplies of productive factors. Some areas have relatively more of one set of factors and less of another. Thus some areas may be abundantly supplied with land, but have a relatively scarce labor supply. This has traditionally been the case in North America, and parts of South America, Africa, and Oceania. In contrast, the reverse holds for China, which has been characterized by a relative scarcity of land and a relative abundance of labor. Therefore each area is best equipped to produce those goods that require large proportions of the factors relatively abundant there. It will tend to export such goods and import those in which other countries have a comparative advantage and which are therefore relatively cheaper abroad.

These advantages of specialization are particularly pronounced for small as compared to large economies. Large economies usually contain within their national boundaries varied and reasonably abundant natural resources. Moreover, large economies provide ample opportunity for regional specialization and an internal division of labor. Given the size of their markets, they can also take advantage of economies of scale within their national units. Therefore it is not surprising to find that, typically, large countries have small foreign trade shares in relation to GNP as compared to small countries. Thus foreign trade turnover (exports and imports combined) ratios have been around 10 to 15 percent for the United States, less than 10 percent for India, and around 15 percent for Brazil, as compared to over 80 percent for the Netherlands, 30 to 40 percent for the United Kingdom, and about 20 percent for Japan. They have possibly been around 6 percent for China and 5 to 6 percent for the Soviet Union.[2]

These ratios are necessarily subject to sizable margins of error arising from several sources. The GNP estimates for China are subject to considerable uncertainty. Moreover, these are derived in Chinese prices expressed in yuan values. However, as will be shown later on, China's foreign trade has to be reconstructed from the trading-partner side, all expressed in U.S. dollars. It is far from clear at what rates these dollars should be converted into yuan, that is, whether it should be the official exchange rate or some estimated purchasing-power parity rate. Depending on what conversion method is used, China's foreign trade ratios could range between 2 and 20 percent. More realistically, they probably fall within a 4 to 8 percent range.

Of course, these ratios are not constant from year to year nor over longer periods. They reflect changes in economic structure, stages of development, and economic policy. In the Chinese case, it is quite clear that, in the 1950s, the economy was becoming gradually more foreign-trade-oriented. This is evidenced by the fact that China's foreign trade (imports and exports combined) rose at an average annual rate of close to 14 percent between 1952 and 1959, while GNP grew at a 10 to 11 percent rate. This trend was reversed in the 1960s. Thus while GNP continued to grow, although at a significantly lower rate, in 1970 foreign trade turnover measured in constant dollars (i.e., adjusted for price changes) was still below 1959 levels. However, in the early 1970s foreign trade began to expand once more quite rapidly. As a result, for the 1952–1974 period as a whole it seems that foreign trade rose only somewhat more slowly than the average annual GNP rate of about 6 percent.

Although foreign trade was relatively unimportant for the Chinese economy in aggregate terms, imports played a most significant role in structural and development terms. Imports of capital goods served as a major avenue for the transfer of advanced technology from abroad. During the 1950s these imports played a very large role in China's investment program, contributing about 40 percent to the equipment component of investment. These ratios declined significantly in the 1960s, but recovered somewhat in the 1970s. Thus the import component of investment in recent years may be around 10 percent.[3] It has been estimated that if China had completely cut itself off from imports between 1953 and 1957, the country's economic growth would have been reduced from an average annual rate of about 6.5 percent to possibly 3 to 5 percent.[4] Presently available data are insufficient to make a similar estimate for the 1970s, but China's industrial progress over the past twenty years would make the cost of total autarky almost certainly substantially less. Import supplies also played an essential role in the provision of military matériel, particularly in the 1950s, and probably still do, although to an unknown and probably smaller degree. In sharp contrast, food imports were quite unimportant at that time, but acquired great significance in the 1960s.

With the onset of an acute agricultural crisis between 1959 and 1962, China began to experience very severe shortages of food. Large-scale grain imports were initiated, at first on an emergency basis, which relieved the situation relatively easily and quickly. However, these imports, which at first contributed to China's economic and political stability, became a normal part of the country's food supply. They were particularly important in provisioning the cities and in building up and maintaining grain reserves. They served to ease the burden on the country's transport system and reduce the extraction pressure on the peasantry. Thus it may for instance be simpler and less costly to ship grain from Vancouver to Shanghai than overland from the remote surplus-producing province of Szechwan.

This is illustrated by the fact that during the depth of China's economic and agricultural crisis in 1961–1962, food grain imports may have augmented domestic supplies available to the army and the urban population by about 30 to 40 percent, although they constituted less than 4 percent of total output.[5] In the 1970s the latter ratio was only about 1 to 2 percent, while the share of food grain imports in the urban food supply may at most constitute 10 percent.

In addition to grain, machinery and equipment, metals, and chemical fertilizer have continued to be of crucial importance in China's economic development, particularly in the 1970s. Between 1970 and 1974, China imported about 35 million tons of fertilizer (in terms of gross weight); in nutrient content this provided one-quarter of China's total fertilizer supply. Although imported machinery and equipment played a much smaller role in total capital formation than in the 1950s, it was very important as a means of transferring advanced technology from abroad and thus accelerating China's technological progress. Its importance is also attested to by the fact that in the 1970s one-fourth of China's total imports went into machinery and equipment, that is about the same share as during the First Five-Year Plan (FFYP) period (1953–1957). In marked contrast, imports of metals, particularly specialty iron and steel products as well as non-ferrous metals, rose greatly in importance from about less than 10 percent of China's purchases abroad in the FFYP period to about 25 percent in the 1970s.

The foreign trade policies of the People's Republic of China

Since the founding of the People's Republic, China's foreign trade policies reflect a complex interaction between its foreign policies, its internal political developments, and the dictates of economic necessity or comparative advantage.

In the 1950s, when China pursued a very active foreign trade orientation, this occurred within the context of a rather tightly knit Sino-Soviet alliance on the one hand and an ambitious industrialization program on the other. A policy directed toward maximizing the rate of industrial growth and building up China's defense establishment could at that time be implemented only by large-scale imports of capital goods and military matériel from the Soviet Union and Eastern Europe. This was further reinforced by the fact that strategic trade controls by the United States and its allies denied these products to China.

Therefore economic and foreign policy combined led China to a preponderantly Soviet trade orientation. However these policies not only shaped the direction of trade and its commodity composition, but minimized the resistance to foreign trade dependence itself. As Sino-Soviet tensions mounted there was some rising concern about China's preponderant dependence on a single trading partner, but there were no signs of animosity toward the import of foreign technology or the "worship of foreign things," nor were there any strong pressures for autarky at that time.

These attitudes changed radically following the Sino-Soviet split of 1960. China's dependence on the Soviet Union was clearly evidenced by the fact that from 60 to 80 percent of its trade was with the Communist Bloc in the 1950s. During the same period the Soviet Union extended credits of $1.4 to $2.2 billion (depending on how these are estimated and converted from rubles and yuan into dollars), and sent about 11,000 Soviet specialists and technicians to China; to this must be added another 1,500 technicians from Eastern Europe.[6] The credits were phased out by 1957, and the technicians were withdrawn suddenly and abruptly in 1960 with attendant disruptions in Chinese industry, in some other sectors, and most notably in defense. This experience dramatized to the Chinese the high potential costs of dependence on any one country or any one source of supply.

This sharp turnabout happened to coincide with a profound agricultural and economic crisis in China reflecting the far-reaching planning and technical errors during the Great Leap, which contributed to a series of very poor harvests. There is no doubt that the economic crisis was further aggravated by the sudden Soviet withdrawal. Thus the marked reduction in foreign trade between 1959 and 1962 (as shown in Table 7-1, p. 246) was a reflection of the depressed state of the Chinese economy which affected its import demand as well as its export capacity.

As the Chinese economy recovered from this deep depression, foreign trade was being restored as well, but at a slower pace than GNP. Thus while trade was leading growth in the 1950s, it was lagging behind it in the 1960s. In part this was due to the fact that a large number of complete plants imported in the late 1950s were still in the process of construction when the Soviet technicians suddenly left in 1960. Many were left standing in this uncompleted stage since even existing and completed plants were at that time operating well below capacity. As a result, there was no need to complete them until recovery was well under way in the mid-1960s.

The completion of these plants greatly expanded China's domestic capacity to produce machinery and a wide assortment of investment goods. Other things being equal, this in itself would have contributed to at least a temporary reduction in import demand. However, this tendency was reinforced by a strong emphasis on self-reliance, buttressed by a series of major campaigns. At least initially, this clearly represented a strong reaction to the Sino-Soviet break. However this policy was gradually broadened to encompass internal as well as external economic policy considerations and as such became firmly institutionalized.

Self-reliance never meant complete autarky, but rather a deliberate pursuit of an import substitution and import minimization policy. The pursuit of this policy entailed at least some isolation of Chinese science, technology and industry from the rest of the world in the 1960s. It also meant that China was cutting herself off from the world's capital markets and from access to even short- or medium-term commercial loans, not to speak of long-term credits. Under the impact of this policy foreign purchases of machinery, transport equipment, and other capital goods were probably reduced to lower levels than might otherwise have prevailed.

To the extent that capital-goods imports serve as a major highway for the transfer of technology, this must have been a factor slowing down the rate of technological progress. At the same time, this posture left many enterprises to their own devices, forcing them to improvise or, to use the Chinese phrase, "take the initiative in their own hands." This meant that, for instance, in a number of cases if certain components of machinery became worn out they had to be replaced by domestically manufactured components. This led to "learning by doing." Although this may have initially led to quite high-cost and inefficient methods of production in many places, it almost certainly stimulated the rapid diffusion of production techniques already known and in process somewhere within China, including those that were relatively advanced. Therefore it is difficult to assess whether on balance self-reliance retarded or accelerated technological progress.

Self-reliance rhetoric and campaigns attained their height during the Cultural Revolution. As the active phase of the Cultural Revolution came to a halt in 1968–1969 and normalcy gradually gained ground, Chinese policy makers began to weigh the costs of self-reliance against those of economic dependence on others. Out of this search for a new policy optimum there gradually crystallized a series of decisions, apparently made at the highest levels, between 1970 and 1972, which involved a reinterpretation of the concept of self-reliance. These trade-policy issues were, however, faced in the broader context of China's domestic and foreign policies, in both their economic and political aspects. To understand this process we must reach back into the Cultural Revolution, its aftermath, and some of the events that led to the fall of Lin Piao.

The fall of Lin Piao in September 1971 – and his death in an airplane crash between China and Russia – marked the culmination of a period in which the role of the military in China had been very much enlarged. With the virtual disintegration of the Party apparatus during the Cultural Revolution (1966 to 1968), the army was called upon to perform many Party roles and to serve as the integrating cement holding the polity and economy together.

This enlarged political role of the army was reinforced by rising Sino-Soviet tensions, aggravated by the enunciation of the Brezhnev doctrine and the Soviet invasion of Czechoslovakia in 1968. The perception of a grave Soviet threat apparently spread and gained increasing credibility in China thereafter. The accumulated tensions exploded in the Chenpao (Damyanski) Island incident of March 1969, leading to large-scale border clashes between Soviet and Chinese troops along the Amur River border. All these developments seem to have prompted a rapid rise in military outlays between 1969 and 1971.

However, following Lin Piao's death, the Chinese leadership appears to have engaged in a fundamental reappraisal of its internal and external policies. In part, of course, this reappraisal must already have been under way, as shown by Mao's interview with Edgar Snow in December 1970, in which he indicated that then-President Nixon would be welcome to visit China "either as a tourist or as President."[7]

Perhaps most notably, the steep rise in military expenditures was not only halted but reversed, so that since 1972 – according to analyses recently published – Chinese military expenditures may have declined by as much as 25 percent, measured in constant dollars.[8] Never formally announced by the Chinese leaders, the reasons for this abrupt change can only be surmised: one, quite possibly, was that the perception of a direct Soviet threat seemed less acute, with the reopening of relations with the United States virtually assured after the secret Kissinger trip of mid-1971. Chinese policy makers may have begun to rely implicitly and tacitly at least on American deterrence to check incipient or overt Soviet expansionist tendencies in Asia, at least in the short run; in the longer run they would seek to build a "powerful, modern, socialist state."

Internal needs and developments must also have contributed to the shift in the allocation of resources. As the Party was being reconstituted in the post–Cultural Revolution period, it once more bid for supremacy of control over all institutions, including the army. Shrinking military expenditures would have necessarily involved some reduction in the army's control over resources. At the same time, the Cultural Revolution–engendered disruptions had led to a decline in the non-agricultural sectors of the economy, and there was also an accumulated backlog of investment foregone during this period. These deficiencies had been made more acute by the subordination of economic requirements to military claims on resources, particularly between 1969 and 1971.

It seems probable that debate on these issues was acute while Lin was still alive and in good standing, and that he himself was deeply involved. Whether his fall reflected or triggered a denouement we shall perhaps never know. In any case, the full thrust of a new line of policy began to emerge after his death. It was apparently decided that China would once again pursue a more open foreign trade orientation and launch an active program of technological imports from abroad. At the same time, in order to minimize the vulnerabilities and risks of dependence, China would limit its reliance on any single source of supply and its overall financial or credit dependence on foreign countries.

Basically, this new line raises the priority ranking assigned to sustained and long-range economic development. It is evidenced by the new wave of economic expansion experienced in China since 1970, and by the large number of new projects launched since early 1972. This reordering of priorities can at least in part be traced back to the receding sense of a direct Soviet threat referred to above. It was most clearly, explicitly, and authoritatively enunciated in the late Premier Chou En-lai's "Report on the Work of the Government," delivered at the National People's Congress in January 1975, in which he sketched his hopes for China's future economic development. He spoke of turning "a poverty-stricken and backward country into a socialist one *with the beginnings of prosperity in only twenty years and more.*" Before the end of the century – according to Premier Chou's program – China "is to *accomplish the comprehensive modernization of agriculture, industry, national defense and science and technology so that our national economy will be advancing in the front ranks of the world.*"[9]

From the standpoint of foreign economic policy, the key point is that the leadership seems to have recognized that the central elements in the new policy – increased investment, stress on more fertilizer production and other agricultural assistance, and advanced technology generally – inevitably called for increased imports of capital goods and even of some capital (i.e., some forms of foreign credit). It was not possible to proceed very far along this road without coming into conflict with the more or less autarkic Chinese foreign trade policy that dominated the 1960s.

Consequently, the self-reliance policy had to be reformulated. One of the most tangible signs of a policy shift was the reactivation of the Technical Export–Import Corporation in late 1972 and the very large number of orders placed by the Chinese for the importation of complete plants. It is estimated that the aggregate value of these turnkey contracts concluded between late 1972 and late 1974 is around $2.5 billion.[10]

The new policy was also articulated explicitly in several publications, of which perhaps an article in the *People's Daily* of October 15, 1974, is one of the most significant. It states that

> the basic principles of our socialist foreign trade are maintaining independence, keeping the initiative in our own hands, relying on our own efforts, *achieving equality and mutual benefit, and each making up what the other lacks*. . . . By advocating the principle of maintaining independence and keeping the initiative in our own hands, *we never mean that we advocate a policy of exclusion*. . . . We have consistently held that *it is necessary to vigorously develop commerce and trade and carry out economic and technical exchanges with various countries and that these are necessary for and conducive to promoting the economic development of various countries.*

This was then further elaborated a few days later in an NCNA (New China News Agency) broadcast indicating that "*China uses foreign trade to stimulate production, scientific research and internal trade. . . . China imports certain new techniques and industrial equipment in line with* the principle of '*making foreign things serve China.' This serves* to reinforce the country's potentials of self-reliance *and accelerate* her socialist construction."[11]

However, this policy shift encountered greater or lesser resistance all along from the ideological "left," who were strongly opposed to "worshipping foreign things." Thus several articles appeared in the *People's Daily* and in *Red Flag* attacking a more open foreign trade orientation during the anti-

Confucian campaign in 1974. Similar voices cropped up periodically during 1975.

This anti-foreign-trade campaign gained in vigor and virulence after the death of Chou En-lai and the attendant purge of Teng Hsiao-p'ing. For example, the April 1976 issue of *Red Flag* carried an article entitled "Criticize the Slavish Compradore Philosophy" attacking that "unrepentant capitalist roader" who, it said, last year called for "pinning hope on foreign countries for the development of production and the development of science and technology"; at the same time he clamored for "bringing out more things to exchange for the latest and best foreign equipment." *Red Flag* then went on to argue that to exchange exports for imports in an unprincipled way would invariably lead to a situation where

> . . . we import everything that we can produce without restriction, export everything that is badly needed in the country without restriction, buy what is advanced from others, produce what is backward ourselves, and *even give to others the sovereign right to open up mineral resources*. Then, as time passed, would we not turn our country into a market where the imperialist countries dump their goods, a raw material base, a repair and assembly workshop, and an investment center?

What has been the impact of these sharp controversies on actual trade policy and behavior? As noted above the series of decisions made between 1970 and 1972 led to a greater involvement of China in the world economy. This is clearly illustrated by the very rapid growth in exports and imports – both in terms of current and constant prices – between 1970 and 1973. Why the slowing down in 1974 and 1975 (see Table 7-1, p. 246)?

Under the impact of a large new investment program in the Fourth Five-Year Plan the imports of machinery, equipment, and other producer goods were greatly stepped up, particularly in 1973. Moreover due to an inferior harvest in 1972, imports of agricultural products – grain, cotton, and soybeans – were sharply increased. Therefore, in 1973 there was a marked expansion in both industrial and agricultural imports at one and the same time. This was also the year that marked the height of the world economic boom, so that China readily found markets for its expanding exports, thus earning the necessary foreign exchange with which to cover its growing import needs.

This situation was radically altered by the onset of a prolonged world *stagflation*. Given the development priorities set by the Fourth Five-Year Plan, China continued its large investment program linked to the importation of complete plants and other types of investment goods. At the same time it was found necessary to continue agricultural imports at record levels. Amidst a raging world inflation all these products had to be imported at high world prices. At the same time in the face of a world recession, and an attendant decline in effective demand in most markets, China encountered great difficulties in placing its exports. As a result, imports expanded much faster than exports in 1974, thus producing China's largest trade deficit since 1949, of about one billion dollars.

This required a curtailment in import orders as a means of narrowing the trade gap. This was evidenced by a very sharp reduction in the placement of new complete plant import contracts and the stretch-out of grain shipments, both evident in the last quarter of 1974. This policy was continued in 1975, so that exports and imports rose very little in terms of current prices and almost certainly declined in real quantum terms.

There has been a great deal of speculation that the slowing down and virtual halt in new complete plant contracts reflected a shift back to a more autarkic trade policy under the pressure of the anti-Confucian campaign and the attacks on foreign trade dependence cited above. And that the same reasons explain the general slow-down in China's trade in the last year or two. While this possibility cannot be ruled out, as I tried to show above, recent foreign trade trends seem to reflect an interaction between China's internal development requirements and world economic trends rather than a shift in trade policy back in an autarkic direction.

This conclusion is buttressed by the fact that even amidst these vituperative attacks on foreign trade, even in the early months of 1976, both high-ranking and working-level officials of the foreign trade ministry and of the ministry of foreign affairs have repeatedly gone out of their way to reassure visiting foreign statesmen as well as businessmen that China plans to continue an active import and export program without any marked shifts in overall trade policy. This of course does not mean that the possibility of a shift can be eliminated, but merely that thus far the anti-trade opposition does not seem to have prevailed. At the same time, it is not entirely clear how seriously or literally these attacks are meant. Many statements are full of ambiguities and contradictions; moreover they must be interpreted as part and parcel of a much broader political struggle for the succession to Chou and Mao in which a great deal of exaggerated rhetoric is used to attack former Vice-Premier Teng Hsiao-p'ing and other opponents.

Irrespective of these controversies, it is striking that Chinese statements concerning trade policy and the potential gains from trade seem to place primary stress on the role of imports rather than exports. This is in contrast to conventional and traditional approaches to foreign trade, which place the emphasis on the role of exports and export-led growth.

This attitude is in part a reflection of the fact that in general centrally planned command economies tend to have a pronounced autarkic bias. Therefore foreign trade policy controversies revolve around the margin, that is not around questions of "either-or," but rather "how much more or less." This bias is motivated by several types of considerations. Trends in the world economy are much more difficult to forecast than at home; therefore involvement in the international economy adds an element of uncertainty and unpredictability that is necessarily disconcerting from a planner's point of view. Moreover in such a system enterprises are not aggressively sales-and-profit-maximization oriented; they produce for the plan, based on certain targets, with outlets for their products guaranteed. They have no incentive to seek markets for their products abroad. In essence, they are supply- rather than demand-oriented.

This tendency is strongly reinforced by the sharp separation in China and in many other command economies of producers and traders. That is, producing enterprises are not in any way involved in foreign trade. They virtually never deal directly with foreign buyers or sellers. Rather, they deal with foreign trade corporations that have a sole export–import monopoly in a broad product line (e.g., cereals, machinery, etc.). Therefore the whole marketing burden falls on these corporations rather than on the producing enterprises.

The planner charged with maximizing the rate of economic growth or some alternative economic goal articulates and elaborates the production or other plans. In the process he discovers certain shortages in raw material supplies either because certain minerals or other natural resources are not found within the country's boundaries, not available in the requisite quantities, or obtainable only at unusually high costs of extraction and/or transport. At the same time, for output to grow as production ceilings are reached with existing plant capacity, the pressures mount for new investment, and for expanding plant and equipment. In developing economies many types of machinery and equipment either cannot be produced at home or can only be produced with great difficulty, at high cost and poor quality. The more complex and technologically advanced such machinery is, the more probable that it will have to be imported from abroad.

In addition, imports can alleviate certain rigidities in the planning process. As certain anticipated and particularly unanticipated shortages or production bottlenecks develop, they can often be more quickly and easily removed –

and with less disruptive consequences for the planning process – by imports than by reallocations of domestic supplies. Therefore imports may play a crucial role in supplying raw material and food, in alleviating short-term bottlenecks, in supplying some major investment components, and in serving as the highway for the importation of technology. This imported technology is of critical importance in pacing the rate of technological progress in the developing country, both in its embodied form as machinery and in its dis-embodied form as know-how, blueprints, and other kinds of technical information.

In this type of economic system, under the conditions of an underdeveloped and continental economy, and for all the reasons cited above, the motivating force for foreign trade comes from the import rather than export side. The need to import provides the inducement to search for export supplies and export surpluses in order to finance imports. This seems to have characterized the approach of Soviet planners earlier and of Chinese planners since their First Five-Year Plan (1953–1957).

The evolution of China's foreign trade

China's foreign-trade pattern is characterized by dramatic contrasts between the 1950s, 1960s, and 1970s, as shown in Table 7-1. Trade rose very rapidly in the first decade, more or less stagnated in the second, and expanded again in recent years. Between 1952 (used as a reference year because by then the Chinese economy had recovered from war devastation) and 1959, foreign-trade turnover rose by about 140 percent (i.e., at an average annual rate of about 13 to 14 percent) while GNP increased by 100 percent. As a result, China's trade expanded much faster than total world trade, the trade of all underdeveloped countries, or the trade of all Asian countries as a group. During this same period world trade rose at an annual rate of about 5 percent, that of underdeveloped countries more than 2 percent, and that of Asia (excluding Japan and China) less than 1 percent.[12] Also in these years the Chinese economy was becoming more open, more foreign trade oriented; in a certain sense it experienced trade-led growth. How can one account for this?

This foreign trade performance appears somewhat less impressive when viewed from the vantage point of a longer-run historical perspective. China's trade had attained a peak level in 1928 and 1929. These trade volumes (in terms of constant prices) were then not surpassed until 1954 on the import side and until 1955 or 1956 on the export side. Therefore the unusually rapid trade expansion of the early 1950s was undoubtedly in part paced by a recov-

Table 7-1. *China's foreign trade, 1952–1974 (in millions of U.S. dollars)*

	In current prices			In constant 1963 prices		
Year	Exports	Imports	Total turnover	Exports	Imports	Total turnover
1952	875	1,015	1,890	795	1,005	1,800
1955	1,375	1,660	3,035	1,295	1,715	3,010
1959	2,230	2,060	4,290	2,315	2,085	4,400
1961	1,525	1,490	3,015	1,540	1,520	3,060
1962	1,525	1,150	2,675	1,585	1,180	2,765
1966	2,210	2,035	4,245	2,155	1,915	4,070
1967	1,945	1,950	3,895	1,930	1,840	3,770
1968	1,945	1,820	3,765	1,920	1,735	3,655
1969	2,030	1,830	3,860	1,920	1,690	3,610
1970	2,050	2,240	4,290	1,865	1,890	3,755
1971	2,415	2,305	4,720	2,180	1,880	4,060
1972	3,085	2,835	5,920	2,570	2,115	4,685
1973	4,960	5,130	10,090	3,039	2,847	5,886
1974	6,515	7,490	14,005	2,856	3,200	6,056

Sources: Current price series from N. R. Chen, "China's Foreign Trade, 1950–74," in *China: A Reassessment of the Economy,* Joint Economic Committee, U.S. Congress, July 1975, p. 645. Constant price data based on deflators derived by A. Eckstein, "China's Economic Growth and Foreign Trade," in *U.S.–China Business Review,* vol. 1, no. 4 (July–August 1974). For 1973 and 1974, trade data in current prices obtained from Central Intelligence Agency, Research Aid, *People's Republic of China, International Trade Handbook,* October 1975, p. 9; these were converted into 1963 prices for 1973 and 1974 on the basis of deflators derived by N. R. Chen in the article cited above.

ery element. However, trade continued to rise at an only slightly less speedy rate between 1954–1956 and 1959.

To explain these trends, we must look to the relationship between domestic levels of economic activity and imports. As noted earlier, in China exports seem to follow imports. Their primary function seems to be the financing of current and past purchases from abroad. In the early 1950s, the Chinese received sizable credits from the Soviet Union, which enabled them to maintain a trade deficit, with imports exceeding exports. These credits then began to be repaid in export shipments so that, beginning in 1955, we see the emergence of trade surpluses. However, these surpluses in effect represented payments for past deficits.

The 1950s represented a period of rapid, forced-draft industrialization, more or less on the pattern of the first two Soviet five-year plans (1928–1937). This meant that preponderant emphasis was placed on the development of the basic industries: electric power, coal, iron and steel, cement, and machine building. Rapid industrial expansion could only be achieved by greatly extending the country's production capacity. This, in turn, was reflected in the very sharp rise of both the levels and the rates of investment. That is, investment was not only increasing, but was growing much more rapidly than GNP. It rose from an estimated 8 billion yuan in 1952 to 35 billion in 1959, that is, at an average annual rate of about 24 percent.[13]

To finance such a marked investment rise, rates of saving had to be stepped up greatly. Therefore one of the major functions of the institutional transformation analyzed in Chapters 3 and 4 was to create the conditions of control over the economy that would guarantee a high rate of saving by households and particularly by agricultural collectives and non-farm enterprises.

Just as China was building its industrial base, so was it creating a modern military establishment. To support this establishment required rapid expansion of defense production and of factories producing military matériel. However, large-scale production of fighters, bombers, tanks, and other major elements of modern warfare was beyond the capability of the People's Republic in the early 1950s. Consequently, these items had to be imported, mostly from the Soviet Union and Eastern Europe. As a result, the two major sources of import demand were rapidly rising investment and the import components associated with it, and the rise of a modern military establishment. Therefore, machinery, equipment, and intermediate products for the manufacture of these and military items combined, accounted for approximately 70 percent of China's total imports in the 1950s.

In marked contrast, we encounter an entirely different pattern of trade behavior in the 1960s. Food crop production declined by about 25 percent between 1958 and 1960. Three successive bad harvests, due partly to bad weather and partly to errors in planning and economic management, produced an acute agricultural and food crisis. This gradually spilled over into the rest of the economy and was reflected in declines in industrial production, consumption, and trade. The process of contraction led to a curtailment of investment and industrial raw material demand, which was reflected in a sharp drop of imports, by about two-fifths between 1959 and 1962.

Thus we see a new pattern emerging, in which machinery and military imports recede in importance and their place is taken by foods, at a time when total purchases from abroad are shrinking. However, declining imports not only reflect a contracting domestic demand under the impact of the depression but also a decreasing export capacity. Amidst substantial drops in farm and industrial production, export supplies were also falling, affecting China's ability to finance imports at pre-depression levels. This condition was aggravated by the fact that the Chinese felt compelled to maintain trade surpluses even during these depression years as a means of repaying Soviet loans. Therefore export supplies available for financing import purchases were even more limited.

The 1962 harvest marked an upturn in China's agricultural production, and by 1963 grain production had virtually recovered to the pre–Great Leap and pre-depression level of 1957. A general economic recovery followed suit, as analyzed in greater detail in the preceding chapter. By 1966 foreign trade recovered close to the former 1959 peak level. It then experienced a temporary setback under the impact of the Cultural Revolution. Trade volumes declined in 1967 and 1968 partly due to some decline in industrial production and partly to disruptions in transport and shipping. By 1969 and 1970, however, exports and imports began to rise once more.

Between 1970 and 1974 China's foreign trade has been expanding very rapidly due to a combination of three factors: (1) the increasing pace of domestic investment and economic activity in general, contributing to rising import demand and the availability of more export supplies, (2) a new international economic posture on the part of the People's Republic of China, and (3) world-wide inflation combined with dollar devaluation. This last factor is reflected in a growing divergence between foreign trade values stated in current prices and in deflated constant prices since 1971–1972. Nevertheless, even in quantum terms, China's foreign trade turnover rose by more than 25 percent between 1972 and 1973. But China's whole world trading position began to change, at least temporarily, under the impact of world *stagflation*. This was reflected in a slowing in the rate of trade expansion in 1974. Preliminary data available in mid-1976 suggest that this may have led to a possible decline in the actual trade volume in 1975.

As one surveys the evolution of China's foreign trade since 1952, several key characteristics stand out. This trade grew rapidly and virtually continuously up to 1959, that is, until the onset of the agricultural crisis. It then declined, recovered, declined again, and finally increased again. Under the impact of this fluctuating pattern, total trade turnover adjusted for price changes remained below the peak 1959 level right up to 1972. What accounts for this contrasting pattern of foreign trade behavior in the 1950s as compared to the 1960s? Some of the reasons and factors have already been touched on earlier in this chapter. I would now like to analyze these more specifically.

In the 1950s the high rate of economic growth led to a marked expansion in import demand. This rapid growth was in turn propelled by a sharp rise in fixed capital investment, from about 10 percent of GNP to 25 or perhaps even 30 percent in 1958–1959. Capital investment had a high built-in import component, reflected in a brisk demand for machinery, transport, and other kinds of equipment and raw materials. At the same time, the demand for imported military matériel was rising in order to supply the People's Liberation Army with modern weapons and equipment. Rapid economic expansion also led to the growth of manufacturing and mining, which supplied exports required to finance imports.

Economic growth then slowed down considerably in the 1960s. The rate of investment leveled off, ranging probably from 20 to 25 percent. In contrast to the 1950s, investment did not rise more rapidly than GNP. Consequently, even if the import component of investment had remained high, the slower rate of investment growth alone would have been a factor in slowing import growth. However, the import component of fixed capital investment also diminished in the 1960s. But import demand was not only depressed by economic factors. On the contrary, this tendency was reinforced by the policy of self-reliance, based on the deliberate pursuit of an import-substitution policy. Finally, the commitment to this policy combined with the Sino-Soviet break forced a drastic reduction of military imports from the Soviet Union and Eastern Europe.

The commodity composition of China's foreign trade

The contrasting patterns of economic development and trade witnessed in the twenty-five-year life span of the People's Republic were necessarily reflected in significant shifts in the commodity composition of exports and imports. The structural transformation of the economy, with agriculture diminishing in importance relative to GNP while industry's weight was rapidly rising, combined with a deliberate import-substitution policy, had a profound impact on the character of import demand and the availability of export supplies.

The much more highly industrialized state of the economy reinforced by self-reliance is most clearly reflected in the fact that the importance of machinery and equipment imports declined both as compared to total imports and domestic production. At the same time, imports of semi-manufactured metals were rapidly rising in the 1960s, both in absolute and relative terms. These are mostly high-quality iron and steel materials and non-ferrous metals used in the production of machinery and military end-items. China was in effect reducing her import dependence, substituting the relatively less costly semi-manufactures for imported end-items in the capital-goods industry. As a result, more than one-quarter of China's import bill was composed of these products in the early 1970s, as compared to less than 5 percent in the early 1950s, as shown in Table 7-2. Correspondingly, while the share of machinery, equipment, and military goods combined comprised at least 50 percent of total imports in the first decade, they constituted around 20 percent or less throughout most of the 1960s and the early 1970s.[14]

While the importance of capital goods and military imports declined, that of foods, particularly grains, rose. The turning point came at the depth of the agricultural depression in 1961. Food imports jumped almost tenfold in value between 1960 and 1961, while capital goods and defense items shrank to about one-third of their former level. To a considerable extent, foods replaced capital goods as the leading import category until about the mid-1960s.

In the 1950s China exported between 0.5 million and 1.6 million metric tons of rice and imported virtually no grains at all. Therefore, both in quantity and value terms, China was a significant net grain exporter. Beginning in

Table 7-2. *Commodity composition of China's imports, 1955–1973*[a] *(in percent)*

Commodity category	1955	1959	1966	1970	1973
Food, beverages, and tobacco	2.2	0.3	27.1	19.2	18.7
Crude materials, inedible	11.1	13.4	16.4	11.3	17.8
of which, textile fibers	(8.0)	(5.6)	(7.1)	(5.4)	(9.5)
Mineral fuels and lubricants	7.4	6.5	0.2	0.2	0.1
Animal and vegetable oils and fats	0.5	0.2	0.2	0.3	1.0
Chemicals	9.6	8.1	12.6	15.5	10.0
of which chemical fertilizer	(3.7)	(2.5)	(7.1)	(7.5)	(4.3)
Manufactured goods, by material	12.4	17.9	18.7	33.3	31.0
of which metals and metals manufactures	(8.9)	(15.4)	(16.2)	(29.1)	(28.2)
Machinery and transport equipment	22.4	40.0	19.1	15.1	15.6
Miscellaneous manufactures	2.6	2.2	2.4	1.3	1.1
Goods not elsewhere specified	31.8	11.4	33.3	3.4	4.7

[a]Figures in parentheses represent sub-categories.
Sources: These percentages were derived by the author from annual commodity composition data published by the U.S. Department of Commerce for non-Communist world trade in annual *Reports to Congress* by the U.S. Mutual Defense Assistance Control Administrator; these were combined with Soviet data for their trade with China published in *The Foreign Trade of the USSR, Statistical Handbook* for various years. Non-Communist world and Soviet trade combined accounted for 79 to 88 percent of China's total imports between 1952 and 1973.

1961, this picture was drastically reversed. Between 1961 and 1966, China imported from 4.5 to 6.5 million tons of grain, mostly wheat. These imports then declined to a 3 to 5 million ton level, until a poor 1972 harvest forced China to step up her grain purchases once more. They then rose to a record of nearly 8 million tons in 1973 and 7 million tons in 1974. As the harvests improved, they dropped back to around 3 million tons in 1975. In the meantime, rice exports shrank under the impact of the crisis in the early 1960s, but then gradually recovered and even exceeded their former peak levels.[15]

The food energy values of rice and wheat are roughly equivalent. At the same time, since the world price of a ton of rice is appreciably higher than of a ton of wheat, China could obtain a net foreign exchange gain in a rice export–wheat import transaction. Since 1961 and up to 1973 it seems, however, that rice exports consistently lagged behind other grain imports both in tonnage and value terms.

Other significant changes in commodity composition of China's trade revolve around chemical fertilizer and petroleum and its products. In the 1950s China imported rather small quantities of chemical fertilizer, ranging well below 1 million metric tons. As indicated in the preceding chapters, China sharply redirected its development strategy under the impact of its agricultural and economic crisis. As a result, much higher priority in the allocation of resources was assigned to agriculture and the development of those industries that support agriculture, that is, that supply production requisites to agriculture. This led to a very rapid expansion of domestic fertilizer production capacity and a stepping up of fertilizer imports. These imports were gradually raised from about 1 million tons (in terms of gross weight) in the early 1960s to more than 7 million tons in the early 1970s.

The opposite happened in the case of petroleum and its products. For a long time it was thought that China was poorly endowed with oil resources. The country's domestic production was small and it was quite dependent on imported petroleum supplies. This is evidenced by the fact that about a quarter of crude oil requirements and well over half of domestic gasoline, kerosene, and diesel oil needs had to be met through imports in the mid-1950s. In the face of strategic trade controls prevailing at the time, China could obtain these petroleum products only from Russia and Rumania. However, following the Sino-Soviet break, the People's Republic was determined to emancipate itself from any dependence on foreign oil.

With these considerations in mind, an active program of geological exploration was launched and as a result several major oil-producing fields were discovered in the 1960s. Moreover, U.N. surveys found large off-shore oil deposits on the continental shelf. With the exploitation of the new fields in the Northeast and the North, oil production has been rising very rapidly, at an average annual rate of about 20 to 30 percent since the early 1960s. Consequently China, which spent about 10 percent of its export earnings for the purchase of oil and its products in the 1950s, has become an exporter of petroleum in the 1970s.

The transformation of China from a net importer to a net exporter of petroleum and the reverse change in respect to grain are but examples of structural shifts in China's trading patterns rooted in its economic development. As noted earlier, increasing industrialization and the growth of a sizable domestic machine-building capacity led to some decline in the relative importance of machinery imports. However, these were replaced by imported semi-manufactures, which gained in importance precisely in response to the expansion of machine building since they constituted primary inputs into the production of machinery end-items.

Corresponding shifts are visible in other imports and exports. Agricultural products – both foodstuffs and raw materials – which dominated China's exports in the 1950s, receded in relative importance in the 1960s and early 1970s, as may be seen in Table 7-3. A major reason for the decline in food exports has been the steady erosion of soybean and oilseed surpluses. In the late

Table 7-3. *Commodity composition of China's exports, 1955–1973*[a] *(in percent)*

Commodity category	1955	1959	1966	1970	1973
Food, beverages, and tobacco	32.8	26.2	30.8	29.1	25.2
Crude materials, inedible	36.9	24.4	18.7	18.6	17.6
of which, textile fibers	(8.0)	(7.2)	(4.6)	(5.7)	(8.5)
Mineral fuels and lubricants	0.6	0.4	0.9	0.5	1.3
Animal and vegetable oils and fats	3.5	1.3	1.9	1.0	0.6
Chemicals	2.1	2.6	3.3	5.0	4.8
Manufactured goods, by material	18.3	25.8	20.4	25.8	25.6
of which, textiles	(8.8)	(18.1)	(11.6)	(17.7)	(15.7)
metals and metals manufactures	(7.9)	(5.0)	(4.8)	(3.2)	(4.4)
Machinery and transport equipment	1.1	1.5	1.2	2.6	2.3
Miscellaneous manufactures	1.8	12.9	7.9	9.2	13.3
Other	2.9	4.9	14.9	8.2	9.3

[a]Figures in parentheses represent sub-categories.
Sources: Same as Table 7-2.

1950s, China exported about 1 million or more tons of soybeans. These shipments shrank drastically during the agricultural depression years. While they turned up again in the mid-1960s, they never recovered. On the contrary, they declined more or less continuously to the point that China's net soybean exports in 1973 dwindled to 37,000 tons, and in 1974 China became a net importer instead of a net exporter of soybeans, at least temporarily.

In the mid-1950s, soybeans, oilseeds, and their products contributed close to 20 percent of China's export supplies. By the 1970s this dwindled to about 2 percent. These declines were more than offset by the increasing role of textiles – yarn, fabrics, and clothing. Textile exports were sustained at high levels throughout the agricultural crisis years (1960–1962), and played a crucial role at the time in supplying the foreign-exchange earnings required to finance China's grain purchases abroad. Textile shipments were maintained at a high level even when the country's total imports were shrinking. As a result, the relative importance of textiles rose from about 25 percent (including fibers) in 1959 to about 40 or more percent in 1961 and 1962. Since then they have stabilized within a 20 to 25 percent range, as compared to around 10 percent in the early 1950s.

This high level of textile exports could be maintained through the depression years only by cutting domestic textile rations to the bare bones. But significantly, these rations were greatly liberalized as China's economic situation improved. As textile production recovered and expanded, most of the increase in output apparently went into domestic consumption rather than exports. Consequently the volume of textile exports adjusted for price changes was in 1973 probably not significantly above the earlier peak 1959 level or much above the levels of the mid-1960s.

Another category of goods that exhibited a steady export rise is manufactured consumer goods such as watches, ball-point pens, thermos bottles, furniture, as well as some durables like bicycles. These grew in absolute terms as well as in relation to total exports.

China's foreign trade in the 1970s

As shown before, under the impact of these sharply contrasting trends the Chinese economy became less self-contained and more involved in the world economy in the first post-revolution decade, while this trend was reversed in the second decade. As a result, China gained in world trading rank in the 1950s but slipped in the 1960s. China was the world's eleventh- or twelfth-largest trader in 1959, but only twenty-second or twenty-third in the early

1970s. Consequently China's total foreign trade turnover in 1972 or 1973 was less than that of the small European countries such as Denmark, Belgium, or the Netherlands. It was also more or less on a par with that of Taiwan – an island of about 16 million people compared to China's approximately 800 million.

China's foreign trade was not only profoundly affected by its industrialization but also by its foreign policy. This is clearly dramatized by the data in Table 7-4. Although China's trade with the Soviet Union and Eastern Europe was quite unimportant during the Republican period (1911–1949), by 1950 the Soviet Union had become China's dominant trading partner. This was a reflection of the friendship and alliance treaties concluded between the two countries in early 1950, supplemented by aid and trade agreements. It

Table 7-4. *Direction of China's foreign trade in selected years (in percent)*[a]

	1955		1965		1974	
	Exports	Imports	Exports	Imports	Exports	Imports
Socialist countries of which:	70	78	32	28	21	13
Soviet Union	48	57	11	10	2	2
Eastern Europe	17	18	7	7	5[c]	4[c]
Other[b]	5	3	14	11	15[c]	7[c]
Non-Socialist countries of which:	30	22	68	72	79	87
Japan	6	2	11	14	19	28
Hong Kong	11	2	17	negl.	13	negl.
Western Europe	8	7	15	19	13	18
United States	–	–	–	–	2	13
Other	5	13	25	38	32	28
Total	100	100	100	100	100	100

[a]All percentages are rounded to the nearest number.
[b]Includes Asian Communist countries, Cuba, and Yugoslavia.
[c]These percentages are not fully comparable with those for earlier years, since Albania is included under Eastern Europe in 1955 and 1965, but is ranged under other Communist countries in 1974; as a result the 1974 figures under-state the share of Eastern Europe and correspondingly over-state it for the other Communist states.

Sources: A. Eckstein, *Communist China's Economic Growth and Foreign Trade*, New York, 1966, Table 4-3, p. 98; R. Dernberger, "Prospects for Trade Between China and the United States," in A. Eckstein, *China Trade Prospects and U.S. Policy*, New York, 1971, Appendix Table A3, pp. 280–297; *People's Republic of China: An Economic Assessment*, Joint Economic Committee, U.S. Congress, May 18, 1972, Table 10, pp. 350–351; Central Intelligence Agency, Research Aid, *People's Republic of China: International Trade Handbook*, Washington, D.C., October 1975, Table 2, pp. 10–11.

was reinforced by the Korean War, which increased China's dependence on Soviet deliveries of supplies and matériel for its armed forces.

From 1951 to 1961 well over half China's trade was with other socialist countries. For most of these years, between 60 and 80 percent of it was with the Soviet Union and Eastern Europe. In part this was a reflection of the close Sino-Soviet ties and in part a result of the U.S. embargo and the associated strategic trade controls by other industrialized countries. As these controls were relaxed in the late 1950s, the role of the Soviet Bloc in China's trade began to gradually decline. This decline became precipitous after the Sino-Soviet break. Therefore while the Soviet share was around 50 percent or more in the 1950s, it decreased to between 20 and 30 percent in 1962, and dwindled to 1 percent at its low point in 1970. It has recovered slightly since. During the same period, Eastern Europe's share declined from around 15 to 18 percent to about 5 to 10 percent, clearly a less drastic drop.

However, Sino-Soviet relations not only affected the direction of China's commerce but its trade policy as well. In the 1950s trading patterns were profoundly affected by the extension of Soviet credits and in the late 1950s and until the mid-1960s by China's repayment of those credits. Through the pursuit of the self-reliance policy, in part influenced by the break, Sino-Soviet relations affected China's trade level as well.

Sino-Soviet relations went from bad to worse, culminating in the Chenpao (Damyanski) Island incident and the sharp border clashes of 1969. These developments apparently convinced the Chinese leadership to seek improved relations with the West, particularly the United States, just at a time when the United States was also moving in this direction. As a result, we see the removal of the U.S. embargo on trade and payments with China in mid-1971 and the opening of commercial and other kinds of relations between the two countries. These changes were occurring when the Chinese economy was recovering from the disruptive consequences of the Cultural Revolution and was launched on a new wave of expansion. Therefore economic and foreign-policy factors converged in prompting closer commercial, scientific, and technological relations with Western Europe, Japan, and the United States. These considerations, in turn, apparently led to a reexamination of the self-reliance policy at the highest level and its reinterpretation in 1971 or 1972. Consequently, just as the Sino-Soviet break contributed to the formulation of the self-reliance policy, so did the further deterioration in these relations play a part in the reinterpretation of this policy.

The abandonment of a narrowly autarkic policy was reflected in a large increase in the country's foreign trade in 1973, followed by slower growth in

1974. Perhaps even more dramatically, it involved a most substantial commitment to the importation of complete plants and foreign technology on the one hand and rising oil exports on the other. At the same time, total trade turnover with the United States rose from zero in 1970 to $5 million in 1971, $111 million in 1972, and about $880 million in 1973. Within two years the United States emerged as one of China's largest trading partners, second only to Japan. To place these developments in perspective, one must take a closer look at four major elements that seem to shape China's trading patterns in the emerging 1970s: its agricultural and food situation; its investment plans and the complete plant purchases associated therewith; its oil production and trade; and its economic relations with the United States.

Agricultural development and trade

It seems that China's farm production has been expanding at an average annual rate of slightly more than 2 percent between 1952 and 1974. To sustain and maintain this rate demanded rapidly increasing fertilizer applications, which was made possible in part by expansion of domestic fertilizer output and in part by imports. These imports provided about one-third to one-half of the manufactured nutrients to the soil in recent years.[16]

The Chinese are clearly committed to further stepping up the quantity and quality of chemical fertilizer applications as a means of raising yield per acre. This is most clearly reflected in the fact that, between December 1972 and September 1974, the Chinese Technical Export–Import Corporation purchased altogether 13 chemical fertilizer complexes, each encompassing an ammonia and a urea plant from firms in the United States, Japan, Netherlands, and France valued at between $500 and $550 million.[17] It is estimated that when these plants are fully operational, between 1977 and 1980, China's modern chemical fertilizer manufacturing capacity will be doubled in terms of nitrogenous nutrient content. Clearly this is a program designed to reduce China's dependence on imported fertilizer. Whether in fact such imports will be reduced is, however, far from certain, given the continuously high fertilizer requirements of Chinese agriculture in the future.

In a certain sense there is a trade-off between the quantities of imported grain and fertilizer, not in any one year, but over the medium or long run. Rising fertilizer imports and its increasing applications to the soil provide an opportunity for increasing yield per acre and thus expanding domestic grain production. This may then reduce the demand for imported grain. The terms of the trade-off will naturally depend on how much additional grain can be produced with an additional ton of fertilizer and on the relative price of these two imports.

It seems that, through the 1960s, the Chinese may in fact have substituted, to some extent at least, rising chemical fertilizer imports for grain purchases. This may be illustrated by the trends in Table 7-5. These data show that grain imports gradually declined from about 6 to 7 million tons to 3 to 5 million between 1961 and 1972. In contrast, during the same period fertilizer purchases from abroad quadrupled. Clearly, the very large imports of grain in the early 1960s were an emergency measure designed to quickly alleviate an acute food crisis in China.

Why did China continue to import grain even after the country's agricultural situation improved? This is far from clear and only speculative hypotheses can be advanced. Chou En-lai stated on several occasions that grain stocks of 40 million tons were accumulated. This would constitute 15 to 20 percent of the total annual supply. One can safely assume that Chinese policy makers

Table 7-5. *China's grain and fertilizer imports, 1961–1973 (in millions of metric tons and millions of U.S. dollars)*

	Grain		Chemical fertilizer[a]	
Year	Quantity	Value	Quantity	Value
1961	6.2	435	1.0	40
1962	5.3	370	1.0	40
1963	5.7	400	2.0	85
1964	6.8	475	1.2	65
1965	5.7	400	2.3	145
1966	5.6	400	2.5	155
1967	4.1	295	4.3	200
1968	4.4	305	4.0	200
1969	3.9	260	4.1	205
1970	4.6	280	4.3	230
1971	3.0	205	4.2	200
1972	4.8	345	4.2	190
1973	7.7	840	4.1	220
1974	7.0	1170	3.0	230

[a]Excludes phosphate rock.

Sources: A. H. Usack and R. E. Batsavage, "The International Trade of the People's Republic of China," in *People's Republic of China: An Economic Assessment*, Joint Economic Committee, U.S. Congress, Washington, D.C., May 1972, Table 9, p. 348 and Central Intelligence Agency, *People's Republic of China: International Trade Handbook*, September 1974, Table 10, p. 15 and October 1975, Table 8, p. 16.

are determined to avoid a repetition of the food crisis of the early 1960s at all cost. Therefore one source of demand for grain is maintenance of reserves to cushion the impact of periodic shortfalls in the harvest.

Another major source of growing demand for agricultural products is population growth. Scattered references in Chinese sources suggest a population of around 800 million in 1973–1974. This would mean a rate of growth of about 1.5 percent between 1953 and 1973. Chou En-lai in his conversations with many visitors usually referred to a growth rate of around 2 percent a year. In that case China's population in 1973–1974 should have been approximately 900 million, based on the Chinese census figure of 583 million in 1953. Whatever it may be, this would indicate that for the two decades as a whole, grain production may have kept slightly ahead of population, or at worst kept pace with it. However, for the last decade or so, between 1963 and 1974, the outcome may have been more favorable, with average annual grain production growth of about 3 percent and population growth of about 1.5 to 2 percent.

If grain output is rising faster than population, this compounds the puzzle of continuing grain imports, unless two other factors are operative that may be decisive. Per capita demand for grain and other foods may be expected to rise in China in response to rising incomes and a gradually rising standard of living. Moreover quite irrespective of this, given the country's sparse railroad network, it may be cheaper and easier to ship grain to the coastal cities of China in vessels across the oceans than in railroads from let us say the hinterlands of Szechwan in the Southwest. Finally, while imported grain accounts for only 1.5 to 2 percent of total supply, it constitutes a much larger share of the marketed grain in the areas easily accessible to the major marketing centers. To extract this additional grain from these particular areas may be much too costly, both in economic and political terms.

On this basis, one might speculate that under normal conditions of domestic production and growth, China's long-term demand for grain may fluctuate between 3 and 5 million tons. However, when crops are poor this demand rises rapidly, as happened in 1973 and 1974. A poor harvest, such as occurred in 1972, probably leads to a drawing-down of stocks, which are then replenished through increased imports in subsequent years. This would explain the jump from 4.8 million tons in 1972 to 7.7 million in 1973 and close to the same in 1974. It would also explain the rapid decline in grain imports in 1975.

Another factor to be considered is the sharp rise in world grain prices. While the grain tonnage imported by China rose by 60 percent between 1972 and 1973, the foreign-exchange cost shot up by over 140 percent. Almost certainly this generates pressures to curtail grain purchases as rapidly as possible. In contrast, the rise in fertilizer costs per ton has been much more moderate. Therefore if these trends continue, other things being equal, it may make sense to step up fertilizer imports until the new fertilizer production capacity being installed between 1974 and 1977 becomes operational.

Other farm products besides grains assume importance in China's trade in agricultural products. First of all, although China imported grains valued at $840 million in 1973, it exported rice and small quantities of other grains valued at $535 million. Therefore, in quantity terms the import–export ratio was about 5:1 but in value terms it was approximately 5:3.

There were two other major developments in China's agricultural trade in the 1970s. These relate to soybeans, as indicated above, and cotton. Up to 1973 China was a net exporter of soybeans. However in 1974, probably for the first time in decades, China became a sizable net importer. Thus a *small net export* surplus of 37,000 tons in 1973 was converted into a *net import* of about 550,000 tons. It seems that China's whole soybean position has become quite uncertain, shifting year by year. In 1975, it was a small net exporter, and in 1976 it may revert to a small net import position.[18]

China has been a net cotton importer ever since the 1949 revolution and during much of the inter-war period. These imports attained their highest levels of about 200,000 tons in the early 1930s. Their next highest peak came during 1963–1965, with an average of about 150,000 tons purchased. China also exported small quantities of cotton, but except for 1959, remained a net importer throughout. During the high-import years, purchases from abroad contributed about 10 percent of total cotton supply. However, these purchases began to rise sharply in 1969 to well over 400,000 tons in 1973–1974, probably contributing about one-quarter of the country's cotton supply. But, they too dropped in 1975, reverting approximately to the level of the mid-1960s.[19]

In the face of sharply rising agricultural imports in 1973 and 1974, it is terribly important to place these recent developments in a longer-term perspective. According to one set of estimates, food exports and imports were nearly balanced in 1965, a year by which Chinese agriculture had fully recovered from the earlier crisis and was launched on a new path of expansion. Between 1965 and 1972, *exports of foodstuffs rose* from $530 million to $955 million. During the same period *food imports declined* from $520 million to $455 million; between 1967 and 1971 they never exceeded $410 million, and as a matter of fact averaged around $357 million. This means that between 1965 and the poor 1972 harvest year China was building up a sizable trade surplus in its food accounts. This situation was temporarily changed in the subsequent two years, when food imports rose much faster than food exports, rising to $1 billion and $1.6 billion respectively. Yet even during these years a surplus on food account was maintained, although it was relatively smaller than in the preceding years. This, combined with the drop in 1975 food imports, strongly suggests the possibility that the marked upsurge in China's agricultural import demand in 1973–1974 may have been temporary.

The complete-plant purchases

In retrospect, the decision to revive the Technical Export–Import Corporation clearly signaled a series of high-level decisions to embark upon importation of foreign technology and foreign plant equipment. It must have represented a clear recognition by the policy makers that in this way the technological gap between certain industries in China and in other countries could be narrowed much more rapidly than through piecemeal purchases of individual components.

Between December 1972 and September 1974 this new corporation placed 41 contracts for the construction of a total of 95 plants valued at approximately $2.1 billion and according to some calculations as high as $2.5 billion. The Chinese had twice before placed major plant orders – once before the Cultural Revolution, between 1963 and 1966, when orders valued at more than $200 million were placed in Western Europe and Japan.[20] Virtually all these contracts were in fact implemented. More importantly, the Chinese entered into a vast complete-plant import program in the 1950s with all the orders placed in the Soviet Union and Eastern Europe. A total of 291 such agreements was concluded with the Soviets and an additional 100 with Eastern Europe. By the time of the Sino-Soviet break in 1960, 130 Soviet plants were completed or well advanced. The total value of these has been estimated at 6 billion (old) rubles or $1.5 billion.[21]

By the same date, 27 Eastern European plants were completed out of the 64 under construction. The cost of these is not known. Assuming that the average cost per plant was the same for those from the Soviet Union and Eastern Europe, their total value would be $1.8 billion. These complete-plant projects constituted the core of China's industrialization drive in the 1950s. Deliveries started in the early 1950s and cumulative complete-plant imports from Russia to China between 1955 and 1962 amounted to $1.6 billion.[22] This would approximate the 6 billion ruble figure referred to above.

Translating the $1.8 billion figure into 1973 dollars yields a total of about

$3 billion. Adjusted for price changes, the Soviet and Eastern European complete-plant projects actually completed may have exceeded the value of orders placed in 1973–1974 by as much as 50 percent. However, the construction of the Soviet and Eastern European plants was stretched over a seven- to eight-year period, while the contracts concluded in 1973–1974 are to be completed within three years. Translating these aggregate values into annual averages at comparable 1973 prices suggests that the current contracts imply a yearly activity rate of about $700 million, as compared to about $430 million for those installed in the 1950s.

The figures cited indicate that, just as the complete-plant purchases of the 1950s made a decisive contribution to building a significant industrial base in China, so may one expect a massive expansion of capacity in selected industries due to the very large infusion of such plants in the 1970s. It was indicated above that the 13 ammonia and 13 urea plants to be built are expected to double China's capacity to produce nitrogenous fertilizer in modern plants and in terms of nutrient content. In addition, a number of major projects were started in the iron and steel industry, in petro-chemicals, synthetic fiber manufacture, petroleum exploration and extraction, and power generation. Not unexpectedly the largest project is in iron and steel manufacture, involving a very sizable expansion of the Wuhan steel complex with the addition of a cold strip, hot strip, and continuous casting mill with a number of additional processes associated therewith. These iron and steel plants purchased from West Germany and Japan are priced at about $550 million and may add about 25 percent to Chinese rolled-steel capacity.

A portion of these complete-plant purchases are on a cash-and-carry basis, with an initial down payment followed by payments upon actual delivery of equipment and final installments paid after the plant goes into operation. However, quite a few are handled on a deferred-payment basis, involving medium-term credits of five or more years, with payments usually to start following plant completion. Through these China is gradually accumulating some fairly substantial debt obligations over the coming years.

China's oil production and trade

As indicated above, China was a substantial importer of crude oil until 1960 and of refined products until 1964. This was at a time when Chinese oil production was low. The expansion in China's petroleum production represents one of the outstanding achievements of the People's Republic. It increased over 3.5 times between 1952 and 1957, nearly 4 times between 1957 and 1962, 2.4 times in the next five-year period, and another 3 times between 1967 and 1972. As a result, China's crude oil production rose from about 440,000 tons in 1952 to an estimated 77 million tons in 1973.[23] This means that it multiplied about 180 times in 23 years, or at an average annual rate in excess of 20 percent.

The scope of the new oil discoveries became apparent in the mid-1960s when the Chinese ceased to import crude oil. However, their full impact began to be felt only in the 1970s as China's production approached – and as of 1976 possibly exceeded – Indonesian levels. As a result, by the early 1970s China was exporting small marginal quantities and the leadership must have been aware that they had, in oil, a major potential asset that could transform the country's capacity to earn foreign exchange and pay directly for its new capital imports. It is intriguing to speculate on the weight this revelation may have had in setting the new overall foreign-trade policy outlined above; what is clear is that the Chinese have for some years been making the heavy investments – in exploration and drilling, and later in shipping – required to develop and sell their oil in quantity abroad.

China began to export oil in commercial quantities in 1973. Oil first became a substantial entry in the Chinese trade ledger in 1974; about 6.5 million tons were exported, and the return to China was an estimated $500 million, or approximately 8 percent of China's total export earnings. These exports rose to an estimated 10 to 11 million tons in 1975, valued at around $850 million. They contributed about 12 to 13 percent to China's total export earnings that year.

Japan was the principal market for Chinese oil, with about 1 million tons shipped in 1973, 4.5 million in 1974, and 7.8 million in 1975. The rest went to North Korea, Vietnam, Hong Kong, Thailand, and the Philippines.[24] It was generally expected that these oil exports will continue to grow rapidly, with Japan serving as the largest customer. It was estimated that by 1980 China would export between 30 to 50 million tons of oil. Both Japanese and Chinese sources encourage such estimates. Even the lower figure would yield export earnings of $2.2 billion to $2.6 billion in terms of 1975 prices. This in and of itself would serve to relieve balance of payment pressures, thus enabling China to pursue an active import program. It should also enable China to finance fairly sizable trade deficits with the United States. Therefore such an outlook could create rather favorable prospects for our exports to the People's Republic.

A number of more recent indications suggest that these projections were perhaps over-optimistic. A recently published and detailed study of China's energy balance demonstrates that the country's domestic energy needs are likely to grow more rapidly than was previously estimated. At the same time, it is most doubtful that the exceptionally rapid rates of oil production growth experienced in the last ten to fifteen years can be sustained over the next five to ten years.[25] These doubts seem to be borne out by a number of reports from Chinese official sources in the first half of 1976, suggesting a slowing down in the rate of extraction. On the basis of presently available information it is impossible to tell whether these slow-downs reflect changes in economic policy with a reduced emphasis on investments in oil production and exports, temporary technical problems, or changes in methods of extraction.

In 1976 complications also seem to be developing on the oil export front. Rather unexpectedly the Chinese reduced their oil shipments to Japan this year (1976) and the negotiations for a long-term oil export agreement are tentatively providing for guaranteed Japanese purchases of only 15 million to 18 million tons rather than the 30 million to 50 million talked about earlier. In part these changes in signals may reflect a Sino-Japanese bargaining process concerning price and other terms of the agreement. However they may reflect more fundamental problems as well.

In any case, based on the aforementioned study of China's energy balance, it seems quite doubtful that China could spare oil export surpluses of more than 30 million tons by 1980. Actually, in projecting China's oil-export capabilities and Japanese purchases of this oil over the next five to ten years, a number of complex factors must be taken into account. As indicated above, China's 1975 oil production was estimated at 77 million tons (or about 1.5 million barrels per day). There seems to be a fair degree of consensus among oil industry and energy specialists who have followed Chinese developments that 200 million tons may be a reasonable production estimate for 1980. This is projected on the assumption that output will grow at an average rate of 20 percent per year and that virtually all of it will come from fields in which drilling is already under way.

These fields are preponderantly on-shore, with some drilling anticipated in the shallow waters of the Pohai Gulf, close to shore. To attain these production levels will require additional investment in drilling facilities, pipelines, and harbor facilities to transport the oil produced. On present indications, these investments do not seem to be beyond China's capabilities either in terms of the resources or technology required.

This process could be greatly accelerated if the Chinese wished to commit themselves to rapid development of off-shore drilling. Correspondingly, it could be slowed down if the necessary investments for further expansion of on-shore drilling and for transport were not sustained. The convergence of quite powerful economic and foreign-policy considerations prompts a high priority for the development of the petroleum industry. Rising oil exports can greatly augment China's foreign-exchange earnings. At the same time they can minimize Japan's inducements to invest in the development of Siberian oil resources, thus also diminishing Japan's interest in seeking closer economic and political links with the Soviet Union. However, China's interest in the development of its oil resources has, at least up to now, not gone so far as to encourage a large-scale program of off-shore exploration and drilling, which could significantly accelerate the rate of China's oil production growth. Given the highly complex technology involved, this would require some form of technical assistance, perhaps based on co-production or similar types of arrangements with the major international oil companies, apparently on terms that are not compatible with China's self-reliance policy, even with the more liberalized interpretation of that concept prevailing recently. On the basis of present indications, the Chinese prefer to embark on this effort by themselves, purchasing drilling rigs, other equipment, and technical assistance abroad as needed but managing the whole enterprise themselves. This will necessarily be a slower development, but in light of the considerable potential for on-shore exploitation in at least the next five years, there is no great pressure to accelerate the off-shore program.

This analysis of China's oil export potential has thus far only considered factors bearing on supply availability. What about the character of demand and markets for this oil? Given Japan's geographic proximity and almost total dependence on imported oil, it can be justifiably viewed as the most natural or logical outlet for China's surplus. But, there are a number of conflicting considerations that must be taken into account in assessing China's prospects in the Japanese oil market.

First of all, Chinese oil has certain peculiar characteristics. Some of it is of low quality (e.g., Shengli oil), and primarily suitable for burning as fuel. This does not apply to most of the exported product, which has a low sulphur but high wax content and leaves a heavy residue after refining. It is quite similar to Indonesian but different from Middle Eastern oil. Since Japanese refineries are largely geared to processing Middle Eastern oil, Chinese oil presents special problems and requires special refining equipment or devices. Therefore the market for this type of oil is limited and must be shared with Indonesia.

Since the Japanese have a strong interest in maintaining close links with Indonesia, they consider it most important to continue importing sizable quantities of oil from there. This further constrains the demand for China's oil in Japan. The problem is further complicated by shipping bottlenecks; specifically the inability of Chinese ports to accommodate large tankers, so that most of the oil has to be shipped in smaller bottoms, driving up the transport costs. However, there are several counteracting factors at work. Viewed from the perspective of the Japanese government, an important national objective is to diversify the country's sources of oil supply and thus minimize the risks attendant upon primary dependence on Middle Eastern oil. Therefore, from the standpoint of long-run energy policy, there is a strong incentive for the Japanese government to subsidize the importation and/or refining of Chinese oil and in fact various schemes designed to accomplish this have been under active consideration.

There is also a serious concern that unless the Chinese can find an outlet for their products, they will not have the purchasing power to buy Japanese machinery, equipment, steel, and other products. In these terms too Chinese oil imports are much more welcome than textile shipments, which compete directly with Japanese textile manufactures. Finally, political considerations reinforce the economic factors cited. There seems to be a strong and deep commitment in Japan today to develop closer links with China and to use trade as perhaps the most important avenue for building a long-term relationship between these two neighbors.

What may be emerging in China's foreign trade is a new pattern. Until recently China has been selling agricultural products – including rice – and textiles, the proceeds of which are used to purchase wheat, some other grains, chemical fertilizer, machinery, and a variety of other products. However, the Chinese have experienced increasing difficulties in placing their cotton textiles, silk, and some other products in recent years. The types of products exported have found limited world markets and this in turn has placed definite constraints on the level of trade. Viewed from this perspective, China's rapidly rising oil production and exports provide an opportunity for breaking away from the old constraints on China's trade. In effect, the new oil exports may pave the way for a continued high level of imports of plant and equipment.

This transformation in trading patterns must pose some political dilemmas for the Chinese leadership. It could significantly augment China's involvement in the international economy and this in turn may expose the economy to the vagaries and uncertainties of the world market and render it more vulnerable to its influences – as was amply demonstrated in 1974. An enlarged international sector may also entail more contact between foreigners and

Chinese businessmen, officials, technicians, scientists, and others. One of the prime avenues for extensive contacts is provided by the complete-plant program. For instance, the construction of the large steel complex in Wuhan – being jointly installed by DEMAG from Germany and Nippon Steel – will require the presence of 20 German and 200 Japanese technicians in China and a six-month stay for training by Chinese technicians in Japan. There will be approximately 250 to 300 Americans engaged in the installation of 8 fertilizer plants, with perhaps a maximum of 100 to 120 present at any one time for periods ranging from two to fifteen months. It has been crudely estimated that a cumulative total of 2000 to 3000 foreign technicans will be stationed in China between 1974 and 1977. This may not only bring with it a transfer of foreign technology, but also a transfer of foreign ideas, approaches, and influences.

These issues have clearly been debated in the top ranks of the leadership, as evidenced by occasional attacks on this policy in the Chinese press and by periodic rebuttals and counter-attacks. They almost certainly constituted one of the foci of policy conflict between the contending groups in the leadership. Nevertheless, the course that took shape in 1971 and 1972 seems to have been followed until the death of Premier Chou and the purge of Vice-Premier Teng Hsiao-p'ing in early 1976, and the subsequent death of Chairman Mao himself. Their disappearance from the scene introduces some uncertainty as to how consistently this policy will be followed in the future.

The development of oil resources and the rapid expansion of foreign trade imposed very heavy strains on China's port and shipping facilities. In 1973 and the first half of 1974, the China trade was replete with complaints of port congestion, long turn-around time for ships, the shallowness of ports so that large tankers could not use the harbors, and poor bulk loading and unloading facilities. Given the character of Chinese ports, Chinese oil is shipped in 20,000- to at most 30,000-ton freighters rather than 100,000- to 200,000-ton tankers. This raises transport costs and somewhat reduces the competitiveness of Chinese oil as compared to other sources of supply available to Japan. At the same time, lack of container port and bulk handling facilities has slowed down the delivery of grain, iron ore, and a number of other products.

Against this background, Chinese planners have allocated substantial resources to correct this situation. Chinese ports were deepened, and in this connection large orders for port dredging equipment were placed abroad. They also built a major container port near Tientsin and possibly in one or two other harbors. An off-shore oil loading facility was completed near Dairen which can accommodate large tankers. An oil pipeline network is under construction in North and Northeast China, with a long spur from the Taching oil field to the port of Chinghuangtao and another running from this port to a refinery on the outskirts of Peking that was recently completed.

As part and parcel of this effort to create the necessary infra-structure for the support of a foreign-trade expansion program, the Chinese have invested heavily in expanding their merchant marine. Since 1971 or 1972 they have added about 1.5 to 2 million tons to their shipping fleet, about 1.1 million of which is based on 64 secondhand ships mostly bought from Japan, Norway, Poland, and Yugoslavia.[26]

Sino-American trade relations

Contrary to all earlier forecasts and projections, China's trade with the United States rose dramatically between 1971 and 1974. Once the trade embargo was lifted by the United States in mid-1971 and the Shanghai Communiqué defined the character of the relationship between the two countries, the major barriers to Sino-American trade relations were removed. Moreover, the removal of these barriers proceeded much more rapidly than had been anticipated.

A second factor that propelled Sino-American trade far beyond projected levels was China's willingness to tolerate a highly imbalanced trade, as may be seen from Table 7-6. It had been generally assumed that two-way trade would more or less have to be in balance and therefore, to the extent that the U.S. market for Chinese goods is quite limited, this would limit not only U.S. imports from China, but U.S. exports as well. In fact this did not turn out to be the case.

Probably the most crucial factor propelling United States–China trade was the coincidence in time of the opening of relations and a poor harvest in China. Until 1972 China purchased its grain – principally wheat – from Canada and Australia and occasionally smaller quantities from Argentina and France. However, with China increasing its grain imports by more than 50 percent between 1972 and 1973–1974, Australia and Canada could not supply these large additional quantities, particularly in a tight world grain market. Thus of the 7.7 million tons delivered in 1973, about 4 million came from the United States, over 2 million from Canada, and close to 1 million from Australia. In 1974 close to 3 million tons were shipped from the United States, about 2 million from Canada, 1.5 million from Australia, and smaller amounts from Argentina and France.

Following the inferior 1972 harvest, China stepped up her other agricul-

Table 7-6. *U.S. trade with the People's Republic of China, 1971–1975 (in millions of U.S. dollars)*

Year	Exports	Imports
1971	negl.	5.0
1972	63.5	32.4
1973	740.2	64.0
1974	820.5	114.7
1975	303.6	158.3

Sources: For 1971 to 1974: William Clarke and Martha Avery, "The Sino-American Commercial Relationship," in *China: A Reassessment of the Economy*, Joint Economic Committee, U.S. Congress, Washington, D.C., July 1975, p. 512. For 1975: United States Department of Commerce, Bureau of East-West Trade, *U.S. Trade Status with Socialist Countries*, Washington, D.C., June 15, 1976, p. 2.

tural purchases as well, particularly – as noted above – soybeans and cotton. These too could most readily be obtained in the United States, thus driving up further our exports to China. It is not surprising therefore that over 80 percent of U.S. exports to China have been agricultural and less than 20 percent have consisted of industrial and transport equipment and other manufactures, as shown in Table 7-7. But this too is completely contrary to earlier expectations, when it was generally assumed that if and when trade opened up, the United States would become a major capital-goods supplier to China. Instead Japan has continued to play this role since the 1960s.

The expected pattern was more closely approximated in 1975, when U.S. exports to China were sharply curtailed. In late 1974 the Chinese began to reduce the quantities of farm products they ordered and deliveries on contracts already firmed up were stretched out. In large part this was due to a succession of two good harvests in 1973 and 1974. However the sharp curtailment of agricultural imports from the United States was also prompted by the fact that much of the wheat delivered by us to China contained some insects and other impurities, while the corn was high in moisutre content so that some of it arrived sprouting. Under these conditions China naturally

Table 7-7. *Commodity composition of U.S. exports to China, 1973–1974 (in percent)*

Commodity category	1973	1974
Wheat	41.5	28.6
Corn	19.1	11.7
Cotton	13.6	22.7
Aircraft and parts	8.4	9.3
Soybeans	7.5	16.9
Iron and steel scrap	3.3	1.6
Fertilizer	0.6	negl.
Telecommunication equipment	0.6	0.1
Other	5.4	9.2

Source: William Clarke and Martha Avery, "The Sino-American Commercial Relationship," in *China: A Reassessment of the Economy*, Joint Economic Committee, U.S. Congress, July 1975, Table 4, p. 513.

looked first to its traditional sources of supply, Australia and Canada, and only then to the United States, which in effect came to play the role of a residual supplier.

As a result of this drop in our exports, the United States–China trade imbalance was also markedly narrowed from about 11:1 in 1973 and 8:1 in 1974 to approximately 2:1 in 1975. This reflects a marked reduction in agricultural shipments on the one hand and some continued growth in our imports from China on the other. Moreover the commodity composition of our exports has changed, with capital goods, transport equipment, and other manufactures looming larger as these continue to rise even in the face of reduced farm shipments. When trade with China opened, the United States gained a rapidly increasing share of that trade. From a negligible level we moved into eleventh place among the People's Republic's trading partners in 1972, only to rise to second place by 1973 and 1974. However, with the decline in 1975, the United States ranked fifth as China's trading partner.

This analysis clearly suggests that the dynamic factor in United States–China trade has been the Chinese demand for our products. Fluctuations in this demand are producing fluctuations in total trade turnover. In marked contrast, U.S. imports from China have been much more stable and have risen continuously but quite slowly. In effect, the earlier projections concerning the market prospects for Chinese products in the United States have turned out to be fairly valid. Thus U.S. imports from China are comprised of textiles, some raw materials, a variety of minor consumer items, and some luxury products, illustrated by the data in Table 7-8. However, none of these can count on large mass markets in the United States, so the opportunities for a dramatic expansion of Chinese sales to us are limited.

In effect, the limiting factors in Sino-American trade have been twofold: the market for China's products in the United States, and China's capacity to sustain a large and continuing deficit in her trade with us. China's ability to sell in the United States is in turn constrained by the country's total export level, and more importantly by the limited market in the United States for the products sold by China. For instance, one of China's major exports has been textiles. However, a number of countries, notably Taiwan, Hong Kong, Singapore, and Korea, are competing for sales in a protected American market. Moreover, the Chinese are handicapped in the competition by virtue of the fact that their products have to bear the burden of the full U.S. tariff, while most of the other countries are allowed MFN (most-favored-nation) treatment.

Several attempts have been made to estimate the potential impact of MFN treatment on Chinese exports to the United States. Unfortunately, these stud-

Table 7-8. *Commodity composition of U.S. imports from China, 1973–1974 (in percent)*

Commodity category	1973	1974
Tin	12.0	8.2
Bristles, feathers, and down	10.5	6.9
Cotton fabrics	10.3	22.3
Works of art, antiques	8.6	6.8
Raw silk	6.8	2.4
Pyro-technical products	4.9	1.0
Rosin	8.6	6.8
Clothing and other textile products	3.1	6.0
Essential oils	2.3	4.2
Wood- and resin-based chemicals	2.4	6.0
Wool and other animal hair	2.8	1.7
Fish and shellfish	1.5	6.2
Tobacco	1.5	2.3
Other	24.7	19.2

Source: William Clarke and Martha Avery, "The Sino-American Commercial Relationship," in *China, A Reassessment of the Economy*, Joint Economic Committee, U.S. Congress, July 1975, Table 5, p. 514.

ies, based on widely varying assumptions and methodologies, arrive at sharply differing results. According to one, the MFN impact would be rather modest, with U.S. imports from China rising by an estimated 16 percent.[27] An entirely different approach, based on the assumption of full normalization of relations in all respects – i.e., full diplomatic recognition, settlement of the claims and assets problem, granting of MFN, and removal of all other trade barriers – concludes that our purchases from the PRC might be trebled or quadrupled.[28] A new and more systematic study of this problem is under way at the present but its results will not become available for some time.

In light of all these considerations, one can certainly conclude that granting MFN would increase Chinese exports to the United States, but by an unknown amount. On the one hand it would increase the quantities of products already being sold and on the other it would open the way to new products that cannot now compete in the U.S. market. At the same time it must be recognized that at least in the short run Chinese export supplies tend to be quite inelastic, so that substantial increases in sales to the United States would require diversion from other markets. This could still contribute to an increase in China's export earnings if prices in U.S. markets were higher than elsewhere.

Nevertheless, there is no doubt that even in the face of existing trade barriers (including MFN), Chinese exports to the United States could be increased with additional effort by all concerned. This would require aggressive salesmanship by the Chinese, extensive advertising of their products, and some further accommodation by China's trading corporations to the requirements of the American market. For instance, they may need to show greater readiness to grant special trademarks to large-quantity buyers and adapt to certain special styling and labeling requirements. Some progress along these lines has already been made as Chinese trading officials have come into increasing contact with American businessmen at the Canton Fair and elsewhere. This process has also been facilitated by the visits of Chinese trading delegations in certain special fields such as textiles, minerals and metals, and several others.

Expanding the market for Chinese products in the United States would not only represent a commercial gain for the PRC but could greatly contribute to raising the exports of our products to China. Trade does not need to be balanced, but the smaller the deficit the less the strain on China's balance of payments and the greater the inducement – other things being equal – for them to buy in the U.S. Therefore it is in the interests of certain American exporters to promote Chinese sales in our markets. This has been recognized by the Japanese some time ago and it is beginning to be understood by some American businessmen as well.

Realistically, all these efforts combined can at best be expected to yield only modest increases in Chinese sales in the United States. Therefore if trade is to be balanced, or even if the imbalance is not to exceed a 2:1 ratio, U.S. exports to China will necessarily be limited unless the PRC were to find means for financing this trade deficit. China maintains a sizable surplus in its trade with Hong Kong and Southeast Asia. In recent years the PRC has also obtained one or another form of banking credit in Japan and Western Europe. Thus the foreign exchange earned through a combination of these means can be applied to covering deficits in Sino-American trade, which is precisely what happened in 1973 and 1974. But China also incurs deficits in its trade with Japan and in recent years with Western Europe as well. This necessarily limits its capacity to finance trade deficits with the United States.

These balance of payment constraints were particularly pronounced in 1974 when the PRC incurred a record trade deficit of about 1 billion dollars, followed by another deficit of about 400 million in 1975. This necessarily influenced China's ability and willingness to continue to finance a large trade deficit with the United States. These balance of payment constraints limiting the expansion of U.S. exports to China could be alleviated or removed if the United States would be in a position to extend credits to China and China would be prepared to receive such credits. For the time being, political and institutional barriers preclude this possibility. The Trade Act of 1974 passed by the U.S. Congress bars the extension of government or government-backed credits to countries that limit emigration. Intended as a measure to induce liberalization of Soviet emigration, it automatically applies to China. At the same time, private bank credits to China are complicated by the claims–frozen assets problem. The U.S. Foreign Claims Settlement Commission awarded a total of about $176.4 million in private claims against the PRC. In turn, the United States has blocked Chinese assets in the United States valued at approximately $76.5 million.[29] Both these figures refer to principal exclusive of accumulated interest. Until this issue is resolved, direct banking relations between the two countries are precluded, since any new Chinese assets (e.g., bank deposits) and commodities could be attached by private claimants in the United States. For this same reason it would be difficult to mount Chinese trade exhibits in the United States.

The absence of direct banking relations between China and the United States is not too serious a problem, because financial transactions can be carried out through subsidiaries of American banks abroad or through third-country banks. Yet, due to a combination of these legal and institutional barriers, neither the U.S. Export-Import Bank nor private banks are in a position to directly extend trade or other credits to China. This places American exporters at a competitive disadvantage in the China market since such credits can be and are indeed extended by the Export-Import Bank of Japan, by other Japanese banks, and by Japanese corporations. Typically these are intermediate-term (usually for five years) supplier credits designed to finance complete-plant sales or large contracts of capital goods. This, combined with geographic and cultural proximity and frequently greater cost competitiveness, provides the Japanese with considerable advantages over the United States in the China market.

Progress in Sino-American trade is also hampered by the absence of full, formal, diplomatic relations between the two countries. Thus the Chinese as a matter of policy seem to be deliberately limiting and constraining their economic relations with the United States as a way of inducing us to move more speedily toward recognition. Therefore, they regard the United States not only as a residual supplier of agricultural products but of capital goods as well. That is, the Chinese are apparently interested in purchasing from the United States only those products they cannot obtain in the desired quantities elsewhere or in which we enjoy a very substantial technological lead.

Conclusions

Foreign trade serves as an indicator of both policy – domestic and foreign – and performance. At the same time it serves as an input into the growth and development process. Changing trade policies in China reflect shifting economic needs in different phases of the development process. They also reflect shifts in China's foreign policy and international relations. Moreover, foreign-trade movements serve as a fairly good index of domestic economic trends in China.

Thus in the 1950s, when China's GNP was growing very rapidly, foreign trade was expanding even more speedily. This was due to the very character of China's development process at the time, greatly reinforced by certain foreign-policy factors. One of the necessary conditions for growth acceleration was a rising rate of investment. This meant that investment was increasing more rapidly than GNP. A very large share of this investment was embodied in modern factories, railways, and other facilities. These in turn required modern, technically advanced machinery, equipment, and other installations which could not be produced in China and therefore had to be obtained abroad. For this reason alone the import component of investment was high, and with investment rising rapidly imports increased rapidly as well. To sustain this pace of expansion, exports had to increase rapidly as well to provide the foreign exchange necessary for financing these imports. As a result, this was a period which in a sense could be characterized as one of foreign-trade-led growth.

However, in the Cold War atmosphere of the time U.S. exports to China were totally embargoed and those of the other non-communist countries were subject to stringent controls. Many types of machinery and capital goods of all types could not be sold to China or sold only in limited quantities. This was also a period when the People's Republic was for reasons of its own – ideological, political, and military – following a "lean-to-one-side policy," based on a close Sino-Soviet alliance. This led to Soviet credits, which enabled China to finance trade deficits for a number of years. It also led to an open foreign-trade orientation in relation to other socialist countries. This orientation enabled China to obtain the machinery, equipment, and technical assistance required for rapid industrialization. But at the same time this opened the way to Soviet influence in many key posts of China's planning, management, and educational systems and in its defense establishment.

For that very reason the break in Sino-Soviet relations aggravated a sharp economic downturn experienced by China between 1960 and 1962. This was followed by a period of slower GNP growth in the 1960s and 1970s (see Table 6-7), that is, about 4 to 7 percent per year (depending on what period we are referring to) as compared to almost 11 percent between 1952 and 1959. These years of more moderate expansion were coupled with no net rise in the quantity of goods exported and imported between 1959 and 1971 (see Table 7-1). Therefore, this could be characterized as a period of trade-lagged rather than trade-led growth.

A number of factors combined to produce this result. The rupture of Sino-Soviet relations meant that many projects under construction were disrupted and thus not completed until some years later. At the same time, due to China's greatly enlarged capital-goods-producing capacity (resulting from the large plant-construction program started in the 1950s and completed in the 1960s), domestic output could meet a much larger share of the country's domestic requirements. During this period of more moderately paced growth, investment was rising more slowly, while the import component of investment was reduced as well because of the enlarged domestic machine-building capacity. For both these reasons the demand for imported capital goods lagged considerably.

To some extent, reduced capital-goods imports were replaced by imports of food and fertilizer. The first of these can be considered as an investment in economic and social stability, particularly for the crisis years. The second represented an investment in agricultural development. However, neither of these led to a rapid expansion of total imports. This lag in imports and in exports as well was reinforced by a deliberate policy of import minimization, that is, the so-called self-reliance policy. The pursuit of this policy almost certainly represented a reaction to the Sino-Soviet break, which had brought home to the Chinese the costs of preponderance or dominance by a single trading partner.

Perhaps, paradoxically, the further deterioration in Sino-Soviet relations in the late 1960s contributed to a reversal of this self-reliance policy. Once more, economic-development requirements combined with foreign-policy considerations, inducing a shift toward a more open foreign trade orientation – now directed at Japan, Western Europe, and the United States, rather than the Soviet Union. Undoubtedly an urge to again accelerate growth and technological progress so that the Chinese economy "will be advancing in the front ranks of the world" by the year 2000, must have played a major role in this latest policy shift. It was reinforced by China's need to seek closer relations with Russia's actual or potential adversaries as insurance against a possible Soviet threat.

However, this new policy also involves some built-in dilemmas. Due to the turnkey projects ordered from Japan, Europe, and the United States, engineers and technicians from these countries are coming to China to assist in the installation of the complete plants. This injection of foreign capitalist influences, techniques, and ideas has become a cause for concern by the Chinese authorities. However, they have minimized the actual or potential impact of this incursion by fairly effectively isolating these technicians from extensive contact with the Chinese people.

Probably a more serious problem is that the new foreign-trade orientation subjected the Chinese economy to the uncertainties and vagaries of the world market, as was amply demonstrated between 1973 and 1975. A booming world economy created a strong demand for many types of products, including those exported by China. Therefore the PRC had no difficulties in placing its rapidly rising exports and using the foreign exchange thus earned to finance a marked increase in imports. China incurred a small, but easily manageable, trade deficit in 1973. But the situation deteriorated under the impact of the world recession in 1974 and 1975. In 1973 China concluded a large number of contracts for the purchase of complete plants, transport equipment, and agricultural products, which began to be delivered in 1974. Moreover China had to buy these at high prices in a period of double-digit inflation.

At the same time, the world recession led to a sharp decline in the world demand for Chinese products. The country's non-oil exports, such as textiles and raw silk, were particularly hard hit. As a result, China incurred a record trade deficit of $1 billion in 1974. This deficit would have been even much larger if China had not exported about 6.5 million tons of oil that year. Thus the experience of 1974 and 1975 suggests that, as long as the world recession lasts, China's trade prospects will be unfavorably affected, except for oil. However, once an upturn in the world economy gains momentum, China's trade prospects should be quite favorable. Sales of non-oil products will almost certainly rise again, while oil exports may also be expected to continue increasing.

To pursue its goal of becoming a powerful, modern socialist state, China will have to rely on imports as a marginal but essential input. These imports serve as both a cushion and a stabilizer for the economy, and at the same time supply its advanced technology. China's foreign trade may be expected to expand as its economy grows. For the 1952–1974 period as a whole, GNP rose at an average annual rate of 6 percent, while foreign trade (adjusted for price changes) increased at a somewhat slower rate, that is at 5 percent a year. In spite of short-term problems imposed by a world economy subjected to a combined inflation and recession, and barring some unforeseen collapse or profound disruption in China, it would be reasonable to suppose that this pattern of expansion can be sustained during the coming decade.

8

The Chinese development model

Introduction

China's economic performance – based on the criteria of growth and stability – and the elements shaping it were appraised in the preceding chapters. The role of the past in conditioning ideological pre-dispositions, in imposing resource constraints, and in shaping institutional arrangements was explored in Chapter 1. This legacy combined with the prevailing ideology defined the goals and to some extent the policy and institutional instruments chosen for their implementation. This in turn required a far-reaching transformation of economic institutions to assure a high rate of resource mobilization and control over resource allocation. The latter issues were explored in Chapters 3 and 4.

To what extent can the combination of ends and means, objectives and instruments, used by the Chinese in the course of their economic development during the last quarter of a century be characterized as a distinct development model? What are the key elements of this model and is it transferable either as a whole or in part to other underdeveloped areas? These are the questions to be explored here based on the different strands of analysis in the earlier chapters.

It would be misleading to think of the Chinese development model as a static, frozen, unchanging system. On the contrary, as was indicated in Chapter 2, the Chinese have experimented with three or possibly four models since 1949. The original First Five-Year Plan strategy based on a more or less Stalinist development pattern was gradually modified through a process of trial and error until it evolved into the model associated with the 1970s, that is, the period since the Cultural Revolution. The focus throughout this chapter will be on this particular post–Cultural Revolution phase of China's development, recognizing that it too is bound to change in the future under the impact of leadership and policy shifts on the one hand and economic transformations generated by the very process of economic growth and structural change on the other.

This exploration of the currently prevailing model will proceed in steps. The goals and objectives of the post–Cultural Revolution regime will be examined first. This will be followed by an analysis of (1) the country's factor endowments and how these have conditioned the strategy adopted, (2) the incentives and institutional mechanisms used to mobilize and allocate resources consistent with the goals and the strategy adopted, (3) the economic performance generated by the interplay of objectives, strategies, and factor endowments, (4) the extent to which one can speak of a distinct Chinese development model and its applicability to other less developed countries, and (5) the dilemmas posed by the development approach adopted in the 1970s.

Objectives

The late Premier Chou's statement to the National People's Congress in January 1975 that China wants to build a powerful modern socialist country by the end of this century probably encapsulates Chinese Communist objectives in their clearest and most succinct form. The pursuit of power requires rapid growth of the economy as a whole; more specifically it requires rapid industrialization, with particular emphasis not only on military goods but also on those branches of industry that serve as inputs for defense production such as steel, fuel, and machinery.

However, rapid industrialization carries with it certain implications for agricultural development. An expanding population and labor force must be fed, a growing industry must be supplied with agricultural raw materials, and imports of machinery and other types of industrial equipment must be financed through exports. A developing country such as China could, if it wished, follow a quite open foreign trade orientation based on the principle of comparative advantage. That is, it could specialize in the production of certain types of farm products for which growing conditions are particularly favorable, use these both for home consumption and exports, and rely on imports to meet a significant share of food-supply requirements. While the Chinese import some foodstuffs, as shown in Chapter 7, these are marginal. Major reliance on imported farm products would violate the principle of self-reliance enunciated on many occasions as a major objective in addition to those mentioned by Chou. In the Chinese view, a foreign trade oriented farm policy would expose the country to the risk of sudden supply embaroges, rendering it thereby vulnerable to foreign pressures.

All of this means that agricultural development cannot be neglected lest it hamper and retard industrial growth. For essentially the same reasons consumer-goods production cannot be neglected either, even though it may be assigned a lower priority than expansion of producer-goods output. Increases in the output of texiles, daily necessities, other wage goods, and even some semi-luxuries (e.g., radios, watches, bicycles) are called for in part to keep pace with population growth and in part to permit at least a modest rise in the standard of living. Such increases are necessary as incentive measures for the labor force and as a means of sharing the fruits of development with the population at large.

The meaning of "modern" as used by Chou En-lai in his report to the National People's Congress is far from clear. This is not too surprising. Industrialization automatically implies a certain measure of modernization. At the minimum it implies a gradual spread of modern technology in industry and transport and also, although at a slower pace, in agriculture. It also means the rise of an army based on modern weapons, the spread of literacy, better health care, and the spread of modern science and its application to agriculture and industry.

However, the application of this concept to the process of production raises a number of dilemmas that have plagued Chinese policy makers throughout the history of the People's Republic. They also plagued Chinese statesmen and modernizers in the nineteenth and twentieth centuries. In the contemporary Chinese context the commitment to modern technology has to be reconciled with simultaneous commitments to "walking on two legs" and to the relative importance of being "red" versus "expert."

A key programmatic slogan of the early modernizers was: "Chinese learning for its fundamental principles (or its fundamental value) and Western learning for its practical use (or practical application)." In a basic sense one could similarly sum up Mao's value orientation and that of most of his associates as a counterpart of this. One could perhaps paraphrase it as "Marxist–Leninist–Maoist learning (or ideology) for its fundamental principles and modern technology for its practical application."

The dilemmas thus posed are clearly reflected in the meanings and connotations associated with the Chinese word *yang,* which can be interpreted as "modern, developed, strong," and as such it is a goal to be achieved. But it also suggests "foreign, alien, westernized" and as such may be associated with the restoration of capitalism, revisionism, and a feeling of inferiority as compared to technologically more developed economies and societies.

In contrast, *t'u* is or can be translated as "native, indigenous" and as such is identified with the common people of China, with the masses, and thus represents a positive value. But it can also mean "backward, primitive" and as such is a phenomenon to be overcome, to be conquered.

Perceived from this vantage point "experts" are to be prized; but this is coupled with a lingering suspicion that they are expert in "modern" and therefore "foreign" technology. They are divorced from the masses and tend to look down upon the cruder, more backward, and primitive methods used by them. Therefore, in Chinese Communist perceptions there may be some association between "red" and "native" on the one hand and "expert" and "foreign" on the other.[1]

Regardless of how interpreted, the pursuits of power and modernity are, of course, not unique to China; these objectives are shared by many other developing countries imbued with a strong sense of nationalism. However, the combination of power and modernity with a strong commitment to socialist values and to the spirit of self-reliance lends China its peculiar distinctiveness as a development model.

From the standpoint of the Chinese Communist leadership one of the most crucial aspects of socialism is the striving toward egalitarianism. There has been no pretension that egalitarianism has already been attained, but there was a determination by Mao and some other leaders as well, especially after the Cultural Revolution, to avoid programs and methods that lead away from rather than toward this ideal. Therefore, measures that may speed industrialization and modernization but contribute to a widening of income differentials encountered resistance. Similarly, the pursuit of socialism without regard of its impact on economic growth was also likely to be opposed. At any one time and in a specific situation there may be definite trade-offs between these two sets of objectives. Some leadership figures and cadres may be expected to assign a higher priority to growth and modernization in a particular situation than to egalitarianism and/or self-reliance. This leads to periodic shifts in policy as leaders are realigned and their power and influence either waxes or wanes. Such shifts may also occur as perceptions of key policy makers change over time and in response to changing conditions.

At least on Mao's part, the pursuit of egalitarianism involved a constant struggle against the rise and crystallization of a "New Class." However, many elements of the bureaucracy are anxious to protect their power and privileged position. Moreover given Mao's adherence to the principle of "democratic centralism," reduction of status differences did not mean a dispersion of political power, even in his own mind. This has led to ambiguities and a series of built-in contradictions, which have become the source of a multi-dimensional struggle. In the course of this struggle, some elements emphasize the "democratic" aspects involving mass participation and the reduction of status differences, while others stress "centralism," that is, the need to concentrate power.

This continuing struggle is also reflected in periodic drives to compress the wage structure and to narrow wage and salary differentials. The 1975 campaign against "bourgeois rights" was in part directed at these income differentials both in industry and agriculture. In agriculture this is to be accompanied by reducing and eventually abolishing the private plots, by gradually substituting the brigade for the team as the basic unit of accounting and income distribution in the commune, and by developing the backward areas.[2]

It is far from clear to what extent such compressions in income differentials narrow the scope of material incentives and thereby undermine work effort and the pursuit of higher skills and labor productivity. In the absence of firm evidence to the contrary, it could be argued that even if differentials were narrowed but not eliminated they could still serve as incentives, particularly if material rewards are supplemented by psychic appeals. Therefore, the narrowing of income differentials – depending on how far it goes in the direction of leveling – need not in and of itself retard industrialization and modernization.

As noted above, even Mao and his closest allies recognized that "democratic centralism" requires concentration of political power at the top. However, they wanted to prevent differentiation in power, role, function, and income from becoming frozen into status and class differentials. In spite of the Cultural Revolution, this objective does not seem to have been realized thus far. On the contrary, as one travels around China and meets peasants, workers, cadres, and high ranking government officials, status differences are clearly apparent in many subtle ways, such as dress, bearing, deference by others, and many other privileges that surround power positions in all societies.

These are among the considerations that have prompted periodic campaigns to break down the barriers between mental and manual labor on the one hand and urban and rural areas on the other. These campaigns and measures have contributed to a development approach that might be considered characteristic of a Chinese model. This concern with status differences was also one of the reasons for abolishing all insignia of rank in the army and for discouraging too explicit identifications of roles and titles since the Cultural Revolution. These considerations also play a role in the periodic attacks on the technocratic approach to economic, military, and administrative management, on professionalism and expertise in contrast to "redness." They also must have influenced the drive for the expansion of rural small-scale industries. While this is prompted by many other considerations (to be brought out in the next section), it serves to narrow the social and cultural distance as well as the technological and the "modernity" gap between factories and farms, city and country.

These concerns are also reflected in the *hsia fang* (down to the country) – the rustication – movement, which leads to the mass migration of youth from the city to the country. This more or less involuntary movement transfers a relatively well-educated manpower pool to the countryside and thus provides a resource for developing leadership and skill and for raising the educational levels of the peasantry. At the same time it deprives the city of a potential pool of talent and creates on the part of some of this youth a sense of frustration and alienation, brought about by difficulties of adjustment to an unfamiliar and harsh physical and cultural environment.[3]

Perhaps the most significant aspect of the rustication movement is that it reverses the flow of migration normally associated with the process of economic development. Large-scale rural–urban migration under the impact of rapid industrialization caused a great deal of concern in China in the 1950s. The press and official statements were replete with complaints concerning the "blind migration to the cities." More remarkable, and probably unprecedented in contemporary development experience, is the fact that an estimated 12 million young people have been "sent down" to the country from the city since 1968.[4]

However, this movement was not only prompted by a desire to break down barriers between city and country. Chinese planners and policy makers have for some time wanted to check the further growth of their largest cities for a number of reasons. They recognize that urban growth requires large-scale investments in social overhead capital such as schools, hospitals, new housing, and other facilities, none of which are directly or immediately productive. For instance, one of the vice-chairmen of the Shanghai Revolutionary Committee told the author in December 1972 that the population of Shanghai city has decreased in recent years; as of that time the population of the city proper was 5.7 million, that is, it was reduced to the 1953 level. He then went on to point out that administering a large city like Shanghai is an enormous and complex task. In his view it would be desirable, but unfortunately not possible, to reduce Shanghai to a city of 2 to 3 million.

At the same time, there are a number of indications that while the largest cities have stopped growing, intermediate and smaller cities are continuing to expand. In this way there is a continuum of cities in terms of size, a hierarchy of national, regional, provincial, district, and local centers. This hierarchy facilitates the communication and diffusion of new ideas and influences from above and needs, aspirations, and demands from below. In effect it also serves to narrow the distance between the largest centers and the masses.

The reduction of barriers between mental and manual labor is also fostered by the periodic tours of duty of urban cadres in communes. These tours may range from one to several months of farm work. However, since the end of the Cultural Revolution they have become more routinized and ritualistic, typically involving temporary duty of at most a few months. They are paralleled by the sending down of agricultural and other scientists to factories and farms to carry on either highly applied research specific to the locality or to adapt research findings to local conditions. Agricultural scientists are thus sent down to the countryside to perform what in effect amounts to farm extension tasks. Similar considerations may lead to the assignment of physical scientists to factories. In the same spirit, as a general rule, students are not admitted to universities unless they have had at least two years of experience on farms, in factories, or in the army. Moreover, while studying at universities they are once more assigned to factories for periodic tours of duty. At the same time, so-called workers' universities have been established in a certain number of advanced factories to raise the technical and educational level of the workers.

These measures clearly entail both benefits and costs. They undoubtedly contribute to the more rapid diffusion of advanced methods in factories and on farms. They may also reduce the psychological and attitudinal barriers between manual and mental workers. However, this has almost certainly led to a watering down in the academic and scientific quality of university training since the Cultural Revolution. Available evidence suggests that at least in some fields scientific research has also suffered.

It could be argued that an optimal strategy for an underdeveloped country would be to let industrially advanced countries bear the full cost of advancement in fundamental science and then merely borrow the findings and apply them to local circumstances. While this approach makes a lot of sense, it must be applied judiciously in a large country which is in the pursuit of increasing its power. Thus not all scientific findings travel freely across boundaries. Some have sensitive security implications and therefore may need to be developed by a country such as China more or less independently. But perhaps more importantly the adaptation of scientific findings to local conditions may require considerable scientific capacity itself. For instance, by assigning agricultural scientists to what may amount to extension work, Chinese planners may have contributed to yield improvements in the short run at the expense of the long run. That is, continuing yield improvements in China will require fundamental advances in plant breeding, in farm practices, and in agricultural science. If scientists are in communes instead of laboratories, then the development of agricultural science is bound to be retarded.[5]

In Chinese official pronouncements and statements the goal of self-reliance is usually linked to the pursuit of a "powerful modern socialist country." The self-reliance policy as usually stated in recent years involves "maintaining independence, keeping the initiative in our own hands and relying on our own efforts."[6] In fact, self-reliance as a development objective was already brought to the fore in the late 1950s. However, its salience and importance were markedly increased following the Sino-Soviet break in 1960. It encompasses several concepts and traits, with the prominence and emphasis given to each of these changing from time to time.

Thus self-reliance as an operational policy has been applied in several different contexts and for different purposes. First of all, it can serve as an important source of normative appeals, as can so many of China's long-range objectives. That is, it is used as one of the means for building pride in individual accomplishments by workers and peasants, factories and communes, cadres at all levels, and state organs. In this way it serves as a means of exhortation to maximum effort.

It also can carry with it a strong autarkic connotation. In a national sense it implies minimizing China's vulnerability to foreign economic pressure, particularly in the light of the Sino-Soviet break in 1960. In this sense self-reliance carries with it strong nationalist, exclusionary, and security (defense) connotations. These are explicitly brought out in another of Chairman Mao's frequently quoted directives, "dig tunnels deep, store grain everywhere, and never seek hegemony"; "be prepared against war, be prepared against natural disasters, and do everything for the people."[7]

Self-reliance is also intended to provide a means for minimizing the importation of foreign ideas, influences, and aspirations. In this sense it can serve as one of the means for preserving the purity of China's social system. This leads to minimizing contacts between foreign visitors and their Chinese counterparts – be they businessmen, engineers, and technicians helping in the installation of complete plants; scientists; diplomats; or just plain tourists. Of course, as shown in Chapter 7, this policy is not interpreted precisely the same way and enforced with the same vigor at all times. Thus it was interpreted more strictly and narrowly in the later 1960s than in the early 1970s.

However, self-reliance also has many connotations for domestic economic policy, primarily relating to regional and local self-sufficiency. This striving for self-sufficiency is largely rooted in transport barriers and bureaucratic resource-allocation bottlenecks inherent in a central planning system. Both of these stand in the way of supplying local needs. For instance, an American delegation of rural industry specialists visiting China in the summer of 1975 found that "even when communes are prepared to pay the going price for some desired item, it will not be necessarily available and they may get it faster if they produce it themselves."[8] Therefore, even if the manufacture of producer goods by rural industries may initially be high-cost and inefficient, this is likely to be out-weighed by the high costs of transporting raw materials and finished goods over long distances and by the administrative delays in obtaining these products from higher-level organs. These considerations then create strong inducements for the expansion of local industries to meet local, agricultural demand for these products.

The desire for self-reliance is reinforced by other considerations as well, such as the urge to decentralize industrial locations and to develop the more backward regions. As with all of the other objectives and policies discussed above, self-reliance too involves some costs and benefits. To the extent that the objectives spelled out above are actually attained, they can be included in the benefits column of this balance sheet. Depending on how rigidly the policy of self-sufficiency is enforced, it almost certainly entails some sacrifice of the advantages of international and/or inter-regional specialization and division of labor. If these costs outweigh the economic benefits of self-reliance, this would be reflected in a reduction in China's economic growth rate. Furthermore, local and regional self-sufficiency could favor the more advanced as compared to the underdeveloped areas of the country. Consequently, unless there are counteracting policies and tendencies at work, self-reliance policies could lead to a widening of local and regional income disparities.

An attempt to measure the net impact of this policy, the benefit–cost balance, would go well beyond the scope of this interpretative synthesis. Such an undertaking would be fraught with a host of conceptual and statistical pitfalls even if the data were available. Factor and commodity price distortions rooted in China's economic system provide an example of one set of problems. Difficulties of measuring long-term training and learning effects resulting from locating industries in rural areas, or of measuring the impact of such policies on regional income distribution, may serve as other examples. Moreover, even if the self-reliance policy were to lead to some sacrifice of growth it could still be pursued for the benefits it offers in terms of socialist, nationalist, or other goals.

Factor endowments

One of the most striking and crucial traits of Chinese agriculture is that it feeds about one-quarter of mankind on about seven percent of the globe's cultivated land. This necessarily means that the cultivated land area per capita is small, so that China is a very land-short economy. This is greatly accentuated by an acute scarcity of capital – less acute now than twenty-five years ago – as evidenced by a relatively small capital stock or small annual additions to capital stock per person. This may not be so small in comparison with other less developed countries near the bottom rungs of the world development scale, but it is quite small as compared to the more developed countries.

Therefore, the Chinese economy is characterized by an acute scarcity of land and capital and a relative abundance of labor. This was evidenced in the 1950s by remnants of open unemployment in the cities and at least seasonal underemployment in the rural areas, particularly during the winter months. In addition, there must have been pockets of disguised unemployment in all economic sectors. Some of this underemployment was gradually absorbed in the 1950s, as irrigation and other capital projects were introduced in agriculture and as capital plant was rapidly expanding in industry, transport, and other sectors.

However a systematic, conscious, all-out campaign to use labor in order to create capital was not launched until the Great Leap. In this sense the Great Leap represented the first comprehensive attempt in China to substitute on a mass basis a relatively abundant factor for a scarce one. As shown in earlier chapters, this attempt failed due to many errors in planning and implementation. However, the Great Leap concept as a development strategy well suited to China's factor endowments left an indelible imprint on Chinese planners and policy makers. It has been gradually rationalized since, through a process of trial and error.

As a result, we see in the 1970s a whole series of programs designed to convert labor into capital and in a certain sense even into land, that is, cultivated land. However, as these programs expand, more and more labor is absorbed so that labor shortages are becoming pronounced and labor too is developing into a scarce factor, although still relatively abundant as compared to land and capital.

These rationalized Great Leap–type programs of agricultural development (usually identified with Tachai as a model) involve land improvement, irrigation, and generally a marked intensification in the patterns of land use. This involves "*farmland capital construction*" based on "*self-reliance* and hard struggle transforming China in the spirit of the Foolish Old Man who removed the mountains."[9] More concretely, it indeed means reshaping the geographical features of an area to provide the physical conditions necessary for the application of an appropriate mix of other inputs – labor, machinery, fertilizer, and improved seed strains – to bring about high and stable yields. This often requires squaring or terracing the land; at times it involves leveling mountains and transporting the soil manually in baskets for several kilometers to build a huge dam or to cover some areas with top soil. In many areas it means constructing underground drainage channels, reservoirs, canals, irrigation channels, pumping stations, and tube wells.[10]

The major effort in this renewed and expanded movement to learn from Tachai seems to be concentrated in North China, where the water supply has in the past been highly variable, unreliable, and short. Precisely for this reason grain yield per acre of cultivated land has generally been lower in the North than in the South. Correspondingly, the opportunity for raising yields with large investments in land improvement may be expected to be considerably greater in the North. Therefore, it seems that this is the region the Chinese leadership is relying on to raise agricultural output significantly beyond current levels. A larger, more regular, and better distributed water supply combined with improved seeds and more fertilizer could lead to a spread of rice production in the North and a significant rise in multiple cropping per acre.

These massive "farmland construction" projects clearly absorb masses of labor – much of it utilized during the slack season. At the same time, the intensity of land use is also being greatly stepped up in areas that have been traditionally irrigated. More and more of the single-cropped areas are being double cropped and double-cropped areas are being converted to triple cropping. In addition, there is more inter-planting and transplanting of crops that heretofore had not been subject to this practice such as wheat, corn, and cotton. All these measures are designed to increase yields per acre; therefore they are in effect land-saving, but they also absorb a great deal of labor.

Labor is also being claimed by the rapidly expanding rural industries. As noted in earlier chapters these produce fertilizer, cement, farm machinery, bricks, iron and steel, pumps, and other types of equipment needed as inputs in farm production. As a result of all these measures, rural labor seems to be quite fully employed all year round. Moreover, there are repeated signs of marked labor shortages in at least some rural areas and during some periods of the year. This has greatly increased the pressure for mechanizing some of the production and processing operations in farming, particularly those that absorb a lot of labor during harvesting and cultivating time. Thus, the emphasis on selective mechanization of agriculture has been quite pronounced in recent Chinese statements and official pronouncements.[11]

Grain milling provides a telling example of how much labor can be saved even by quite modest measures of mechanization. According to data collected by the American Rural Small-Scale Industry Delegation, hand pounding of rice requires 400 man-hours per ton in some of the places they visited in China. A simple pedal-operated device can do it in 120 man-hours while a commune-run rice mill requires 10 man-hours.[12] Similarly, a lot of labor can be saved by the mechanization or semi-mechanization of threshing; therefore it is not surprising that mechanization has progressed furthest in these two types of operations.

However, the adaptation of production and capital formation technology to the country's factor endowments is not confined to agriculture. It is also quite apparent in Chinese industry, although perhaps in a less dramatic form. In industry it is manifested by the simultaneous application of a spectrum of technologies, based on different factor proportions. This "walking on two (or several) legs" is demonstrated by the rise and spread of rural industries on the one hand and the rapid expansion of large-scale factory industry on the other. At the same time it is illustrated by the simultaneous utilization of both highly mechanized, capital-intensive and preponderantly manual, labor-intensive processes within the same factory, each used for particular operations. But this latter phenomenon is not unique to China. To a greater or lesser extent it is a familiar feature of the development landscape in all industrializing countries.

In this respect the distinctiveness of the Chinese development model is derived from the scale of and approach to "farmland capital construction" and the close integration of rural industrial and agricultural development analyzed in greater detail in Chapter 4. In the Chinese case this process of adapting technology to the prevailing factor endowments is carried well beyond the formation of physical capital; it is applied to human capital formation as well.

Perhaps the scarcest resource in China – even scarcer than land and capital – is highly skilled manpower such as scientists, engineers, and medical personnel. This scarcity was of course much more pronounced before 1949, since the supply has been significantly augmented in the past twenty-five years. In the face of such scarcities, the training and utilization of this type of manpower – particularly the technological aspects of this utilization – can have far-reaching implications not only for economic growth and military security, but also for income distribution and the welfare of the population at large.

Perhaps this can be most clearly demonstrated in the field of health care and delivery systems. In many less developed areas a significant share of the physicians tend to be trained in advanced countries or in medical schools at home that emulate their practices. Frequently this means that the physicians are trained to work with complex and very expensive medical equipment, relying on elaborate hospital facilities and highly advanced methods of health care. Medical personnel thus trained are strongly tempted to reproduce these facilities and practices at home.

Low-income countries, however, can at best afford only a small number of such health care units. This then becomes one of the factors that may lead to the concentration of physicians and health facilities in the cities at the expense of the countryside. In the absence of strong counter-measures, this leads to situations in which the urban upper-income groups are relatively well provided for with medical care while only minimal provisions may be made for the care of the rural masses. Therefore, in low-income countries capital-intensive health care systems tend to favor the rich as compared to the poor.

The Chinese seem to recognize this quite clearly and thus have adopted a strategy designed to produce a mass base for the wide distribution of health care.[13] By training a sizable pool of para-medical personnel, they have built a hierarchy of manpower and facilities ranging from the most advanced in the large centers to the quite simple or even primitive in the villages. However, this does not necessarily mean that complete egalitarianism in health care quality and delivery has actually been attained; it rather means that as compared to the past these differentials have almost certainly been narrowed both inter-personally and inter-regionally.

The same general strategy characterizes the Chinese approach to manpower training and utilization in other fields. For instance, it applies to agricultural scientists and farm extension workers, as indicated above. It is also evident in industry in the technical education provided to workers, thus creating a continuum extending from the highly trained engineer, to the less well trained who are educated in so-called workers' universities, to the skilled worker, and to the unskilled laborer.

In many ways, the picture presented here is a highly simplified and idealized blueprint, which in its present form is largely the child of the Cultural Revolution. Although some programs can be traced back to the early 1960s, others were introduced only since 1968–1969 or even later and thus some have not yet become diffused all over the country. It will take time to train people in sufficient numbers to implement this strategy fully. Beyond this, there are inevitably some costs as well as benefits built into this approach. The recognition of these costs and dilemmas has apparently produced some resistance to the implementation of these programs in universities and scientific laboratories.

In a certain sense the strategy of human resource development adopted in China tries to substitute a mass-based system for an elite-based one. To accomplish this the top of the educational and manpower pyramid is faced with the risk of becoming diluted in several ways. On the one hand, the energies of the people at the top tend to become scattered as they are induced to perform a variety of tasks. They have to spend some time in the rural areas, with the masses; often they have to concentrate on highly applied research, development, or extension work rather than on basic research. They also have to devote time to political education and discusssion. As a result, their own scientific and advanced technical development may suffer. The scientific and technical advances in their own fields may thereby be retarded.

On the other hand, the educational policies adopted since the Cultural Revolution seriously undermine the possibility of replacing those at the top with equally well trained people. This is due to the fact that admission requirements to universities, including the leading institutions, have been appreciably eased. Elementary and secondary schooling combined were reduced from twelve to nine or ten years. At the same time the university curriculum was shortened from four to six years to three or three and a half years. Moreover, university students have to spend some time in factories and on farms and in political education. It may very well be that this system turns out students of greater dedication and commitment – although there is no way of assessing this one way or another – admirably suited to occupy a range of intermediate technical, scientific, and leadership positions. However, it is doubtful that it can produce a generation of high-grade scientists, physicians, and engineers.

This is clearly recognized by many scientists and academicians in China, as evidenced by the fact that these practices have been a subject of continuous debate, with considerable pressure to upgrade academic standards. As a result, visitors to Chinese universities are always told that they are still in a state of "struggle, criticism and transformation." Based on all these considerations combined it could be argued that the pattern of manpower training and utilization adopted since the Cultural Revolution is well designed to adopt and distribute rapidly technology and knowledge that is well developed. However, this could be at the expense of borrowing from the future in the sense that this strategy, if sustained over a long period, may undermine China's capacity to push forward the frontiers of science and technology.

Institutional mechanisms and incentives

The adoption of production and investment technologies designed to implement societal objectives in ways suited to China's factor endowments required the crystallization of a system of economic organization for resource mobilization and resource allocation. It also required a set of incentives to motivate the human actors in the system to contribute to the best of their ability.

Thus farm production was collectivized so as to facilitate consolidation of land holdings, gain economies of scale, obtain more ready access to agricultural produce, accelerate the flow of new ideas and techniques to rural areas, and prevent the rise of a "kulak" class in the countryside. Collectivization did not entail institutional innovation, since it was adopted from the Soviet Union. However, while collectivization in the Soviet Union was preponderantly extraction-oriented, the Chinese were equally concerned about promoting production. But collectives – agricultural producers' cooperatives later transformed into production teams – were too small to manage an integrated approach to agricultural development involving farm production, capital construction, and rural industrialization at one and the same time. This, combined with several other considerations, led the Chinese to bold innovation in the form of communes, which turned out to be counterproductive in their initial and experimental forms; but following a process of trial and error, they seem to have evolved into quite effective instruments for the mobilization of labor and other resources and its allocation to competing tasks.

With the team and the village remaining the basic units of social organization and production, the close links between reward and effort could be preserved. This was reinforced by the continued maintenance of private plots and rural markets, which served to reinforce material incentives. There are definite indications that some leadership groups are pressing for the collectivization of private plots and the simultaneous transfer of the income-accounting functions from the team to the brigade. These measures would inevitably disturb the currently prevailing reward system. How this would affect peasant incentives, if these changes were introduced gradually and combined with persuasion and indoctrination, is impossible to forecast. They would almost certainly be disruptive and counter-productive if introduced suddenly and simultaneously in the country as a whole.

Agricultural collectivization and communization in agriculture were paralleled by nationalization of industry and the other non-farm sectors. In this way the state and its subordinate organs assumed direct control over the management of industrial, banking, trading, and other kinds of enterprises. Broadly speaking, in all these sectors the Chinese adopted institutional forms pioneered by the Soviet Union in the 1920s and 1930s. As described in Chapters 3 and 4, these enterprises bought from and sold to each other intermediate and producer goods. They sold consumer goods to households and, in turn, purchased labor from them. All transactions between enterprises and households were in cash, while inter-enterprise payments were made through a system of bank clearings.

Prices of most commodities were fixed and controlled by central or local state organs. Most producer goods and the most essential consumer necessities were subject to "unified distribution," that is, distribution through licensing and rationing. The market as a mechanism for distributing goods and services played a limited and supplementary role. It was used to distribute producer goods not subject to licensing and consumer goods not encompassed by rationing. Within this limited purview, prices played a significant role as allocators of the goods and services distributed through the market mechanism. They also played at least an indirect role in the allocation of goods subject to "unified distribution." That is, prices may have exerted some influence over the particular factor combination and raw materials mix actually used by an enterprise even if these were subject to administrative allocation.

Irrespective of their potential function as allocators, prices served as a basis for valuing all goods and factors and of measuring enterprise performance based on profit or loss accounts. Enterprises turned virtually all their net earnings into the state budget in the form of profits and taxes. The budget, in turn, served as a source of investment finance for all but the locally administered enterprises. These institutional arrangements represent familiar features of economic organization in all socialist countries although there are naturally considerable differences in detail between the Soviet Union, Eastern Europe, and China.

None of these institutions or instruments – in agriculture, industry, and the other sectors – could serve as a means of implementing leadership and societal objectives without a planning system to provide the framework and the direction for this resource-allocating process. Unfortunately, available information concerning the nature and organization of the Chinese planning system is very limited and highly fragmentary, especially for the 1960s and 1970s.

As indicated above and in Chapter 4, it is a system based on a mixture of price and physical-planning elements, combining administrative and bureaucratic command allocation with market allocation of factors, goods, and services. It represents a blend of decentralized and highly centralized traits, combining central control with more or less decentralized administration. Thus, as shown in Chapter 5, central authorities maintain a tight control over budgetary outlays at all levels of government down to the county. This provides them with control over the major sources of funds with which to influence and shape the resource-allocation process.

This control is probably most pronounced in the field of fixed capital investment, since state enterprises are totally dependent on the government budget for financing these. However, communes and sub-commune enterprises retain their earnings after taxes and thus generate their own investment funds. To this extent the state's control over the pattern of investment is less complete in agriculture than in the other economic sectors. Central control is also much less far-reaching in the allocation of other factors, that is, land, labor, and raw materials.

Thus the patterns of land use are largely locally determined. For non-farm tasks, labor is mostly allocated by provincial, county, and municipal labor bureaus, while in agriculture this function is performed by the communes, brigades, and teams. Centralized and decentralized approaches seem to be combined in the allocation of fuel, power, and materials, although the precise mechanics of distribution and the division of labor between central and local government organs is quite obscure in this field. A certain number of commodities are subject to national distribution. As suggested in Chapter 4, this is probably a smaller number than in the past, possibly over 100 items of great national importance such as iron and steel. This reduction in the number of commodities subject to national materials-supply allocation in itself represents a move in the direction of decentralization.

This tendency is reinforced by the fact that the distribution of all other producer goods and a wide range of consumer goods is delegated to provincial, municipal, and county authorities. There is also a category of goods which, as noted above, are distributed by the market but on the basis of prices fixed by the planning organs. Decentralization is also fostered in China by the considerable transport barriers referred to earlier and by the recognition that a highly centralized system of resource allocation could cause enormous delays in the delivery of goods and in general produce far-reaching inefficiencies. These high transport costs and administrative bottlenecks provide local industries with what in effect amounts to high tariff-like protection from potential competition by large-scale urban factories.[14]

Decentralization is further encouraged by the spirit of self-reliance, which exhorts local organs to "take the initiative in their own hands." All these considerations combined induce local enterprises to meet their needs from their own resources or resources already placed at their disposal, rather than wait for additional allocations. Such initiatives are, in turn, made possible by the fact that no enterprise or government jurisdiction is barred from producing any above-plan or outside-plan items as long as it does not lay claim on additional outside resources.

However, decentralized allocation of land, labor, and materials does not preclude *central or national planning and control* over this allocation process. Not only does the budget serve as a powerful central control lever, but the Chinese Communist Party apparatus with its network of cadres reaching down to all enterprises, government organs, villages, and production teams provides a powerful unifying thread. This network provides an *informal channel of communication and command* through which central authorities can shape and influence the planning process. This informal channel is in part based on *administration by moral example* and on *model emulation* guided by the prevailing ideological precepts and value system.[15] Positive reinforcement is complemented by various forms of pressure or coercion. One of the overwhelming impressions one gains from documentary evidence and from first-hand observation in China is that this seems to be a society without an escape. An individual is rarely permitted to retreat into his private self; on the contrary, he is constantly exhorted to participate. Deviant behavior is severely punished, not necessarily through incarceration but by denial of material and other benefits and by what amounts to humiliation, excommunication, and a range of more or less subtle pressures exerted through small neighborhood groups in the city and small work groups in the village.

Moral example and model emulation as a basis for guiding proper conduct are deeply rooted in Chinese tradition and in the Confucian ethic. They have been transformed by the Chinese Communists into potent guides to action. Positive models such as the Tachai production brigade in agriculture or the Ta-ch'ing oil fields in industry are widely publicized. They are combined with negative examples as a means of communicating to the cadres and the masses what is considered approved as compared to anti-social behavior and what practices are to be emulated or avoided. Moral exhortation and model emulation reinforced by education and indoctrination are designed to bring about a convergence in the value systems of the leaders, cadres, and masses. To the extent that they do indeed lead to such convergence in reality they can greatly ease the administrative burdens of central planning and bureaucratic resource allocation.

Moral example, model emulation, and normative appeals in general, while important in the Chinese planning process, would not in and of themselves suffice to motivate cadres, workers, and peasants. They need to be supplemented by both material incentives and the more or less subtle forms of pressure referred to above. Actually, the relative weight to be placed on normative appeals as compared to material incentives has been one of the most contentious issues in the policy debates waged during the life span of the People's Republic. In spite of these debates, occasional fluctuation, and pressures, the basic character and structure of material incentives and the reward system as a whole have not changed very much since the mid-1950s.

As noted in earlier chapters, China's industrial wage structure is based on an eight-grade classification which has prevailed since the wage reform of 1956.[16] It provides for a 3:1 to 4:1 wage span, which in some quite extreme cases may go up as high as 5:1. Super-imposed on this wage structure are rates for administrative, technical, scientific, and political cadres which start higher and rise above the top industrial wage. This widens the wage and salary span to about 7:1. At its extremes it may go as high as 13:1 or even 20:1. Clearly, these are quite sizable differentials. However, as will be shown below, there are countervailing forces at work which lead to a narrowing of this span, particularly at the extremes. Moreover, even at its extremes these wage and salary differentials are narrower than those prevailing in Republican China (1911–1949) or in many other underdeveloped countries.

Upward movement along this wage scale is apparently based on seniority, skill, performance, and political attitude. Thus wage and salary differentiation serves as an important spur to better and higher quality effort, that is, to raising labor productivity, unless seniority becomes the predominant criterion for promotion. On the other hand wages play a very limited role as allocators of labor. This is evidenced by the fact that inter-industry and inter-regional wage differentiation is quite narrow and frequently based on cost of living differentials.[17] It is also borne out by the fact that labor tends to be moved from place to place and sector to sector by assignment rather than by free movement.

In assessing the role of material incentives, it must be remembered that management bonuses have never played an important role in China, in contrast to the Soviet Union and other socialist countries in Eastern Europe.

They have not been distributed at all since the Cultural Revolution, and possibly since the 1950s. At the same time, premiums were occasionally distributed to workers in enterprises that fulfilled their plans. It is unclear whether this practice has been continued since the Cultural Revolution.

Conjoined with material incentives, normative appeals are not confined to moral example and model emulation. They are translated into tangible psychic rewards based on many different forms of recognition which carry prestige, special titles such as "model worker," or other types of distinction. Some of these may in addition yield material benefits as well. Psychic rewards may be reinforced by a commitment to "serve the people." Neither documentary sources nor visitors' observations can provide conclusive evidence as to the depth of this commitment by the cadres and the masses. To the extent that this is the case it can serve as a powerful lubricant in the functioning of the planning system and the whole process of bureaucratic resource allocation.

Performance

The actual behavior of the development model sketched in the preceding sections can best be gauged by assessing China's economic performance during the past twenty or twenty-five years. As noted before, China's economic development during this quarter of a century was actually based on several alternative models. However, the basic development approach utilized since the Cultural Revolution can be traced back to at least the Great Leap, and in many of its aspects even to the mid-1950s. The successive models tried represented more shifts of emphasis than totally new departures. Therefore it may be both legitimate and useful to assess the development experience as a whole, rather than confine this appraisal to the much too brief span of the post–Cultural Revolution years.

Given the objectives spelled out above and in Chapter 2, the most relevant criteria for appraising China's economic performance may be considered stability, growth, income distribution, standard of living, and self-reliance. Each of these will be reviewed here in the light of the more detailed analysis in the preceding chapters.

Economic stability

As indicated in Chapter 5, the objective of economic stability involves the maintenance of both full employment and a stable price level. It can also be viewed as the unfolding of a reasonably stable growth path associated with relatively mild or minimal fluctuations in output and employment.

In China there was clear evidence of open urban unemployment in the early 1950s when the economy was still recovering from war devastation and was thus operating at less than full capacity. Open unemployment appeared again in the crisis years between 1960 and 1962 or 1963. During the rest of this period China was experiencing no large-scale unemployment. Inevitably there was some seasonal underemployment in agriculture and some wasteful or inefficient utilization of labor in industry and other sectors. For instance, anyone visiting Chinese factories in recent years must have been struck by the relatively large and often not fully utilized pool of labor one encounters in these plants.

More remarkable than the record of employment has been the course of price stability in China. However, it must be stressed that this finding is based on an official index which may understate price rises of unrationed commodities, although it seems to be borne out by comparisons of samples of commodities and of wages for the 1950s and 1970s. China's performance in containing inflation becomes even more impressive when viewed in the perspective of the country's experience in the past, Soviet pre–World War II experience, and the double-digit inflation raging in the contemporary world.

On the other hand, China's economic development was characterized by marked fluctuations in rates of growth, as shown in Table 6-7. This was most clearly illustrated by the explosive growth during the Great Leap years of 1958 and 1959 and the drastic collapse during the crisis years between 1960 and 1962. There were milder dips during the Cultural Revolution, and throughout the years rates of growth alternatively accelerated and decelerated. For this reason, China's economic performance must be judged as somewhat mixed if based on the criterion of stability. It was remarkable in terms of avoiding the pitfalls of inflation, but it was subject to marked fluctuations in rates of growth – and sometimes even in levels – of production and at times in employment as well.

Economic growth

In spite of these fluctuations, the growth performance of the Chinese economy can be considered very impressive when compared to that of (1) Republican China (1911–1949) or some sub-period thereof or (2) presently developed countries that were in the process of industrialization between the late eighteenth and twentieth centuries. In contrast, it is less exceptional in comparison with the post-war experience of other underdeveloped areas, particularly in Asia (e.g., South Korea, Taiwan).

As shown in Chapter 6, measurement of growth in China and some other countries as well is greatly complicated by the absence of reliable statistics. However, if we accept the reconstructed official data as a basis for analysis (as summarized in Table 6-7), China's average annual rate of growth between 1952 and 1974 may be estimated at around 6 percent. If the country's GDP estimates were expressed in terms of more recent prices (e.g., 1970, 1971, or 1975 prices), the growth rates would be somewhat lower. Presently industrialized countries have attained their mid-twentieth century level of development with an average rate of growth which, in most cases, was not much above 3 percent per year. It is of course true that these countries started their industrialization process in the late eighteenth and early nineteenth centuries at a level of per capita income probably higher than that of China today. Even so, it must be remembered that a 3 percent rate of growth produces nearly a twentyfold increase in GNP over a century; a 4 percent rate yields almost a fortyfold rise; and a 6 percent rate leads to an increase of over 300 times in a century.

One cannot sufficiently emphasize the fact that growth rates of 4 to 4.5 percent, which appear moderate by contemporary standards, were characteristic historically of the most rapidly expanding and dynamic economies. This is the rate that transformed Japan into a major industrial country between 1870 and 1940. If China were to grow at the same historical rate as Japan (about 4 percent), then its GNP would be approximately 14,000 billion yuan (at constant prices) in 2075 as compared to an estimated 350 billion in 1975. At today's exchange rates, Chinese product would be approximately equivalent to 7,000 billion U.S. dollars, that is, close to five times the 1975 GNP level for the United States. This would necessarily mean that China would be an enormous economic power, at least in absolute terms. Whether this would also be true in a relative sense will necessarily depend on what happens in the coming century in the United States, the Soviet Union, and Japan. Indeed, if these countries follow their past growth patterns, the gap between them and China will increase, rather than diminish. All this, however, constitutes a very artificial projection, given the enormous imponderables of China's and these other countries' future. Therefore, it is only intended as an illustration of what may be the implications of a 3 to 6 percent growth rate over a century.

Income distribution

Having explored in some detail the problems of stability and growth in Chapters 5 and 6 and more briefly above, it is most essential to review some of the fragmentary evidence concerning income distribution in China. Direct quantitative measures of China's income distribution are precluded by the lack of relevant statistics. Nevertheless it is possible to illuminate this question, at least partially. For this purpose three kinds of information are presented in this section. First, some data on the comparative wage structure of China and certain other countries are discussed and analyzed. Second, the implications of the income redistribution resulting from land reform, collectivization, and nationalization are analyzed in somewhat hypothetical terms. Third, the trends in inter-regional per capita product differentials are assessed as a possible means of illuminating changes in income distribution between the 1950s and the 1970s.

One of the most striking characteristics of Chinese society as seen by virtually any visitor is its apparently egalitarian character in terms of income. As one travels around China, be it in the city or in the countryside, one sees poverty but very rarely abject misery or degradation, so frequently associated with the extremes of deprivation. One certainly has the impression that the Chinese have succeeded in placing a floor on real incomes. Firsthand visual impression, at least in areas to which foreigners have access, also shows that people seem well fed, adequately clothed – at times with a relatively narrow band of differentiation in quality of dress, be it men or women. This impression is reinforced by the fact that one very rarely is exposed to extremes of luxury and high living. It is also particularly striking if one has been to India or some other parts of Asia.[18]

More tangibly, however, during a month-long visit to China it is possible to collect wage and salary data, as did a group including the author in December 1972 and January 1973. The data thus gathered in factories, local industry, schools, universities, and other institutions suggest certain patterns. It became clear that the wage span of industrial workers in factories varied from about 3:1 to 5:1. Based on an eight-grade classification, industrial wages would usually range from about 30 yuan to 100 or 120 yuan a month (as illustrated in Table 8-1) to which were added certain payments in kind. Similar data were gathered by other visitors and can also be confirmed from evidence in Chinese documentary sources.[19]

A very similar wage structure was encountered in a Shanghai textile mill, in a pottery factory near Canton, and in several factories in Nanking. The average wage in these factories was given as 60 to 70 yuan a month, that is, within Grade 5 and closer to the bottom than to the top of the scale. Interestingly enough, this range of wage differentials is quite typical for industries in many other countries, both developed and underdeveloped. For instance, in Guatemala the ratio of average hourly earnings of electrical fitters to laborers

Table 8-1. *Monthly wage in two Chinese factories in 1972*

Grade	Wage in yuan: Shenyang No. 1 Machine Tool Plant	Wage in yuan: Anshan Rough Rolling Mill
Apprentices	22.00	19–21
Workers' Grade: 1	33.00	34.50
2	38.90	40.00
3	45.80	48.13
4	54.00	56.82
5	63.60	67.10
6	74.90	79.25
7	88.20	84.50
8	104.00	110.00

Source: A. Eckstein, *China Trip Notes* (mimeo), Ann Arbor, Mich., December 1972 and January 1973.

was 7:1 in the early 1960s. The ratio of carpenters' wages to unskilled laborers' in construction was 5:1. In Singapore, the ratios between government skilled and unskilled rates was 2.5:1. In Egypt, average weekly earnings of semi-skilled workers in all industries were more than three times as high as unskilled earnings in 1960.[20] In the U.S. and Europe the wage spread within industry seems to be typically around 3:1. All these examples suggest that the Chinese industrial wage structure is not significantly more egalitarian than that of other countries. Yet this conclusion must be treated with caution since many of these wage data are not fully comparable.

For technical and engineering personnel, the salaries would usually start at about 50 to 80 yuan and go up to 150 to 200 yuan a month. For instance, a chief engineer would frequently be in this top range. However, for very senior management, technical, and professional personnel, including senior full professors, we were quoted salaries of 300 to 400 yuan. This suggests that a wage and salary span of 10:1 can at least occasionally be found in China. Moreover, if we compare the polar ends of these scales, ranging from an apprentice to that of senior professional or political figures, differentials of 20:1 can also be encountered. There is no doubt that the number of people in these top ranges must be very small.

What would this mean in terms of U.S. equivalents? According to the *Handbook of Labor Statistics*, the average farm wage rate in the United States in 1972 was about $360 per month.[21] The lowest union wages quoted in the same *Handbook* were $2.11 per hour for truckers' helpers in Birmingham, Alabama. Translated very crudely to an annual rate, this would mean roughly $4,000 to $4,500 a year. Starting with a base rate of $4,000, a ratio of ten to one would call for an income of $40,000 a year and twenty to one for an income of $80,000 a year. Since there is no income tax in China, these would have to be net spendable incomes, which according to recent U.S. tax rates for a family with two children would be equivalent to a gross salary of about $160,000 a year. Of course there are some, but very few, chief executives in the United States who are earning gross salaries and bonuses (i.e., before paying taxes and exclusive of property incomes) of perhaps as much as $500,000 to $800,000 a year.

Therefore, at these very extremes the U.S. wage and salary span may go as high as 50:1 or even 75:1 (on a net, after-tax basis). In most African countries, where the disparities tend to be largest, the ratio between the usual starting salary of a university graduate in the civil service and an unskilled laborer in the capital city was between 8:1 and 11:1 in 1963. In India, the comparable ratio was 5:1 in 1958. However, if we take the top of the scale reached by the numerous graduate cadres and compare it to unskilled labor rates, the differential is much more striking – about 30:1 in Africa and roughly the same in India. In fact, a young university graduate may be paid ten times more than an unskilled worker, a permanent secretary (the top career in the civil service) thirty times more, and an industrial manager in the private sector eighty times more.[22]

All of this suggests that at the extremes the wage and salary spread in the United States and in many underdeveloped countries is much wider than in China. Of course, if property incomes are added, the gap between China and the other countries becomes even wider. At the same time, the spread in China is significantly greater than one would pre-suppose on the basis of visual observation alone. Of course, wage and salary data in and of themselves do not tell us much about distribution, since we do not know how many people are encompassed by each income-earning class. Beyond that, wage and salary spreads of 10:1 or 20:1 may represent very differing degrees of real income differential in China as compared to the United States, India, or other underdeveloped countries. One would expect this to be true for a number of reasons. Housing rentals are nominal in China, very rarely exceeding 2 to 4 percent of monthly income. Health services for all factory workers are free and for workers' dependents provided at nominal rates. Prices are fixed in such a way that all necessities are priced very low, while luxury goods are priced very high. As a result, the price structure itself has built into it certain elements of progressivity that tend to narrow the real purchasing power differential between the top and the bottom of the income scale in China. This is further reinforced by the fact that consumer necessities, the purchases of which loom large in consumer budgets, are rationed so that higher income groups cannot bid them away. Moreover, the range and quantity of luxury goods obtainable at any price is quite limited in China. Finally, luxury consumption is frowned upon, particularly since the Cultural Revolution, so that even if the luxury goods are available and people can afford them, they are discouraged from buying them.

In addition, there are continuous pressures to narrow the wage and salary spread. Thus, workers in grades 1 and 2 are periodically promoted en masse. Monthly salaries of 300 to 400 yuan for senior personnel result from the fact that some individuals were raised to these levels in earlier years and have not been reduced since. At the same time, people now appointed as senior engineers or professors obtain top salaries of around 200 yuan a month. This would suggest that the wage and salary span could be considerably compressed in the future, possibly to 5:1 or 7:1 unless current wage policies are markedly reversed. On the other hand all the data cited thus far relate to the urban sector, while based on available indications, peasant incomes and wages in the rural areas seem to be considerably lower. If this is taken into account, even if top salaries do not exceed 200 yuan, wage differentials of at least 10:1 may be expected to prevail for some time to come.

One may also assume that people near the top of the managerial, professional, and political-cadres scale also receive sizable perquisites or payments in kind. If these are included, spans of 10:1 may be on the low side. In spite of this, income differentials both in money terms and in real terms are almost certainly higher in the United States or in India than in China. This is of course what one would expect. The purpose of the comparison is not to suggest that the two spans or distributions are comparable but merely to illustrate that the degree of inequality in China is probably significantly greater than visual impression or ideological commitment would suggest. This also implies that the Chinese clearly must be relying to a much greater extent on material incentives as a means of motivating workers, technicians, managers, and professionals than is often sanctioned by official statements. At the same time, in the face of this reality, it is not surprising that Mao and many of his associates see the need for periodic campaigns designed to inculcate egalitarian values as a means of countering inegalitarian trends built into the wage and salary structure.

Nevertheless, although China's wage and salary – and therefore probably also its household income – structure is characterized by considerable inequalities, these are almost certainly smaller than in the 1920s, 1930s, or 1940s. The far-reaching confiscation, nationalization, and collectivization of private property must have led to major changes in the distribution of income between 1949 and 1955 or 1956. As shown by Perkins, even if GDP per capita did not rise appreciably between the 1930s and the 1950s, the consumption levels of the poor could have increased significantly just through this redistribution.[23] Thus based on hypothetical but not unrealistic calculations and some simplifying assumptions, if the top 5 percent of the population receives 25 to 30 percent of the national income and the bottom half receives only 15 to 20 percent, one can reduce the top 5 percent to the national average and have enough left over to raise both investment and consumption.

This would mean that after the redistribution, the 5 percent who were formerly on top would receive only 5 percent of the national income, while the share of the bottom half would now be 30 to 40 percent. Thus their incomes and consumption levels could be doubled, assuming that per capita product rose at least marginally between the 1930s and the 1950s; that is, by at least 10 to 15 percent to absorb the additional investment.

There is also some limited evidence that suggests that the process of income redistribution was continuous, not confined to the 1945–1955 period. Necessarily the radical transformation in the income structure was a hallmark of the initial years of Communist rule. Therefore to the extent that there may have been additional changes, these were much more gradual and incremental. The evidence for some further redistribution of income is both qualitative and quantitative.

It seems that while real wages of workers and all employees in industry rose rapidly between 1952 and 1957, they did increase only marginally between 1957 and 1972.[24] There is some evidence to suggest that this virtual standstill in real wages produced some industrial-worker dis-satisfaction and unrest during the Cultural Revolution and again in 1974–1975. At the same time agricultural purchase prices were raised almost 65 percent, while the prices of industrial products sold in rural areas have been increased less than 15 percent.[25] As a result, the real incomes of the rural population must have been raised, although we have no clear indications whether the benefits of this improvement were distributed more or less equally between the different elements of the rural population.

Regardless of how they were distributed, this must have led to a compression of average urban–rural income differentials. A possible narrowing of income differentials also seems to be borne out by possible changes in the inter-regional distribution of income. It appears that regional income disparities were quite wide in China, even as late as 1957, possibly wider than in Italy, Yugoslavia, or India. However, available data seem to indicate that these disparities were diminishing, even if only quite gradually, between 1952, 1957, and 1971.[26] It is of course possible that a Chinese province is much too large a unit in terms of which to measure these disparities. Therefore, it is conceivable that these conclusions would be modified if per capita income or product indicators were readily available on a *hsien* or commune basis.

What conclusions can one draw from these explorations of China's income redistribution? Following the birth of the People's Republic a far-reaching program of income redistribution was carried out which must have raised the living standards of the lower-income groups. However, this did not by any means eliminate all income differentials, nor was it so intended. It still left wide disparities between rural and urban areas as well as within each of these broad sectors and between different provinces and regions.

Government policy was directed to a gradual narrowing of these disparities between the 1950s and the 1970s. The tentative evidence presented suggests that wages and salaries were compressed in the urban sector as a whole. Periodically workers in the lowest two grades were raised a grade or two en masse so that at a particular time the number actually tied down in these bottom grades may have been small. At the same time, at least since the Cultural Revolution, the numbers in the top salary scales of 300 to 400 yuan must have diminished considerably through a process of attrition. Concurrently, average urban–rural income differentials were almost certainly narrowed in the past twenty years. On the other hand, it is far from clear what happened to income disparities within rural areas. Finally, inter-regional income differentials were narrowed. At best this could have had only an indirect effect on inter-personal income distribution.

What then is the net impact of these changes on income distribution? It is reasonably clear that there are still considerable disparities in the mid-1970s within industry, between urban and rural areas, and inter-regionally. However, these disparities are probably less pronounced than in the mid-1950s and these in turn were significantly diminished in comparison with the mid-1930s. Beyond this, it would not be possible to derive any precise measures of China's income distribution during any of the aforementioned periods due to the paucity of available data.

Standards of living

Just as with income distribution, data limitations do not permit any hard and fast measurements of China's living standards and their trend over time. However, as with incomes, these may be illuminated at least partially and indirectly.

A very crude measure of trends in Chinese standards of living may be obtained by comparing the estimated products per capita in 1933, 1952, 1957, and 1974 and then deducting from these investment and defense expenditure. The residual would then be a composite of household, that is, private, and collective consumption; the latter referring to health, education, recreational, and similar services financed out of the government budget. Based on the estimates in Table 6-8, supplemented by Perkins's derivations for 1933, it seems that per capita product may have declined slightly between 1933 and 1952 but by 1957 exceeded former levels. It then continued to grow, with some interruptions. As a result, by 1974 it exceeded the 1957 level by perhaps more than 90 percent.[27]

As shown in the highly tentative estimates presented in Table 8-2, per capita consumption may have declined much more substantially than product between 1933 and 1952 and then recovered more slowly. This was largely due to a very dramatic rise in investment, which increased from about 5 to 6 percent of national product in 1933 to about 16 percent or more in 1952 and 20 to 25 percent in 1957. However, by the 1970s average per capita consumption standards had exceeded 1933 and 1957 levels by about 50 and 70 percent, respectively. This suggests that the bulk of the Chinese population must have

Table 8-2. *Conjectural estimates of per capita product and consumption in China, 1933–1974*

Year	GDP per capita (in 1952 yuan, rounded)	Nonconsumption[a] share (in percent)	Consumption per capita[b] (in 1952 yuan, rounded)
1933	140	10	126
1952	130	20–25	98
1957	160	25–30	112
1974	310	35–40	186

[a]Refers to total investment, defense, and government administration.
[b]Based on the higher share of these ranges.

Table 8-3. *Relative purchasing power of an average industrial wage over a sample of consumer goods in China and the United States*

Category	Amounts the average wage can purchase		
	In China	In U.S.	Ratio (rounded)
Foodstuffs in pounds	*per hour*		
Rice (long grain)	2.0	14.2	7:1
Wheat flour	1.8	23.9	12:1
Irish potatoes	4.8	30.5	6:1
Carrots	4.8	12.4	25:1
Cucumbers	5.5	10.9	2:1
Chicken	0.26	6.9	26:1
Beef	0.48	2.0	4:1
Pork	0.34	2.7	8:1
White sugar	0.44	20.4	46:1
Fabrics, clothing, and footwear	*per week*		
Cotton prints (per square meter)	7.0	129.2	18:1
Corduroy fabrics (per square meter)	2.7	81.9	30:1
Unpadded cotton cloth jackets	1.6	6.4	4:1
Cotton work pants	2.1	26.9	13:1
Corduroy jackets	1.6	5.6	3.5:1
Corduroy trousers	2.3	19.2	8:1
Cloth coats with lining	0.2	2.9	14:1
Blue cotton work shirts			
Good quality	3.2	19.2	6:1
Poorer quality	5.0	33.6	7:1
Cotton flannel colored western-style shirts	2.5	44.6	18:1
Light wool sweaters	0.7	10.7	15:1
Men's cotton socks (pairs)	11.3	206.7	18:1
Tennis shoes:			
Basic quality	3.1	33.8	11:1
Sturdier	1.5	21.3	14:1
Cloth shoes with rubber or synthetic soles	2.3	48.8	21:1
Miscellaneous consumer manufactures			
Three-gallon pots	1.2	29.8	25:1
Drinking glasses	49.4	1,344.0	27:1
Simple alarm clocks	1.0	16.8	17:1
Very simple bedside lamps	1.3	29.8	23:1
Metal folding chairs	0.7	22.4	32:1
Wooden straight-back chairs	1.5	12.2	8:1
Umbrellas	1.7	26.8	16:1
Ball-point pens	13.8	149.3	11:1
Plastic 4-ounce baby bottles with nipple cap	34.6	336.0	9:1

Table 8-3. (*cont.*)

Category	Amounts the average wage can purchase: In China	In U.S.	Ratio (rounded)
Durable consumer goods			
Bicycles	0.4	9.1	23:1
12-inch TV sets	0.14	6.5	47:1
Small transistor radios	1.6	84.4	53:1
Watches			
Swiss	0.11	5.9	53:1
Domestic	0.54	32.8	60:1

Sources: The figures in this table were derived by the author based on price data for China and the United States. For China these data were collected by Professor Robert Scalapino and the author during a visit in December 1972 and by Bruce Reynolds on a visit in the fall of 1973. For the United States, they are average 1972 prices based on *Retail Food Prices* (monthly), published by the U.S. Bureau of Labor Statistics; non-food prices were obtained from Sears Roebuck and J. C. Penney catalogues.

begun to reap substantial material benefits from the process of economic development. Based on these conjectural estimates, per capita consumption may have risen at an average annual rate of close to 3 percent since 1952, and at a rate of 1 percent since 1933.

What was the living standard actually attained as a result of this development process? One way of gauging this could be to develop at least a partial measure of the comparative living standards in the United States and in China in the 1970s. Admittedly the consumption patterns in the two countries are so divergent that they may be difficult to compare. However, relevant data in the same form as those obtainable for China are more readily available to us for the United States than for other countries. Bearing these considerations in mind, the comparative purchasing power of an average industrial wage was estimated for China and the United States as shown in Table 8-3.

The comparison is based on retail price quotations in markets, department stores, and other shops compiled by the author during a month-long visit to China at the end of 1972. These were combined with prices collected by a group of economists from Yale who visited China in the early fall of 1973.[28] As a result, a total of about 210 price quotations were gathered for 110 different items. In a number of cases prices for several different varieties or qualities and from several different Chinese cities were obtained.

The Chinese goods for which price data were available were first matched by U.S. equivalents in terms of size, weight, and quality. Only consumer items for which reasonably close equivalents could be found were used. Then the U.S. retail prices for these were compiled. These two steps reduced the number of items from 110 to 38 – 9 entries for foodstuffs, 15 for fabrics, clothing, and footwear, 9 for miscellaneous manufactured consumer goods, and 5 for durable consumer goods.

The quantity that could be purchased with the average industrial wage at the prices prevailing in China and the United States was then derived. The calculations in Table 8-3 are based on an average monthly wage in Chinese industry of 60 yuan. Since there are no income taxes, this is a net wage. In contrast, average weekly earnings of production and non-supervisory workers were $154.69 in the United States in 1972. However, this is gross income. The *Handbook of Labor Statistics* gives the gross weekly earnings of production and non-supervisory workers on private agricultural payrolls as $135.78 in 1972. The corresponding income, net of taxes, for a wage earner with three dependents was $120.79. This 88 percent ratio was applied to the $154.69 figure to obtain a net average weekly wage in U.S. manufacturing of $134.40. This is equivalent to $2.84 per hour, assuming a 40 hour week, and $591.00 a month. If one were to convert the monthly Chinese wage into dollars at the exchange rate prevailing in late 1972, it would be about $24. On this basis the American worker would be earning 25 times more than his Chinese counterpart. As may be seen from Table 8-3, this probably overstates the purchasing-power gap.

Table 8-3 shows that for foodstuffs the purchasing-power ratios range from 2:1 for cucumbers to 46:1 for white sugar. For staples, the largest consumption items in China, the ratios range from 6:1 for potatoes to 12:1 for wheat flour. For meats the range is 4:1 for beef, 26:1 for chicken, with pork – a popular consumer item in China – 8:1. The median ratio for all foods is 7:1.

For fabrics, clothing, and footwear the range is from 3.5:1 for corduroy jackets or 4:1 for unpadded cotton cloth jackets to 30:1 for corduroy fabrics. However, cotton cloth prints were 18:1 and so were several other items. The median was 11:1. In the miscellaneous manufactures category, wooden straight-back chairs were relatively cheapest with an 8:1 ratio, while metal folding chairs were relatively dearest at 32:1. The median of these nine items was 17:1.

The purchasing-power gap was greatest for durable consumer goods, which ranged from 23:1 for bicycles to 60:1 for domestic watches. The median was 53:1. Ideally, one would want to have a much larger sample of observations for each category. Thus, undoubtedly, the small number of comparable items reduces the validity of the generalizations one would wish to make. Nevertheless, the data exhibit a consistent pattern.

The purchasing power of the American industrial wage is a multiple of the Chinese for all the listed items and a sizable multiple for most. The differential is relatively narrowest for foods and widest for durable consumer goods, with fabrics, clothing, footwear, and miscellaneous manufactures between these two in the order cited. This is precisely what one would expect a priori, on the basis of international cross-section comparisons of consumption patterns.

Of course, from these data we cannot derive a single index or derive a single measure of the relative purchasing power of the two wages in their own price settings. However, one is strongly tempted to conclude that the purchasing-power gap is likely to be at least 7:1, since this is both the median for foods and the ratio for rice. Almost certainly this is on the low side in the light of the data in the table. One might speculate that, based on Chinese tastes, habits, and consumption-expenditure patterns, a U.S. wage in manufacturing might buy ten times the quantity that could be obtained in China. However, based on U.S. tastes and patterns, the purchasing-power multiple could go as high as 20:1 or higher. In making this comparison, one must also bear in mind that the average industrial wage represents a far higher position in China's total income scale than would be the case for the corresponding U.S. wage on our income scales. This is primarily due to the fact that average farm wages and incomes are perceptibly below the average industrial wage in China, while the bulk of the population and labor force is in agriculture and not in industry.

Self-reliance

As pointed out before, self-reliance refers to two different but inter-related aspects of the economy. The first relates to international trade and the degree of foreign trade dependence, while the second refers to the extent of local or regional self-sufficiency. On the basis of the available data for China, crude assessments of foreign trade dependence are possible but the same cannot be said for regional self-sufficiency. Therefore, this analysis of self-reliance will be confined to the first aspect.

As indicated in Chapter 7, foreign trade is necessarily a small sector relative to GDP in any large continental or sub-continental economy. However, depending in part on which of the estimates is used, it seems that China's foreign trade dependence is low, even in comparison with other large countries. Actually, foreign trade ratios rose in China during the 1950s, declined in the 1960s, and may have been rising once more in the 1970s without recovering to their 1959 peak importance. Under the impact of these contrasting trends, these ratios may not have been too different in 1974 than in 1952. They may have declined slightly, since for this period as a whole GDP seems to have been rising somewhat faster than foreign trade volume, that is, at an average annual rate of 6 and 5 percent respectively.

China's decreasing import dependence is borne out by another series of measures as well. Imports, particularly of machinery and equipment, represent a major avenue for the transfer of foreign technology. Moreover, imported capital goods can play a most significant role as a component in domestic investment. This indeed was the case in the 1950s, when close to 40 percent of China's total investment in machinery and equipment was based on imported capital goods. This ratio was about 6 percent in the 1970s, having declined to around 4 percent during the Cultural Revolution period.[29] During these same years the share of machinery and transport equipment in China's total import bill declined from 35 to 18 percent.

This, of course, does not deny the importance of capital-goods imports for some branches of industry during some periods. For instance, such imports from the Soviet Union played a crucial role in the development of a number of basic industries in the 1950s. Complete-plant imports from Japan, Western Europe, and to some extent the United States are making a major contribution to the expansion of production capacity in the chemical fertilizer, petrochemical, and iron and steel industries, as well as in power generation and commercial aviation, in the 1970s.

Even in these terms China's import dependence must be considered modest in comparison with other underdeveloped countries. China's self-reliance is most pronounced when gauged by the criterion of international financial dependence. As may be seen from Table 7-1, China incurred sizable trade deficits in the 1950s amounting to a total of about $1.2 billion. These were financed by Soviet credits, which were beginning to be repaid in 1955. In 1956 this situation was reversed, and since then and until 1972 China accumulated trade surpluses totaling about $2.3 billion, which were used to repay the Russian aid and finance a Chinese foreign aid program.

Therefore, until recently China was a net exporter of capital, a most unusual situation for an underdeveloped country and particularly for a country experiencing rapid economic growth. As a result, China is one of the very few developing economies free of any long-term debt. However, since 1973, under the impact of a relatively ambitious import program combined with world-recession-induced export difficulties, China incurred large trade deficits, which reached a record of about $1 billion in 1974. These are being financed by a combination of short-term and intermediate-term credits. These balance of payment difficulties may be expected to be of a transitory character. Once world economic recovery gains momentum, the demand for China's traditional exports may be expected to rise. Such increases combined with a gradual growth in oil exports should enable the Chinese to maintain trade surpluses again, which then could be applied to repaying the debts incurred in 1974 and 1975.

Distinctiveness and transferability of the Chinese development model

China's economic performance must be considered as impressive, based on the overall assessment in the preceding section. There is very little doubt that the Chinese economy has been growing quite rapidly, so that a marked rise in per capita consumption was sustained despite a significant increase in the rate of investment. At the same time the very wide disparities in income characterizing Chinese society before 1949 have unquestionably been narrowed; precisely to what extent cannot be ascertained on the basis of the available data. Based on partial and tentative evidence, it seems that income inequalities may today be narrower in China than in many – but not all – of the other developing countries and perhaps also in the Soviet Union.

This suggests that after a process of trial and error, Chinese leaders and planners evolved a set of development policies that worked and in essence achieved their principal objectives. This does not mean that no other policies could have been adopted or that the development strategy pursued was necessarily the optimal one. For instance, theoretically, instead of investing so heavily in the intensification of land use in North China where natural conditions are unfavorable and where therefore capital–output ratios are bound to be high, they could have embarked upon an ambitious and far-reaching program of railroad development. Construction of a wide-ranging and reasonably dense transport network would permit much greater inter-regional specialization and economic integration. This would enable China to substitute what may turn out to be relatively cheaper grain imported from overseas, instead of expanding grain production under the rather inhospitable conditions of the North. Under these conditions, resources released in "farmland capital construction," could be devoted to producing farm and industrial products in which China enjoys a comparative advantage.

Such an approach would automatically mean a sacrifice of agricultural self-sufficiency and a much more open foreign trade orientation. It would represent not only a change in strategy but a shift in the Chinese leaders' objectives. It would not only dilute the pursuit of self-reliance but would almost certainly lead to some major changes in rural–urban relations and employment patterns in ways that would run counter to the planners' preferences. At the same time the leaders could not be assured that this alternative development path would lead to greater stability, higher growth, and better income distribution than the strategy pursued since the early 1960s. In the transition period, while the railroads were being built, China could be exposed to more or less severe balance of payment pressures since food imports would have to be increased before new export commodities were produced with which to pay for these expanded purchases from abroad. This in turn might require foreign loans to bridge this gap, which would also run counter to leaders' objectives.

Even if the policies and measures adopted were reasonably well designed to accomplish the principal leadership objectives, how efficiently were resources utilized in China? On the basis of the highly fragmentary evidence at our disposal, no conclusive judgment is possible. Nevertheless, there is no doubt that the process of resource allocation in China is peppered with numerous instances of inefficiency. This is apparent in the allocation of factory labor, with hoarding of labor and its underutilization in a number of cases. It is also evidenced by the frequent accumulation of large inventories of finished products crated in factory yards but not shipped for considerable periods. It is also illustrated by periodic breakdowns in the production process, particularly in the initial stages of plant operation.

These examples and a number of others one could cite clearly demonstrate that the Chinese economy is not operating at full efficiency. In many instances it may be operating quite inefficiently; but so is every living economic system. The crucial question one would need to address is whether the Chinese economy is operating less efficiently than those of other less developed countries. This question is impossible to answer, not only due to inadequate data but also because of some very complex conceptual problems. All of the instances cited represent cases of static inefficiency. However, in a rapidly growing and changing economy we must consider dynamic efficiency as well. An operation that seems high-cost, inefficient, and technically deficient at one moment in time may become quite efficient over a period of time. Among the crucial variables in this context are learning effects, that is, the capacity to "learn by doing," to learn from mistakes, and the speed at which this can be accomplished. In this respect, however, cultures, societies, and economic systems differ a great deal.

Irrespective of whether China's development strategy is in some sense optimal or whether it is implemented with a high degree of efficiency, the question that needs to be addressed now is in what ways can this strategy be considered as distinctive in comparison with other developing countries on the one hand and socialist economies on the other. As noted earlier, China shares two major objectives with other less developed countries: the quests for increasing power and modernization. This leads all of them to pursue rapid economic growth and technological progress, as the necessary bases for a share of power in the international system and for modernity in the contemporary world. For most of the less developed countries these goals are coupled with a strong striving for a rapidly rising standard of living. This objective is more muted in the Chinese case, at least as an explicit, high-priority one.

On the other hand, the strong commitment to self-reliance and to a socialist and egalitarian pattern of development is a distinctive feature of China's approach to development. Many other developing countries talk of socialism, but only rarely is this translated into concrete operational policies and programs for narrowing inequalities of income. On the basis of partial evidence at least, it seems that in most low-income countries the development process may be associated with growing disparities between regions and between different income groups.

The periodic attacks on status barriers represent perhaps one of the most striking features of the Chinese model. There are no counterparts to the rustication movement in other socialist countries – in the Soviet Union or in Eastern Europe – or in other underdeveloped areas. Nor does one find elsewhere institutionalized measures designed to systematically break down the role differences between mental and manual labor.

In a most fundamental sense China's development strategy rests on a mass-based mobilization approach evidenced not only in the policies referred to above but also in the distribution of communal services, most notably in the field of health delivery and technology. This is reflected in mass involvement and mass participation not only in the construction of the health delivery system, but also in the diffusion of new technology, in farmland capital construction, in the development of rural industry, and in a wide variety of other measures that are ultimately designed to substitute labor for land and capital.

This whole mass-based development drive seems to be infused with a powerful set of motivations in part based on material aspirations and expectations of a rising standard of living. But these material incentives are combined with strong normative appeals rooted in a vision of a powerful China in which indignities, major inequalities, poverty, human misery, and deprivation will have been eliminated. This combination of material and normative appeals also characterizes the development process in other low-income countries, and in the Soviet Union and Eastern Europe as well. However the weight of patriotic and other ideological appeals as motivators of this drive seems to be much more pronounced in China, at least at this stage of development. Moreover, the whole process is reinforced and lubricated by a continuous push for model emulation and an exhortation to serve the people.

All these features, combined with China's approaches to agricultural development, rural industrialization, methods of industrial planning, and economic administration, do add up to a distinctive development model. Basically this model reflects an interplay between scarcity, ideology, and organization. The harsh realities of poverty and of scarce land, capital, and highly skilled manpower are imposed by China's factor endowments. The objectives of development, stressing a strong, powerful, self-reliant, egalitarian state and society, grow out of China's modern history and contemporary ideology. The systematic massing of labor and its substitution for land and capital is a manifestation of the scarcity of these resources. The methods of mobilizing and motivating labor and all of the human actors in the system is a function of ideology and organization.

To what extent is this model transferable? Are there any lessons to be drawn from the Chinese experience that could be applied in formulating development programs for other low-income countries? The model is the product of a socialist economic system in which the means of production are publicly owned, that is, property is nationalized and collectivized. The economic activities of factory enterprises, communes, and production teams are planned and carried out within a framework of controls. Resources are allocated principally through administrative channels rather than through the market, and prices are for the most part fixed by state authorities.

Moreover, the economic system is permeated from top to bottom with ideology and political organization. Ideology defines values, objectives, models, and attitudes, while organization provides the avenue for indoctrination, education, peer pressure, and more or less subtle forms of coercion (if necessary) through which these are transmitted to and inculcated in the masses. This then becomes manifested in certain patterns of human behavior absolutely critical for the functioning of the economic system and the success of the Chinese development model. These include a highly pronounced work ethic, a capacity for hard work, dedication, self-abnegation, subordination of the self, and willingness to sacrifice for the common good. The Communist Party constitutes a most essential ingredient in this process, both as the source of the ideology and the agent for its dissemination.

In exploring the question of transferability, it is essential to identify the settings in which the Chinese experience might be applicable. In China, the development process is unfolding in a country of unprecedented size; the territorial expanse of the Soviet Union is much larger, while the United States mainland encompasses roughly the same land area as China. However, in terms of population China is in a class by itself, approximated only by India. Size in and of itself carries with it many crucial implications for economic development.

A large country is likely to be endowed with considerable mineral resources and a sizable internal market. Therefore, it is much easier for a large country to pursue a self-reliance policy without sacrificing economies of scale or efficiency. At the same time, a large country necessarily faces much more serious internal transport barriers, which may serve to reinforce the advantages of a regionally based self-reliance policy. These options are not open to a small economy which, given its limited resources and internal markets, must necessarily take advantage of international specialization and international division of labor if it is to develop. Therefore the issue of self-reliance poses itself in a quite different way for a small country. It does not mean reducing its involvement in the international economy, but rather maximizing the degree of national control over the process of resource allocation so that the benefits of development will be distributed to the population at home rather than be transferred abroad. As a result, self-reliance policies as implemented in China are applicable only to a limited number of countries. Other less developed economies may still wish to adopt this posture but its implementation requires a rather different set of policies.

There are also underdeveloped countries that are not as land-short as China. In parts of Africa and Latin America land is a relatively abundant resource. In these cases great reliance can be placed on bringing new lands under the plough, in extending the cultivated land area, and in this way increasing farm production. Since all underdeveloped economies are more or less capital-scarce and such new land programs require vast investments, they may call for a far-reaching substitution of labor for capital. For this reason a major emphasis on "farmland capital construction" may be a necessary feature of development programs in these areas as well, although their form would necessarily differ from that carried out in China.

Therefore, differences in size and resource endowments limit the transferability of China's development model and some of its features to other developing areas. However, there are many more fundamental constraints to this transferability, even to settings in which resource configurations are more akin to those prevailing in China. These limits are largely imposed by systemic differences, although cultural factors may also play an important role here. For instance, in the case of India, transferability may be impeded not only by its vastly different economic system but by the lack of linguistic unity, the persistence of the caste system, and a number of other differences in the two traditions.

Leaving aside these very important but quite elusive cultural elements, one of the most crucial questions to be faced is whether the Chinese development model can be transferred to more or less private-enterprise-oriented market economies embedded in a variety of non-communist political and social systems. As indicated above, the Chinese redistributed income through a series of confiscatory measures which then gradually led to the virtual elimination of private property. To the extent that regional disparities in stages of development and per capita income levels were narrowed, this was achieved through a highly centralized fiscal system with vast resource-allocating powers.

Can inter-personal and inter-regional income inequalities in other developing economies be narrowed without these vast controls over resource allocation and without resorting to these confiscatory measures? Can status barriers between peasants, workers, and intellectuals be attacked on a purely voluntary basis without ideological indoctrination, peer pressure, and a vast organizational effort by a highly disciplined and dedicated political movement? Can the spirit and motivation for hard work, maximum effort, innovation, and self-abnegation be replicated in other developing economies?

There are a number of underdeveloped countries, including Asian countries (e.g., Taiwan, South Korea, Thailand, Malaysia, Indonesia) that have experienced rapid economic growth, marked structural transformation, and a gradual process of modernization since World War II. However, they have accomplished this through development strategies, policies, and instruments markedly different from those applied in China. Except for one or two countries (e.g., Taiwan), in most cases this development was not associated with improvements in the distribution of income. On the contrary, available evidence tends to suggest that growth was coupled with a widening of income inequalities in the less developed countries.[30]

While it may not be too difficult to design redistributive tax or income-transfer policies for these developing economies, there are enormous political and administrative obstacles to implementing these. Tax morale in these countries tends to be low, the administrative capacity of the government bureaucracies tends to be limited, and last but not least, powerful vested interests can and do bar the implementation of such programs. It is also very doubtful that the kind of spirit, motivation, and social controls prevailing in China can be transferred to the entirely different systemic settings of other developing areas. In essence it is difficult to visualize how particular elements of the Chinese experience can be pulled out of their total context for possible inclusion in the development programs of other countries. The different facets of what may be termed the Chinese development model are quite interdependent and deeply imbedded in the economic, political, and social system as a whole. Therefore it is not at all clear how elements of the model or the model as a whole can be transferred without adopting the essential features of this system as a whole.

Prospects and dilemmas

The year 1976 may present a particularly uncertain vantage point from which to forecast China's future course of development. With the passing of both Mao and Chou En-lai, it marks a major change in China's top leadership. Nevertheless, even if the succession were marked by far-reaching political instability, it is improbable that this would lead to a major upheaval and break-up of the country.

However, during this succession period and particularly in a post–Mao-Chou era, power struggles and policy disputes – including economic policy differences – could become seriously aggravated. Therefore, it may be particularly difficult to forecast the future course of China's economic policy. Nevertheless, barring a repetition of Great Leap Forward – or Cultural Revolution – type measures or China's involvement in a major international conflict, the country should be in a position to sustain over the coming decade approximately the same average rate of economic growth as in the past twenty-five years. This would mean that by the end of this century China's gross domestic product could be quadrupled. In terms of total size it would still lag far behind the United States and the Soviet Union, but could easily be among the five largest economies in the world.

Nevertheless, just as in the past, it will be no easy task to sustain a 6 percent rate of growth. Based on past performance, this will require a rise in farm production of about 2 to 3 percent a year assuming (1) a continued commitment to basic self-sufficiency in food supply, and (2) a rate of population growth of not less than 1.5 to 2 percent a year. This will necessarily pose a major challenge to Chinese agriculture. Over time it will require very large investments in the farm sector and its far-reaching technical transformation. It is far from clear whether such a major transformation can be accomplished within present patterns of economic organization and employment in agriculture. This range of issues will necessarily constitute one of the continuing problems facing the Chinese Communist leadership for the rest of this century and probably beyond.

The successor generation in China will also have to face up to the challenge of sustaining the Revolution, it values and spirit, in the face of rapid economic growth. As industrialization proceeds the processes of production are bound to become more complex. Technical training requirements may also be expected to grow, thus posing a number of dilemmas. Will the educational system as reorganized after the Cultural Revolution be capable of training the advanced engineering, scientific, and technical manpower required for an industrial society? If not, can that system be reshaped in such a way as to continue producing "reds" and "experts"? Can status and income differences be fairly narrowly confined in the face of the growing specialization, division of labor, and functional differentiation associated with industrialization?

Another and closely related range of questions revolves around consumer aspirations. With a fairly rapidly rising product, can household purchasing power in the cities and in the countryside be kept stable or rise only quite slowly and gradually? Alternatively, will increasing product be gradually translated into increasing consumer appetites? Can consumerism be contained and the spirit of frugality and self-abnegation be preserved?

It is also very unclear whether China can maintain a 10 percent rate of industrial growth for several decades with a preponderantly rural population. This of course will crucially depend on the pattern of industrialization, that is, the technologies used, the scale of plant, and the degree of capital intensity. It may also depend on whether it is possible to design a highly decentralized pattern of industrial development in China that would economize on transport and be partly regionally based. Such a pattern might slow down the rate of urbanization and at the same time alleviate some of the dilemmas posed above.

In essence, the fundamental challenge confronting China's leaders in the coming decades will be to maintain the tempo of economic growth, to build a strong and modernizing China, while preserving socialist values and not only socialist forms of organization. It remains to be seen whether China can become a modern industrial state without perpetuating the "new class" that has been gradually emerging since the 1950s and without following the "revisionist" road. If China's far-reaching experiment were to succeed, it would indeed be a historic contribution to the process of modern economic growth.

Notes

1 *The economic heritage*

1 For a most penetrating analysis of these issues see Alexander Gerschenkron, *Economic Backwardness in Historical Perspective*, Cambridge, Mass., 1962.
2 This analysis is largely based on John K. Fairbank, Alexander Eckstein, and L. S. Yang, "Economic Change in Early Modern China," in *Economic Development and Cultural Change*, Oct. 1960; also reprinted as Chapter 4 in Alexander Eckstein, *China's Economic Development*, Ann Arbor, Mich., 1975.
3 Eli F. Heckscher, *An Economic History of Sweden*, Cambridge, Mass., 1954.
4 Joseph Needham, *Science and Civilisation in China*, vol. 1, Cambridge, Eng., 1965.
5 R. H. Tawney, *Land and Labor in China*, Boston, 1966, p. 11.
6 Simon Kuznets, *Modern Economic Growth, Rate, Structure and Spread*, New Haven, Conn., 1966, Table 2.3, p. 42; and *Economic Growth of Nations, Total Output and Product Structure*, Cambridge, Mass., 1971, Table 2, p. 24.
7 This is referred to as a "restoration" since it led to the reinstatement of the Meiji emperor's prerogatives. Between 1601 and 1868 Japan was ruled by the House of Tokugawa, who were hereditary rulers of the realm in the name of the emperor, with the latter relegated to a shadow. The restoration brought the emperor into the forefront and led to the fall of the Tokugawas.
8 See John W. Hall, *Japan, From Prehistory to Modern Times*, New York, 1970, Chapters 10–13.
9 Thomas C. Smith, *The Agrarian Origins of Modern Japan*, Stanford, Calif., 1959, pp. 67–68.
10 Hall, *Japan*, pp. 211–213.
11 Based on D. H. Perkins, *Six Centuries of Agricultural Development in China* (1368–1968), Chicago, 1969, Table II.1, p. 16 and E.1, p. 295.
12 Perkins estimates that prior to 1900 farm sales within a limited region a few tens of miles in diameter probably amounted to between 20 and 30 percent of farm output ". . . but that *only about 7 or 8 percent of all farm output entered into long-distance trade.*" (*Agricultural Development*, p. 115). Henry Rosovsky indicates that in the early Meiji period about 25 to 30 percent of agricultural produce was sold off farms in Japan ("Japan's Transition to Modern Economic Growth, 1868–1885," in *Industrialization in Two Systems, Essays in Honor of Alexander Gerschenkron by a Group of His Students*, New York, 1966). On the face of it, the total amount sold off farms seems very similar in the two settings. But the bulk of the 25 to 30 percent in the Japanese case is probably rural–urban trade, rather than primarily sales within a local rural area. However, since long-distance trade constituted only 7 to 8 percent of output in China, one might presume that total rural–urban trade (including short hauls from farms in the vicinity of cities) could not have exceeded 10 percent.

13 In Japan about 43 percent of males and 10 percent of females had some form of schooling around 1868 according to R. P. Dore, *Education in Tokugawa Japan*, Berkeley, Calif., 1965, p. 321. In contrast, even as late as the 1930s (that is about sixty years later) only 30 percent of the males and 1 percent of the females could be said to be literate in China, according to J. L. Buck, *Land Utilization in China*, New York, 1964, p. 373.

14 For a highly sophisticated analysis of the traditional market framework see G. William Skinner, "Marketing and Social Structure in Rural China, Part I," *Journal of Asian Studies*, no. 241, 1964, pp. 3–43. The estimates of the degree of commercialization are based on Perkins, *Agricultural Development*, pp. 114–115.

15 See Perkins, *Agricultural Development*, Chapter 7.

16 D. H. Perkins, "Growth and Changing Structure of China's Twentieth-Century Economy," in D. H. Perkins, ed., *China's Modern Economy in Historical Perspective*, Stanford, Calif., 1975, Table 3, p. 122.

17 These are based on the work of Dwight Perkins cited in Table 1-3.

18 This conclusion is based on Perkins, *Agricultural Development*, Table II.1, p. 16, on the basis of which it seems that cultivated acreage per capita declined continuously from 3.45 mou (one mou is roughly 1/6 of an acre) in 1873 to 2.6 mou in 1957. Given the margins of error in both the cultivated land and population figures, this decline could of course be more apparent than real. On the other hand it could also be larger than these figures suggest.

19 Based on Perkins, *Agricultural Development*, Table II.12, p. 35.

20 For a more detailed analysis of the evolution of treaty ports see John K. Fairbank, *The United States and China*, Cambridge, Mass., 1971, Chapter 6.

21 Based on T. C. Liu and K. C. Yeh, *The Economy of the Chinese Mainland, National Income and Economic Development*, 1933–1959, Princeton, N.J., 1965, Table F-1, pp. 586–588.

22 See A. Eckstein, Kang Chao, and John Chang, "The Economic Development of Manchuria, The Rise of a Frontier Economy," *The Journal of Economic History*, March 1974, Table 5, p. 253.

23 Thomas Rawski, "The Growth of Producer Goods Industries, 1900–1971," in Perkins, ed., *China's Modern Economy*, pp. 207–210.

24 B. L. Reynolds, *The Impact of Trade and Foreign Investment on Industrialization: Chinese Textiles*, 1875–1931, unpublished Ph.D. dissertation, University of Michigan, 1975, Table B-4, p. 254.

25 All rates of industrial growth cited are based on John K. Chang, *Industrial Development in Pre-Communist China, A Quantitative Analysis*, Chicago, 1969.

26 For an interesting analysis of textile industry development see Kang Chao, "The Growth of a Modern Cotton Textile Industry and the Competition with Handicrafts," in Perkins, ed., *China's Modern Economy*, pp. 167–201.

27 Based on E. W. Pauley, *Report on Japanese Assets in Manchuria*, Washington, D.C., 1946.

28 U.N. Economic Commission for Asia and the Far East, "Economic Development in Mainland China, 1949–1953," *Economic Bulletin for Asia and the Far East*, November 1953.

29 Simon Kuznets, *Modern Economic Growth, Structure and Spread*, New Haven, Conn., 1966, p. 1.

30 Based on Perkins, *Agricultural Development*, and his recent synthesis, "Growth and Changing Structure of China's Economy," in Perkins, ed., *China's Modern Economy*, Table 3, p. 122.

2 *Development strategies and policies in contemporary China*

1 Mao Tse-tung, *Selected Works*, vol. 4, Peking, 1961, p. 454; this is an extract from an editorial dated September 16, 1949.

2 Wu Chiang, "Theorists of Uninterrupted Revolution Must be Thorough Theorists of Dialectical Materialism" (in Chinese) in *Che-hsueh yen-chiu*, No. 8, 1958, p. 54. It is very interesting to note that this transformist view of man, society, and nature assumed growing importance in Stalin's mind after World War II. This was evidenced in the so-called Stalin Plan for the Transformation of Nature formulated in 1949, and in Stalin's approach to biology, linguistics, and psychology. This view of man was perhaps emphasized more during the Great Leap (1958–1960) than at other times, but it certainly was not confined to that period as evidenced by the quote cited in the following footnote.

3 "Preface by Mao Tse-tung to the book *Socialist Upsurge in China's Countryside*, December 27, 1955," reprinted in R. R. Bowie and J. K. Fairbank, *Communist China 1955–59: Policy Documents with Analysis*, Cambridge, Mass., 1962, p. 118.

4 A. S. Chen, "The Ideal Local Party Secretary and the 'Model' Man," *China Quarterly*, no. 17, January–March 1964, pp. 229–240.

5 For the quotation from Liu see Conrad Brandt, Benjamin Schwartz, and J. K. Fairbank, *A Documentary History of Chinese Communism*, Cambridge, Mass., 1952, p. 336. For the quotation from Ch'en Yun see the same source, pp. 330–331.

6 Lin Chung-hsien, "Psychological Disposition Necessary for the Study of Flying," *Hang-k'ung chih-shih* (Aviation Knowledge), March 1960, in *Joint Publications Research Service* (JPRS), Washington, D.C., no. 2973, July 6, 1960, pp. 9–10. My attention to this article was directed by Donald Munro's unpublished manuscript on *The Concept of Man in Contemporary China*, Ann Arbor, Mich., p. 156.

7 *The Four Firsts* (Ssu-ke ti-i), collection of articles reprinted for the most part from the *Liberation Army Daily*, Shanghai, 1965, p. 32.

8 Mao Tse-tung, "Reading Notes on the Soviet Union's 'Political Economy' " in *Miscellany of Mao Tse-tung's Thought* (1949–68), *Part II*, JPRS 61269-2, Arlington, Va., 1974, pp. 302, 307.

9 Mao Tse-tung, "Speech at the Hangchow Conference," May 1963, JPRS 61269-2, pp. 322–323.

10 For a more detailed analysis of these concepts see G. W. Skinner and E. A. Winckler, "Compliance Succession in Rural Communist China, A Cyclical Theory," in Amitai Etzioni, ed., *Complex Organizations, A Sociological Reader*, New York, 1969.

11 I am indebted for this further refinement of the normative concepts to Donald Munro, who developed these in his most stimulating manuscript on *The Concept of Man in Contemporary China*.

12 This essay was published in B. F. Lippincott, ed., *On the Economic Theory of Socialism*, Minneapolis, 1938.

13 Max Weber, *The Protestant Ethic and the Spirit of Capitalism*, Talcott Parsons, trans., New York, 1958; and R. H. Tawney, *Religion and the Rise of Capitalism*, New York, 1926.

14 The first of these quotations is from Mao, "Reform in Learning, the Party and Literature" in Boyd Compton, ed., *Mao's China, Party Reform Documents, 1942–44*, Seattle, 1952, p. 21. The second quotation is from Mao, "Where Do Correct Ideas Come From," in K. Fan, ed., *Mao Tse-tung and Lin Piao, Post-Revolutionary Writings*, New York, 1972, pp. 267–268.

15 For a brief sketch of the comparative wage structures in China and other less developed countries see A. Eckstein, *China's Economic Development, The Interplay of Scarcity and*

Ideology, Ann Arbor, Mich., 1975, pp. 346–350. For data on the Soviet Union see Edmund Nash, "Purchasing Power of Workers in the U.S.S.R.," *The Monthly Labor Review*, April 1960, p. 362; and Mervyn Matthews, "Top Incomes in the USSR," in *Economic Aspects of Life in the USSR*, published by NATO Directorate of Economic Affairs, January 1975, pp. 134–139.

16 Included in *People's Communes in China*, Peking, 1958, pp. 9–16.

17 Quoted from Mao's speech at the Supreme State Conference on January 28, 1958 in Stuart Schram, ed., *Chairman Mao Talks to the People*, New York, 1974, pp. 91–92.

18 In his unpublished Ph.D. dissertation (University of Michigan, 1971) on *Rural Policies and the Distribution of Agricultural Products in China, 1950–59*, David L. Denny marshals a great deal of evidence showing that farm retentions per capita at worst did not decline and may actually have increased in the 1950s.

19 Based on C. M. Hou, "Manpower, Employment, and Unemployment," in *Economic Trends in Communist China*, A. Eckstein, W. Galenson, and T. C. Liu, eds., Chicago, 1968, p. 342.

20 "Talks at the Chengtu Conference," March 1958, in Schram, *Chairman Mao*, p. 98.

21 Ragnar Nurkse, *Problems of Capital Formation in Underdeveloped Countries*, New York, 1953.

22 R. S. Eckaus, "Factor Proportions in Underdeveloped Areas," *American Economic Review*, September 1955, pp. 559–560.

23 This was spelled out by Liu Shao-ch'i in his *Report on the Work of the Central Committee* delivered at the Second Session of the Eighth Congress of the Chinese Communist Party on May 5, 1958.

24 "Communiqué of the 10th Plenary Session of the 8th Central Committee of the Chinese Communist Party," New China News Agency (NCNA), Peking, September 28, 1962, U.S. Consulate General, Hong Kong, *Current Background*, no. 691, p. 4.

25 Benedict Stavis, *Making Green Revolution, The Politics of Agricultural Development in China*, Ithaca, N.Y., 1974, p. 1; see also A. L. Erisman, "China, Agriculture in the 1970s," in *China: A Reassessment of the Economy*, Joint Economic Committee, U.S. Congress, July 1975, p. 332.

3 *Property relations and patterns of economic organization in China*

1 Ch'en Nai-ruenn, *Chinese Economic Statistics, A Handbook for Mainland China*, Chicago, 1957, p. 367; and *Hung Chi* (Red Flag), 1961, no. 7. See also Audrey Donnithorne, *China's Economic System*, New York, 1967, pp. 92–111.

2 According to Table 1–2, 65 percent of NDP was derived from agriculture in 1933 and 56 percent in 1952 in 1933 prices. According to Carl Riskin's study of "Surplus and Stagnation in Modern China" (in D. H. Perkins, ed., *China's Modern Economy in Historical Perspective*, Stanford, Calif., 1975, p. 74), rent plus tax in agriculture absorbed about 10 percent of NDP in 1933. According to Chinese official statements, about 12 percent of farm output went into agricultural taxes in 1950; this means that 7 to 8 percent of NDP went into taxes in the early 1950s.

3 Peter Schran, *The Development of Chinese Agriculture, 1950–1959*, Urbana, Ill., 1969, p. 21.

4 K. R. Walker, "Organization for Agricultural Production," in *Economic Trends in Communist China*, A. Eckstein, W. Galenson, and T. C. Liu, eds., Chicago, 1968, p. 431.

5 K. R. Walker, *Planning in Chinese Agriculture*, London, 1965, p. 43.

6 It is interesting to note the term *production brigade*. The concept of a brigade, borrowed

from military terminology and practice, underlines the mobilization character and campaign approach that characterized the Great Leap and the birth of the communes.

7 Donnithorne, *China's Economic System*, p. 147.

8 For a more detailed analysis of these problems see Kang Chao, *Agricultural Production in Communist China*, 1949–1965, Madison, Wis., 1970, pp. 46–58.

9 For a good, detailed discussion of commune, brigade, and team organization see Frederick W. Cook, "The Commune System in the People's Republic of China, 1963–74," in *China: A Reassessment of the Economy*, Joint Economic Committee, U.S. Congress, July 1975, pp. 366–410.

10 Barry M. Richman, *Industrial Society in Communist China*, New York, 1969, p. 676.

11 Most of the evidence for this approach is based on criticism of Cultural Revolution practices and the remnants thereof in Chinese official sources since 1969 or 1970. See, for instance, the following: Ts'ai Cheng, "Put Mao Tse-tung Thought in Command of Economic Accounting," *Jen Min Jih Pao* (*JMJP*), Nov. 29, 1970; Joint Investigation Team of Liaoning Provincial Revolutionary Committee, Shen-yang Municipal Revolutionary Committee, and the Army Command of Shen-yang, "Rely on the Working Class to Institute Rational Regulations and Systems," *Hung Ch'i*, no. 12, 1970, pp. 57–62; Joint Investigation Group of the Ministry of Light Industry, The Kiansu Provincial Light Industry Bureau, and the Nan-t'ung Municipal Revolutionary Committee, "Make a Success of Enterprise Management in a Down-to-Earth Manner," *JMJP*, March 2, 1972.

12 Richman, *Industrial Society*.

13 Donnithorne, *China's Economic System*; Franz Schurmann, *Ideology and Organization in Communist China*, Berkeley, Calif., 1966, Chapter IV; Dwight H. Perkins, *Market Control and Planning in Communist China*, Cambridge, Mass., 1966; Joan Robinson, *Economic Management, China 1972*, London, 1972.

14 *Kung-jen jih-pao*, July 19, 1955.

15 The names, precise functions, and jurisdictions of these organs and agencies change frequently with periodic government reorganizations. It is for that reason that they are identified in these general terms, rather than by name.

16 Richman, *Industrial Society*, p. 713.

17 Nicholas Lardy, "Centralization and Decentralization in China's Fiscal Management," *China Quarterly*, March 1975.

4 *The resource-allocating system*

1 Foreign Languages Press, *The Eighth National Congress of the Communist Party of China*, Peking, 1956, vol. I, pp. 261–328.

2 *Peking Review*, vol. XVIII, no. 4, January 24, 1975.

3 Foreign Languages Press, *The Draft Program for Agricultural Development in the People's Republic of China 1956–1967*, Peking, 1956.

4 For a more detailed analysis of these relationships see Dwight Perkins, *Market Control and Planning in Communist China*, Cambridge, Mass., 1966, pp. 32–38; and Kang Chao, *Agricultural Production in Communist China*, Madison, Wis., 1970, Chapters 8 and 11.

5 Based on D. H. Perkins, "Constraints Influencing China's Agricultural Performance" in *China: A Reassessment of the Economy*, Joint Economic Committee, U.S. Congress, July 1975, Tables 7 and 8, pp. 362–363. All of these price indices must, however, be treated with caution since in the absence of detail data on how they were constructed, it is difficult to assess their validity.

6 Based on A. L. Erisman, "China, Agriculture in the 1970's," in *China: A Reassessment of the Economy*, p. 332.

7 The supply of mechanical pumps increased from 90,000 in 1957 and 560,000 in 1959 to 3.47 million in 1966. The use of electric power in the countryside rose from 1.5 billion kilowatt-hours in 1962 to 4.6 billion in 1970 and 5.5 billion in 1971. Tractor production, expressed in "standard units," rose from 9.4 thousand in 1959 to 58.6 thousand in 1970 and 68.3 thousand in 1971. For fuller details see A. L. Erisman, "China, Agricultural Development: 1949–70," in *People's Republic of China, An Economic Assessment*, Joint Economic Committee, U.S. Congress, May 1972, pp. 134–140.

8 Based on A. Eckstein, *China's Economic Development, The Interplay of Scarcity and Ideology*, Ann Arbor, Mich., 1975, Chapter 8, Table 1, p. 264.

9 D. H. Perkins, "Growth and Changing Structure of China's Twentieth Century Economy" in D. H. Perkins, ed., *China's Modern Economy in Historical Perspective*, Stanford, Calif., 1975, Table 6, p. 134.

10 Field, "Civilian Industrial Production in the People's Republic of China, 1949–74," in *China: A Reassessment of the Economy*, Table B-4, p. 168.

11 C. R. Roll and K. C. Yeh, "Balance in Coastal and Inland Industrial Development," *China: A Reassessment of the Economy*, Table 3, p. 88.

12 Sidney H. Jammes, "The Chinese Defense Burden, 1965–74," *China: A Reassessment of the Economy*, pp. 459–466.

13 For a further analysis of these policies see A. Eckstein, "China's Trade Policy and Sino-American Relations," *Foreign Affairs*, October 1975, pp. 134–154.

14 For further detail see Chapter 7.

15 Ishikawa Shigeru, *Economic Development in Asian Perspective*, Tokyo, 1967, Chapters 3 and 5.

16 Jon Sigurdson, "Rural Industrialization in China," in *China, An Economic Assessment*, pp. 411–435; and Thomas G. Rawski, "Chinese Economic Planning," *Current Scene*, vol. 14, no. 4, April 1976, p. 5.

17 Based on the report of an American Rural Small-Scale Industry Delegation which visited China in the summer of 1975 under the auspices of the Committee on Scholarly Communication with the People's Republic of China.

18 Based on "Proclamation of the National People's Congress of the People's Republic of China," NCNA, Peking, January 18, 1975.

19 Perkins, *Market Control*, Table 9, p. 109.

20 The data for 1952–56 are based on Perkins, *Market Control*, p. 101. Information for 1958 and 1959 can be found in She I-san, "A discussion of the reform of the commodity distribution system," *Planned Economy* (Chi-hua ching-chi), no. 10, 1958, p. 34. The 1972 estimates are based on interviews with Shanghai planning officials in December 1972.

21 David Novick et al., *Wartime Production Controls*, New York, 1949.

22 In Chinese sources there is no single place as far as I am aware in which this system is fully described. It is referred to by Audrey Donnithorne in *China's Economic System*, New York, 1967, pp. 459–460 and by Barry Richman in *Industrial Society in Communist China*, New York, 1969, pp. 707–708. Aspects of it are also dealt with in *Planned Economy* (Chi-hua ching-chi), January 1958, pp. 38–41 and October 1958, pp. 34–35, in *Planning and Statistics* (Chi-hua yu t'ung-chi), no. 13, July 1959, and in *People's Daily*, November 12, 1957, p. 7.

23 C. Y. Cheng, *Scientific and Engineering Manpower in Communist China, 1949–1963*, Washington, D.C., 1965, p. 110.

24 Donnithorne, *China's Economic System*, pp. 177–180.

25 See National Academy of Sciences, *Plant Studies in the People's Republic of China*, A Trip Report of the American Plant Studies Delegation, Washington, D.C., 1975.

26 Richman, *Industrial Society*, p. 376.

27 Anna Louise Strong, *Letter from China*, Peking, no. 13, December 30, 1963, p. 2. Quoted in Donnithorne, *China's Economic System*, p. 186.
28 Perkins, *Market Control*, p. 110.
29 Donnithorne, *China's Economic System*, p. 451.
30 Perkins, *Market Control*, p. 151.
31 Based on briefings in ten Chinese factories during my month-long visit to China in December 1972 and January 1973 with a delegation from the National Committee on United States–China Relations.
32 N. R. Lardy, *Central Control and Redistribution in China, Central–Provincial Relations Since 1949*, unpublished Ph.D. dissertation, University of Michigan, 1975.
33 I am indebted to Professor Thomas Rawski for calling this to my attention. In any case this is a subject that will require much more research.

5 *The quest for economic stability*

1 John K. Fairbank, *The United States and China*, Cambridge, Mass., 1971, pp. 90–94; and Chang Kia-ngau, *The Inflationary Spiral*, New York, 1958, p. 3.
2 Much of the data and analysis in this section is based on Chang Kia-ngau's book on *The Inflationary Spiral*.
3 S. H. Chou, *The Chinese Inflation, 1937–1949*, New York, 1963, p. 23.
4 Chou, *Chinese Inflation*, pp. 34–35.
5 See Chou, *Chinese Inflation*, Table 7.1, p. 243; and Chang, *Inflationary Spiral*, Table 21, p. 63.
6 The monthly price quotations for Shanghai are based on *A Collection of Shanghai Price Data Before and After the Liberation* (1921–1957), compiled by the Shanghai Economic Research Institute of the Chinese Academy of Sciences and the Economic Research Institute of the Shanghai Academy of Sciences, Shanghai, pp. 454–459.
7 For further details see Y. L. Wu, *An Economic Survey of Communist China*, New York, 1956, pp. 397–403.
8 Based on Chung Kan-en, "The Success of the State Bank's Policy on Interest Rate," *Economic Weekly*, Shanghai, July 3, 1952.
9 *Ta Kung Pao*, Shanghai, June 10, 1949.
10 Based on *Two Kinds of Societies, Two Kinds of Wages*, Shanghai, 1973, p. 16, quoted in D. H. Perkins, *China's Modern Economy in Historical Perspective*, Stanford, Calif., 1975, Table A4, p. 153.
11 Based on Franklyn D. Holzman, "Soviet Inflationary Pressures 1928–1957, Causes and Cures," *The Quarterly Journal of Economics*, May 1960, pp. 167–168.
12 Christopher Howe, *Wage Patterns and Wage Policy in Modern China*, Cambridge, Eng., 1973, Tables 17 and 19, pp. 31–33.
13 Holzman, "Inflationary Pressures."
14 These are estimates derived from Katharine H. Hsiao, *Money and Monetary Policy in Communist China*, New York, 1971, Table IX-2, p. 232. The index of repressed inflation is estimated by relating the index of commodity retail sales to an index of currency in circulation, both at current prices. Total inflation is measured by comparing trends in retail sales at 1952 constant prices with the currency index.
15 Howe, *Wage Patterns*, Table 19, p. 33.
16 Hsiao, *Money and Monetary Policy*, Table V-5, pp. 130–131. In some cases loan charges fell below and above this range.
17 The data cited in the last two paragraphs are based on Hsiao, *Money and Monetary Policy*, Tables VI-15, VIII-4, VIII-5, VI-11, and VI-9.

18 Based on GNP estimates in Table 6-6.
19 Kang Chao, *Capital Formation in Mainland China 1952–65*, Berkeley, Calif., 1974, Table 31, p. 112.
20 N. R. Chen, *Chinese Economic Statistics*, Chicago, 1967, Table 3.39, p. 169.

6 *Economic development and structural change*

1 State Statistical Bureau, *Ten Great Years*, Peking, 1960.
2 For a fuller exposition of these hypotheses see Alexander Eckstein, *China's Economic Development*, Ann Arbor, Mich., 1975, Chapter 2.
3 See Simon Kuznets, *Modern Economic Growth, Rate, Structure and Spread*, New Haven, Conn., 1966.
4 See N. R. Chen, *Chinese Economic Statistics, A Handbook for Mainland China*, Chicago, 1967, Table 1.5, p. 127; and Ernst Ni, *Distribution of the Urban and Rural Population of Mainland China, 1953 and 1958*, International Population Reports, series P-95, no. 56, Washington, D.C., 1960.
5 A National Conference on Learning from Tachai attended by First Vice-Premier Teng Hsiao-p'ing and other leaders was convened in October 1975; see *Peking Review*, vol. 18, no. 44, October 31, 1975.
6 See Alexander Eckstein, *The National Income of Communist China*, New York, 1961, Table A-1, p. 92; and T. C. Liu and K. C. Yeh, *The Economy of the Chinese Mainland*, Princeton, N.J., 1965, Table 36.
7 Hua Kuo-feng, "Mobilize the Whole Party, Make Greater Efforts to Develop Agriculture and Strive to Build Tachai-Type Counties Throughout the Country," *Peking Review*, vol. 18, no. 44, October 31, 1975, pp. 7–10, 18.
8 D. H. Perkins, "Constraints Influencing China's Agricultural Performance, in *China: A Reassessment of the Economy*, Joint Economic Committee, U.S. Congress, July 1975, Table 5, p. 356.
9 A. L. Erisman, "China, Agricultural Development, 1949–1971," in *People's Republic of China: An Economic Assessment*, Joint Economic Committee, U.S. Congress, 1972, Table 12, p. 138.
10 D. H. Perkins, ed., *China's Modern Economy in Historical Perspective*, Stanford, Calif., 1975, Table A-5, p. 154.
11 Perkins, "Constraints," Table 2, p. 351.
12 D. H. Perkins, *Six Centuries of Agricultural Development in China, 1368–1968*, Chicago, 1968, Table II. 8, p. 30.
13 K. Ohkawa and H. Rosovsky, *Japanese Economic Growth, Trend Acceleration in the Twentieth Century*, Stanford, Calif., 1973, Table 4.9, p. 96.
14 See Kjeld Bjerke, "The National Product of Denmark, 1870–1952," in *Income and Wealth*, Series V, London, 1955, Table II, p. 125; and Phyllis Deane and W. A. Cole, *British Economic Growth, 1688–1959*, Cambridge, Eng., 1962.
15 Subramanian Swamy, "Economic Growth in China and India, 1952–1970," *Economic Development and Cultural Change*, vol. 21, no. 4, part II, July 1973, Table 5, p. 11.
16 For a more systematic and extensive discussion of textile imports and the rise of a domestic factory-based textile industry see R. F. Dernberger, "The Role of the Foreigner in China's Economic Development, 1840–1949"; and Kang Chao, "The Growth of a Modern Cotton Textile Industry and the Competition with Handicrafts"; both in Perkins, *China's Modern Economy*, pp. 19–47 and 167–201, respectively.
17 For a further elaboration see Thomas G. Rawski, "The Growth of Producer Goods Industries, 1900–1971," in Perkins, *China's Modern Economy*, pp. 203–233.

18 The presently most highly industrialized countries do not seem to have attained this stage until after World War I, and in some cases not until after World War II, according to W. G. Hoffmann, *The Growth of Industrial Economies*, London, 1958, Table 23, p. 89. However, this results in part from the particular definitions of producer and consumer goods and the comparability of Hoffmann's definition with that on which the data in Table 6-3 are based.

19 Alexander Gerschenkron, "Economic Backwardness in Historical Perspective," in Bert F. Hoselitz, ed., *The Progress of Underdeveloped Areas*, Chicago, 1952.

20 For a description of methods used in deriving his index, see R. M. Field, "Civilian Industrial Production in the People's Republic of China, 1949–74," in *China: A Reassessment*, Appendix A, pp. 160–164. It should be noted that this is a most complex index, based on different and at times inconsistent weighting systems.

21 See J. K. Chang, *Industrial Development in Pre-Communist China*, Chicago, 1969, p. 73.

22 These data are based for the Soviet Union on Norman M. Kaplan and Richard H. Moorsteen, "An Index of Soviet Industrial Output," *The American Economic Review*, vol. L, no. 3 (June 1960), Table 1, p. 296; for Japan on Ohkawa and Rosovsky, *Japanese Economic Growth*, Table 4.4, p. 81; for India on Swamy, "Economic Growth," Tables 25 and 26, pp. 44–45; for the United States on U.S. Department of Commerce, Bureau of the Census, *Long-Term Economic Growth, 1860–1965*, Washington, D.C., October 1966; for Germany and France on League of Nations, *Industrialization and Foreign Trade*, New York, 1945, Table 1, p. 130; for Great Britain on Deane and Cole, *British Economic Growth*, Table 38, p. 170.

23 For more detail on these definitions see N. R. Chen, *Chinese Economic Statistics*, p. 29.

24 The 1952 and 1957 estimates are based on T. C. Liu and K. C. Yeh, *The Economy of the Chinese Mainland, National Income and Economic Development*, 1933–1959, Princeton, New Jersey, 1965, Table 8, p. 66. These are in terms of value added; there are later estimates but these are in terms of gross factory output and are therefore not comparable. One of the latest is by T. G. Rawski, who estimates that about 6 percent of gross factory output was derived from "small industries" in 1972. (See his article "Chinese Economic Planning" in *Current Scene*, Hong Kong, vol. 14, no. 4, April 1976, p. 5). In value-added terms this ratio could very well be significantly higher.

25 For a further analysis of the underlying strategy see Jon Sigurdson, "Rural Industrialization in China," in *China: A Reassessment*, pp. 411–435.

26 See Central Intelligence Agency. Research Aid, *China, Role of Small Plants in Economic Development*, Washington, D.C., May 1974.

27 See T. C. Liu and K. C. Yeh, "Chinese and Other Asian Economies, A Quantitative Evaluation," *The American Economic Review, Papers and Proceedings*, May 1973, Table 3, p. 219; Thomas Rawski, "Recent Trends in the Chinese Economy," *China Quarterly*, no. 53, Jan.–March 1973, Table 12, p. 21. It should be noted that the data presented in Tables 6-6 and 6-7 represent substantial revisions of my earlier estimates in my article "Economic Growth and Change in China, A Twenty Year Perspective," *China Quarterly*, no. 54, April-June 1973, Table 6, p. 232. These present revisions are based on a great deal of subsequent research, which has convinced me that the official reconstructed grain series and gross individual output value series may be fairly reliable and thus may better serve as a basis for GDP estimates than independently estimated farm and industrial production.

28 Liu and Yeh, "Chinese and Other Asian Economies," Table 5, p. 222.

29 For both Aird and Orleans estimates see Leo A. Orleans, "China's Population, Can the Contradictions Be Resolved?" in *China: A Reassessment*, Tables 2 and 3, pp. 75–77.

30 A quite crude adjustment based on 1971 prices is possible using the price indices in Perkins, *China's Modern Economy*, Table 8, p. 139. Agricultural procurement prices have risen much faster than industrial prices. Moreover, in 1952 industrial prices relative to farm prices were high compared to earlier periods. Since the industrial sector has been growing most rapidly, if it is weighted in terms of these high prices its share of GDP will loom very large and that of agriculture will appear correspondingly smaller. These suggest that the price-adjusted ratios may be around 25 to 30 percent for the A sector, 45 percent for the I sector, and 25 to 30 percent of the S sector.

7 *The role of foreign trade in China's economic development*

1 This brief outline of the advantages of international specialization is largely based on Bertil Ohlin, *Interregional and International Trade*, Cambridge, Mass., 1967.
2 These ratios are based on the sum of imports and exports combined in relation to GNP. The data are from the United Nations, *Statistical Yearbook*, 1974, New York, 1975, pp. 406–413, 644–646. Data for China are from A. Eckstein, *Communist China's Economic Growth and Foreign Trade*, New York, 1966, Table 4-9, pp. 120–121; those for the Soviet Union are from F. D. Holzman, "Foreign Trade," in Abram Bergson and Simon Kuznets, eds., *Economic Trends in the Soviet Union*, Cambridge, Mass., 1963, Table VII.3, p. 290.
3 Based on an as yet unpublished study by Robert Michael Field on *Real Capital Formation in the People's Republic of China: 1952–1973*, April 1976, Table 8, p. 30 and Table 19, p. 60.
4 Eckstein, *Communist China's Economic Growth*, p. 124.
5 Eckstein, *Communist China's Economic Growth*, pp. 127–128.
6 See Eckstein, *Communist China's Economic Growth*, Table 4-3, p. 98 and pp. 167–169.
7 *Life*, April 30, 1971.
8 Sidney H. Jammes, "The Chinese Defense Burden, 1965–1974," in *China: A Reassessment of the Economy*, Joint Economic Committee, U.S. Congress, July 1975, pp. 459–566.
9 "Report on the Work of the Government," *Peking Review*, no. 4, January 24, 1975, pp. 23–25.
10 Hans Heymann, Jr., "Acquisition and Diffusion of Technology," in *China: A Reassessment*, p. 701.
11 Foreign Broadcast Information Service, *PRC Daily Broadcast*, vol. I, no. 203, October 18, 1974.
12 See Eckstein, *Communist China's Economic Growth*, Table 4-2, p. 96.
13 Based on Field, *Real Capital Formation*, Table 19, p. 61.
14 In compiling these import shares it was assumed that the large "other" (commodities not specified) import category consisted for the most part of military goods. Virtually all these "other" imports came from the Soviet Union; they dwindled after the Sino-Soviet break. For a discussion of this problem see Eckstein, *Communist China's Economic Growth*.
15 A. L. Erisman, "China, Agriculture in the 1970s," in *China: A Reassessment*, Tables 3 and 4, pp. 343–344.
16 A. L. Erisman, "China, Agriculture," Table 2, p. 333; and D. H. Perkins, "Constraints Influencing China's Agricultural Performance," in *China: A Reassessment*, Table 5, p. 356.
17 Based on information in *U.S.–China Business Review*, vol. 1, no. 1, Jan.-Feb. 1974, pp. 363–373 and vol. 1, no. 6, Nov.-Dec. 1974, pp. 8–9.
18 Based on U.S. Department of Agriculture, Foreign Agricultural Service, *World Agricultural Production and Trade, Statistical Report*, October 1975, pp. 12–13.

19 U.S. Department of Agriculture, *Agricultural Trade of the People's Republic of China, 1935–69*, Foreign Agricultural Report No. 83, Washington, D.C., 1972, Tables 5, 8, 31, and 62 on pp. 15, 20, 52, 76. Also, USDA, *The Agricultural Situation in the People's Republic of China and other Communist Countries*, Washington, D.C., May 1974, Table 6 and USDA, Foreign Agriculture Circular, *Cotton*, Washington, D.C., June 1976, Table 4, p. 15.

20 See A. H. Usack and R. E. Batsavage, "The International Trade of the People's Republic of China," in *People's Republic of China: An Economic Assessment*, Joint Economic Committee, U.S. Congress, 1972, p. 349; and R. F. Dernberger, *The Transfer of Technology to the PRC*, unpublished paper, August 1975.

21 Eckstein, *Communist China's Economic Growth*, p. 143.

22 Eckstein, *Communist China's Economic Growth*, Table 4-5, pp. 106–107.

23 Bobby A. Williams, "The Chinese Petroleum Industry: Growth and Prospects," in *China: A Reassessment*, Table 1, p. 228 and National Council for U.S.–China Trade, *China's Petroleum Industry*, Washington, D.C., 1976, p. 25.

24 *China's Petroleum Industry*, p. 50.

25 Central Intelligence Agency, Research Aid, *China, Energy Balance Projections*, Washington, D.C., November 1975.

26 Based on information provided by Japanese shipping and commercial sources in interviews with the author in April and May of 1975.

27 Steven C. Hass, *Impact of MFN on U.S. Imports from the People's Republic of China*, Office of East-West Trade, Department of State, August 1973 (mimeo).

28 David Denny, *The Effect of Normalized Commercial Relations on PRC Exports to the U.S.*, Bureau of East-West Trade, Department of Commerce, 1973 (mimeo).

29 See Charles H. Bayar, "China's Frozen Assets in the U.S., Their Present Status and Future Disposition," in *U.S.-China Business Review*, vol. 2, no. 5, Sept.-Oct. 1975.

8 *The Chinese development model*

1 This juxtaposition of *yang* and *t'u* and its possible meanings, connotations, and significance is based on a seminal paper by Lyman P. Van Slyke, "Culture and Technology," prepared for a conference on *Sino-American Relations in Historical and Global Perspective* (mimeo), Wingspread, Wis., March 1976.

2 This was clearly brought out in Vice-Premier Hua Kuo-feng, "Summing-up Report at the National Conference on Learning from Tachai in Agriculture," *Peking Review*, vol. 18, no. 44, October 31, 1975, pp. 7–10, 18. This was a high-level conference concerned with agricultural policy and agricultural development strategy convened for a whole month in September-October 1975.

3 These frustrations and difficulties of adjustment occasionally surface in the Chinese press. They are buttressed by accounts of Overseas Chinese who have an opportunity to visit their native village and by the high incidence of this youth among the Chinese migrants to Hong Kong.

4 *Peking Review*, vol. 19, no. 2, January 9, 1976.

5 This was identified as a key problem by a delegation of American plant scientists visiting China in August-September 1974; see National Academy of Sciences, *Plant Studies in the People's Republic of China, A Trip Report of the American Plant Studies Delegation*, Washington, D.C., 1975.

6 Li Chiang (Minister of Foreign Trade of the PRC), "New Developments in China's Foreign Trade," *China's Foreign Trade*, no. 1, 1974, p. 4.

7 Chou En-lai, "Report on the Work of the Government," *Peking Review*, vol. 18, no. 4, January 24, 1975, p. 25.
8 American Rural Small-Scale Industry Delegation, *Rural Small-Scale Industry in the People's Republic of China*, Berkeley, Calif., 1976 (forthcoming), Chapter 1, p. 8.
9 Hua Kuo-feng, "Summing-up Report," p. 9.
10 These major construction projects have been under way for some time. They could be observed during my visit to China in December 1972. They were given a renewed impetus by the National Conference on Learning from Tachai held in September and October 1975 and were described in some detail in American Rural Small-Scale Industry Delegation, *Rural Small-Scale Industry*, Chapter 5, pp. 2–5 and Chapter 6, p. 7.
11 A note of urgency concerning the need for farm mechanization is quite pronounced in Hua Kuo-feng's report.
12 American Rural Small-Scale Industry Delegation, *Rural Small-Scale Industry*, Chapter 4, p. 25.
13 For a sophisticated analysis of the relationships between technology and health care strategy in China see Peter S. Heller, "The Strategy of Health-Sector Planning," in M. E. Wegman, T. Y. Lin, and E. Purcell, eds., *Public Health in the People's Republic of China*, New York, 1973; especially pp. 85–90.
14 I am indebted for this insight to the members of the American Rural Small-Scale Industry Delegation.
15 For a most suggestive elaboration of this notion of *administration by moral example* see Arthur Stinchcombe's chapter (Chapter 2) in American Rural Small-Scale Industry Delegation, *Rural Small-Scale Industry*. The concept of *model emulation* has been articulated by a number of sinologists, most notably by Donald Munro in *The Concept of Man in Contemporary China* (forthcoming), Chapter 6.
16 Carl Riskin, "Workers' Incentives in Chinese Industry," in *China: A Reassessment of the Economy*, Joint Economic Committee, U.S. Congress, July 1975, Table 2, p. 216.
17 Riskin, "Workers' Incentives," Table 3, p. 217.
18 For instance, I recall my first visit to Hong Kong in December 1952, when I saw many people homeless, sleeping in the streets or inhabiting miserable squatters' settlements on the outskirts of Kowloon. (This, of course, no longer applies to Hong Kong today.) Similar impressions, even worse, could be gathered on a visit to Calcutta or some other parts of India in 1966. I saw nothing even remotely corresponding to these symptoms in any part of China visited.
19 See Riskin, "Workers' Incentives," Tables 2 and 3, pp. 216–217; Christopher Howe, *Wage Patterns and Wage Policy in Modern China, 1919–1972*, Cambridge, Eng., 1973, Chapter 3; Charles Hoffman, *The Chinese Worker*, Albany, N.Y., 1974, Chapter 4.
20 Elliott J. Berg, "Wage Structures in Less Developed Countries," in A. D. Smith, ed., *Wage Policy Issues in Economic Development*, London, 1969, p. 303.
21 U.S. Department of Labor, Bureau of Labor Statistics, *Handbook of Labor Statistics, 1973*, Washington, D.C., 1973, Table 45, p. 108.
22 Berg, "Wage Structures," p. 320.
23 D. H. Perkins, "Growth and Changing Structure of China's Economy," *China's Modern Economy*, pp. 125–127.
24 See Howe, *Wage Patterns*, Table 17, p. 31 and D. H. Perkins, "Growth and Changing Structure," Table A-4, p. 153.
25 Perkins, "Growth and Changing Structure" and *Peking Review*, no. 31, October 10, 1975, p. 9.
26 This is based on the findings of Nicholas R. Lardy in "Regional Growth and Income Dis-

tribution, The Chinese Experience," Economic Growth Center, Yale University, Discussion Paper #140, October 1975.

27 The point of departure for these calculations and those in Table 8-2 was provided by the per capita estimates in Table 6-8. The 1933 estimate is based on Perkins, "Growth and Changing Structure," on the assumption that the rate of change between 1933 and 1952 would be the same if calculated in 1957 or in 1952 prices. Investment, defense and government administration shares in GDP are based on estimates by Perkins, T. C. Liu and K. C. Yeh, *The Economy of the Chinese Mainland*; Kang Chao, *Capital Formation*; and the U.S. Government.

28 The prices obtained by the Yale group were compiled by Bruce Reynolds who at that time was a graduate student in economics at the University of Michigan and is now Assistant Professor of Economics at Union College.

29 Based on an unpublished paper by R. M. Field, *Real Capital Formation in the People's Republic of China: 1952–1973*, April 1976, Table 19, p. 60.

30 See Hollis Chenery, ed., *Redistribution with Growth*, London, 1974, pp. 3–27; Simon Kuznets, "Economic Growth and Income Inequality," *American Economic Review*, vol. XLV, no. 11, March 1955, pp. 1–28; Simon Kuznets, "Quantitative Aspects of the Economic Growth of Nations, Distribution of Income by Size," *Economic Development and Cultural Change*, January 1963, Part II.

Index